G000065277

Corfe Castle 2000

A diary of the village

Published by the Corfe Castle Millennium Association

First published in 2001

by

Corfe Castle Millennium Association,

Corfe Castle, Dorset

England

Copyright Corfe Castle Millennium Association

http //www corfecastle-diary2000 co uk

All rights reserved No part of this book may be

reproduced in any form or by any means

without permission in writing from the publisher

Printed by Optichrome Ltd , Maybury Road, Woking, Surrey

ISBN 0-9540932-0-8

Foreword

In 1996 the Corfe Castle Parish Council held a public meeting to discuss how to celebrate the Millennium As a result, the Corfe Castle Millennium Association was formed

The aims of the Association were to commemorate the year 2000 in the village To do this, we organised religious and artistic activities, held social events, and undertook the planning of a sports pavilion, which was chosen to be the capital project

Within the pages of this Diary you will find the words and thoughts of the people of Corfe Castle, as well as descriptions of all the Millennium activities, which took place during the year 2000 Pages of the Diary were sold to people who live within the parish of Corfe Castle including Kingston and to people who were staying in the village or who were related to villagers Once sold, what went onto the page was entirely up to the author The reader will see from the Diary the wide variety of contributions, which include factual records, personal thoughts, historical information, drawings and a host of interesting and memorable ideas

The village of Corfe Castle is in the Isle of Purbeck, in the County of Dorset The population of the whole parish is about 2,000 people The ruins of the Castle, now owned by the National Trust, draw many tourists throughout the year and dominate the village

Traditionally the village was a mainly agricultural, stone working and clay mining community, now it relies heavily on tourism, the oil industry, which is centred on Wytch Farm, and work in the neighbouring towns of Poole and Bournemouth

The village has a cricket club and a football team Both, however, lack facilities A major objective of the Millennium year was to raise money to build a new pavilion on the West Street sports field The sale of this Diary is intended to help raise money for this project

Activity during the lead up to the Millennium was intense and involved much hard work by all members of the Committee The idea for this Diary came mainly from Eileen van Lelyveld, who has done much of the work in putting it together She has also liaised with our sponsor Sam Chalmers, to ensure that the brilliant idea of the Diary became a reality Without Sam's financial backing, publication of the Diary would not have been possible

We all hope you enjoy reading the Diary

Stephen Dru Drury

Chairman of the Corfe Castle Millennium Association

NEW YEAR'S EVE AT THE FOX INN

In the early days of 1999 we decided that we would not open on New Year's Eve but as time went on it was suggested that as everybody wanted to have a get together, we would use the pub as a place to hold a party. All those who wanted to come would provide food so there would be a running buffet through the night. That was the easy bit! What could we do to make it a night to remember? We decided to cram 1000 years into one night with the help of props, costume, music, lighting and .... Roger White.

The stage was set for a 9 p.m. start time and finish – well that was anybody's guess. Our thanks must go to the following, for without their help and support none of the evening's events would have been possible – Drew Thompson, Roger and Patricia White, Joe, Monica and David Williams, Ian Harris, Marita Shaw, Nick Moss, Fiona Hewitt, Joe Crackle, Neil Windsor, Trevor Hendes, Charles Spinney, Wayne Tarbotton, Chris White, Jan and David Birnham, Nigel Dragon, Doreen White and Jeremy Figgins.

Rehearsals for the short sketches started in November, with kind permission from Roger and Patricia, whose carpet will never be the same again. Costumes, props and lighting effects were being made and Ian produced a magnificent paper sculpture above the fireplace with the castle soaring up, welcoming the new Millennium, surrounded by angels blowing trumpets.

About 50 people attended with a dress code of black, white and silver. White depicting purity, silver charity as we passed into the new century. The scene was set with white table cloths, overlaid with iridescent silver centre mats and silver and white candles and black, silver and white rosettes adorning the Christmas decorations. The overall effect was stunning. Everyone sat waiting as the lights turned green – a smoke machine filled the room, so much so that we had to open the doors!

The show opened with Drew reading the first six verses of Genesis (*In the beginning God created the earth* ...) then with the music of Egdon Heath, thunder flashes and lighting, from out of the smoke arose two huge dinosaur heads, while two screaming pterodactyls flew down, their wings flapping – that made them look up!

As we progressed through the century in music, the next piece of history was the Egyptian period, alias Trevor and Charles, who were both decked out in shimmering gold from head to foot – apparently the gold wouldn't come off their legs for two days, even with a scrubbing brush! Their grand entrance was a candle lit procession to the music, "Arrival of the Queen of Sheba" carrying a 6 foot replica of Tutenkhamun. They then returned to the well, changed their hats to fezzes and broke into YMCA, which had everyone dancing in the aisle and joining in.

As war approached there were wonderful choruses from Vera Lynn, Glenn Miller, Churchill's speeches, tank gun fire, sirens  and to the tune of "Spitfire Prelude" the lights went out and four blow-up spitfires flew through the bar, picked up in spotlights, which got a standing ovation and the atmosphere turned electric. The mood changed just as quickly when we had a minute's silence. Nigel Dragon played "The Last Post", Annette had arranged a beautiful poppy and laurel display, which with more smoke I placed on the well, surrounded with crosses. Looking back, I think this was probably the most moving point I have ever experienced – you could have heard a pin drop. And during the silence we scattered over 500 poppy leaves. The silence was unbelievable, an emotion stirred and I was conscious of three people in tears.

Today's weather: A dry cold day.

Name: FOX INN

House: " AND COMPANY "

Year of birth:

Street: WEST

The music continued through a period of time, with excerpts from some of the more modern musicals. The first was from Riverdance (this needed and impact – but what?) It must have been about 6.30 a.m. one morning, it struck me, why can't we do it in puppet form, leprechauns even? Ian designed a structure that he could step into and have 2 puppets either side, so when he moved, they all moved, and it worked perfectly. Nobody had an idea of what was about to happen. So we built up a one night only, no expenses spared, image, and to drums and flashing lights everybody waited with anticipation. Then, in the distance, above all the noise, I could hear, "help, help, help", only to find when I went to the kitchen that Ian's head had moved round so his eye holes were near his ears. With one quick twist he was off, dancing the night away with footwork that would have made an Irishman cry. The laughter and applause were tremendous – it nearly took the roof off!

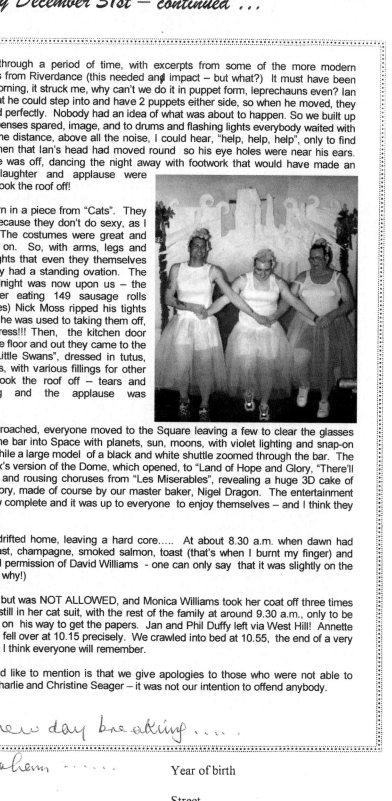

Now it was the girls' turn in a piece from "Cats". They dance superbly (only because they don't do sexy, as I was repeatedly told). The costumes were great and the make-up was spot on. So, with arms, legs and tails, they reached heights that even they themselves were surprised at – they had a standing ovation. The last section before midnight was now upon us – the lads' turn. Well, after eating 149 sausage rolls (obviously due to nerves) Nick Moss ripped his tights and was mumbling that he was used to taking them off, not putting them on, Tress!!! Then, the kitchen door opened, smoke filling the floor and out they came to the music, "Dance of the Little Swans", dressed in tutus, head-dresses and boots, with various fillings for other parts. Yet again, it took the roof off – tears and laughter were falling and the applause was humungous.

As the hour rapidly approached, everyone moved to the Square leaving a few to clear the glasses and try and transform the bar into Space with planets, sun, moons, with violet lighting and snap-on iridescent necklaces, while a large model of a black and white shuttle zoomed through the bar. The centrepiece was the Fox's version of the Dome, which opened, to "Land of Hope and Glory, "There'll Always be an England" and rousing choruses from "Les Miserables", revealing a huge 3D cake of Corfe Castle in all its glory, made of course by our master baker, Nigel Dragon. The entertainment for the evening was now complete and it was up to everyone to enjoy themselves – and I think they did!

Gradually the masses drifted home, leaving a hard core….. At about 8.30 a.m. when dawn had broken, we had breakfast, champagne, smoked salmon, toast (that's when I burnt my finger) and scrambled eggs, by kind permission of David Williams - one can only say that it was slightly on the rubbery side (can't think why!)

Phil Duffy tried to sleep but was NOT ALLOWED, and Monica Williams took her coat off three times before returning home, still in her cat suit, with the rest of the family at around 9.30 a.m., only to be met by Drew Thompson on his way to get the papers. Jan and Phil Duffy left via West Hill! Annette remained standing and I fell over at 10.15 precisely. We crawled into bed at 10.55, the end of a very long but perfect day that I think everyone will remember.

The final thing we would like to mention is that we give apologies to those who were not able to attend, particularly to Charlie and Christine Seager – it was not our intention to offend anybody.

Today's weather: *A new day breaking …..*

Name *by Graham ……*   Year of birth

House   Street

My day started with the treble bell-rope in my hand. As the last stroke of Big Ben rang out at midnight, I was privileged to give the traditional call of "Look to, treble's going, she's gone" and lead the six bells of St. Edward, King & Martyr into rounds. Twelve Corfe Valley Ringers were there and David, our Tower Captain, gave each one a chance to ring. Half an hour later we stood the bells and wished each other 'A Happy New Year'. The champagne bubbled, accompanied by Mary's sausage rolls and Annie's mince pies. Nearly a month earlier, on Dec. 5th., the restored ring of bells was triumphantly dedicated. The bells had been silent since 1957 when the wooden bell-frame believed to date from the 16th. century became unsafe. Fund raising to restore the bells formally started in 1992 with the forming of the Belfry Fund Committee, At that time the cost of repairing the bell-tower, overhauling and resiting the clock mechanism, a new steel bell-frame and two new bells was set at £84,000. By 1999 that estimate had doubled. With a Millennium Fund Grant of £56,000 the money was raised and work started in April '99 to be completed in time for the dedication.
The ringers, mostly trained by David Langford and Ben Dames, were new to ringing, their experience ranging from a few months to four years. We all felt elated to finally have such a beautiful ring of bells

Corfe Valley Ringers
Carol Dean
Brian Dean
Jill Foley
Lynn Higgens
David Langford
Ken Lees
Hazel Parker
Ian Parker
Rodney Parker
Mary Rosewarn
Martin Smith
Peter Smith

Woke at 6.30am for a cup of tea followed at a reasonable interval by turkey dripping toast with the jelly that I think is the best bit of the turkey! Out at 9.0am into a misty, muggy morning to walk/ mud-paddle through the saturated fields with Jay, our dog. Everything very still and quiet, the only living thing the abundant lichens on the trees showing that our air is good and clean. The sky cleared to patches of blue and the light increased - short lived but heart-warming for the moment.

12.00pm. The Millennium ring. The culmination of the many restorations and augmentations of church-bells in Britain and the frantic training of sufficient people to ring them. Every bell capable of being rung was pulled into action at midday for a short ring followed by a 1/4 hour service. At the end of the service our Rector asked us to ring again. Fortunately six of us were still there and we dashed up to the ringing room for another short ring. Home to lunch of home-made soup and salad.

2.00pm. The Corfe bells rang out again, this time for an attempt to ring what is believed to be the very first full peal of 5040 changes ever to be rung in Corfe. For Ian Parker it would be his first peal. At intervals during the afternoon I went outside to listen - the bells rang on. At 4.15 I took Jay out to record the sound of the bells and the lights in the square. At 4.42 the bells came round, 7 extents of Bob Minor. Great excitement from the 'groupies' gathered outside the church and no doubt relief from the band as they stood their bells as one. Well done!

5.00pm. Home to tea and a quiet evening to reflect on a very eventful day for all those involved in getting the bells of St. Edwards up and ringing. All the frustrations of the Belfry Fund Committee and their dedication to the project. The struggles of the learner ringers. Finally, we have our bells. May they always bear witness, pleasurably.

THE PEAL BAND
1. Ian Parker
2. Sue Smith
3. Ben Dames
4. David Langford
5. Graham Elmes
6. Martin Hough.(C)

Plain Course of Bob Minor

Today's weather: Overcast, mild, occasional rain

Name JILL FOLEY

Year of birth 1932

House 57

Street WEST STREET

Sunday January 2nd

I was woken up by the radio alarm at 6.30 am as usual. Today, though, I continued to doze while listening to odd snippets of news. I had only three hours sleep the previous night so I was still catching up. My wife, Linda, and I eventually got up just before 9.00am. Everything was very quiet. Nellie, our eleven-year-old daughter, was up watching television, but still in her night clothes. Alice, Linda's mother who has been staying with us during the Christmas holidays, was soon up and about also, but there was no sign yet of Tom our 16-year-old son, or Belle our 14-year old daughter.

It was a lovely, bright, clear morning with very little wind. Linda and I strolled down to the bottom of the garden with a cup of coffee. We were glad to get some fresh air as we hadn't been outside at all the previous day. From the end of the garden, looking out across the halves, we could just about hear the church bells. We decided that it would be a good idea to go for a walk.

Linda and I set off across the halves towards the village. The field was very wet. As we got to the square there were several people on the streets and one or two shops were open. We could obviously hear the bells clearly now. This was the first time that I had heard them since they had been replaced. I had intended to come to The Square on New Year's day but I was still recovering from the previous night. We carried on walking through the village and then took the permissive path up to the top of East Hill. From the top of the hill, as we looked down on the village, we could still hear the church bells. It was a perfect scene, quintessentially English. I never get tired of the countryside around the village, and from up there it all looks like its almost a model. I was struck by the thought that the scene had changed very little during the last century. Also, I thought what a disaster it would be if a by-pass were ever to be cut through it. As we walked along the ridge towards the TV mast we watched the steady progress of a steam train as it came along the valley and into the station. This only seemed to make the scene more complete. We took a different path down the hill and then across the railway towards the back of the village hall and then home.

For the rest of the morning I sat and watched the cricket. It was the fourth test between England and South Africa. England made their usual impressive start followed by the fall of several quick wickets. During this time the weather outside had rapidly deteriorated. Although it was still fairly mild for the time of year, it was now very dull and there was a steady drizzle which set in for almost the rest of the day.

The lounge still needed a good clean after our New Year celebrations. We had a large Christmas tree in the corner which was losing all its needles, so we decided to take it down at the same time. The children weren't entirely happy about this as it meant that Christmas was now all over.

At the beginning of the afternoon I drove into Swanage with the children. We needed to get a small amount of shopping and we were also hoping to find a photo booth open as we need to get our passports renewed. We knew this would have to be done all through the Christmas holidays but it got forgotten about with all the other things which were going on. There was nowhere open so it had to be put off to another day anyway. There was a lot of traffic on the roads and plenty of people in Swanage, all of whom looked very wet in the constant rain.

We took it very easy for the rest of the day. Some friends from Swanage called in to see us for a short while in the afternoon. Nellie went out to a garden centre with a friend. Tom sat up in his room for most of the time doing his best to revise for his mock GCSEs. By now Linda wasn't feeling too well. She had a headache and was continually sneezing. She felt she had a cold coming on. We had dinner in the evening, as we would on a normal Sunday, but it didn't really feel like a Sunday as we were all so much out of our routine. After we had cleared up and watched a little television together we all went to bed, apart from Tom who was still struggling with revision.

Today's weather: Bright at first, little wind, very mild. Later there was rain for the rest of the day. 8°C

Name STEPHEN PERRIN   Year of birth   1951

House   120   Street   EAST STREET

The Nineham girls return to the village for the turn of the century.

Coming back to the village to hear the church bells ring was Eileen's wish.

A bonus of staying at 36 East Street as it was the home of our great grandfather's brother and wife. George and Eliza Wills. It is almost opposite Morton Cottage where we lived following our move from Sandy Hills after our only brother was killed in an accident.

Our parents final home in the village was at 162 East Street until 1983.

Local visitors to the cottage included Mrs. G. Welsh, Betty Groves [Brinton], Barbara Cannings [Chaffey], Linda Applin [Hoare] and Mary Wills who all dropped in for a mince pie and a drink.

Several groups of the family joined us in walks around the village during the stay recalling childhood memories and noting the growth and and changes, some good, some not so good.

We joined with many others to see in the new Millennium in the Square which, as usual was beautifully lit, defying the damp conditions.

It was very pleasing to return and we are grateful to the old established families who made us welcome.

Today, 3rd January, is the last full day, we will be packing now the last visitors have left.

Today's weather **Generally wet and windy**

Name EILEEN CUNNINGHAM
GWEN COX (née NINEHAM)
House FARRIERS LODGE

Year of birth 1934

Street 36 EAST STREET

Tuesday January 4th

Alarm went off at 5.30am as usual. Down in shop by 6.30am Still very dark + damp outside but not raining.

First job this morning was to dismantle the old 'pounds + ounces' weighing machine + place the new gleaming metric scales on the counter. Required by law now + costing £500.00 we struggle to convert our daily fresh vegetable invoice into kilograms. We press on, however, we could be fined £2,000.00 if we do not comply with the new regulations.

Fresh bread daily from Whites Bakery at Langton Matravers arrives at 7.00am followed shortly by Williams Bakery at Wool with their selection of bread, cakes, pastries + crumpets. Derick the milkman from Swanage prompt at 7.15 with creams + yoghurts – an ideal time for a quick cup of coffee before pressing on.

The morning was fairly quiet, the first normal working day for the majority of people after the long Christmas + Millennium Celebrations – the longest Public Holiday ever.

Tuesday in the shop is a delivery day (also Thursdays + Fridays) and normally fairly busy. Customers ring with their grocery orders and we provide a free delivery service to Corfe Castle and the surrounding villages. Today there are not so many orders – larders still stocked up from the Christmas Holidays + funds being low! However, there is plenty to keep us busy – Christmas decorations + gifts to put away for another year, dates to be checked on all food items constantly, and new orders to be completed for the next main wholesale order which arrives once a week.

Mid afternoon, and with the sad tolling of the new church bells, a funeral is taking place at St. Edwards opposite. Friends and relations filing into the church for the service of a well respected man who had lived in the village for 50 years. In keeping with the sombre theme, the day became more overcast. There are still a few visitors in the village, faces not recognised, until shortly before we close when a flurry of customers, remembering the time, hurry through the door for last minute goods and video's.

The new Video Department has been a great success for the shop. Customers are able to hire out the tapes for a 24 hour period at a cost of between £1.50 – £1.95. Previously, this service was only available in nearby Swanage or Wareham so we feel has proved beneficial for both local people and the shop. We close the doors at last at 6.30pm. It is dark and cold. We clean and tidy the shop and climb the stairs. Another day – a new year and a new millennium in the story of Clealls Stores (Est 1881). Good luck to her, may she always continue to serve the villagers of Corfe Castle.

Today's weather: Some Sun; Some Cloud but DRYish.

Name CLEALLS STORES   Clealls Year of birth 1881. Established.
       JOHN + CAROL ELMES (from 4th July 1994)
House 25   Street East Street

Most of Corfe Castle people were in the square .Just before twelve o'clock the lights went out.The bells were ringing .At twelve o'clock the lights came back on.Then we could hear the bells of Big Ben.At each chime of a bell a rocket went up.
    by Geoffrey Dragon.

Dad lifted me up on to his shoulders so I could see everything.
Then some music came on and everyone did a dance.
And I was still on his shoulders!
By Canna Hazuki Whyte

I stayed up until half past two in the morning because I was at the village hall at Kimmeridge. We went outside to see fireworks at midnight. It was good fun. By Sam Dallisson.

On New Years Eve me ,mum Rosie and Dad all went to Sarah's house for a party. Mum dressed up as a flapper girl. At ten to twelve we all went down to the square and took our party poppers down as well. All the lights went off and then fireworks went off. At the first chime of midnight all the lights came back on and we got our party poppers out and popped them. by Poppy Davis.

At Bushey we all got together at Paul's house for a big party. Nearly everyone who lives in Bushey was at the party. When it was 12 o'clock we ate a grape each time we heard Big Ben chime on the television. We also had Champagne.   by Daniel Naptin.

Today's weather: Temp 13°C. Rainfall 0mm. Damp and Dull.

Name   Children from Class 3   Year of birth   7-9 yr olds

House   Corfe Castle First School   Street   East Street.

Corfe Castle School

Mr Nigel Dragon, Chairman of the Governors of Corfe Castle First School, distributes a Childrens illustrated Bible to all the pupils to mark the Millennium

Today's weather:

Name   Year of birth

House   Street

When we had our Carol Service and Nativity on The last day of term Dec. 16 th. we were all Presented with Bibles Because it was going To be the new Millennium. This picture shows Lyndsey O'Brien ,Michael Morris And George Goodall from The Reception class with Their Bibles.
Mr. Dragon Chairman of Governors helped Give out The Bibles. All the Bibles Had silver covers and They had wonderful Pictures inside.
By Georgina and Ellie.

Today is the first day of the Spring Term in the year 2000. Some of the children in class have been telling us what they did on December 31st.

MY MILLENNIUM. My mum and dad dressed up as the Flintstones and I was Pebbles. We went to the square. My little brother slept all the way through the celebrations. by Chloe Morgan.

Today's weather: Temp. 13°C. Rainfall 0.mm. Damp and Dull.

Name *Children from Class 3.* Year of birth *7-9 yr olds.*

House *Corfe Castle First School.* Street *East street.*

DATE
5,1.00

After break we did Dividing by 5 and 10. We found the multiples of 5 and 10. I got onto remainder sums.

Mariko Whyte.

10 20 30 40 50
60 70 80 90 100

5 10 15 20 25 30 35
40 45 50 55 60 65 70 75
80 85 90 95 100

$5\overline{)35} = 7$ $5\overline{)10} = 2$

$5\overline{)95} = 19$ $5\overline{)90} = 18$

$10\overline{)60} = 6$ $5\overline{)70} = 14$

In the afternoon we had History and Jade and I Were finding out about The Romans.

We found out about what the Romans ate.
They ate stuffed dormouse.
They ate freshly picked salad.
They ate freshly killed snails.
They ate stuffed peacock.
They ate oysters and mushrooms.
They ate wet red mullet.
They ate bay leaves and mint!
by Jade Hedges and Eleanor Wallace.

MENU

Today's weather: Temp. 13°C. Rainfall 0mm. Damp and Dull.

Name Children from Class 3.

Year of birth 7-9 yr olds.

House Corfe Castle First School.

Street East Street.

What a start to the New year the Village is full of Cold and flu bugs Not Millennium Bugs.

Its Granny churchills 86th Birthday to day how things have changed since she was born, but she has had the church bells ring again.
We where going to have a tea party today but as Grannys got the cold bug as well as Steven my son and her doughter Shirley & grandson Ben has the flu we have had to Cancell it until everyone is better, so this year granny will have Two birthdays like the Queen.
We drove the Car into poole to do some shopping and get her present a New Telephone to go by her bed.
As there was no tea party 9 went to the Village Bingo with my sister Ros and freinds Mooter & Jan, What a lot of people there (about 40).
Harry Corter came from Swange to do the Calling we had a cup of tea in the interval (Cost 20p) and 9 won a draw Prize. They hold a bingo every fortnight and all profits go to help run the Village Hall.

Today's weather: Showers again we have had so much rain this Winter but it was frosty when we came out of the Hall at 10pm

Name RITA CHURCHILL   Year of birth 1950

House 21 West Street   Street

Corfe Castle Congregational Church
Cameo Club 6.30pm - 8.00pm

CAMEO are the initials of the Young peoples Club of our Church, it means **Come And Meet Each Other.**

Tonight is the first evening meeting after the Christmas and New Year holiday. We meet each week during term time and do a lot of things which are of interest to children and young teens. We are a younger group than the Youth Club which meets in the Village Hall each week.

We are church based which means that a lot of what we do is of a spiritual nature and is based on the Bible. Also, we do preparation and practising for special events in the Church such as family services and a Nativity play at Christmas and a Special Easter presentation.

Our Cameo Club is open to all Young People, whatever their church - or no church connections. We also have young people from surrounding villages and Wareham and Swanage usually friends from schools. Our numbers vary of course from 12 or 15 up to nearly 30

We have craft evenings, water colour painting, cooking, competitions and of course plenty of games especially when we hire the village hall.

Our regular attendees are: Joanna Watson, Judy Spinney, Catherine Restevick, Charlie and Lorna Wareham, Navelle Joy, Tania Davies (all young teenagers). The other children by Christian names: Emily & Amber, Sheriden and Nicole, Lawrence & Sam, Sarah &Adam, Joss, Joshua & Michael, Alex and Felix, Rosie & Tom and several others not so regular.

We have four leaders at the moment: Mrs. Dorothy Longhurst, Mrs. Megan Methan and the Minister and his wife - David & Pam Foot.

Today's weather: DRY, MILD with some WIND.

Name CAMEO CLUB

Year of birth

House CONGREGATIONAL CHURCH

Street CORFE CASTLE

Today, the Corfe Castle Christmas Festivities Committee will remove the Christmas lights and decorations that adorn the buildings of The Square, East Street and West Street.

Following the best year ever, with new lights up to Morton's House Hotel in East Street, and along West Street to The Fox a great deal of work has to be done in order to take down all the decorations within one day. It might even take longer.

As usual, Joe Williams and Geoff Windsor are first on the scene at around 8.15. Others drift in to The Square from about 8.30. Perfect weather, blue sky and the sun is shining. Work starts immediately to remove the 14 small trees donated by Malcolm Ramm of Norden Farm, and individual special festive light features made by Justin Cross. Soon we have about 15 Committee members working in The Square, including Chairman George Preston. As soon as the crane arrives, everyone is hauled off their tasks to deal with the big tree against the cross. The crib below is dismantled quickly and the power supplies to the tree disconnected. There is some debate as to whether the lights from the tree should be removed before the tree is lowered to the ground or after. The latter is decided upon so the brackets and wire stays are loosened to allow the tree to be lifted out of its fixings by the crane. Whilst in a suspended position the lighting is removed. Branches of the magnificent tree provided by the Rempstone Estate are then unceremoniously cut off, and the tree loaded on the crane and carted away.

It's 10am and a call goes round that coffee and hot buttered toast are being served in the National Trust tearoom. Very welcome! Rumour has it that the Bankes Arms are preparing bacon sandwiches and coffee; a member of the Festivities Committee is asked to ask them to delay until 11am. That gives us another 40 minutes work before the next break! By now our numbers have swelled to 19 – what a turnout! Jane Windsor takes notes on improvements to be made next year.

Three work parties form, each tackling different sections of the decorations. The remaining small trees and festive lights come down very quickly. The trees are loaded on to a pick-up truck for disposal and the lights and crib are taken to the Bankes Arms Stable for storage.

Now to tackle the main lighting looms. One groups starts from the Bankes Arms and works up East Street, another starts at the Townhouse and works towards West Street, and the third concentrates on The Square. 40 minutes have disappeared and everyone heads for the Bankes Arms for a second or perhaps a third breakfast. Another 3 members have miraculously arrived – did they smell the sizzling bacon? Doesn't take long for the blarney to start, but that's the fun of this committee. Twenty minutes later we all tumble out of the building and get back to work. Two looms are taken down from across the road with the minimum of difficulty. Everyone seems to know what to do. All the looms are now in short sections making handling much easier and each is wound on its own drum. Ends are labelled to make things easier next year for when they are put up again. Lucas van Lelyweld is doing his usual clearing up job with brooms and dustpan and brush. A star!

Just after 1pm it's all over – the lights and decorations are all down. The Square looks bare. It is hard to believe that it happened so quickly and efficiently. A quick check around The Square to make sure that everything is accounted for and put away. Some have to disappear to meet other commitments, the rest of us go into the Greyhound Inn for a well deserved drink. Once again, the Greyhound does us proud and feeds us.

The sun is still shining.

The following evening, Sunday 9th January, is cold and frosty. A number of Committee members take down the Christmas decorations in the Village Hall. Warm and lively inside with all the usual banter. Within an hour the task is complete. Our Chairman, George Preston, thanks everyone for their help.

The Festivities Committee is thankful of all the support it receives from the village that make the decorations possible, and especially grateful to those who water and feed us whenever work is going on.

Another year is over, and planning for next year is already underway!

Name ~Dougles Whyte~   Year of birth 1953

House ~Secretary CCCFC.~   Street 3 West Street.

Name *Ian Harris* Year of birth *1946*

House *Castle View Florist & Cafe* Street *East Street*

The first day back to work after having the flu.

Wots that noise – oh no it's morning, not 5.30 a.m. already. Reluctantly slipped out of bed, threw on my clothes as central heating still not working. Quick wash in cold water, not a nice experience but did the job, woke me up!

Dark outside, scraped the car windscreen and set off to work. News on radio about a flu epidemic across the country, drove across the Square, nobody about. Saw Mark Hathaway baking in Dragon's Bakery. Corner shop open, turned left and set off to work at Holton Heath.

Went out at dinner time for petrol £3.94 per gallon (that's 78.9p a litre). Paid in cash and then back to work.

Finished work at 5 o'clock, drove home in the dark – can't wait for the clocks to go forward an hour. Daffodil and tulip bulbs already shooting, checked mail (good, no bills) and took over from my wife Debbie with our little horrors, Luke and Kieran. Sat around the table for tea (things looking up, no arguments between the boys). Deb went out to work so I washed up and got the boys bathed and ready for bed. How many times have I got to read Thomas the Tank Engine? Good, eyes shut --went downstairs. Deb arrived home so I got ready for the Millennium meeting in the Bankes Arms at 7 o'clock (no, not the Fox with sidekick Doug Whyte).

Mike, Stephen, Eileen, Doug, Tina and myself. Main topic was the Mid-Summer Ball, disco, Church service and children's party in June/July. We chatted about New Year's Eve and how great it was to see so many villagers dressed in fancy dress, singing and dancing. The fireworks were spectacular (wot a night!). Meeting closed and home we went, well nearly! Right hand turn and into the Fox for a quick pint.

Phil Duffy was in there telling jokes and stories of times gone by, laughing and joking. And so ends my day.

GOOD COMPANY – GOOD BEER – AND LET THE WORLD GO BY

Today's weather: Cold and dry

Name   Kevin Reynolds   Year of birth   1963

House   17   Street   West Street

'He MUST be delirious — he said he wanted to visit the Dome'

THE DAILY TELEGRAPH

TUESDAY, JANUARY 11, 2000

* * No. 44,966

Just go to bed: there's no cure for this horrible flu

Keep warm, have plenty to drink and treat the symptoms, advises our doctor **James Le Fanu**

THOSE hit by flu this winter can expect to suffer from a range of unpleasant symptoms.

Unlike the localised infection of a cold, the flu virus gets into the bloodstream and travels round the body.

Sufferers get what is known as a viraemia, caused by the virus circulating and reproducing as it progresses. They develop a temperature, aches and pains in the muscles, a bad headache and profound weakness.

Despite the publicity surrounding Relenza, the new anti-flu "wonder drug", the best way to cope with flu is to retreat to bed and, as there is no cure, treat the symptoms. Take temperature-reducing drugs (such as paracetamol), lots of cough medicine and hot drinks.

This winter's flu epidemic is caused by the Sydney strain of the Influenza A virus, which is more virulent than normal.

Whereas flu usually lasts five days, this year quite a lot of people are getting residual symptoms including a persistent, unpleasant cough that can last up to three weeks.

Although the flu is not dangerous, its complications certainly can be.

Those most at risk are the elderly and people with chronic heart or respiratory illnesses. They are particularly susceptible to bronchitis and can develop pneumonia.

Those in the high-risk categories are advised to get themselves vaccinated against the virus, although this is not guaranteed to protect them.

100th birthday coin minted

Queen Mother: in profile

Today's weather:

EIGHT months ahead of the big occasion, formal celebrations of the 100th birthday of Queen Elizabeth the Queen Mother began yesterday with the issue of a £5 centenary crown, writes Robert Hardman.

Flanked by flag-waving crowds, a smiling Queen Mother is seen in profile above her signature.

The coin's designer, Ian Rank-Broadley, said yesterday: "I wanted to portray a realistic portrait which showed Her Majesty's dignified bearing, but retained the elegance and grace for which she is so admired."

Having won the competition to design the crown for the Royal Mint, Mr Rank-Broadley was granted a special sitting at which he took the photographs on which his design is based.

Initially, the silver-coloured coin will be on sale in a presentation folder for £9.95.

Name   A Day in the life of a Committee Member of The Millennium Association!

House

Stand in for the would-be Diarist for today; ...down with the Flu.

CORFE CASTLE WOMEN'S INSTITUTE

On this day a post-Christmas lunch was enjoyed by the members, some with their husbands, organised by the Corfe Castle Women's Institute at "Kemps", a very pleasant country hotel on the Wareham to Wool road.

The menu was as follows -

Chilled Fans of Galia and Charentais Melon with a Peach & Honey
Yoghurt Dressing
OR
Cream of Mushroom and Tarragon Soup

Steak & Kidney Pie topped with a Stilton Crust
OR
Roast Delice of Salmon with a light Lemon Grass & Dill Cream
<<<< >>>>

Selection of Fresh Vegetables and Potatoes

<<<< >>>>

Profiteroles served with Chocolate Sauce
Fresh Fruit Salad and Cream

<<<< >>>>

The cost was £12.00 per head, including a "tip".

Those attending were -

Elizabeth Crabbe (our President) with husband John, Margaret & John Cooper, Kate Murphy, Doreen Neilsen, Tess Robinson, Em Reed, Dr.E.A.Richardson, Ruth and Rev.Herman Nuttall, Vera Clark, Betty Carter, Esme Woodland, Molly Miller, Sybil Windsor, Bettine Simpson, Kathleen Cowley, Joan Dunne, Eileen Alcock, Beryl Pyle. Our Secretary, Stella Gibson, was unfortunately unable to attend as she had recently broken her hip.

Today's weather: Typical English winter day: cold, drizzling, dull and dreary.

Name CORFE CASTLE WOMENS INSTITUTE Year of birth FOUNDED 1946
House MEETING IN THE VILLAGE HALL Street 2nd THURSDAY MONTH

Today is my 19th Birthday. I was born in Epsom, Surrey on a Tuesday. We moved to Corfe in 1993. My mother, who is a sculptor, used to come here in the summer to work and buy Purbeck Stone. We had many holidays in this area and always loved coming here.

I am in my final year at the Purbeck School in Wareham, doing A-Levels in Art, English and Economics. I am hoping to do a Foundation year at the Arts Institute in Bournemouth in the autumn and then go on to University.

I didn't celebrate my birthday much today, as I was working after school. I have a part-time job as Second Chef at the Bankes Arms here in Corfe. (Not very busy today). But we had a few beers and some darts practice in the British Legion after work. I am playing in the Legions Team and so far we are doing very well in the League. However, I will celebrate more thoroughly on Saturday, when I'll be going to the Opera House in Bournemouth with my mates. Inspite of its name, this is a very large nightclub, with many dancefloors, disco music and it holds hundreds of people.

Slinky

Today's weather: Cold, Dry, Sunny

Name Quentin D.R. Seik   Year of birth 1981

House No. 8   Street Halves Cottages

Friday January 14th

I woke up in time for Elaine,, our cleaner, to arrive and remove the layer of dust that causes everyone in the house to sneeze.

I walked in to the village wrapped up in a fleece and scarf in an attempt to reduce the effects of typical January minus figure wind chill factors.
In Clealls I bought a couple of birthday cards, wrapping paper, a box of Maltesers (unfortunately they were for some one else), and some polo's for me, to compensate for the lack of feeling in my fingers.

An hours revision for a university exam on the speculated impacts of Global Warming. Is this problem still escalating or has it been decided to act on significantly reducing greenhouse gas emissions?

Had lunch while watching a television programme about people on holiday in Mallorca in the hot sun by a beautiful blue sea. Meanwhile, I'm eating a cheese, ham and tomato sandwich in England, in January - but I'm not bitter!

More lovely revision.

Braved the cold and almost darkness again to walk the 'far too energetic' dog on the common, as the sun set behind the tumuli on the ridge.

At the end of the day, a meal at Mama's Cuisine in Swanage with five friends to say good-bye before going back to university. Calamaris and tagliatelle with prawns and salmon beats sandwiches but I'd still prefer Mallorca!

Today's weather: Lovely Cold and Sunny

Name ALISON LOUISE KEMP   Year of birth 6/12/1980

House 7   Street COLLETTS CLOSE

St Edward, King and Martyr
Corfe Castle

Evensong for the 17th Annual General Meeting
of the
Dorset County Association of Church Bell Ringers

Saturday 15th January - 4pm

The Dorset County Association of Church Bell Ringers held their Annual General Meeting at Corfe Castle on January 15th, 2000. The DCA chose Corfe for their meeting as the bells had previously been silent for 43 years. The day commenced with a Church Bellringers service conducted by Rev. Maurice Strike and this was followed by tea in the Village Hall prepared by the Corfe Valley Ringers. After tea there was the business part of the day the AGM which was attended by:
Chaiman, Deryk Bugler from Toller Porcorum
Vice Chaiman, Philip Reoch from Blandford Forum
Ringing Master, Alan Frost from Dorchester.
This meeting was supported by a further forty-six members and five Corfe Valley Ringers were proposed and accepted for membership.
During the evening we ended with excellent ringing from all the DCA members – a wonderful day blessed by beautiful spring-like weather.

David Langford

```
O Mighty God, the joy is ours
To sound Thy welcome from our towers;
And when, at last, Thou callest 'Stand'
Let Mercy rule at Thy right hand.

                 Hymn: 'O Mighty God this Earth is Thine'
                      (to Wareham)
```

Today's weather: Clear crisp air on a Spring - like day.

Name   Year of birth

House   Street

TO-DAY WE ARE IN TORQUAY, DEVON, VISITING THE TRADE FAIR "TORQUAY FAIR 2000". THIS IS A NEW EXPERIENCE FOR US, NEW TO THE BUSINESS AS 'SHOPKEEPERS'! ON RETURNING HOME FROM WORKING OVERSEAS (1977 to 1996), WE DECIDED TO OPEN A SMALL SHOP IN THE PART OF OUR HOUSE THAT WAS ONE OF THE FORMER SMITHIES IN THE VILLAGE! LAST WORKED IN THE 1930'S BY THE MOSS FAMILY.

THE BLACKSMITH'S SHOP
CORFE CASTLE
DORSET

(opposite Mortons House Hotel, East Street)

AN INTEGRAL PART OF THE HOUSE, THE OLD FORGE, (AND SAID TO BE THE OLDEST SURVIVING HOUSE IN THE VILLAGE) THE OPENING OF THE BLACKSMITHS SHOP HAS ENABLED VISITORS TO SEE INSIDE THIS 15th CENTURY BUILDING AND THEY ARE MOST INTERESTED IN ITS HISTORY. THE SHOP OPENED IN APRIL 1999.

We Strike whilst the iron's hot! ... whilst the weather is cold and less visitors around! ... in search of Unusual gifts.

Wrought Iron for home & garden; and Metal craft,

Genuine horseshoes always in stock!

WE NOW REALISE HOW TIRING IT IS TO TRAIL AROUND TRADE FAIRS! WE WERE ABLE TO SOURCE SOME INTERESTING GIFT IDEAS TO ADD TO OUR VARIETY OF GOODS. THE BRIGHT CRISP CLEAR SUNNY JANUARY DAY MADE THE JOURNEY A PLEASURE, BUT NICE TO GET BACK HOME!

Today's weather: A BEAUTIFUL BRIGHT DRY DAY.

Name EILEEN & LUCAS VAN LELYVELD-CRONE Year of birth 1932/1933

House THE OLD FORGE (Residence) Street 38 EAST
also housing THE BLACKSMITH'S SHOP.

I live in Studland and have been Parish Clerk since 1996. This day was chosen for the Diary as it was the first Parish Council meeting of the new Millennium. The Parish Council meets on the third Monday of every month, in the Town Hall in West Street, starting at 7 pm with a chance for members of the public to raise anything of concern. During the afternoon I prepare for the meeting, writing up a "clerk's report" summarising "matters arising" and other correspondence, etc. I also need to prepare cheques for signing and check out any last minute background information about matters on the agenda.

The morning had been spent meeting with Jon Pack and Lesley Brown, of BP. The Parish Council had discussed the future of Furzey Island (which lies within the Parish) at our December meeting. The island had been previously mentioned by BP at the Wytch Farm Consultative Committee and the way that this had been reported suggested that its disposal was very imminent. Although no specific proposals were discussed at this time, the Parish Council felt strongly that it should come to a locally based organisation for some sort of community-based use. As a result of this morning's meeting I was able to report back to the Parish Council in the evening about the process of decommissioning, restoration and monitoring the success of the restoration. This will take quite a while. It will therefore be several years before any alternative use for the island can be considered. Members certainly felt clearer about what is happening and it was agreed that Jon Pack and Lesley Brown (together with Jon Pack's replacement, Eamon Naughton) be invited to the March meeting to discuss the matter further.

One of the main items to be considered at the January meeting was the Parish Council's budget for next year and the consequent Parish precept which is raised through the council tax. With an increase purely to allow for inflation the precept was set at £12,170. This of course is only a minor part of the total council tax collected by the District Council (which also includes the County Council and Police Authority precepts). The Parish Council has no other source of income and it relies on the 22p (Band A) to 65p (Band H) per week per property from the council tax for all of its activities.

Following several requests for a pedestrian crossing in East Street, the Parish Council decided to ask the County Council for a feasibility study. We would not want to lose the school crossing patrol, and so we have asked the County to look at the possibility of a pedestrian crossing for the library and Village Hall rather than further towards the school.

The formal agreement with the County Council for the Parish Council to carry out minor highway maintenance was signed and consequently we expect to be doing this work as from April. Under the agreement, we will be responsible for clearing gutters and gullies, clearing weeds from the pavements, etc. Cutting the verges will still be the responsibility of the County Council, as will repairing potholes.

The Parish Council discussed the County Council's Local Transport Plan, which is now required by the government for every county. The final plan which will be published later this year will set out the County's policies and programme for transport projects for the next five years. We submitted lengthy comments on the draft: we felt the plan was rather too woolly and general and there is very little mention of the specific situation in and around Corfe Castle. We expressed the expectation that the final plan would be far more detailed about problems and projects for individual parts of the County.

The Parish Council also responded to Purbeck District Council with our views on waste collection, street cleaning and public toilets. The government is requiring all Councils to review all their services, under the "Best Value" regime, and this is the first round of services to be looked at. In summary, we replied that waste collection operated reasonably well apart from some details, but expressed concern over the emptying of litter and dog bins and the prospect of public toilets being closed.

The Council considers all planning applications. At the January meeting, it submitted objections to the District Council on applications for an extension and garage for a cottage in Kingston, and for antennae and cabin for Vodaphone at the Rollington Transmitter (we are trying to get the ground equipment better camouflaged).

Today's weather: **Bright but cold**

Name **Stephen Yeoman**   Year of birth **1954**

House **Town Hall**   Street **West Street**

Tea in bed? Suspicious!　.　Cooked breakfast? Very suspicious!!

Hang on! Today is the Anniversary of Captain Scott reaching the South Pole in 1912 and that means it's my 'Birthday' So why no cards? I must have words with the Postman So how shall I celebrate? There's nothing on in Corfe today as it's always very quiet at this time of the year Still, its a lovely day but cold, so I'll wrap up, and walk up to The Sweet Shop and get my 'Telegraph' newspaper [45p] and seek some inspiration

I see National Express Coaches are advertising a £10 deal to any UK destination for the over 50's, so I could go to London and ride on the 'London Eye' ferris wheel. That would be nice but the 'Eye's not working yet due to mechanical problems A visit to the Millennium Dome is also a possibility, but I fear that I might be the only one there!! Attendance is below expectation and it is due to close at the end of this year I wonder if it will ever host the Olympics?

Alternatively, I could go and see the tigers at London Zoo in Regent Park I better hurry, as tigers are an endangered species, and due to poaching there are now less than 5,000 in the wild compared with 80,000 in 1900 Then I could follow that with an evening visit to St Martin's Theatre in West End to see the 'Mouse Trap', a fine play now in its 48th year You might have thought that someone would have let the cat out of the bag by now!!

Of course, I could stay at home and just listen to cybergirl 'Ananova', the world's first digital newscaster, but unfortunately she's only being unveiled today

On the financial front I see that the pound has soared to a 11 year high, and as the euro sinks to a new low, I sometimes wonder if the euro has a future Still we have been offered a referendum before we adopt the euro, and currently a majority of the country are against it. However, I fear politics and big business will prevail

I hear today that England have won an historic Test Match in South Africa It's historic, not only because it's a rare England victory, but because for the first time, both sides forfeited an innings in a Test Match Unfortunately, we still lost the series!

Decision Time I shall drive down to Chardstock, a little village in Devon where my family have lived since the early 1600's Many years ago today, I was born in Chardstock Post Office [second delivery]. So a lunch of beef-on-the-bone, now that the Government ban has been lifted, at the village pub that Mum and Dad used to run, followed by a walk around the village to reminisce on my misspent youth, seems a good idea

A very good idea as it turned out　.　the rest of the family suddenly arrived [with cards] from all over, for a surprise birthday luncheon at the pub!

So back to Corfe and just time for some more birthday cake [courtesy of Dragons Bakery] and another Gin and Tonic WHAT A GREAT DAY!

Today's weather.
SUNNY · BLUE SKY · COLD · MAX TEMP 8°C · CLOUDED OVER

Name   APSEY PETER   Year of birth   1940

House   THE OLD BAKEHOUSE* : WEST Street . CORFE CASTLE
* PRIOR TO BEING CONVERTED INTO PRIVATE ACCOMODATION IN 198
THIS BUILDING WAS DRAGON'S BAKERY [AND PREVIOUSLY HIBBS'S BAKERY

A telephone is ringing by my bed. Where am I? I grope for the handset. An American voice tells me that it's six thirty on Wednesday the 19th of January, and the outside temperature is twenty degrees below zero — "have a nice day sir". My wake-up call. In the darkness I replace the phone and remember yesterday's drive to the airport and the eight-hour flight. If this is Wednesday I'm in New Jersey, at the IBM Conference Centre where American Express Bank is holding its annual management meeting. It promises to be a grim affair.

I shower, dress and head down for breakfast - a vast buffet of dishes of fried and scrambled eggs, bacon, potatoes, fruit of all kinds, bagels the size of dinner plates, yogurt pastries, and a dozen or so cereals. My body clock says it's lunchtime, and I'm hungry after breakfast, with time to kill before the first session, I wander into the Web Room, where twenty or so computer terminals crouch in the twilight, waiting for human contact. Each displays the menu of an Internet search engine. I approach one and type in the words 'Corfe Castle'. After a few moments the screen shows one hundred and forty-seven sites.

Outside the sleet is driving against the window. I click on one of the sites, and the screen fills with a familiar image: a brilliant summer's day, with the sunlit castle on the crest of its hill. This is how it will look when we walk up to the May Fair with the children. Figures mill around the gate and small groups sit on the grass of the inner bailey. In the foreground, below the screen, my imagination can extend the picture: cars are crowding the square, while tourists, villagers and perhaps a few costumed members of the Sealed Knot are drifting up towards the castle or standing in groups around the square. Then a vicious gust rattles the Web Room window, and I log off and walk over to the meeting room.

In the morning session there's bad news about the Indonesian loans. In the afternoon there's bad news about the Hong Kong mortgage book. But in the evening there's good news: in the bar and during dinner, a famous magician is working his way round the room. Moving from group to group he performs incredible tricks at very close quarters. A guest selects a playing card and replaces it in the pack. Seconds later it is found under a chair on the other side of the room. A ring disappears from a lady's finger, then turns up attached to the magician's key ring. The audience of hard-boiled bankers gasps with wonder like a party of little children. Back home my own children will be reading about Harry Potter. On Saturday I'll be there.

Today's weather:

Name Frank Spooner   Year of birth 20 - 5 - 1951

House Meadowside   Street East Street

I'm not actually in Corfe today. Michael (my husband) and myself are staying with my brother, sister-in-law and nephew up in Sheffield. That is where I originally come from. We are up here because Michael is doing a central heating job, no doubt in years to come it will all change to a different source from gas.

Got up this morning to a nice, dry, cold but sunny day. May father came and took be to Chesterfield Market. Looked for good bargains but failed. Went out for lunch. Food cheaper up here in some places.

Volunteered to help 5 – 6 year olds make Chinese lanterns. Great fun – got glue every where!

Didn't do much in the evening. Michael was working late so did my crosswords. Then watched "Who Wants to be a Millionaire" – I wish!! and a couple of other programmes.

Today's weather: Dry, cold but sunny

Name	Mrs. Janice Harriott	Year of birth	1954
House	Lagney Court	Street	Jubilee Gardens

06.30: Rose after good nights sleep to find wife already busy downstairs. Washed & had quick breakfast. Removed car from garage.

07.10: Drove to work at Winfrith, via A351 and Holme lane – nothing much to see, dawn not yet broken.

07:30: Arrived at work for an early start, before the others get in. Cant say much about work, it is classified, but involves computers. Morning fairly uneventful.

12:00: Nip over to canteen or the "Casterbridge Centre" as it is now known, for lunch. Have a reasonable meal of broccoli & pasta bake. Dive back to base to collect car for quick trip into Wareham. I need to get there to collect a book from Wareham Bookshop. Manage to arrive at 12.45 and in luck to find a handy parking space. Collect book & decide to call at Lloyds Bank for some cash as I am down to £1.40.....

13:05: Back at work. Send off some mail and book hire car for trip to Portsmouth on Monday. Complete time sheet for week & other routine bits & pieces.

16:00: Leave work for the weekend – bless the flexitime system!

16:20: Arrive home & park car. Wife presents me with list of calls from the day. Open post. Various Council documents, including a planning proposal for the clay pit at Trigon and an appeal document relating to a Kingston application.

17:00 Eat evening meal, braised celery, potatoes, onions and a Linda McCartney pie – No, I do not eat meat.

18:00 Further office work at home, including a glance at the planning agenda for next Wednesday. do some odd jobs, check email then watch some TV for rest of evening. Look forward (not!) to some decorating work tomorrow.

22:00 Bed, and a little more T.V.

Today's weather: FAIRLY FINE

Name LEJ. HAYWARD   Year of birth 1943

House TILIA HOUSE   1   Street EAST STREET.

Today we held the draw for the Carved Owl this was carved by myself, Ken Miller, from an original oak beam taken from the Belfry of St. Edwards Church during restoration of the bells. The reason my wife Molly suggested the carving, was that her first husband's family The Scadden's had lived in Corfe Castle for many generations and had been Bell Ringers.

£1000 was raised and given to the Belfry Fund, thanks to the people of Corfe Castle and Bell Ringers around the County.

Local girl Samantha Burgess won the owl. She has asked that it be displayed in the Corfe Museum for all to see.

Today's weather Cloudy morning, sun later.

Name	Ken & Molly Miller	Year of birth	1935 - 1933
House	The Haven	Street	Jubilee Gardens

Sunday January 23rd

Yesterday, was my Mums' 63rd birthday! I am Sharon Brown (nee Applin) and Mum is Linda Applin of West Street She was born in Corfe Castle and now, after having her family and career has retired to the very house that she was born and brought up in
I live in South Woodford, North East London and work for Abbey National on a project as a Business Analyst in Marylebone. I came to Corfe Castle for the weekend, with my flatmate Kathy, to make Mums birthday a special day. I had driven down on Saturday morning, stopping at Sainsburys on the way to purchase food and wine for the evening meal.

I woke to find Sunday had arrived with clear skies and a blaze of winter sunshine, cold but dry, the perfect weather for a long walk. First of all we all had breakfast of croissant, orange juice and coffee looking out into the garden where a selection of birds were greedily eating from the seed and nut feeders hung in the garden. We decided that we would drive to a local craft shop called Hobbycraft to get some ideas for Valentines day craft activities for my Guide unit in Woodford Green. I found many ideas and purchased much pink and red card, tissue paper, sticky hearts and lots more We also visited the garden centre next door and bought lots of plants for the garden back in South Woodford They were much cheaper than in London and looked much more healthy than any I have seen in my local area.
We drove back to Corfe Castle for lunch for and then went to Arne Nature Reserve for a walk The sun was still shining but it was bitterly cold and windy. I was glad that I had remembered all my windproof clothing and walking boots. We found a birdwatchers 'hide' and stopped there for a while to view across the wetlands and spot a variety of birds. We continued our walk in the direction of the shore when unfortunately Kathy tripped and fell over a tree root - she fell flat on her face in a huge muddy puddle She was okay, if a little shocked and recovered quickly after a bit of a clean up. We all made it to the view point and then to the sand at the sea shore. We all threw a few pebbles to see how many times we could make them bounce on the water Kathy was the expert at this and won by far We had slower walk back to the car to make sure that there were no more accidents and then drove back to Corfe Castle for a hot drink (and for Kath to wash properly).
Back at the house we drank hot coffee and lounged around a bit reading the Sunday papers - a luxury I very rarely have time to do at home. Feeling refreshed and ready for the 3 hour drive home we said our goodbyes and set off for London. The drive home was busy but not as bad as it has been in the past - at least the traffic was moving on the motorways! Even so, we decided to do the route through London rather than take the M25 around London

Once arrived back at home and the unpacking was done it was a quick get ready for work on Monday, grab something to eat and then an hour infront of the television to relax before retiring to bed.

I hope Mum enjoyed her birthday- I certainly enjoyed the weekend and will try to spend more time visiting Corfe Castle this year.

Today's weather Sunny but cold.

Name Sharon Brown   Year of birth 1962.

House Visiting Corfe   Street West Street.

I heard Joanna's alarm, and she came down for her breakfast soon after, watching TV. She let me out for my morning constitutional, but I had to bark to come in again because she'd gone upstairs by then, to get washed and dressed. Boss and the Missus said 'Hello' when they came down. Until people started leaving I stayed curled up on my rug, but the last one to go gives me 2 dog-biscuits so I need to be alert for that!

Elaine came to do some cleaning today. I think she likes me because she chats away to me, but shuts me out in the utility area when she's doing her stuff downstairs. The good news is she gives me 2 biscuits too when she goes!

I spent most of the long afternoon asleep, just fighting with my rug from time to time. They all came home at about the same time today, and we had a good bonding session. Usually I don't get my supper till they have had theirs, but I was in luck today, as they gave me mine first. That's good, because it's tough being hungry and having to put up with the smells and sounds of their cooking and eating! Anyway, my meal was OK - no extra snippets of uneaten cat food (Jo is feeding neighbours' cats while the humans are on holiday, and because cats are stupid and leave some I often get it). They give me a few handfuls of meal (Tesco's cheap stuff at the moment - I prefer Winalot), half a small tin of meat and a third of a big tin. I reckon that's about 140 grams of meal which costs about 12p, and 600 g of meat which costs about 43p. With 9 Shapes as well (about 7p) I only cost them 62p a day to feed! Oh, a smidgen of milk at bedtime, and water (they're on a meter), but that wouldn't come to much, would it?

They were all in this evening, which is unusual. But it wasn't that good, as they are doing something very smelly upstairs (painting the bathroom I think) and that confounded computer takes them away from my attentions too. To make it worse, Jo had her school textiles all over my lounge floor so I was not allowed in most of the evening. The good news is that she didn't have any time for ear-piercing practice on flute or saxophone.

When we all eventually settled in the lounge I got my own back by asking to go out, then barking to come back in- three times! It's a good game to keep my profile up. When in the garden I terrified the various neighbourhood cats, and I spent a little while exchanging abuse with Jock at No 5.

I'm a bit concerned as I heard them talking about taking me to the vet for a kennel cough squirt up the nose next Friday. No way! I'm sorry, I'm happy to cooperate on most things, but NOT THAT! They'll have to find another way, or better still not go on holiday and stay with me. Anyway it didn't work last time - my voice still hasn't recovered properly. I feel a bit of a fool - a pedigree golden retriever yelping like a puppy-dog!

Today's weather: Cold, no wind, cloudy - good for smells in the garden. Dry, so I wasn't kept in the utility room to dry off!

Name	Happyland All Gold (but call me Jaffa)	Year of birth	1994
House	7	Street	Colletts Close

Tuesday January 25th

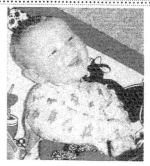

I was woken at 3.30am by my 16 week old baby boy, Adam, in need of some nourishment. Fifteen minutes later he had had his fill and quietly drifted off for another sleep, I did the same. 6.30am another alarm call from Adam, more sustenance please. Fed and changed him then popped him back into bed as he was still sleepy. I went back to bed for a couple of hours then woke at 8.30, dressed and busied myself with some chores untill Adam woke at 9.30 to rise bright and bubbly.

Once awake, changed his nappy, washed his face and hands and gave him his breakfast, which consisted of a milk feed from me then got him ready for the day. No play time this morning as we had to go to Tescos for the weekly shop, managed to leave the house by 11.00am. Adam enjoys shopping at the moment, so much to look at, fascinating shapes and colours in rows of groceries which made up for the play time missed at home this morning.

We arrived home by about 12.30 put away all the shopping and prepared lunch for Adam. He has just started solids, consisting of baby rice and breast milk mixed to a puree and absolutely adores it. He polished off the lot and followed it with a quick drink of milk. It won't be long before he is eating proper meals.

Having met the needs of my son, it was now time to get ready to go over to Corfe to feed my pony, Sally. Sally needs to be fed every day during the winter until the grass begins to grow again on the common. We mixed up food for Sally and drove over to Corfe at about 2.00pm. Adam usually stays with Granny and Grandad, my parents who live in Corfe, while I walk up to the common. As it was such a gloriously sunny day I put Adam into the sling, collected Mums dog, Jay, walked up to the common and had a short walk round before feeding Sally. Adam fell asleep. We met Sally on the walk and she followed us to the gate. We stood in the sunshine with the warmth on our backs while she ate her food. We arrived back at my parents house in time for a lovely cup of tea, and a play with Adam followed by a drink to keep him going until tea - time.

We left Corfe at about 4.45pm to get back home to prepare food for a small dinner party for my Brother Andy, who is over from Singapore for a week of business conferences and my sister Jenny and her husband Graham who live in Corfe.

Having prepared dinner, I bathed Adam. Ben, Daddy, arrived home at about 6.00pm and gave Adam his evening feed while I got on with the dinner. While the food cooked I showered and got myself ready for the evening ahead.

Jenny arrived at 7.00pm straight from work, followed shortly by Andy and Graham. A pleasant evening was had by all. Adam joined us for the whole evening, which is not unusual at the moment and entertained us with his vocals as the evening progressed. 10.00pm, time for his last feed of the day and bed. Andy, Jenny and Graham left shortly after and Ben and I retired to a very welcome bed.... I wonder when I will be woken, not too soon I hope!

Today's weather: Very cold, frosty ,sunny and blue skies.

Name Jacqui Seal

Year of birth 15/06/1965

House 2.

Street East Walls (Wareham)

(visiting 57 West St Corfe Castle)

My main activity today was a meeting of the Corfe Castle Methodist Church Council – at my flat, as it's more comfortable than the church on a cold January day – so first I had to tidy my lounge. My 11-week old puppy Lisa leaves such a lot of rubbish around the floor – bits of fern fronds, snail shells, sticks & paper as well as the odd puddle & pile of poo!

A quick spell at the word processor to create an Agenda as I'm the Hon. Sec., then a calming mug of black coffee and I'm ready.

The Meeting was fairly well attended – 6 out of 11 members present, plus the Minister (Rev. Sylvia Garrett) and 2 Circuit Stewards. Routine business easily dealt with, but the hard part was to decide whether to continue as a church or to close down.

After very frank discussion, and with much heartache, we decided to ask the Poole & Swanage Circuit to sell the premises – which are a heavy burden for such a small elderly band of members. We also decided to continue as a church using other premises – either my lounge, or hiring a room – and to go forward out in the world rather than stuck away in a big inflexible building.

After an emotional morning I was only fit for playing in the garden with Lisa. This was no hardship, it being a glorious sunny day.

One of my other jobs as a Methodist is to edit our local church magazine (covering Swanage, Herston, Studland, Corfe Castle, Wareham & Wool) and I collected the pages for February's issue yesterday. I counted out 35 for Wareham & 5 for Wool (leaving me 20 for Corfe) and drove over to Wareham to give theirs to Margaret James for distribution.

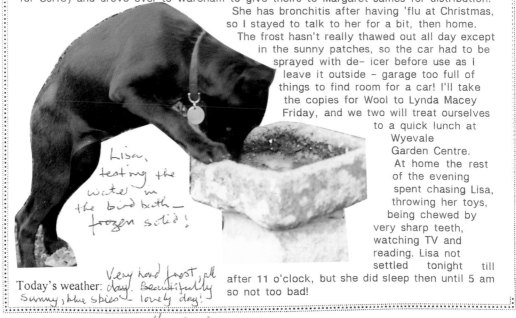

She has bronchitis after having 'flu at Christmas, so I stayed to talk to her for a bit, then home.

The frost hasn't really thawed out all day except in the sunny patches, so the car had to be sprayed with de- icer before use as I leave it outside – garage too full of things to find room for a car! I'll take the copies for Wool to Lynda Macey Friday, and we two will treat ourselves to a quick lunch at Wyevale Garden Centre.

At home the rest of the evening spent chasing Lisa, throwing her toys, being chewed by very sharp teeth, watching TV and reading. Lisa not settled tonight till after 11 o'clock, but she did sleep then until 5 am so not too bad!

Lisa, testing the water in the bird bath – frozen solid!

Today's weather: *Very hard frost, all day. Beautifully Sunny, blue skies – lovely day!*

Name *Mary Wills (Helen Mary Wills)* Year of birth 1938

House *Kestrel Court, 56 A (ground floor)* Street *East Street*

Thursday January 27th

I woke at the usual time of 07.30am but was in no hurry to get out of my warm bed as I knew that the very cold weather which we had been experiencing was expected to continue. However, I knew that I had a busy morning ahead so made the effort. As I expected, on looking out of my bedroom window the hoar frost was so thick that it looked like snow (Temperature - 4 °C).

After breakfast of cereal with semi-skimmed milk and black coffee (200 Calories!) I went to the swimming pool at the Vista caravan park in Swanage where I swam about ½ mile. Before leaving home it took me several minutes to clear the ice from my car (a 'S' Reg. 1998 Ford Focus) - even spray de-icer was not very efficient.

After swimming I went to May's flat in Swanage where we meet each Thursday morning to continue with our hobby of calligraphy. The flat is situated high on the south side of Swanage bay with marvellous views. The building was once a Children's hospital and converted into flats some years ago. Our project for this week was to make and use our own pens from a bamboo stick (with a reservoir made from an aluminum drinks can); another from 'all purpose J cloth' and cardboard. Besides managing to cut my finger on the metal both methods produced very satisfactory instruments.

Returned home to lunch of Salmon Mornay (a packaged 'ready meal') and fresh vegetables followed by yogurt. This is quite a normal sort of meal for me as I **hate** all forms of cooking and spend as little time as possible in the kitchen!
As usual I watched the 'News at One' whilst I ate my lunch - the headlines were concerned with the news that a surgeon in Wales had removed the wrong kidney from an elderly patient; the repeal of the bill which bans the promotion of homosexuality in schools; the war in Chechnya and the start of the American Presidential campaign.

By the time I had finished, copies of the February edition of the Corfe Valley News had arrived for me to post (at a cost of 31p each) to the many 'out of district' subscribers. The Corfe Valley News, of which I am the current editor, is a monthly magazine delivered to 900 homes in Corfe Castle and the surrounding villages.
On my way to the post office I called on Mary with my old newspapers (The Independent) which she finds very useful now that she has a new puppy which is not yet house trained. Then on to the post office, next to the bakers to deliver a letter to Nigel Dragon a fellow Parish Councillor and finally to the local shop, Cleall's Stores, to do some grocery shopping.

By the time I arrived back at home it was nearly 4.30pm and time to watch 'Countdown' on the television whilst having a cup of hot chocolate to warm me up.

As I was expecting email I logged on to the Internet on my PC. There were several messages including the one I was expecting. After replying it was time for tea and a relaxing evening watching television, reading the newspaper and my library book 'The Remorseful Day' by Colin Dexter - and so to bed at 11.00pm (23.00hrs)

Today's weather: *Sunny, clear skies, very cold - frost continuing all day in sheltered spots*

Name	Linda Applin	Year of birth	1937
	64, West Street		
House		Street	

C O R F E   C A S T L E

JUMELAGE

P O N T   H É B E R T

President : Victor Valle.
Chairman : Richard Piercy
Vice Chairman: Mike Perry.
Secretary: Herman Nuttall.
Treasurer: Barry Wilson

The Twinning Association of Corfe Castle held a Cheese and Wine Evening at the Bankes Arms Hotel to raise money for a proposed visit of children from Corfe Castle to stay with French families in the town of Pont Hébert, Normandy. This follows a very successful visit made by 16 children from our twin town last June.

The Chairman, Richard Piercy, welcomed the 50 guests, including Founder Members, Paul Randall and Victor Vallé. A £4.50 ticket entitled everyone to a free glass of wine, French cheeses and pâté bought from Tesco supermarket and a dessert of trifle, charlotte russe, raspberry pavlova or lemon tart made by the ladies of the Committee.

The Raffle was made up of items with a French flavour. From a selection of wine, chocolates, olive oil, coffee and other delectable French goodies, Diana Dru Drury won a Camembert cheese and Heather and John Dixon won a jar of Soupe à Poissons.

A total of £200 was raised. Mike Perry proprietor of the Bankes Arms, is always very generous towards the Association and allows the Committee to hold its monthly meetings in the Club Room. A cross-section of the village comes to Twinning events, as neither church allegiance, politics or age affects membership.

Last September 30 people from the village crossed the Channel to Cherbourg and we await the return visit of our French friends later this year. See the diary page for 30th September!

Committee: Paul Randall. Ruth Nuttall.Cathy Brett. Gillian Humphries. Ann Preston. Jenny Wilson. and elected officers.

Today's weather: Grey and drizzly.

Name Corfe Castle & District

House Twinning Association

Year of birth 6 months upwa
ellighble for membe
su

Street

"Corfe Castle? Too much of the chocolate box about it" a severe friend, an artist, says. You can see what he means. The village is "themed", like a model of itself; the stern, grey castle walls, the precipitous slopes of the castle grass; all the beautifully maintained National Trust and private property. The buildings are attractive the older ones of doughty enduring stone. The infilling, at least of stone, is generally very smart and cared for. The Greyhound, of itself, is worth the whole of another village.

I have longer memories of Corfe than my friend, and have enjoyed more intimacy with its unlevel pavements and quiet people. I first arrived at the village railway station on the day before Christmas Eve in 1956, expecting to be met by someone I had known during my army National Service. He was to have been there with his father in his father's car. There was no one to meet me; some muddle over a telegram that didn't arrive. The train which had sat steaming and puffing in those days of coal and boilers, puffed a bit more and set off for Swanage. I set off alone for Worth Matravers on foot, beneath the pale light of the full moon, feeling protected and almost becalmed by its presence. Later, in what seemed like the natural course of things, I owned an old car myself; a Morris Eight of 1933 vintage. As I made my way to Swanage or my parents' house in Langton, Corfe had reduced itself to an awkward bend in the road by the Bankes Arms and the Square which involved some double declutching.

So for a number of years, I generally passed Corfe by. But I remember those times in the 1960's with a young family when perhaps we kept the children up too late! I can see in my mind's eye the moth-filled lights of the car, the headlights teeming with self-bodied insect life. When we walked in the dark, the roadside banks were studded with the faint green light of glow-worms, and alive and ticking with the constant sound of crickets.

Time moves on. Though my father died in 1974, my mother continued to live in Langton for another eleven years. My sister Marion and her husband William moved into their home in West St. Corfe in 1983; my mother sooned joined them and my own visiting to Corfe grew more frequent.

Walks on Corfe Common, to the Copper Bridge, to the Civil War batteries, along the railway line, or on the downs leading to Swanage, these gave me new perspectives of Corfe Castle village. On winter evenings exposed to the sugary, coppery artificial street lighting; on fairer days basking in the heat and light of the sun; I observed its two main streets, West Street thronged with pottering visitors, East Street edgy with traffic.

What Corfe was once, a thriving almost self-supporting community, it will almost certainly never be again. So is its air of permanence provided only by the Castle, the Church, the shapely solid dwellings of the past? I don't think so. There are so many people in the village who care about it, and unobtrusively sustain its amenities and attractions.

NOTE

My brother wrote this Millennium Diary page whilst staying with me in West St recovering from pneumonia. He already knew, as I did, that he was terminally ill with cancer, Multiple Myeloma; finally he lost his life on the last day of June 2000. My own Diary entry was written with him very much in my thoughts.

MARION ORMEROD nee ROBBINS

Today's weather:

| Name | MICHAEL JOHN ROBBINS | Year of birth | 1935 |
| House | THE GREY HOUSE, 102 | Street | WEST |

A disastrous start to the day!

The alarm was set for 4 a m. but somehow I managed to sleep through it and woke up with a start at 6.15 a m.

The shop has to be open by 8.30 a.m so a revised production schedule is needed.

One major plus is the fact that we are one of the few remaining bakeries that still produce all the white bread by using the old fashioned method of an eight hour bulk fermentation. This means that the dough is mixed the evening before it is required and allowed to stand and ferment during the night This now allows me a quick start.

Luckily we do not have too many wholesale orders today as this is by far the quietest period of the year.

Deliveries only have to be made to the Isle of Purbeck Golf Club, Manor House Hotel, Studland and Halfway Inn, Norden

Production this morning will consist of :-   White Bread
Soft White Rolls
French Sticks and Crusty Rolls
Brown Bread and Rolls
Wholemeal Bread and Rolls
Malted Grain Bread and Rolls
German Six Grain Bread
Doughnuts, Buns and Danish Pastries

After a hectic morning's work I manage to complete all the production by 11.30 a m.

My parents used to run the village bakery in West Street, Corfe Castle, a different site to the one that I now occupy When they retired from the premises in 1984 and moved back to Swanage, the village was left without a bakery until the National Trust 'offered me my existing premises in 1991, on condition that they were turned into a working bakery.

Sunday is still a special day for our family and we all gather at my parents' house for Sunday lunch Today there were fourteen of the family gathered for traditional roast beef. It seems to be the only time the family manages to get together apart from Christmas   Lunch over with and the washing up completed, the hectic Sunday continues as my family are members of the local branch of the Salvation Army and thus will all be attending our afternoon service at 3.30 p m

Back to my parents' house for afternoon tea and then return to Corfe Castle where I once again change into my bakery clothing and spend the evening making the white bread dough for use the following morning. I also have to spend time prepping up all the puff pastry goods such as apple turnovers, eccles cakes and sausage rolls, so that they too are ready for baking.

Finally roll into bed exhausted but happy at 11 p m satisfied, having spent the day doing what I enjoy!

Today's weather

Name	Nigel Dragon	Year of birth	
House	Dragons Village Bakery	Street	The Square

At work in a lovely place ...

Drove into Corfe Castle from Weymouth early, as usual, I had left an assignment for a course at Bournemouth University to the last minute. As I do every work day, I checked to see if the east wall of the castle was still standing, as it came into view from the Wareham Road. It was!

Today the castle looks square and squat. Some days it looks tall and slim – it all depends on the weather. I noticed that Box and Sons had the digger ready at the barn in North Field. Tim Box came in to see me about a soakaway and water pipeline they want to dig around the barn. It would need to be monitored and recorded archaeologically, it is for me in the end, a new stone store for stone from the Castle excavations. It would have to wait until I got back from Bournemouth Uni.

Had a working! lunch and took a mug of tea over to the Barn to look down the holes the machine had dug. Very black soil, with 17th, 18th, 19th and 20th century finds in it. Blue and white pottery, animal bone, bits of farm machinery and a multi-coloured marble an 8er. It was not very deep in some areas and then it was on to the natural orange sand and clay. Pete Mould arrived at 3 o'clock to talk about the consolidation and work on the ruins of West Mill at the bottom of the Castle mound. He is a worker with lime and stone and had been checking his work on re-pointing (and rebuilding parts) of the lime kiln at South Barn Farm at Langton Matravers, just off the Priests Way. Phil the Warden had been cutting back the scrub to clear the site for the work to be done, re-using stone we had excavated a few years ago. The rest of the stone had been given in 1920 by Mr. Bankes for the building of the War Memorial In the village. The site will be lovely when it's finished and open to people to use for picnics etc. Today the birds were singing and the snowdrops were out in large clumps along the riverside. I thought, I work in a lovely place – how lucky I am.

Today's weather: Sunny intervals, cold wind, cloudy later

Name   Nancy Grace   Year of birth   1963

House   Archaeologist working for the National Trust   Street

It started off as a very dull day - as well as being a very sad one As thirteen years ago today I lost my beloved mother, Winifred Read She lived at No 11 East Street where she brought up my two brothers Brian and Raymond and myself

Brian, who lives in Spain and was over staying in Poole, arrived at my home at 11 am to begin our morning of remembrance First we walked down to St Edward's Church to look at the Book of Remembrance We had a pleasant look around the church and then sat for a while Then we left the church and made our way to God's Acre Cemetery in West Street, where we placed two lovely potted plants We stood and gathered our thoughts before visiting the graves of our other relations, including our grandmother Ida Stockley, who was one of the villages great characters and died in 1982 at the grand age of 96 I said goodbye to Brian and made my way home

After lunch my husband Bert (a local postman of 33 years) and I left the house to visit West Mill We walked down Oliver Vye's Lane and at the end of which we crossed the road and went over the footbridge that crosses the river and takes you directly to my mothers birthplace
My mother was born in one of the small cottages there in 1907 to Ida and Walter Stockley Walter worked at the local clay mines, but having always suffered from bad health he died at the age of 54 leaving his wife to bring up their 8 children alone Going by the stories Mum used to tell me West Mill was a wonderful place to live and grow up - so peaceful and picturesque - nestled at the base of West Hill with the river flowing right past the side of the house The children used to love the times when the farmers would bring their sheep down to be dipped, and when they used to race across the stepping stones, often falling in   When the river used to rise and flood the house, which it did several times, it was another matter. The children would have to climb out an upstairs window onto the bank at the rear of the house in order to get to school Having no husband to support the family meant times were hard, but the family was a very close and happy one   To help support the family Mum went to work as a maid in Bournemouth She did not enjoy this much as it meant time away from the others and West Mill As the years went on the three cottages at West Mill became uninhabitable, so in the 1920's the family moved up into the village, into No 10 West Street My grandmother lived there for the rest of her life while Mum eventually moved to No 11 East Street

As usual this time of year West Mill was abundant with snowdrops If you look across the river you can still see the steps and some of the original stepping stones Also part of the toilet is still standing It was an interesting and exciting time when the National Trust did their archaeological dig there several years ago If you follow the public path that goes around the back of West Mill you will see an information site, which I think is a good reminder of life, as was, all those years ago

On returning home my husband and I sat and and compared life back then with life today How times were hard and money was short but people were happy All the people in the village knew each other and got on well   No one thought twice about going out and leaving their back door open, just one of the things you would not dream of doing nowadays As the time passes by it brings with it many exciting technological concepts such as cars, aircraft, television, computers, the Internet, mobile phones etc   As these things change and progress so do the problems of society When we now have the problems of drugs, killings, bombings, burglary, racial, physical and mental abuse, and people becoming more self-obsessed and money orientated - it makes you realise what a wonderful place and time it must have been to live

Today's weather

Name Johnston Family   Year of birth

House 40 East Street,   Street

Ann Johnston's mother (Winifred) is seen here on the stepping stones at their home West Mill Cottages circa 1912 with sister Bessie in the arms of their mother Ida Ann Stockley (later affectionately known as Grannie Stockley to all in the village)

Today's weather

Name

Year of birth

House

Street

Woken up by the alarm at ten to seven - today is a work day. I now, after 34 years in the RAF, work as an independant IT consultant.

A modest breakfast of Optima and fruit with a couple of cups of coffee. The weather today is beautifully bright and clear; I think that high-pressure is on the horizon. Ready to go by ten to eight; this is the time to leave as I have to get to the Studland to Sandbanks ferry to get the ten past eight crossing. The traffic through Sandford, the long way round, at this time of morning is absolutely impossible, so the ferry is the way to go. Additionaly you travel through beautiful country and have super views over Poole Harbour on the way.

I am on my way to Christchurch for a day's work with BAE SYSTEMS, with whom I have a contract at the moment. I advise them on information technology business. I notice that the traffic on the way to work gets worse each year.

Today the first business is a progress in meeting which we have every Wednesday: today we are going to review the current project through which we are hoping to obtain a Ministry of Defence contract in the near future.

The journey is about 45 minutes and in addition to travelling over the Purbeck Hills to the ferry it also involves going along the Over Cliff Road in Bournemouth, where once again there are beautiful views over the calm sea towards the Isle of Wight.

On arrival I park, stop at the main gate to pick up an entrance pass and then up to the secure area where I will be working today. Just time to make a quick coffee and then straight into the progress meeting. This is followed by a design review and then some commercial business. A very busy morning, which is soon over and it is time for three of us to go to the pub for a quick lunch.

At the pub a pint of lager and a prawn baguette and after about 45 minutes back to start work again on the practical demonstration. The day is a continuous round of busy activity and by about six I am becoming quite exhausted; happily it is time to go home. By then there is not quite time to get to the ferry to return home via Studland; if there is less than 25 minutes it is too difficult to get to Sandbanks and the danger is that I will miss the ferry and have to wait a long time for the next one.

So I decide to do the long way round by Wessex Way. This means that I don't have to wait although it also means that it takes a little bit longer. Never mind, I am soon home to a great welcome from Diana and the dogs.

Today's weather: BRIGHT + CLEAR

Name Stephen Du Drury   Year of birth

House Herons, East St   Street

What fun we are going to have compiling this diary: "Diary 2000" a Millennium Association project ….. and today was most enjoyable and entertaining when I popped in to see Connie and Danny McCrae at 21 East Street. But, oh dear, the traffic on East Street (A351) is unbelievable; it seemed to take ages to get across the road on the bend by the Bankes Arms. The huge vehicles just about miss hitting the pavements and buildings. Connie says she is often picking up bits of kerb stones!

However, once inside I had a really warm welcome in this country cottage (National Trust, formerly Bankes, property). We had a good cosy chat by their real coal fire on this February morning.

I have known Connie and Danny since the 1960s so we had lots of laughs and plenty to talk about. The highlight of my visit was to see the framed "Certificate of Appreciation" recently presented to Connie. Prior to 1951 the (now toilets) building was used by a local builder, George Brinton (Betty Groves' late father) as his office.

● *Connie with her certificate and trophy*

Connie is flushed with pride

A COMMUNITY stalwart in Corfe Castle for more than half a century, Connie Macrae, 79, has been recognised for her tireless work on making sure the village's public loos are always spick and span.

The Kimmeridge-born grandmother lives with her husband, Danny, next to the East Street loos, which she started cleaning when they first opened in 1951.

And Connie is so houseproud she still supplies air freshener and soap – at her own expense!

Her devotion had the parish council scouring their brains for a suitable, but heart-felt, award.

Now chairman Les Hayward – who as a child in the early 1950s used to play in the lavatories and was thrown out many a time by

Mrs Macrae – has presented a surprised Connie with a framed certificate and a gold toilet brush!

"I've done it for so long to keep the toilets going. I enjoy it and have met a lot of nice people whom I regard as friends," explained Connie.

"Connie has cleaned the toilets since 1951 and treated them as an extension of her own home," said Mr Hayward.

"Although Connie is employed by the district council and not the parish, we felt her long service and devotion to the local community should not go unrecognised as we move into the new millennium."

In 1991, judges for the best kept village in Dorset specifically singled out Connie's work for praise.

Along with the late Reg Spiller and Connie's first husband, the late Harold Tatchell, Connie was a founder member of Corfe Castle's festivities committee after the Second World War. It provides the village's Christmas lights display, a children's party and a Christmas function for senior citizens.

Connie was also the caretaker of Corfe Castle village hall and a fundraiser for the Royal Air Forces Association in Swanage for many years.

She served on Corfe Castle's Royal British Legion committee for many years – receiving village and county award certificates for her sterling work a few years ago – and staged bingo evenings and dances.

Today's weather   Remarkably bright, dry and mild

Name	Connie and Danny McCrae (in conversation with Diary Committee Member Eileen Van Lelyveld)

Year of birth   1920 & 1912

House   21   Street   East Street

The Corfe Castle Society

The Society was founded in 1969 at the instigation of the late Mrs Rachel Lloyd According to its Rules, its main objects are to encourage public interest and pride in the Castle, village and civil Parish of Corfe, and to safeguard the character of the village as a place of residence as well as an area of historical interest and beauty Although I was not in the area at the time, I believe the need for such a body sprang from the proposals to construct a bypass to relieve congestion and danger from the traffic through the village Some means of achieving this result was, and still is, very desirable, but much controversy at the time concerned the route a bypass should take Today, the possibility of any such major road construction still looks very remote

All residents of the Parish are eligible for membership, and at present we have about 200 members The annual membership subscription is £2 00 We have a Committee, which meets monthly, and consists of myself as Chairman, Frank Spooner as Vice-Chairman, his wife Karen as Treasurer, Mary Wills as Membership Secretary and Stephen Dru Drury, Roger Free, Tom Hunt and David King as Members At present we have not succeeded in persuading anyone to take up the position of Secretary, this seems typical of many such voluntary bodies, all of whom find difficulty in recruiting people to take on the job of helping to run activities Perhaps it a symptom of the increasing pressures and pace of life and the number of competing leisure opportunities

We arrange a series of Open Meetings each year - usually seven between October and May, each with a speaker or other entertainment, wherever possible with a local flavour One such meeting has taken place tonight Entitled "East of Purbeck", it consisted of a slide show and talk given by two local ladies, Mrs Cynthia Sansom and Mrs Brenda Chappell, who are old friends of the Society and have given us much pleasure over the years They have a remarkable talent for exploring places of interest, photographing them most beautifully, and unearthing the most fascinating facts, which they record on an audio tape as an accompaniment to the sequence of projected slides Tonight we were taken on a visit to places to the East and North of Purbeck, starting with Christchurch - originally called Twynham- and including places as diverse as Bournemouth and the little village of Throop Although many of us thought we knew the area well, they succeeded in revealing something new to us all

We had an audience of about 40, particularly good for a rather dark dank winter night The meeting also provided Eileen van Lelyveld with an opportunity to remind us of this Diary project, and seek sponsors for other dates, and we also served our usual coffee and biscuits to facilitate some neighbourly conversation Perhaps the most important contribution a Society such as our can make is just that, an opportunity to foster a sense of community

Today's weather   Overcast, dry,but humid, 10° C maximum, keen W wind, very dark night,

Name JOHN ANSTEY (CHAIRMAN, CCS)   Year of birth 4/6/1927

House 2 AILWOOD FARM   Street UNDERHILL RD

SATURDAY 5 FEBRUARY, 2000

We arose at about 8.30 a m , had breakfast and fetched the newspaper from the village shop. After completing some work on the document for the visit of the French geologists in June, we made preparations for the long walk along the Dorset Coast that we had planned As it was the weekend, we would be able to walk within the Lulworth Ranges, and we were looking forward to visiting Mupe Bay, one of our favourite places

We prepared our usual sandwiches and drinks, and set off on the eighteen mile car journey to the heights above Ringstead just after 10.30 a m We enjoyed a warming cup of coffee before we set out on the walk to Mupe Bay and back, a distance of some 14 miles We had hoped for an improvement in the weather, but the sun seemed reluctant to break through the veil of cloud that covered all of the coast, although from time to time patches of sunlight appeared briefly on the waters of Weymouth Bay, ruffled by a south-west breeze that was enough to chill us as we stood looking out towards the completely obscured Isle of Portland.

We set off towards the coast and were soon at the gaunt and bleak Nothe Cottages that crown the summit of the great chalk headland of White Nothe We made good progress along the cliff-top path to the stone obelisk, and then began the descent into Middle Bottom Then we climbed up the slopes to the cliffs west of Bat's Head, and there had our first view of Durdle Door, today enshrouded in the unwelcome murky haze that covered all of the coast . Soon we had ascended the easy western slopes of Hambury Tout and were looking down on Lulworth, and thinking of a suitable spot for lunch

We ate our sandwiches on rocks near the western end of the Cove, and after a quick phone call to our daughter Helen, set off for Mupe Bay, some one and a half miles away By the time we reached the cliffs above Mupe, the sun had come out briefly, and we enjoyed the bright view eastwards With the long inland walk back to the heights of Ringstead in mind, we did not linger at Mupe, but set off on the climb up Radar Hill and had soon descended into West Lulworth, and bought some chocolate at the village stores to sustain us on the last leg of the trek westwards A long walk up the road to Winfrith took us to Daggers Gate, and we were soon at the obelisk, where we had the last of the coffee and the very welcome chocolate We were back at our car by half-past four it had been a worthwhile walk, even it was a bit chilly and the views were obscured by the grey winter haze

We were home just after five, and enjoyed a warming cup of tea, and some cakes Saturday evening is usually a special culinary event for us, and we celebrated our walk with a meal that included avocados and prawns, lamb steaks with a fine range of fresh vegetables, and strawberries and cream. A quick read of the papers and we were soon ready for bed, after an exhilarating day out on the coast.

Overcast and quite chilly with the occasional bright spell

Today's weather

Name JOHN and RUTH CHAFFEY   Year of birth 26.3 .1931 and 4. 11. 1936

House 10   Street COLLETTS CLOSE

Sunday February 6th

Awoke at 5 a.m. to prepare for the monthly Antique Fair at Corfe Castle Village Hall which I have been organising since 1996.

Leave home at 6.45 a.m. to travel to Corfe Castle Village and put out signs to advertise the Fair and set up the stalls in the Village Hall.

 Antiques for sale include ceramics, hand embroidered linens, books, postcards and small pieces of furniture.

Example of prices are £3 for 1950s Playing Cards, £25 for a hand painted Chamber Pot, £95 for a Brass Preserving Pan and £600 for a Windsor Chair.

Many of the visitors to the Fair travel on the steam train from Swanage which can be seen from the Village Hall.

It's a very busy venue in the summer when so many people visit Corfe to see the historic castle ruins.

Today's weather: Started fine but rained later

Name   Jeanette Morbey   Year of birth

House   Renaissance Antique Fairs   Street   Corfe Castle Village Hall

Monday February 7th

Today I am 67 years of age I got up about 8·30 AM
I am making seville orange Marmalade today
I prepared and cut up the peel yesterday and left
soaking overnight. Marmalade takes quite a long
time to cook simmering for about 2 hours
before adding sugar. I used 3 LBs of oranges and
6 LBs of sugar. I ended up with 11 LBs of Marmalade
I finished approx. 1·30 PM. All jars labelled and the
washing up completed.

After lunch I visited the library and exchanged
3 books. Whilst I was there I noticed the new
Doctor had started his surgery in the Village Hall
car park. The New Doctor is "Steve Horsnell". He
replaces "Dr. Selwyn."

After tea I went with my youngest brother, Roy
and his wife Angelika to evening class at the
Purbeck school, Wareham. The class is upholstery and
renovation. I am renovating and reupholstering an
old armchair approx. 90 years old. Probably Edwardian
The Tutor is "Adrian Clarke" from Dorchester. He
is very good at the job.

Arrived home approx 9·30 pm. Went to bed about
11·00 pm.

Today's weather: Dull early Morning. Rain with fairly strong wind
brightened up early afternoon.

Name JOHN E. FORD   Year of birth 1933

House 3. JUBILEE HOUSE   Street EAST STREET

It's my birthday!

After an early morning cup of [tea] I was given a mounted photo of Corfe Castle at dusk with the comet Hale Bopp, and a snazzy tie, from Christine and Joanna. After breakfast, off to work as Education Coordinator for the National Trust in Purbeck. Lots of [phone] and [letters] to deal with, about [building] bookings for Corfe Castle and Studland mainly. A group of our Volunteers have a sewing and spinning workshop in the Study Room this morning. At 11am a group of Bournemouth University Heritage Conservation students arrive for a talk by me, so I get into [graduate] mode. They seem satisfied with my comments on why the Castle is here, what it's made of, and so on.

5pm - Home for tea - Joanna's helping out at Rainbows, Chris rushes out to do Brownies, Joanna rushes home for tea. More [phone calls] including one from Alison in Norwich to say Happy Birthday (there was an e-mail from her too) and one from a neighbour asking if I could remove one of our [trees] ,then Jo goes off to Rangers, Chris comes in, and I go off to Badminton in Wareham. A good laugh. A court costs about £5, so 2 courts between 6 people (11/2 hours) isn't bad. Up to the bar afterwards for a [drink] and a packet of crisps. Then home, a small Tunisian liqueur (Thibarine) with Chris, sort out the [cat] , and bed.

Today's weather: Cold, windy, and some light rain in the morning

Name	David Kemp	Year of birth	1946
House	7	Street	Colletts Close

I got up at 7.15 am, put my dressing gown on, and had breakfast
of Bran Flakes, milk and a mug of tea in the sitting room with
the electric fire on. The central heating was only just coming
on. After washing, dressing and clearing away, I was in time
to meet Mr Varney, who was arriving at 9 am to repair a leak
in the flat roof of the garden chalet. We discovered where it
was, and he went up his ladder on to the roof.

There used to be two large garages for coaches between the
boundary of the chalet and East Street, and about eight motor
coaches operated out of them, conveying school-children, private
hire and outings. There were three petrol pumps and a forecourt,
for we sold petrol, but there is no one selling petrol in the
village now, whereas in years gone by there were three, Dave Ford,
Billy Blake, near the site of the Castle Inn, and Sheasbys.
The land was sold and now Uvedale Court flats, built by Corfe
Castle Charities, are there.

Mr Varney finished after a couple of hours, and kindly cut back
a clematis that had grown up the side of the house, got entangled
in a telephone wire, and was growing along the guttering. His
long ladder was very useful!

I was having a 'catching up' day at home, as I had been cleaning
my cottage near the square for four days then been to Poole to
meet some friends the previous day, so I was receiving and making
telephone calls, and had a 'ready meal' lunch, from freezer to
microwave, which only took about ten minutes to cook, followed
by yoghourt. I tried to catch up with some paperwork, pay bills,
etc. (I don't have a computer, although I am going to a computer
class for beginners at Wareham). I do use my electronic
typewriter, though.

I decided a needed some fresh air, so walked down to the village
shop for some free range eggs, etc., had a chat in the shop, then
back to the paperwork.

I made beans on toast for tea, ate it in the sitting room watching
the six o'clock news on TV, decided there wasn't anything I wanted
to watch on TV, so read a book I had got from Corfe Library for a
while, then had an early night.

I hadn't used my car all day!

Today's weather: Dry and sunny in the morning, but becoming
increasingly cloudy and cold in the afternoon.

Name JANICE SHEASBY   Year of birth 1942

House Ashmead, No. 60   Street   East

Corfe Castle Computer Club.

Club members gathered at our comfortable venue above the British Legion in East Street for our regular second Thursday in the month meeting. As ever the discussions ranged from exciting announcements about new hardware or software to dismal news of breakdowns, poor service or other bad experiences. The main feature of the evening was a presentation by Geoff Pyle of ten 10" x 15" professional digitally scanned transparencies and laser printed onto Kodak photographic paper. These were compared with Cibachrome prints of the same size.

Nancy Logue gave us details of her new PC/Scanner/Printer package bought from the Kingston Maurward College, where she has recently attended a computer course. We are always eager to compare quality and prices of new outlets. John Burt gave us information about a new section of the Blandford Camera Club, dealing with the Photographical Digital Imaging by Computer, and interested members have been invited to attend.

The nineteen members who enjoyed the exchange of information and ideas this evening were:-

William Jones - Ken Chirgwin - Ronald Gibson
Ken Watson - Sheila Watson - Nancy Logue - Robin Swaine
Keith Lambert - Keith Dowling - John Burt
Peter Madge - Tony Gopsill - Karel Smits - David Watson
Geoff Pyle - Nick Squirrell - Mike Hawthorne
Ray Harris - Geoff Marshall

The Corfe Castle Computer Club was formed seven years ago, and those seven years have seen huge advances in the power, capability and value for money of the Personal Computer. As more and more people buy computers and existing owners settle down with their machines, the Club enjoys a steady stream of new members to give and take advice and swap tales of triumphs and terrors.

Geoff Marshall <marshalls@bychance.freeserve.co.uk> Secretary.

Today's weather:

Name Corfe Castle Computer Club   Year of birth Every 2nd Thursday each m
House Meeting at the British Legion   Street East,

Friday February 11th

I am writing this diary page in my capacity as Secretary of Corfe Castle Millennium Association. This organisation is responsible for the creation of this diary, with the aim that it shall be stored in the Archives, hopefully at County Hall, Dorchester, where it may become a reference document for future generations.

Firstly, let me say something about the Association. In 1996, The Parish Council considered how the Millennium could best be celebrated. It was decided that a committee should be formed to make all arrangements, thus relieving the council of this responsibility. The inaugural meeting of the Millennium Association was held in December 1996. The officers, who have remained unaltered, were elected. I became the Secretary, Stephen Dru Drury the Chairman, Linda Applin the Vice-Chairman and Mary Wills the Treasurer. Some twenty or so villagers, as individuals or as representatives of the many committees, clubs and societies within the community, form the nucleus of the membership. Our role is to provide celebrations throughout the year 2000 to cater for all ages and tastes, and to co-ordinate events arranged by other organisations.

It was decided at an early stage that we should form a number of sub-committees with responsibility for organising events in the following areas:

Religion – This sub-committee, led by Rev. Maurice Strike, includes representatives of various denominations. The sub-committee will organise a series of interdenominational services throughout the year. Maurice is also instrumental in producing a community play, 'Thy Kingdom Come', which will be held for three nights in April. This will focus on two thousand years of Christianity by highlighting the work of certain individuals.

Entertainment – Having regard to the fact that the Christmas Festivities Committee continue to put on its usual Christmas and New Year functions, the Entertainment Sub-committee is able to concentrate on the Midsummer Celebrations to be held in the Castle. A marquee will be erected for three days of events. Friday 30th June will see a family disco together with live music to be provided by Jim Etherington and his band. A ball, with three course meal, will be the attraction on Saturday, 1st July, followed on Sunday by a religious service in the morning and a children's party in the afternoon. The weekend promises to be a memorable occasion. The Sub-committee will be holding an 'It's a Knockout' competition in September, and in November, a firework display with fireworks launched from the Castle,

Art – A Stone Carving Symposium will be held in July. The public will have the opportunity to experience at first hand sculpting stone, something which is very much part of our heritage here in Purbeck. The Drama Group will be staging '1066 and all That' as well as a series of Murder Mystery Walks.

Environment – We shall be planting trees to commemorate the Millennium and hope to involve the young folk of our community in this project.

Capital Project – We are working towards building a pavilion and enhancing other amenities within the village sports field. This is very much a long term project which, following the dissolution of this Association, will be continued by a Sports Trust.

Our regular monthly meeting, at which the various sub-committees reported their progress, was held last evening . The main topic of debate was the disappointment brought about by the rejection of our application to the Millennium Commission for funding to stage the community play and the stone carving symposium both mentioned earlier. This being so, we shall now finance the events from our own resources accumulated by our fund-raising efforts. This will require careful financial planning in order that we are able to meet our many commitments and still have funds to pass to the Sports Trust.

The first part of today was spent recording the minutes of the meeting. Accuracy is important as the contents will be regarded as the final word in any legal dispute. I used my Canon 'Starwriter Jet 500' word processor, which has many features of a computer but is less sophisticated. The minutes, together with letters generated by the discussion during the meeting, took much of the morning. Having spent this time indoors at a desk, my wife and I decided to take advantage of the fine weather for the time of the year and took a stroll over Corfe Common with its fine views of which one never tires.

Today's weather: Dry, Sunny and bright. Chilly westerly wind. 8 degrees max.

Name Jim Rosewarn   Year of birth 1945

House April Cottage   Street West Street 77

CORFE CASTLE
12 of February 2000

I woke to a wild wind, rain belting down. An hour later not a cloud in the sky, it's going to be one of those thoroughly changeable days.

The postman and the paper-boy have delivered the most amazing amount of bits and pieces of paper along with our letters and papers through the letter-box.

There are insurances, holidays, good causes, financial advisers, stair lifts, walk-in baths, all sending advertisements. Into the bin with it all. It will take all morning to read and we have better things to do today.

My Mum wants to go to Wimborne to collect some new shoes she has ordered. So we bundle into the car and get on the road early. We carefully watch the speed limit as there has been a real crack down lately on observing speed limits through villages, quite right but apparently quite a number of people have been caught. It goes on your licence, you can only have three offences and you are banned from driving which would life very difficult around here.

It's the Coffee Morning at the Village Hall in aid of the Drama Group, a good cause but we were too late. The next show they are doing is based on '1066 and all that' they are auditioning at the moment so there will be lots of little parts playing all those Kings, Queens and Rogues of the History.

The sun is very low coming into the kitchen. I am cooking baked fennel [a good Delia Smith recipe] jacket potatoes and chicken pie [Mummy got in Swanage] for lunch.

Hugo and I walk Fred up the Halves while it's cooking. The Castle looks like a great ancient old tooth towering over the village.

Mum had a tea party in the afternoon at Sybil's. So Hugo and I took Fred a walk at Studland along the shady beach where my Dad used to keep his boat. The shape of the beach has completely changed since then. There was a rainbow over Old Harry. The woodland path used to be so overgrown and smelly Now it has been widened, the stream is clean, you can easily get boats down there. We came back past Godleston manor and the old brick kilns. We saw little lambs with their legs dancing away with them. When we got back we planted the Catulpa tree Hugo had brought from London

Just an ordinary day at Corfe Castle.

Today's weather

Name   JENNIFER CAREY & BETTINE SIMPSON   Year of birth 1932 + 1911.

House 40 ST KATHERINES COTTAGE   Street WEST STREET

Today I am walking around the village delivering the Diary pro-forma pages and guideline notes to the people in the village who have so far selected a date to record "a day in their life in 2000". In these early months of this Millennium Project there is much explanation needed to encourage village residents, their relations, close friends with Corfe Castle connections and village organisations to be involved in this Diary; a history book for the future.

It is a beautiful day, brilliant sunshine and a canopy of bright blue sky, amazing in mid February. I enjoy my stroll around the village and I spy ....

- ❖ Spring flowers: crocus and daffodils shooting through everywhere
- ❖ Birds singing happily
- ❖ On the Church Noticeboard: 2nd Sunday Parish Communion 10.30 a.m.
- ❖ The village is buzzing with visitors
- ❖ Sunday Lunch advertised at Mortons House Hotel (12.30 – 2 p.m.) £12.50
- ❖ In the Sweet Shop: Walls Ice Cream Solero Exotic £1.10, Cornetto 90p

From about 3 p.m. homeward bound traffic from Swanage is a continuous stream, mostly two people per car and mobile phone chattering!

Other cars are parked outside the rows of cottages, in some cases ranked two deep.

From sitting on the Market Cross in the Square, motor bikers and cyclists gear up and race away.

There is a magnificent sunset heralding another good day tomorrow, St. Valentine's Day. That date for this dairy is already adopted and reserved in my Big Red Book where I keep tabs on everything.

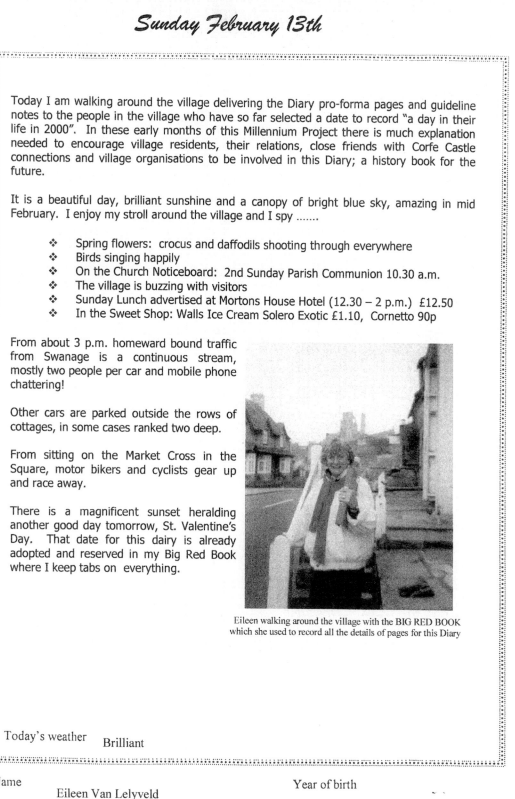

Eileen walking around the village with the BIG RED BOOK
which she used to record all the details of pages for this Diary

Today's weather   Brilliant

Name
          Eileen Van Lelyveld   Year of birth

House   Committee Member Millennium Association   Street

ST. VALENTINE'S DAY! This is the first big day in the florist's calendar and as we'd only introduced flowers to the craft shop shortly before Christmas we didn't know how things would go. Marita, who as a trained florist, had run her own shop before, knew what to expect, but would the amorous swains of Corse shower their young damsels with huge garlands of flowers.. ...or would they forget and have to make do with a late box of chocs How much do we order? Too much?! Too little??! AAAARGH Anyway, quite a few gentlemen had ordered in advance (good planning, lads) — and Marita opened the shop early to get things going. ...And the orders came in — some collected, others to be delivered anonymously to wives or girlfriends. A good day ensued, with lots of cheery banter, and that formidable mass of red roses getting smaller by the hour. Then a brain-wave. We'll stay open later to see if any of the returning "commuters" had forgotten what day it was — and sure enough, in they came — red faced, panting, and everlastingly thankful. "ROSES! HAVE YOU GOT ANY ROSES LEFT?!!" Suffice to say, that extra time we stayed open saved several chaps bacon, averted a potentially nasty evening, and probably threw in a few browny points for good measure. At last we closed, tired but happy. A good day. — Looking forward to next year now!

Today's weather DRIZZLY!

Name IAN HARRIS - MARITA SHAW   Year of birth 1946 - 1955
House CASTLE VIEW FLORIST & CRAFTS Street WEST STREET.

St. Edwards Church Choir Dinner. Why can't we choose the weather for our annual "get together"?! The weather was awful all day Rain poured down as guests leapt out of cars, skirts and trouser-ends held up for puddles, jostling umbrellas ...... but, as ever, the Reception Hall at Morton's House Hotel was warm and welcoming. Soon, accompanied by our guests, we were enjoying aperitifs, conversation and meeting with people. We were then ushered into the Conference Room, beautifully laid out with one huge table for twenty-two. We had a splendid a la carte menu (rather brave of the management, as there were only two waitresses, and one waiter to serve a four course meal) but they managed gallantly.

Maurice, our Rector, said a special Millennium Grace and expressed a hope (silent prayer!) for more people to join our hard-pressed choir. Ken Klaxton, our new organist/choir master, whose determination to raise our standards must seem an uphill task, no doubt silently applauded! We do really need another Bass or two. Where are all the Sid Paynes and George Hoopers of the village? We all enjoyed an excellent meal, some good wine and lots of laughter and ended the evening with coffee and chocolates in the splendid, oak-panelled lounge. How many of us will be attending next year, one wonders?

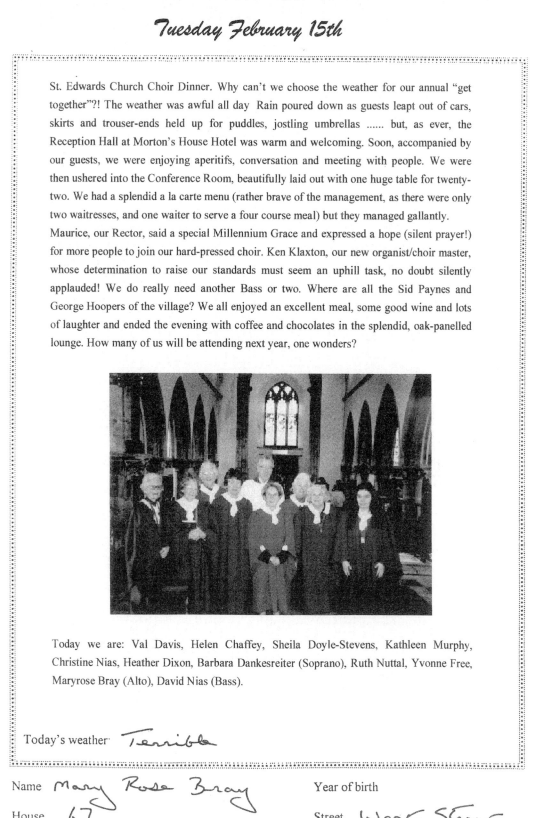

Today we are: Val Davis, Helen Chaffey, Sheila Doyle-Stevens, Kathleen Murphy, Christine Nias, Heather Dixon, Barbara Dankesreiter (Soprano), Ruth Nuttal, Yvonne Free, Maryrose Bray (Alto), David Nias (Bass).

Today's weather *Terrible*

Name *Mary Rose Bray* Year of birth

House *67* Street *West Street*

.... continuing my walkabout with the Big Red Book chasing the Diary Dates!   - so more jottings on a jolly cold day. I am well wrapped up against the biting wind, but full of the joys of spring! There is that special aroma of new mown grass as the Church lawns are being cut.

The Book of Remembrance for this date reads:

George William Fooks Born 8th January 1906 died 1990

.... a well known Corfe Castle name.

Walking along West Street I have time to ponder at the new extension to God's Acre with the young hedge planting; it all looks so serene and green in the winter sunshine, with neat pathways all nestling beneath the castle ruins standing sentinel over the village.

God's Acre has so many lovely colour contrasts with the spring bulbs and always so lovingly cared for.

The Village Noticeboard in West Street announces the next meeting of the Parish Council on Monday 21st February at 7 p.m. in the Town Hall. The Agenda includes:

- Proposed (car) waiting restriction outside the school
- Youth shelter progress report
- New surgery: to consider what, if any, assistance the Parish Council can provide
- Shell Bay to Norden cycle route – consideration of revised route

There are not many folks out today in spite of the bright day. Smoke rises from many chimneys, people are no doubt staying snug indoors. This evening, wearing our other committee "hats", Lucas and I join fellow members of the Corfe Castle Christmas Festivities Committee for our annual "do" at the Fox Inn. We all treat ourselves – giving us a "pat on the back"!

Today's weather   Bright but very chilly

Name   Eileen Van Lelyveld
            Committee Member Millennium Association   Year of birth

House   Street

CORFE COMMON.
HAYWARD TO THE CORFE COMMON.

The position of Hayward to the Common dates back for many centuries. Traditionally, the Hayward represents the Common Right Holders in ensuring that the stock on the Common is managed correctly.

Corfe Common is owned by The National Trust but is managed by the Corfe Castle Common Management Committee. The Committee is keen to ensure that the ancient practice of retaining a Hayward is maintained and one of its responsibilities is to annually appoint a Hayward.

The Committee is asking for nominations from anyone within the Parish of Corfe Castle to put his or her name forward for consideration at their next meeting to be held in the month of March.
The principal duties of the Hayward include:

1. Regularly checking that the animals grazing the Common are healthy.
2. To direct Graziers where they can graze their stock and to request that graziers move stock when necessary.
3. To ensure Graziers are licensed to use the Common.
4. To keep records of the stock on the Common.
5. To attend the Meetings of the Corfe Castle Common Management Committee.

There is a small remuneration of £350 per year plus any telephone expenses.

If you enjoy walking the Common and have an interest in grazing stock, you would be most welcome to submit your application for the Committee's consideration. Applications may be obtained from the Corfe Castle Ticket Office and must be returned to the National Trust Office, Corfe Castle for the attention of Douglas Whyte by Friday 3rd March.

Today's weather: A ☼ BRILLIANT DAY.

Name   EXTRACT from :-   Year of birth

House   CORFE VALLEY NEWS .   Street

FUELLING A THOUGHT !?
AT THIS TIME

Be
prepared
for the future.

'Oil' island not up for sale – yet!

POOLE harbour's 'oil island' of Furzey is not up for sale just yet, says BP Amoco.

But a company spokesman has confirmed that it is possible the island will go on the open market.

Concerns about the future of the island, tucked between Brownsea and the southern shores of the harbour, have come from residents in Purbeck – within whose district boundaries the islands lie.

Parish councillors at Corfe Castle have expressed fears the island could be sold to the highest bidder after the oil company's production comes to an end.

The councillors are trying to win support for a concept that the island could be transformed into a haven for a community-based use involving local organisation. The parish council has appealed for ideas.

Now a spokesman for the oil giant has confirmed that oil production from the island will cease at the end of this year.

The 35-acre island would be restored in what could be a year to 18-month process.

The oil company says the island is within what it recognises as a particularly sensitive and beautiful area, and it is bent on making "doubly sure" that its restoration is appropriate, which could take additional time.

Though it is said the island is not yet up for sale, the company admits: "Our long-term view is that we probably shouldn't be the long-term owner of the island."

Furzey for the people!

I HAVE to agree with Corfe Castle Parish Council and its chairman Les Hayward that Furzey Island should not be allowed to be sold off for private or commercial gain when BP Amoco departs it next year.

When you think of the billions of pounds that BP has made from the oil taken out from under Purbeck since the mid-1970s, the oil company has a moral duty to donate the island to the local community.

I would urge everyone in Purbeck who has a good community idea for Furzey's use to get in touch.

I know it's in the parish of Corfe Castle but it's an asset and potential amenity that could be enjoyed by everyone in Purbeck.

And come on BP Amoco, what do you think Furzey could be used for so it benefits local people and not just a businessman from far away or a fat cat millionaire wanting a second holiday home?

NAME & ADDRESS SUPPLIED
Corfe Castle
■ Editor's note: Ideas for Furzey Island's use should be sent to Corfe Castle Parish Council clerk Stephen Yeoman, at Heligstan, Agglestone Road, Studland, BH19 3BZ.

No firm is an island

REGARDING the disposal of Furzey Island, BP says "we have a responsibility to our shareholders".

I hope that the responsibility can be interpreted by their board as a wonderful chance of enhancing their image to the world, especially now when fears of runaway growth and the power of global business exist.

They could keep Furzey Island and work on with various authorities to establish half the island as a wildlife reserve.

The other half, which includes the large house, cottage and pier, could be used for disabled people and children and organised access for the public under the control of a warden, paid for by councils and the charities concerned.
NAME & ADDRESS SUPPLIED

Today's weather:
DRY, OVERCAST and CHILLY

Name Extracts: Press Cuttings Free Papers (Local) GUARDIAN and ADVERTISER.

House

Year of birth for local oil EXPLORAT
1st stage from the 1970

Street

Saturday February 19th

Out of bed as usual at 4.45am.

Supplements for papers have to be brought in from outside, as they are delivered during the night. Wonderful smell of freshly baked bread, from Dragon's, greets us as we open the shop door. One of the bundles has come open and we have no 'Guardian' magazines. Have to ring wholesaler to bring us some.

We have 500 newspapers delivered which have to be counted & sorted, rounds made up and orders reserved.

It's a lovely, fine & sunny day. The start of half term, so there are plenty of visitors buzzing around the square (especially lots of Japanese today)

Usual chaos with parking – I think 'Road-Rage' originated in Corfe.

Turns out a great day for us trade-wise. Everyone's buying ice-creams and enthusing over the sweets in jars. They can be a real pain to weigh out on a busy day, but it's worth it to hear people reliving their childhood.

The Guardian magazines have turned up. Rita Churchill found them discarded outside her house. Obviously too intellectual for the 'kind person' who took them.

The day's getting even better, Alec has arrived to start improvements in the flat upstairs. He building a fitted wardrobe & putting up a shelf for the Hi-fi.

It feels like our home at last!

Today's weather: Dry & quite sunny most of the day Cloudy towards the end.

Name GILBERT DIXON + JULIE DIXON   Year of birth 1949 + 1960

House THE SWEET SHOP   Street THE SQUARE

St. Edward's Church Sunday School or Junior Church meets every Sunday at 10:30 am in the Robing Room. Barbara and I have been taking care of the young children for many years, and really enjoy this activity. Today we are joining the Church for our monthly informal family service. The Rector has arranged a film showing the story of Abraham and his journey into the desert. The lesson for the children today has been Faith and Trust in God, as was Abraham and his family's trust in God's word. All things they were told to do they did, knowing that they would be guided and protected in every way. Some drawings done by the children will be added to these pages, together with names of some of the Sunday School members. After the service we enjoy a coffee with squash and biscuits for the children, and a friendly chat before a short Communion Service for anyone wishing to participate.

ABRAHAM TAKING HIS FAMILY TO THE DESERT

ABRAHAM AND HIS FAMILY.

Hagar the servant girl with her baby

Hugo Docx   Poppy Davis
Madeleine DOcx
Anastasia Beaumont

Antonia Docx   Hadley Docx
Rosalie   Spike Davis

Christopher Mannello

Carina Whyte shunou whyte
Maribor Whyte

Sarah with Hagar's baby

The burning city of Sodom.

Today's weather: Wet

Name Betty Groves   Year of birth

House 26 Townsend Road   Street

TODAY ON THE VILLAGE HALL NOTICEBOARD

We are sorry for any inconvenience caused to our customers by the temporary reduction of space in our new car park extension. This has been caused by problems outside our control which has left our new village Doctor, Dr. Stephen Horsnell, without a surgery. The Health Authority is urgently arranging a permanent purpose-built surgery in the village. However, in the meantime a temporary Portacabin surgery has to be used.

Your Village Hall Committee was approached at short notice for use of the car park extension to house the Portacabin and were pleased to be able to help. We understand that plans for the new surgery will be drawn up very soon and that a building will be constructed as soon as possible.

(G.E. PRESTON, VILLAGE HALL CHAIRMAN)
FEBRUARY 2000

Dr. Stephen Horsnell commenced his duties on Monday 7th February 2000; his family will join him in the near future.

Today's weather. A lovely day of sunshine

Name	A "roving eye" around the village	Year of birth
	Committee Member: The Millennium Association	
House	Village Hall	Street	East Street

CORFE CASTLE TOWN TRUST

The Corfe Castle Town Trust was established by the Charities Commission in 1889 and continues to be responsible for the administration of the property previously owned by the Ancient Borough of Corfe Castle including the stone cross in the square, the village pumps and the well. The first Trustees were Mr. Ralph Bankes, Rev. E. Bankes, Mr. E> Smith, Mr. S. Paine, Mr. T. Luther, Mr. G Cleall and Mr. F. Bentinck. At that time the main concerns were repairs to the Town Hall and the provision of street lamps. The main income for the Trust was rent for the ground floor of £2.13s per annum!

Many well-remembered names have since contributed, prominent in the Minutes are Dr. G. Dru Drury, Mr. W. Ottaway, Mr R. Spiller, Mr. B. Goodwin, Mr E Moss, Mr. H Hibbs, Mr. E. Holland, Mr. P.A Brown (who started the Museum), Mr. Paget-Bowyer, Dr. Drew Thompson and Mr F. Baxter

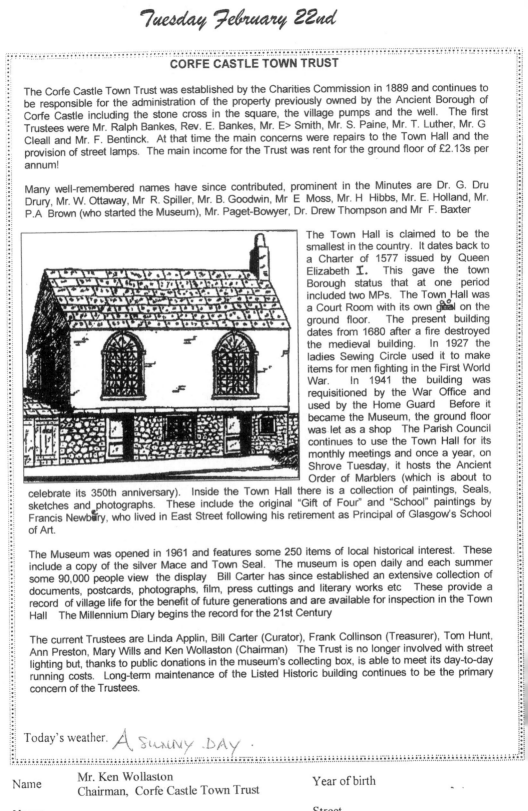

The Town Hall is claimed to be the smallest in the country. It dates back to a Charter of 1577 issued by Queen Elizabeth I. This gave the town Borough status that at one period included two MPs. The Town Hall was a Court Room with its own gaol on the ground floor. The present building dates from 1680 after a fire destroyed the medieval building. In 1927 the ladies Sewing Circle used it to make items for men fighting in the First World War. In 1941 the building was requisitioned by the War Office and used by the Home Guard Before it became the Museum, the ground floor was let as a shop The Parish Council continues to use the Town Hall for its monthly meetings and once a year, on Shrove Tuesday, it hosts the Ancient Order of Marblers (which is about to celebrate its 350th anniversary). Inside the Town Hall there is a collection of paintings, Seals, sketches and photographs. These include the original "Gift of Four" and "School" paintings by Francis Newbury, who lived in East Street following his retirement as Principal of Glasgow's School of Art.

The Museum was opened in 1961 and features some 250 items of local historical interest. These include a copy of the silver Mace and Town Seal. The museum is open daily and each summer some 90,000 people view the display Bill Carter has since established an extensive collection of documents, postcards, photographs, film, press cuttings and literary works etc These provide a record of village life for the benefit of future generations and are available for inspection in the Town Hall The Millennium Diary begins the record for the 21st Century

The current Trustees are Linda Applin, Bill Carter (Curator), Frank Collinson (Treasurer), Tom Hunt, Ann Preston, Mary Wills and Ken Wollaston (Chairman) The Trust is no longer involved with street lighting but, thanks to public donations in the museum's collecting box, is able to meet its day-to-day running costs. Long-term maintenance of the Listed Historic building continues to be the primary concern of the Trustees.

Today's weather. A SUNNY DAY.

Name	Mr. Ken Wollaston Chairman, Corfe Castle Town Trust	Year of birth	
House		Street	

Today I came across this old photograph – a scene depicting the Turn of the Century   NO! Not this turn, but that of the 19th to the 20th. That's my younger sister and me kneeling at the front of the picture. BUT I'm not that old! My Grandmother, Doris Mayo, then a very active member of Corfe Castle Women's Institute (W.I.), involved us, as girls, to take part in the play presented by the W I. in the mid-1970s in the Village Hall. Mrs. Sibyl Windsor was very helpful today in identifying all the players by name and it was very interesting to hear all about their special event. At the time, Mrs. Windsor had in her theatrical costume wardrobe at her house, some lovely Victorian clothes and this led to the idea of the W.I. members writing a play about a typical Victorian family   This photograph of members of the cast, was specially produced in sepia to give an authentic look.   Mrs. Windsor reminded me of how she taught Sharon and me the dances which we performed on stage

Now this year I really have witnessed a turn of the century, the 20th to the 21st and with two young boys of our own, Luke and Kieran. I am sure they, too, will remember this special year 2000 and how they celebrated in Corfe Castle and with lots of photographs for the family album.

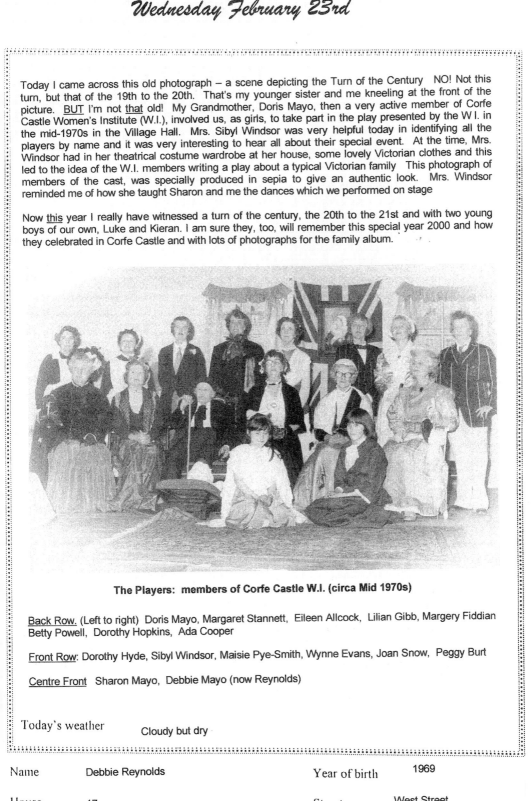

The Players: members of Corfe Castle W.I. (circa Mid 1970s)

Back Row. (Left to right) Doris Mayo, Margaret Stannett, Eileen Allcock, Lilian Gibb, Margery Fiddian Betty Powell, Dorothy Hopkins, Ada Cooper

Front Row: Dorothy Hyde, Sibyl Windsor, Maisie Pye-Smith, Wynne Evans, Joan Snow, Peggy Burt

Centre Front Sharon Mayo, Debbie Mayo (now Reynolds)

Today's weather   Cloudy but dry

Name	Debbie Reynolds	Year of birth	1969
House	17	Street	West Street

Today's daily newspaper sport headlines

Stanley Matthews, legendary football wizard, dies at 85

BY ANDREW MULLINS

SIR STANLEY MATTHEWS, the first footballer to be knighted and one of England's greatest players of any era, died yesterday after a short illness.

The 85 year old was twice made European footballer of the year during a career that spanned four decades. His performances in more than 50 internationals and the moving way in which he at last won a coveted FA Cup winners' medal secured his place in the history of his sport. But the mesmerising skills he showed made him a legend potent long after he retired in 1965, having become the only 50-year-old to play First Division football.

A spokesman for the private North Staffordshire Nuffield Hospital in Newcastle-under-Lyme said last night: "Sir Stanley Matthews died peacefully this evening after a short illness." It is believed he may have had an accident on the island of Tenerife before being flown to the Nuffield for treatment.

Sir Stanley will be remembered for the 1953 FA Cup final. Having lost two previous finals with Blackpool, he reached a third one at the age of 38. With only 20 minutes remaining, his side trailed 1-3. Matthews, who was renowned for his explosive speed and close control, then produced perhaps the most extraordinary quarter of an hour in football history, making two goals as his side recovered to win 4-3 with seconds to spare.

Sir Bobby Charlton said last night. "I loved him. He was an absolutely magical player."

Ken Jones, page
Modest conversion, page

Today I am working two doors down from home. I am a painter & decorator and shall be papering the sitting room at Mrs Aplin's. The children are on half term from Wareham Middle School so my two (Maria and Stephen) are up and down the road with their friends. My wife Angela is at work at Clealls Store the local shop. This afternoon I took Stephen to a football training session at Wareham. This evening is a night at home as I cannot go to football training myself as I am recovering from a broken ankle caused while playing football.

Today's weather:

Name Phil Turner   Year of birth 1962

House No 68   Street West Street

Friday February 25th

I woke up at about 6.15am but mummy didn't come to get me out of my cot until about 6.45 by which time I was really hungry. My nappy is changed and it's quick and easy to do because it is a disposable one. It has pictures of teddies across the front.

I had my breakfast milk and some porridge with fruit in it - today it was apple. I sat in to my blue and white check highchair and could watch what mummy was doing in the kitchen. My breakfast is cooked in the microwave, it is very quick.

After breakfast mummy and I went to Tesco in Poole and to Greenslades the fish shop in Poole. Poole Bridge was closed so we had to go through Hamworthy. We bought some dressed crabs and prawns. This is for a special dinner for my Grandpop and nana who are visiting us this weekend from Cambridge.

In the afternoon I played in my baby bouncer, in my inflatable ring and with my light and sound ball. Unfortunately Nana rang to say that they wouldn't be coming afterall because Grandpop had a stomach bug.

After my tea of vegetables and cheese, mummy + daddy took me for a walk in my new back pack across the Common. I went to bed at 7.15 and not even my down mobile could keep me awake

Today's weather.
A FINE BUT CHILLY DAY.

Name Anna Louise Philps

Year of birth 27/7/99

House 66

Street West Street

Our Wedding Day

Sarah's morning... It was just before 8.00 o'clock when I awoke. My bridesmaid, Dee, and I lay in bed for a few minutes chatting excitedly about the day ahead. We could hear my mum and brother, Peter, in the kitchen downstairs and before long the lure of breakfast and coffee tempted us to join them. It wasn't really a normal breakfast: Dee insisted on opening the first bottle of Champagne for the day. My mother wanted to know what time everything was happening - the hairdresser's arrival, the flowers, when was I getting dressed? the cars, etc. My stepfather was in command of the washing up and Peter was making more tea.....he drinks it by the gallon!

The morning was a sort of organised chaos, with people coming and going all the time: Flowers were delivered. The Best Man came at least once to arrange or do something vitally important. My sister-in-law, Jane, arrived with my niece and nephew Becky and Mark – Becky being my second bridesmaid. Then there was the hairdresser, the make-up lady, the photographer, numerous visits from the Nomad team who were preparing the marquee and barn for the reception, and a number of friends and family just dropping in to say hello! It was hectic, but great fun.

Then all of a sudden it was calm again and just four of us were left; my brother, who was giving me away, my bridesmaids Dee and Becky, and myself.

We arrived at the church on time, the sun was trying to break through the clouds, and the last few guests ran past us to get to their seats. The church was almost full. My handsome husband-to-be stood smiling at the top of the aisle, and so many friends and family were there. I felt so excited as I walked up the aisle to Dougie.

Dougie's morning... Quiet by comparison! I had spent the night with family at Rempstone Hall. After a good night's sleep and a magnificent breakfast I found a comfy armchair, a newspaper and a cigar. Around me everyone seemed very busy doing this and that and constantly checking their watches.......but all I had to do was be ready on time, and I had plenty of time to relax!

At mid day, my Best Man Miles, Mervyn, one of my Ushers, and I went to Mortons House Hotel where we met up with the rest of my Ushers for lunch: A time to double check duties, laugh with friends and wind up an already overstressed Best Man!

Our day together... The service was beautiful – full of magical moments and as we exchanged our rings, the sun shone through the stained glass window above the altar. Leaving the church, we leapt into the air with joy...Fantastic!

Outside the church we excitedly chattered to friends and family – we didn't notice how cold it was but perhaps they did! Time to head back to Rollington for the reception - our chariot awaited: A little grey 'Fergie' tractor pulling a trailer decked out splendidly with a bench seat and table, flowers and champagne in a milk churn ice bucket, and ivy everywhere. It was brilliant! Dougie, cigar in mouth, popped the champagne cork to resounding cheers from our guests and all the onlookers in the square!

The afternoon reception was held in a marquee in the farmyard. We had about 150 guests – It might have been a cold February afternoon outside, but inside it was fairyland! The marquee was completely lined in black, and guests found a forest of trees all cleverly lit with fairy lights and spotlights. I think 'Wow' was the word on most people's lips as they arrived. It was such fun. I think we managed to spend some time with everyone - but time went so quickly.

About 6 o'clock, everyone left.... Us first of course! Dougie and I were booked into Mortons House and we had a couple of hours to relax our aching smile muscles and freshen up for the evening party. Amusingly Corfe Castle suffered a total power failure during this time, but it was very romantic getting ready by candlelight!

Back to the farm for 8 o'clock with shots of Schnapps on arrival. Even Dougie and I could hardly believe how incredibly beautiful the barn looked. A grain and tractor store for most of the year – tonight it was a fantastic dining hall. Fairy lights, candelabras, and hundreds and hundreds of nightlights....the scene was set for quite a party...... There is a saying: *"Live like there's no tomorrow, Love like you've never been hurt, Dance like nobody's watching!"* We did just that – and the party went on through to about 3 o'clock.

A day of all days to be remembered for always.

Today's weather: Cloudy with intervals of sunshine.

Name	Douglas and Sarah Ryder	Year of birth	
House	Rollington Farm House	Street	Studland Road

Sarah and Dougie's Special Day

At 2 p.m. on 27th February Carey Hall became a gathering place for Wareham District Rainbows, Brownies, Guides, Rangers and young Leaders to remember Guiding in other countries and also to view our Guiding Banner to which everyone made a contribution. Each guide unit made a display about a country of their choice, and chose a craft for everyone to try.

The country chosen by the Corfe Castle Brownies and Rainbows was Japan and our joint display consisted of butterflies and peace doves, Japanese Brownie dolls holding the Japanese flag and paper cranes as well as a collection of photographs and postcards.

Two Brownies came dressed in kimonos.

The Wareham Guide District Banner incorporating the embroidery of Corfe Castle Brownies and Rainbows

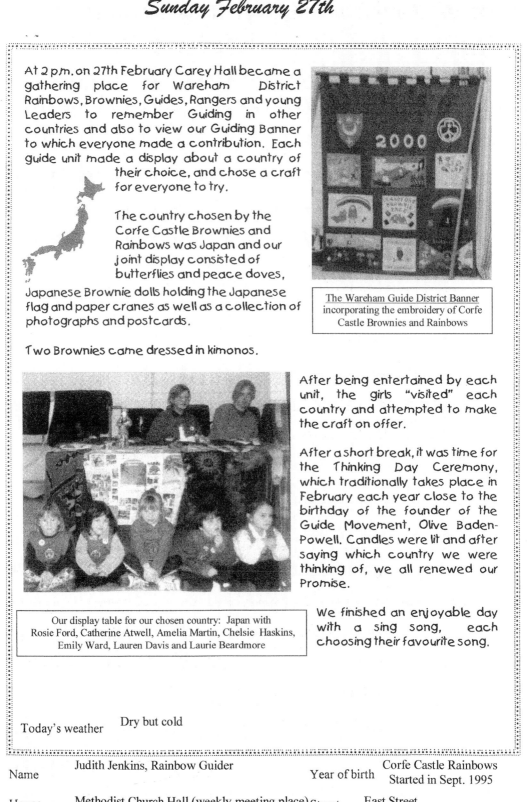

Our display table for our chosen country: Japan with Rosie Ford, Catherine Atwell, Amelia Martin, Chelsie Haskins, Emily Ward, Lauren Davis and Laurie Beardmore

After being entertained by each unit, the girls "visited" each country and attempted to make the craft on offer.

After a short break, it was time for the Thinking Day Ceremony, which traditionally takes place in February each year close to the birthday of the founder of the Guide Movement, Olive Baden-Powell. Candles were lit and after saying which country we were thinking of, we all renewed our Promise.

We finished an enjoyable day with a sing song, each choosing their favourite song.

Today's weather   Dry but cold

Name   Judith Jenkins, Rainbow Guider

Year of birth   Corfe Castle Rainbows Started in Sept. 1995

House   Methodist Church Hall (weekly meeting place)   Street   East Street

To-day is my 70th birthday it also marks 5 years of retirement from Corfe Castle Library which I joined when it opened in March 76 as Assistant Librarian in Charge, I spent 19 very happy and interesting years there, 5 years of retirement have also been very happy enjoying the company of 6 Grandchildren, a move from 'Denehurst', Higher Gardens after 32 years to 'Potters Barn', East Street.

We have had a family lunch to-day prepared by my daughter, I also had a surprise present from John my husband of a framed scraper board picture of a very elegant garden designed and worked by him for an Art School project in 1947 when he was a student. The family gave me a pair of bronze Cranes for the garden, I wonder if they will look very 20th century in years to come.

We also had a beautiful bank of snowdrops outside our bedroom window for the last month, sadly to-day they have all gone.

Today's weather **Sunshine & Showers plus a clap of thunder & lightning**

Name *Margaret Ellen Cooper* Year of birth *1930*

House *Potters Barn* Street *East Street*

Hi I'm Stephen and this is my diary account for my birthday, which this year falls on the real date. Being born on leap year day means for three years I have my birthday as the 28th.

6:45, I woke and opened my presents.

8:15, Left for school, I had quite a good day.

03:45, I looked at my presents more closely and watched Wrestling I had taped two nights ago.

5:30, Had tea.

6:10, I played on the P.C. on Age of Empires.

6:55, Played pool against grandad and Adam with my new cue.

7:40, I done some homework on the P.C.

8:10, Played pool against grandad then gran and grandad went.

8:30, Penn [my half sister] and Paul [her boyfriend] arrived and I opened my presents from them.

9:45, Penn and Paul went and I went to bed. The weather wasn't too bad today, it didn't rain it wasn't sunny and it didn't snow. I say that because it snowed on my birthday before and I broke my wrist.

Today's weather DRY & BRIGHT

Name STEPHEN TURNER   Year of birth 1988

House 68   WEST Street

MArch 1st AD 2000

At the age of 88 I think a description of my life in Corfe rather
uninspiring. However, life goes on a certain routine has to be
observed. I have many blessings.

  After breakfast and the perusal of the death notices in the Daily
Telegraph and other items I feel a gentle tapping on my toe. My black
and white Cavalier Spaniel "Tessa" gazes at me with Appealing eyes.
I capitulate so out we go. How lucky we are to have so many unspoilt
acres on Corfe Common. The sky is blue, a lark hovers above and spring
flowers are in evidence. In the summer we are visited by droves of
Tourists but they frequent the Castle and Village. On the Common one
sees a different world. All is peace and tranquility. The odd dog barks
rabbits scutter into the bushes, horses and cows graze. A perfect
pastoral idyll.

   Now for the excitement of the day. A visit to the British Legion Club
in East Street for refreshment and the latest Village news. Once the Club
was the haunt of elderly warriors re-fighting their battles. Alas nearly
all have faded away. Once six of my 8th Army friends reminisced about
the Western Desert. I am the sole survivor.

  My afternoon nap is disturbed by a welcome telephone call from my
son Matthew, a Mining Consultant at present working in the blistering
heat of the Mohave Desert in California where he is overseeing the
extension of a Borax mine. It is his 44th birthday.
   At six o'clock I return to the Club for my weekly game of bridge
with three friends. I inaugrated this mini club some five years ago.
I am partnered by Dr Drew Thomson and thanks to his expertise We win 5p

  After that a late supper a little television and bed. No, not an
exciting day but I am so fortunate to be greeting by a devoted daughter
and a faithful hound. Their support gives an old man a special quality of
existence.
   A warm house a close family in Purbeck where my family have lived for
three centuries is not a bad end to an eventful life. Daily I count my
blessings.

Today's weather: VARIABLE

Name P. D. RANDALL   Year of birth 1912

House KERILEE   Street WEST ST.

04.00	Up early today – too early!
04.30	Left Corfe for Poole Bus Station. Di driving. Take a drive around by the harbour. Starting to get light – nice morning.
04.50	Seems as though the 05.00 Flight Link bus now leaves at 04.50. Just made it. Feel miserable. 26 years and still hate saying goodbye to Di.
07.30	Arrive Heathrow Terminal 2 for S.A.S. Phone Bob – he's on his way. Check us both in.
08.40	Bob and myself go through departure. Starting to get busy. Business Class tickets so spend our time in S.A.S. Executive Lounge.
10.30	Board flight to Stavanger.
12.30	Arrive Stavanger. Meet the rest of our lads.
13.00	Two hour bus ride up to Sjoard. It's cold. Wish it would stop snowing. (Going to Regalia – a semi-submersible)
15.00	Arrive. Takes an hour to get through security. No chance of getting a beer tonight.
18.00	Stowed my gear in my cabin. First meeting.
18.50	Job = to salvage and lift fast cat ferry "Sleipner" which sank mid November. Loss 16 persons of 82. Speak to Di and Alex on the mobile for an hour.
21.00	Sort out dive gear. Large tall hotwater suit. Using 17c hat - neckdam – liner – boots
22.30	Cup of tea and a shower. Hello bed

Today's weather   Warm and balmy in U.K. Cold and windy in Norway

Name	Philip French	Year of birth	1949
House	The Ragged Cat	Street	West Street

Friday March 3rd

6:00am — I open my eyes for the first time and feel thankful that the mornings are starting to get lighter. Maybe Spring is on the way after all. I wouldn't be without my black labrador, Digger, but on cold Winter mornings the prospect of walking him is not terribly enticing.

8:00am — Up on the Common bundled up with hat and scarf. The beautiful views of the Castle and the Purbeck hills remind me each morning what a lovely place this is to live. My son and daughter tell me that trips to Corfe are like stepping back in time away from the stresses of city life. My husband was desperate to return from Jersey to the Dorset he loved and every morning I feel sad that he only enjoyed a short time here, before he died two years ago.

8:30am — My elderly parents aren't as fit as they used to be, so I make the trip to Hamworthy several times a week to take them shopping and, with my sisters, help them cook and clean. I grew up in the house where my parents live and 50 years on I still see plenty of faces that I recognise from my school days.

Midday — I visit my sisters and we catch up on family news and grab a sandwich before heading over to Poole.

3:00pm — Yoga at Poole Sports Centre. I've found yoga to be a great way to stay supple, not to mention unwind and relax. The class I go to is for "Nifty Fifties", but they haven't thrown me out since I turned 60! We are really put through our paces and I leave tired, but energised and glad that I made the effort.

4:00pm — Rain or shine, Digger the dog will be waiting for his next walk. I might take him to Hamworthy Park or stop in Wareham Forest on the way home.

5:00pm — Roll on the summer evenings! By now it's getting dark and any thoughts of mowing the lawn are gone for another day. I contemplate the battering my garden has taken from the wind as I bring in some coal and logs for the fire. A real fire might be hard work, but it's worth it for the fake sunshine it brings to my evenings.

8:00pm — I've always enjoyed cooking, so I spend some time most days coming up with recipes and ideas from magazines and books and try them out on friends and family. I also use the library regularly for both videos and books and see how many chapters I can manage before my eyelids start to close.....

Today's weather: Dry & Sunny.

Name   JOYCE PRINCE

House   LARKRISE

Year of birth

Street   43 WEST St.

 Today the Village Hall Management Committee held a Coffee Morning at the Village Hall in aid of the Youth Club, under the direction of Betty Carter. The Village Hall has been in existence since 1950. The site was formerly used by the Royal British Legion, which left for its present location.

A Coffee Morning is normally held on the first Saturday of every month – except January – for the purpose of raising funds either for the Village Hall or some other charitable purpose.

Today's contributions, totalling £281.56, were handed to the Youth Club, which regularly uses the Hall on Wednesday evenings during school term time, and sometimes during the holidays.

Stalls at the Coffee Mornings are manned by volunteers, and include home made cakes and scones etc. – prices range from 10p to £2.50 – clothing bric a brac, books garden produce and a raffle. Prizes for the raffle are generously donated by individuals and won on a first come, first served basis.

The Hall is used for social or charitable purposes also by groups or individuals from outside the Parish. Craft Fayre and Renaissance Antiques hold regular displays and from time to time we are entertained by ARTSREACH.

The Village Hall Management Committee today consists of:-

Chairman, Major George Preston
Hon. Secretary, Mrs. Judith Jenkins
Hon. Treasurer, Mr. David Nias
Mrs. Anne Preston, Mr. William Blight, Mrs. Lilian Gibb, Mrs. Betty Carter, Mr. Peter Smith, Mrs. Rosemary Apsey and Mrs. Diana Dru Drury.

Today's weather: Sunny – after early frost

Name	CORFE CASTLE VILLAGE HALL	Year of birth	1950 (opened)
House	Sited at No. 67	Street	East Street

Four children for breakfast – ours and my sister's two (absolute chaos!). all washed, dressed and at Mum's by 10.00. Luke is very excited as it is his 4th birthday today. He got Buzz Lightyear and Woody (toys from this year's hit Walt Disney film) trousers, a quilt set, Buzz pencils and note book, puzzle and an Action Man scooter. After a hurried lunch all children changed, then off to the Party.

Putlake Adventure Farm with 12 children, oh my god! Party cost £5 per child. They fed lambs and goats, played on tractors and in a barn full of straw they all looked like scarecrows. Most of them milked a cow and had a pony ride. A fantastic day was had by all and the children went home tired but happy with party bags and ice cream.

Top (left to right): Hallam Stuckey, Lauren Davies, Luke (birthday boy), Caris Ellison, Joe Grimes, Stuart Viney

Bottom: Joseph Quinn, Shuna Whyte, Connor Martin, Kelly Martin, Lisa Green

We went back to Mum's for home-made scones (made by Dad) and clotted cream. More pressies for Luke.

At last it was time for bed – not a peep from the children until 8.45. Maybe we will invest £30 for a season ticket if this is the result of a day at Putlake!

We checked on the boys before going to bed ourselves. Luke was snuggled down with Buzz and Woody. Both sleeping soundly.

Today's weather: Sunny and dry

Name   Luke Reynolds   Year of birth   1996
          (written by Mummy & Daddy – Debbie & Kevin)

House   17   Street   West Street

Monday March 6th

The weather was beautiful again this morning; perfect for striding out over the hills. Do you remember the path gently sloping up from Hill Lane on to the top of the ridge? It's lovely to hear the whistle of the train and watch it chuffing out clouds of steam in the valley below. We kept up a good pace along the ridge, past 'Nine Barrow Down' and 'Giants Trencher', over the road and up onto 'Ballard Down'. The views from this ridge are superb with Swanage Bay and Studland Bay on either side and the open sea about a mile ahead. I love this long flat walk on the short springy grass heading towards Ballard Point, you feel on top of the world. Now for the best picnic in England: fresh tomatoes, sandwiches, a game pie to share and apples - why does food taste particularly good on cliff tops? We are really lucky in Corfe to have good local butcher, baker and grocery shops in the village. It was great to sit on the headland and see the cormorants flying low over the water and gulls soaring. We enjoyed the rest of the walk along Ballard Cliff and the views down towards Swanage, though I can't remember our route through the houses. We chatted and tramped along the beach, past the pier and the empty Punch and Judy box. It's all very quiet at this time of the year, with few tourists, but we enjoyed an ice-cream any way. After a wander around the shops it was big decision time - bus, train or walk back to Corfe Castle? We took the train - brilliant!!

Today's weather: mild

Name Maureen + Richard COWLES   Year of birth 1953

House Hillview Nº 49   Street West Street

Tuesday March 7th

We are 3 of the 12 children of Victor and Kate Ford and our Birthdays are all today. Peggy is the oldest, Edzell is the 9th child and Roy is the youngest. Our family has lived in this area for generations and our grandfather and father used to farm Woody Hyde Farm at Harmans Cross.

Peggy A.C. Bessant: (68) I am a widow and now live at Furzebrook, where I have a caravan site. This morning I got up at 7.30 am, fed my cat Smokey and Sadie the dog, and then took the dog out. While I had my breakfast, I opened the 12 Birthday cards and presents I had received. Spent the morning with household chores, such as cleaning out the Parkray fire and watering my plants in the conservatory. I put out some seeds and peanuts for the birds and did a few small jobs around the garden. After taking Sadie out for a longer walk, I drove to Canford Heath, to have lunch with my daughter Diana. In the afternoon we went shopping together for lampshades and wallpaper as I am having my sitting room redecorated. Had a quiet evening watching TV and knitting on a blanket for the Red Cross.

Edzell George: (58) I am a self-employed farmworker and gardener and now live at Yeovil. I also work in Yeovil Market some days. I got up at 5.45 am as usual and after breakfast left for the farm. 7.30: started work on the tractor, cleaning up the yards, bedding up the cows, feeding the calves. 9.30: Second Breakfast. 10 am: Clean cubical house for cows. 11 am: Fetch large tractor for cleaning slurry tanks. 1 pm: Lunch Break. 1.30 - 5.30: Hedge Laying. My brother Roy and I often go to Hedgelaying Competitions together, so this will be good practice.
After supper, I went out to the weekly meeting of the Wessex Morris Men. After the dancing practice we all went to the Royal Oak at Cerne Abbas.

David Roy: (53) I am a Garden Design Engineer and I have a small gardening business called "Hedgerows & Rosegardens". Today I finished laying an old hedge at Bucknowle House for Mr. Harvey. To restore it, I had interplanted this with 105 new native hedgerow plants: beech, hawthorn, viburnum opulus, dogwood, hazel and field maple. I layed this hedge in the Dorset style.
Coincidentally, we have an old family photograph of our Greatgrandfather George Ford, when he was tenant at Bucknowle, sitting with his wife Emily and all his children in front of the house, dated Christmas 1912.
Had a relaxing evening at home, as we had celebrated our Birthdays together on Sunday with a meal at the Halfway Inn, with a number of other family members.

Today's weather   Damp, overcast, sunny intervals, drizzle later
                  Wind: westerly, Force 4-5

Name   David Roy Ford

House 8, Halves Cottages

Year of birth 1947

Street Corfe Castle

Christmas 1912
at Bucknowle House, Corfe Castle

George and Emily Ford (née Vincent) – centre front - with their 7 children
Emma, Anna, John William, Elizabeth Emily, George, Emily Isabella and Samuel Charles

George Ford was tenant of Bucknowle Farm
as well as overseer of Eggleston Farm, near Kimmeridge
(Tenant of Lord Eldon)

Wednesday March 8th

Didn't have to go to work today.

  Had two cats keep me company for extra lie in.

Got up, fed cats and chicken.

 Went to plot, fed ponies and sheep. Mother sheep ready to lamb (no babes by midnight)

Rather boring day. Did chores indoors. Jackie brought two rugs to mend (bit sweaty - horse rugs!!). Started on one of them.

 Soon time to feed horses on common and plot.

Sheep making lots of noise - they think their tea is late. All present for tea.

Had our dinner late because Alan was messing about with the car - ready for MOT check tomorrow.

Bedtime, read a book for a little while. Goodnight.

Today's weather: Dry, but nasty cold wind

Name   Patricia Sherwood   Year of birth   1941

House   70   Street   West Street

Thursday March 9th

I got up at 7.00am, fed Minto the cat My neighbour's cat came to visit

Breakfast of coffee and toast

I then read the Daily Mail the main news of the day was that George Brown the Chancellor is to launch an attack on Tax and Benefit Cheats

At 8.30am I got ready to go to the Nursery School where I help There were 18 children present. I read them stories, helped them make up jig-saw puzzles and helped them make paper and glue pictures

At 1030am we sat down with children for drinks

At 11.00am the children were taken out into the school playground for run around as it was a lovely sunny day I stayed inside and helped Louisa, the student, tidy up. We put the chairs into a circle ready for story time The children were collected by their parents at 12 00md

I arrived home at 12 30pm. My husband Peter had put a cottage pie and vegetables ready for lunch

In the afternoon we went over to Holme Nurseries, between Wareham and Wool, where we bought Rose Trees for Kevin and Mandy's 10th Wedding Anniversary on 10th March
We then went into Swanage to do some shopping at Leo's Supermarket

On the way back we picked up Fish & Chips for tea - Cod £2.45 and Chips£1 00.

During the evening we watched T.V. and went to bed at 11.00pm

Sunny and warm for the time of year.

Today's weather

Name MARIE POPE   Year of birth 11/3/42

House 48A   WEST Street

Friday March 10th

Up as usual 6AM, cup of tea, woke Richard for his paper round, feed cats and let them out. Rouse Deborah, breakfast, make sandwiches say goodbye to Terry, off to school.

After dropping Richard and Deborah off, head for Wareham Middle School, where I work as a Learning Support Assistant. Once there after checking if there were any important notices in the staff room, I check the children I support have everything they need for the day. Which was a busy one with Literacy, maths, Science, English and Humanities, my brain was fairly buzzing.

Some problem with a hyperactive child causing chaos with one lesson, but survived the day. 3.15pm home time, picked up Richard and Deborah and head for home. After the usual household chores, making tea, quick bath then change and out to do my night duty at a Nursing Home starting at 8pm. It never ceases to amaze me how it always rains on Fridays and sunny Saturday morning. After listening to report, start medicine round and settling the residents down for the night. Eventually sat down for a quick break 10pm and chat with my other two colleagues, before carrying on with our work. 12mn I'm tired still 8hrs to go but everyones asleep. Can't wait till morning and bed.

Today's weather   Wet and Windy

Name   Judith Jenkins   Year of birth   1951

House   14   Street   East street

Saturday morning! A beautiful, warm, spring day Corfe looks as pretty as a picture and delicious wafts from the bakery encourage the purchase of warm scones to set us all up for the day

First things first – we display as much jewellery as practicable and make sure we get a hot drink   Wash the windows, polish the cabinets, vacuum the floor and feed the fish The four staff in today will be needed to serve customers, put away jewellery not required, take in jewellery repairs and give out as much information as possible In every instance when someone is thinking of buying pearls or diamonds we will spend as much time as possible to make sure they are able to make an informed choice and give them a guide to take away Mrs C wants to know if we have any other sapphire pendants than those on show – we are able to show a fine collection of sapphires of every colour, thus dispelling the common myth that all sapphires are blue and work with her to develop a design specifically for her. It's always exciting to go right back to choosing a stone, choosing the metal, and working out a design Mr and Mrs H want to know if inherited jewellery can be reworked into pieces that can be worn everyday, rather than have jewellery simply sitting in a box. Our pleasure!

The great thing about a Saturday is that it's a much more physical day than the rest of the week. There's no time to work in the office as the shop will be too busy. Today we will see regular clients, those who work weekdays, customers who live out of the area and have travelled down for the weekend, a few more tourists now the weather is getting better, and, of course, couples taking the opportunity to look for engagement or wedding rings All sorts of people of all age groups - and all with differing tastes, opinions and requirements We're all on the alert to make sure everyone feels welcomed – even if they have to wait, and to ensure no-one feels rushed or neglected. We know that couple over there probably want to get a clearer idea of what sort of engagement ring to look for and how much it will cost, without feeling they have to commit to buying now, and we're really very happy to help Jewellery is such an emotional business!

If there is a lull anywhere between 11.30 and 1 00 we try to eat our lunches as quickly as possible On a Saturday you never know when you'll get another chance to eat! In the background we will be constantly making sure we are keeping accurate customer information to make sure the client gets what they need. There's no way we can rely on memory!

Five-thirty and the closed sign is finally turned Feet ache now as everything is made ready for Monday . will it be another lovely Spring day? Anyone fed the fish?

Today's weather   A beautiful, warm, spring day

WHY
DESIGNER
JEWELLERS

Year of birth

Street

HI MY NAME IS DAVE I AM A VOLENTER STATION MASTER ON THE SWANAGE STEAM RAILWAY I NORMALY ARRIVE AT CORFE CASTLE STATION AT 9.30 I ONLY GO THERE AT WEEKENDS WE ONLOCK THE STATION THEN START CLEANING THE TOILETS FIRST THEN ALL THE BRASS WE DO EVERY THING THE SAME AS BRITISH RAIL IN THE 1940s THE FIRST TRAIN ARRIVES AT 10 50 THEN ITS ALL GO WE MEET PEOPLE FROM ALL OVER THE WORLD MY NORMAL JOB I am a DELIVERY DRIVE AND DRIVE ALL OVER ENGLAND

Today's weather: Sunny

Name DAVE WELLMAN

House 72

Year of birth 21/7/44

Street WEST

A cup of tea and a crossword
To get the brain going today.
Go down to get the newspaper,
Have coffee with Pat on the way.

Washing up, washing and gardening.
Well, really, where does the time go,
As soon as I've got the ground ready
There's runner beans and tomatoes to sow.

Switch on the oven for cooking -
Sausage rolls for darts food for tonight -
We're playing at home, for the Legion
Against the "Crow's Nest" - what a fight.

We manage to win, five games to four
Then home, at about eleven-thirty,
Feed the cat, then lock up the door
Another day almost over.

Time to think about bed
A quick crossword, a coffee, a book.
Ah well, time to lay down my head.
Goodnight.

Today's weather: Some sunshine, reasonable.

Name   Joan Marshallsay

Year of birth   1921

House   76

Street   West

Tuesday March 14th

Today I woke up at 6:55a.m. because I was excited about my 10th birthday. I had breakfast and got ready for school, then I was given presents, my best one is a musical Winnie the Pooh jewellery box.

I walked to the bus stop with my sister Holly and the bus took me to Wareham Middle School, I am in year 5 with Mr Casey. After register I went to maths with Mrs Evans. Next it was break, I bought some raffle tickets and gave my prize in, in aid of Mozambique flood relief. Then I had music with Miss Chaudhri and I played the minuet on the key-board. Then I had PE, I tried the high-jump I got over 90cm but I couldn't manage 1m. My friend landed on the bar on her back.

At lunchtime I ate my sandwiches in the hall. Then when I had finished I went to recorder club with Mrs Salter, we practised God Save the Queen for the guide AGM on Saturday.

After the lunch register I had more maths then literacy. We did a narrative Poem called 'Noah' and we had to find rhyming words. I caught the bus back to Corfe and went to a piano lesson at Roger Frost's house. I played my grade 2 pieces and scales then I came back home.

Mum got tea ready while I watched TV. We had Enchiladas followed by strawberry cheese cake. I played on the computer while Holly did her homework then we watched the video of The Prince of Egypt.

I went to bed at about 9pm.

Today's weather·

Name Cherry Smith   Year of birth 1990

House Larksgate   Street Townsend Mead

The Ides of March - and a Lenten Lunch at the Rectory.
Lent, as the days lengthen.

Morning comes early - the first caller at the door at
8:30 - not for lunch, but on Charities business.

While Maurice is at church for the mid-week communion
service, a certain amount of preparation for the lunch
- small tables moved here and there, arrangements of
chairs, the kitchen re-ordered to accommodate more
bustling bodies than the usual one or two. The
committee of the CMS arrive early with thermos flasks
of steaming hot soups, cheese and a large box of bread
of all sorts. Mugs are put out on the kitchen table,
bread sliced into baskets, cheese arranged on plates.

The early-comers arrive, many bearing more flasks of
soup. Soon the Rectory is a-buzz with people meeting
and greeting, chatting over their mugs of soup - and
all generously putting their donations into the basket
for the Sudan Medical Link.

It's all over by two o'clock - mugs washed and returned
to their rightful owners, the money counted and found
to be over £220.00. One late-comer arrives and sits
with us at the kitchen table for a bowl of soup, as
we'd not managed to have ours with the others, what
with serving the soup and looking after the needs of
the gathered flock.

Amid the lightness and generosity of giving for Lent,
the darkness creeps in. We learn of a burglary at St
Peter's, Church Knowle the night before and later that
night, returning, we see the police at Y Jewellers
where, once again, a break-in has been attempted. The
Ides of March, indeed.

But what remains of the day is the conviviality of folk
gathered in the sunny Rectory, on a bright March day,
to support the work of the CMS while enjoying a jolly
good Lenten 'feast'.

CMS - Church Missionary Society

Today's weather: Bright, sunny, warm for March, but a bit of a bite in the wind.

Name Nancy Strike   Year of birth

House The Rectory   Street East Street

I can hear the sound of walking and talking. Its nearly nine am and the noise has woken me up. I am not one of those people that jump out of bed wide awake and ready to tackle anything, rather the sort that winces, mutters and staggers out of bed with all the grace and agility of a nine month pregnant "mother to be". Indeed if I was a "mother to be" you might be sympathetic for an early retired fifty four year old man there is precious little sympathy - it is an offence against nature for a man to be still in bed when his lady is up and completing her first mile on the treadmill while shouting opinion at Killroy a television discussion programme

Radio four is also left on in the bedroom just in case I try to turn over, and the incessant sound of a politician being asked a question and being interrupted before he can answer it, is as resting as an assault on your boxer shorts with a jagged beer glass. I just have to get up !

I start the day by finding my bowl my spoon and my packets of muesli and mixed nuts and pouring my skimmed milk on the top If I am feeling particularly socially aware I make some tea, find a bowl for Lorna, find her a spoon, and find her special choice of cereal. I do have my caring days and these meet with surprise and encouragement when sporty spice bounces into the kitchen to smugly declare that she has already walked two miles and is planning to go swimming She is setting a cracking pace.

After being reminded of the monthly membership charge for the Springfield Country Club I get my swimming kit together and off we drive. We are just in time for the adults only session - children are always to be avoided in a swimming pool, particularly the very young incontinent variety I set about swimming a few lengths when I see Lorna coming down the steps into the pool wearing a large blueberry on her head and a pair of pebble glasses She cannot see much and like a tanker with no one on look out, she sets out to cross the channel. I wave bon voyage, as Lorna causes panic in the regular shipping lane and I am left to hold my stomach to stifle eruptions of involuntary sniggering. Swimming does have its compensations

Today's weather

Name DAVID WALKER   Year of birth 1945

House 55   Street WEST

Friday March 17th

St. Patrick's Day

Woken shortly after 5.30 by a blackbird singing loudly although it's not yet dawn. At 7.15 the sun broke through hazily. Showered then downstairs to first feed the two cats their breakfast of small brown pellets that look just like rabbit droppings but that is all they will at present eat. Cats big black healthy animals, one male, Neil, one female, Milly, both strays from the animal sanctuary in Church Knowle. All this carefully observed by Toby the 2 year old Dobermann who is pretending sleep in his basket by the Rayburn in the kitchen. He doesn't believe in rising before 8.00, much the same as my husband, a retired farmer.

Now a beautiful morning, quite fresh, but blue skies and just a light breeze. At 8.15 off in the car to my job as part-time receptionist for Dr. Stephen Horsnell who took over Corfe Castle Practice in February. We are working in temporary premises, in portacabins in the Village Hall car park, where we are surprisingly comfortable.

The national news today is almost totally concerned by the announcement this morning that BMW is to sell off the major part of Rover Cars. Many redundancies are feared. The news from the local village of Church Knowle, where I live, is that the Church was broken into some time during Tuesday night and a large chest of drawers stolen from the vestry, which was securely locked, as was the Church itself. A small Jacobean table is also missing. There has been a spate of thefts in this area, mostly sheds being targeted for small tools and other items.

During the afternoon I drove into Wareham to shop for a few things I wasn't able to buy locally. In Church Knowle there is only a bus once a week on a Thursday, which is Market Day. We have a fortnightly mobile lending library, which also offers the loan of videos as well as talking books and even jigsaw puzzles.

Spent a very pleasant hour in the vegetable garden , much to Toby's joy as he loves to "help" with the digging.

7.00 preparing supper, listening to "the Archers" on the radio, still going strong after so many years. A full, but definitely not exciting day.

Today's weather: Sunny morning. Cloudy and cooler later. Fine all day

Name	Pauline Freer	Year of birth	1939
House	Corfe Castle Doctor's Surgery	Street	

Saturday March 18th

My day started at about 8.o'clock.
Firstly I helped a neighbour in her garden, later I returned home to start work in my own vegetable garden.

The weather was cloudy with some sunshine but the slight wind was on the cold side.

My two grandchildren stayed with us for the week end, so I had to spend some time with them.

In the afternoon we took the dog for his walk across West Halves and along the river to Copper Bridge. It was nice and peacefull as not many people take that route.

My work is environmental, and I am fortunate enough to be able to visit Furzey Island every other week to carry out maintenance work.

I packed up my work in the garden at 3.o'clock as I wanted to watch the rugby on the television. Wales 26 Scotland 18.

I went to Wool Royal British Legion in the evening to celebrate my birthday.

Today's weather: Cloudy with some sunshine Cold light wind.

Name Ken Williams

House 1, Webbers Close.

Year of birth 18.3.34.

Street West Street.

Saturday March 18th

In Cambridgeshire today. Spending Kierans 2nd Birthday with Kevins family. Going out for a meal this evening. My mum and Dad are with us aswell.

After a restless night with the boys and being dragged from our beds at some unearthly hour we went shopping. It's so different up here not a rolling hill in sight people rushing here and there. Ive seen alot of changes here in the past 15 years housing estates. Industrial areas 3 new landlords at the pub. Its lovely to go home and get back to snails pace with yet another group of grockles looming. Well thats another story. Back to today. After a very wet bath time we eventually got out for our meal all 12 of us. Both boys were very well behaved. Kieran tried to blow out all of his candles but big brother had to step in with a big huff to do the job properly.
Boys shattered. A peaceful night was had by all!

Today's weather: Mild, but overcast

Name DEBBIE REYNOLDS   Year of birth 1969

House 17   Street WEST

Sunday March 19th

Dear Council,
We are writing to you on the behalf of the youths of Corfe castle.

To bring to your attention the fact that we no longer have a place to meet and socialise as the shelter we used to use has now been destroyed, and the church porch is no longer available or suitable for us.

We are asking you if it would be possible to construct a small shelter for us to use as shade from the sun in the summer and shelter from the rain in the winter.

We are well aware of the elderly residents of Corfe castle, which feel intimidated by our presence so a shelter away from the residential areas would save any annoyance.

We have enclosed a page of signatures with this and if needed we will get more.

Yours sincerely
From the youths of Corfe castle.

SIGNED...

Mrs Betty Carter
(Corfe Castle Youth Club)
51 East Street
Corfe Castle

Dear Mrs Carter

REQUEST FOR SHELTER

The Parish Council has received a petition from "the youths of Corfe Castle", which we discussed at last Monday's meeting (copy enclosed). There is support and sympathy for the idea (although the detailed practicalities may not be straightforward to resolve).

Councillors thought that the best way forward would be to meet with the youths, via the Youth Club, to discuss the matter in more detail and we hope that this suggestion meets with your approval. Tom Hunt, Nigel Dragon, Rob Green and Debbie Reynolds have volunteered to represent the Parish Council. It will probably short-circuit things if you were able to liaise directly with some or all of them about a suitable date, but I am happy to act as a go-between if you would prefer

Yours sincerely   Stephen Yeoman
Clerk

CORFE CASTLE PARISH COUNCIL

Today's weather:

Name   **From the youths of Corfe castle.**

House   Street

THE BELFRY MODEL

In 1999, as the old wooden 17th Century belfry in the Church of St. Edward at Corfe Castle was unsafe and was scheduled to be replaced, I decided to build a 1/16 scale working model of it. I had medical problems and needed a long-term project to keep me occupied at home.

In the model belfry, the frames are made of oak, with dowelled tenon joints. The bell-wheels are of cherry wood, and the bells are stoneware pottery. There are 522 wooden parts plus another 103 of steel or brass, 130 fastenings, and 6 bells. Including preparatory work, the model took 300 hours to make and was completed in September 1999.

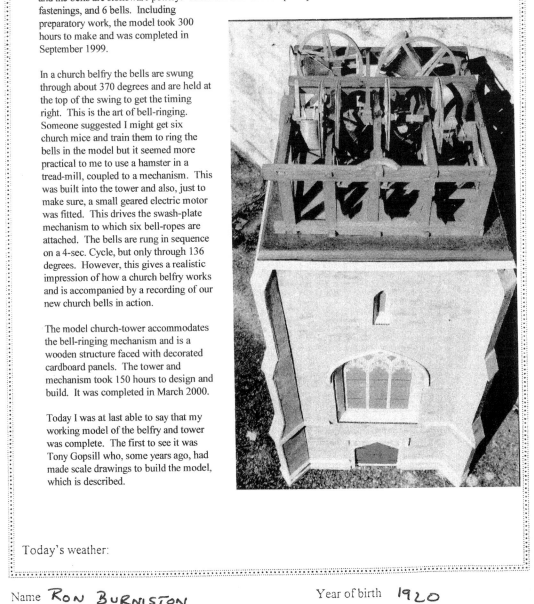

In a church belfry the bells are swung through about 370 degrees and are held at the top of the swing to get the timing right. This is the art of bell-ringing. Someone suggested I might get six church mice and train them to ring the bells in the model but it seemed more practical to me to use a hamster in a tread-mill, coupled to a mechanism. This was built into the tower and also, just to make sure, a small geared electric motor was fitted. This drives the swash-plate mechanism to which six bell-ropes are attached. The bells are rung in sequence on a 4-sec. Cycle, but only through 136 degrees. However, this gives a realistic impression of how a church belfry works and is accompanied by a recording of our new church bells in action.

The model church-tower accommodates the bell-ringing mechanism and is a wooden structure faced with decorated cardboard panels. The tower and mechanism took 150 hours to design and build. It was completed in March 2000.

Today I was at last able to say that my working model of the belfry and tower was complete. The first to see it was Tony Gopsill who, some years ago, had made scale drawings to build the model, which is described.

Today's weather:

Name RON BURNISTON

House FARING

Year of birth 1920

Street HIGHER FILBANK

CORFE CASTLE GARDENING CLUB

The Club met as usual on the third Tuesday of the month in the Village Hall at 7.30 p.m.

This was an evening full of inspiring information. Mr. K. Hix, a horticultural expert and a former lecturer at our County Agricultural College, came to talk to us about "Preparing for the Coming Year in the Garden". Fully aware of our comparatively small gardens. He showed us how to rejuvenate our pots and hanging baskets, our shrubs and our lawns.

Spring is also a time of propagation and he delighted members with his practical expertise in this area, as well as with the many cuttings he produced to which members were invited to help themselves.

Today's weather: Fine and even sunny

Name   D. Parry Jones   Year of birth   03.01.1928

House   Weybac, Norden   Street

Wednesday March 22nd

My birthday today.

Allways have the day off work this day.

Woke up late to a nice sunny morning, looking forward to meeting up with family for lunch.

Down the pub for lunch & a very good time was had by all.

lots of cards and goodies)

A nice walk on the common set the pace for the evening bash to come.

A lovely day

Today's weather: Nice and bright (rain in morning) hope all day

Name E A JARVIS

Year of birth 1951

House 49 HARVEST COTTAGES

Street OFF WEST STREET

Thursday March 23rd

Today is my 50th birthday and weatherwise it is extremely gloomy – absolutely pouring with rain – but I am determined not to feel depressed at having reached this great age!

The doorbell has rung several times - I have been spoiled as a couple of friends have sent me flowers and others have braved the elements to drop in with cards and presents.

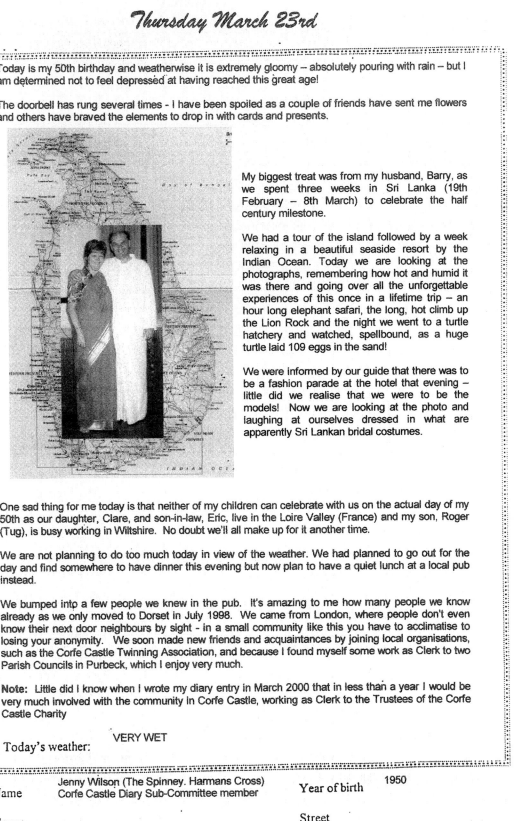

My biggest treat was from my husband, Barry, as we spent three weeks in Sri Lanka (19th February – 8th March) to celebrate the half century milestone.

We had a tour of the island followed by a week relaxing in a beautiful seaside resort by the Indian Ocean. Today we are looking at the photographs, remembering how hot and humid it was there and going over all the unforgettable experiences of this once in a lifetime trip – an hour long elephant safari, the long, hot climb up the Lion Rock and the night we went to a turtle hatchery and watched, spellbound, as a huge turtle laid 109 eggs in the sand!

We were informed by our guide that there was to be a fashion parade at the hotel that evening – little did we realise that we were to be the models! Now we are looking at the photo and laughing at ourselves dressed in what are apparently Sri Lankan bridal costumes.

One sad thing for me today is that neither of my children can celebrate with us on the actual day of my 50th as our daughter, Clare, and son-in-law, Eric, live in the Loire Valley (France) and my son, Roger (Tug), is busy working in Wiltshire. No doubt we'll all make up for it another time.

We are not planning to do too much today in view of the weather. We had planned to go out for the day and find somewhere to have dinner this evening but now plan to have a quiet lunch at a local pub instead.

We bumped into a few people we knew in the pub. It's amazing to me how many people we know already as we only moved to Dorset in July 1998. We came from London, where people don't even know their next door neighbours by sight - in a small community like this you have to acclimatise to losing your anonymity. We soon made new friends and acquaintances by joining local organisations, such as the Corfe Castle Twinning Association, and because I found myself some work as Clerk to two Parish Councils in Purbeck, which I enjoy very much.

Note: Little did I know when I wrote my diary entry in March 2000 that in less than a year I would be very much involved with the community in Corfe Castle, working as Clerk to the Trustees of the Corfe Castle Charity

Today's weather: VERY WET

Name Jenny Wilson (The Spinney. Harmans Cross) Year of birth 1950
Corfe Castle Diary Sub-Committee member

House Street

Friday morning, up at 7.00.

Breakfast for the children (Robert 8 yrs old and Bethany 6 yrs old) and for me two dogs and cat.

Children to school (Old Malthouse Prep school) in Langton Matravers, by car, to be ready for assembly at 8.20.

Usual morning walk for the dogs - park in lay by on Kingston Hill, walk across the common to West St. turning circle, walk back to car.

0.900 - to work, as Nurse Practitioner in the village surgery. Very routine morning.

13.00. Having just finished work, pick Bethany up from school for Exeat Weekend.

Sandwich lunch at home then off to Wareham forest with dogs and Bethanys' bike.

Meet some friends with their children (plus dogs & bikes!) and follow the Sika trail for 2 hours.

16.30 All home to our house for tea - pasta with a cheese sauce and salad.

18.00 Back to school for play performed by pupils - very enjoyable. Julian (husband) manages to join us from work (he is a General Practitioner).

20.30 Home, children have a snack then go to bed.

21.00 Supper for Julian & myself - chicken curry & rice.

I watch television, Julian reads.

23.00 To bed.

Today's weather:
DULL BUT NO RAIN. TEMP - MILD, NO WIND.

Name DEIRDRE SELWYN   Year of birth 1957.

House LONGBARROW   Street MEAD RD.

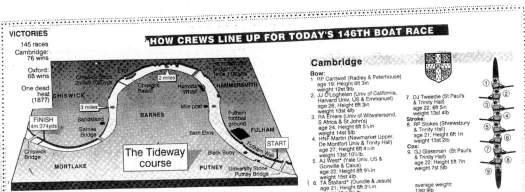

HOW CREWS LINE UP FOR TODAY'S 146TH BOAT RACE

VICTORIES
145 races
Cambridge: 76 wins
Oxford: 68 wins
One dead heat (1877)

CHISWICK · BARNES · HAMMERSMITH · FULHAM · MORTLAKE · PUTNEY

The Tideway course

University Stone Putney Bridge

The boat race was won by Oxford this year - the first time for many years

Cambridge

Bow:
1. RP Cantwell (Radley & Peterhouse) age 19; Height 6ft 3in weight 12st 9lb
2. JJ O'Loghlen (Univ of California, Harvard Univ, US & Emmanuel) age 26; Height 6ft 3in weight 13st 4lb
3. RA Ehlers (Univ of Witwatersand, S Africa & St John's) age 24; Height 6ft 5½in weight 14st 5lb
4. HNF Martin (Newmarket Upper, De Montfort Univ & Trinity Hall) age 27; Height 6ft 4½in weight 13st 10½lb.
5. AJ West* (Yale Univ, US & Gonville & Caius) age 22; Height 6ft 9½in weight 15st 4lb.
6. TA Stallard* (Oundle & Jesus) age 21; Height 6ft 3¾in weight 13st 2½lb

7. DJ Tweedie (St Paul's & Trinity Hall) age 22; Height 6ft 5in weight 13st 4lb
Stroke:
8. RP Stokes (Shrewsbury & Trinity Hall) age 21; Height 6ft 1n weight 13st 2lb
Cox:
9. GJ Glassman (St Paul's & Trinity Hall) age 22; Height 5ft 7in weight 7st 5lb

average weight: 13st 9lb

Oxford

Bow:
1. AGG Dunn* (Eton & Lincoln) age 19; Height 6ft 4in weight 13st 6lb
2. NJ Robinson* (Hampton & Lincoln) age 21; Height 6ft 5in weight 14st 6½lb
3. BJ Burch (Cheltenham & Pembroke) age 20; Height 6ft 5in weight 14st 8½lb
4. MJ Smith (Hampton & St Catherine's) age 18; Height 6ft 1½in weight 12st
5. DR Snow* (St Paul's & Balliol) age 21; Height 6ft 6½in weight 15st 9½lb.
6. TH Ayer* (Massachusets Inst of Technology, US & Worcester) age 24; Height 6ft 5in weight 15st 12½lb
7. EB Lilledahl (Yale Univ, US & Nuffield) age 25; 6ft 4in weight 14st 13lb

Stroke:
8. AM Reid (Yale Univ, US & Lincoln) age 23; Height 6ft 6in weight 14st 5lb
Cox:
9. AK McLaren (King's, Canterbury & Pembroke) age 19; Height 4ft 10½in weight 7st 1lb

average weight: 14st 5⅞lb

*Blue

INDUSTRIES IN THE DOLDRUMS

BEEF INDUSTRY

This sector found itself in crisis on 20 March 1996 when the Government admitted for the first time that "mad cow disease" – BSE – could after all be transmitted to people. The European Union at once banned British beef and an export market worth £200m disappeared overnight. In the four years since then, beef farmers have struggled to cope as millions of cattle have been slaughtered as a precautionary measure, with government compensation covering only a fraction of their former price. Many farmers have had to diversify into activities such as tourism to survive. Now that the EU has lifted the ban, normality is slowly returning.

PIG INDUSTRY

Farmers in this sector have had even worse trouble in the last two years, with the vast majority of pig farmers losing large sums of money. In 1998-99 their average loss was £14,700, while in the current financial year it is expected to be £8,000. In the last year alone, more than a quarter of them – about 1,500 farmers – have been forced to leave the business and it is thought there may be only 3,000 British pig producers by June. By that time the UK pig population may be 25 per cent smaller than in June 1999. Their troubles have been caused by the high pound, but also by Britain's unilateral abandonment of stalls and tethers as ways of keeping pigs, on animal welfare grounds. The change has added large sums to productions costs and the rest of Europe, which continues to use the old methods, can now undercut the cost of British bacon, pork and ham.

Prescott hits out at paternity 'nonsense'

BY SARAH SCHAEFER
Political Reporter

JOHN PRESCOTT yesterday brushed off Tory claims that he could not cope with running the country if Tony Blair took paternity leave.

POULTRY INDUSTRY

Chicken farmers have also been in trouble. Egg producers have suffered tumbling prices over the last two years because of overproduction, with a dozen eggs sometimes costing 45p or more to produce yet fetching only 25p from the packing plant. The causes have included fierce price competition from the supermarkets, and the economic cycle of boom and bust, but the bust has lasted longer than usual. The UK chicken flock has come down from 35 million to 30 million birds and prices are now stabilising.

Tomorrow is the first day of British Summer Time, when clocks will be put forward by one hour from 1am Greenwich Mean Time. BST will end at 2am on 29 October

Tom Craig

Name Compiled by a Committee Member. Year of birth NEWS TODAY
House TODAY'S NEWS IS TOMORROW'S HISTORY! Street wise!

Sunday March 26th

Another morning in Boring Old Corfe Castle. Woken at 6.30 by the boring old birds. Look out of the window at the same boring old view of the hills and fields with boring old animals in them.

Breakfast at 8.30 and somehow we stir ourselves up and go for a boring old walk along the boring old beach at Studland with its boring old views of Bournemouth and Poole. Back at 10.30, then a walk down to the village and meet some of the residents, and greet them in traditional Aussie fashion!

You see, since returning from our holiday in Australia and New Zealand we have tried to introduce some of the finer points of the Down Under culture here in BOCC (Boring Old Corfe Castle) but with as yet little success. When we meet residents, slap them on the shoulder and greet them by roaring 'G'DAY MATE, NO WORRIES' they either fall writhing to the ground, or take no notice whatsoever. A suggestion to a National Trust Official that they re-label the toilets (sorry, lavatories) SHEILAS and BLOKES instead of Ladies and Gents caused his eyes to go permanently much closer together; my car sticker 'WHERE THE HELL IS CORFE CASTLE?' brought forth howls of dismay from the Chamber of Commerce; a proposal to replace our hedges and roof with silver corrugated iron was not received with enthusiasm by the local Planning Authority as it would not blend in well in the Conservation Area and a request to rename our house 'HEREWEAH' or 'GOODONYER' led to angry scenes at the open session of a recent Parish Council Meeting. Because of all this we have been finding life socially quiet in the village, even to being cut completely dead at the W.I Coffee Morning where the Committee were doing a photo-shoot for their 2001 Calendar in the Village Hall yesterday, though the thongs, no shirt and a hat with corks on might have had something to do with it!

Back home then for the afternoon - the sheep are making a lot of noise now, and there is a wretched horse neighing its head off in the field next door. To cap it all there about twelve pigeons honking in the trees and a couple of pheasants rasping at each other. All this noise - can't stand it - animals, birds, bells, trains, and now as it gets dark the owls are starting up!

So another day ends in BOCC. Going to be in dead trouble if anybody in the village gets to read this!

P.S. We jest, of course as we have to admit that it is a really lovely part of the world in which to live, and we enjoy it more and more, and sometimes feel when we are on holiday that we would much rather be at home!

Today's weather: Dull and yes, you've guessed it, boring!

Name Roger Frost   Year of birth 1934

House SPRINGWOOD   Street WEST

I came to Dorset in 1972 from Surrey and moved to Corfe Castle in 1984 with my parents when the cottage was built from local stone and I worked in Poole. At that time I had a Rough Collie dog named Lincoln who was everybody's friend.

I have been working for the National Trust shop in the Square for ten years and I am working this day. I was woken up by my alarm at 6 a.m. It's downstairs for my breakfast of two shredded wheats with honey from the National Trust Kingston Lacy Estate.

 I look out in my garden and see our tame blackbird which sits on the garage roof and sings its beautiful song. Lincoln, my old dog, has now gone and I have this puppy, a miniature schnauzer, Jester. I take him for his morning walk for about an hour on the common and fields around. It looks as if there has been a frost last night, only whilst out I saw Joan Ingerfield with her dog, Monty. I always say "hello" to the dogs and make a fuss of the local horses and Jester likes them and they like him too. I give him his breakfast and my Dad gives me a lift down to the shop in the Square in time for 9.30 a.m. The shop opens at 10 a.m. There are four of us working in the shop today and it's a busy one. The shop is having a complete change round. I am in the stock room in the morning unpacking a delivery of cross stitch books and in the shop after lunch.

Not many people about during my walk to day I looked back at the following. When we moved to this cottage at 156 East Street in 1984 we planted an Irish Yew tree about 2'6" tall at the bottom of the garden. In this Millennium year 2000 it is now 12 ' tall - what is its future? Before this Millennium we planted an oak tree down at the National Trust car park, by the stream to mark the National Trust Centenary in 1995. I also planted a walnut which we picked up at Kingston Lacy. It germinated and it is now 8' tall, again down at the National Trust car park.

We finish work at 5 p.m. in March so its home to walk Jester and get the meal ready and spend a quiet night in..

Today's weather·   Dry and overcast but bright first thing

Name	Georgina Gumbrell	Year of birth	1950
House	Michaelmas Cottage (156)	Street	East Street

Tuesday March 28th

Today is a normal working day for me. I get up at about 6.00am. As I am a diabetic my first job is to inject myself with insulin. I have four injections a day using an insulin pen.. I use two types of insulin - before breakfast, lunch and dinner I use fast acting Humalog insulin and last thing at night I have slow acting Humalin Insulin.

Every fourth morning I test my blood glucose level using a meter. This enables me to monitor my overall general diabetes control.

After breakfast I wash, dress and get ready for work. I wear a uniform of black trousers, white shirt and black blazer. I leave home at about 7.10am to catch the bus to Poole. On the way to the bus stop in east street by the 'Why' jewellers I go via the square to buy a paper which I read on the 50 minute journey. I work as a sales clerk (deputy senior clerk) in the local bus company travel office at Poole bus station.

I work a shift system either 08.30am to 16.36pm or late shift 09,24am to 17.40pm - a 38 hour week.

As a sales clerk my duties include the selling of bus and coach tickets and answering general enquiries. Most bus tickets are bought by passengers for either journeys to work or children/students to school or college. The coach side of the work is varied but most tickets are to London airports or further afield to major cities in Western Europe although some are to eastern Europe and North Africa. We also sell coach holidays, which are popular with the middle aged and elderly to places throughout England, Wales, Scotland, Ireland. and Europe. We also sell promotional items such as model buses which are limited edition collectors items and books.

Some typical fares are:

Local bus - Corfe Castle to Swanage (adult day return) £3.55
        Corfe Castle to Poole (adult day return) £5.00
National Express - Bournemouth to Glasgow/Edinburgh (adult economy) £58.00
        Poole to London (adult period return) £20.00
        Poole to Gatwick (adult period return)   £28.50
Holidays   **Scottish Lochs (7days)   £275.00**
        Paris inc. 1 day at Euro-Disney (4 days)   £145.00
        Italy - Lake Garda (12 days)   £479.00

Lunch is usually between 12.30pm and 14.00pm depending on the shift (this is when I have my second injection of the day) After the 40 minute break it is back to work until time to go home. I usually sleep during my bus journey home the it is time for my third injection and my evening meal.

After dinner I read any mail and answer any letters. I make sandwiches for the following day's lunch. I don't watch very much television although I enjoy my favourite pastime of football either on the Television or on the Radio. 21.30 time for a shower and then it is time for the fourth injection of the day and a small meal before bedtime which I usually eat whilst watching the late evening news on the television and go to bed between 22.30 and 2300

Today's weather:

Name Mervyn Hayward   Year of birth 1961
House 62   Street West Street

Today a friend of mine called Charles Esson came to play. I have a BOYS ONLY camp in our wood. Every time a friend comes over we improve it by making more walls and traps to defend us from girls and adults (water bombs, hidden pits and trip wires). We have made a huge longbow that even Daddy has problems drawing properly. Charles and I went to the camp and tried to build another wall but it started raining heavily so we had to give up and go home. We played snooker 'til lunch time. After lunch Mummy drove us to Nick Spooner's house in Corfe. Nick's Mum drove us to Tower Park in Poole where we went to Giles Malyon's Megabowl birthday party. We all had a great time and then had tea in Burger King before coming home.

Today's weather: Cold, wet and miserable

Name Henry Bond   Year of birth 1988

House Whiteway Farm   Street

Thursday March 30th

The cat woke me up at 6 30am but I went back to bed and got up at 7.30am - my usual time

I had breakfast of cornflakes and toast I then read the daily paper (The Mail) - the Stockmarket was down 51 points

I took my wife Marie to the Nursery School where she helps look after the children

Then to Jill Beavis in East Street for a hair cut On the way home I bought two sausage rolls and two Danish pastries from Dragon's Bakery in the Square

At 9.45am I set off to Wareham for the produce Market in East street (there is no longer a cattle market in Wareham) I met Peter Fenney an old Corfe Castle resident and a member of the Corfe Castle Football team in his younger days. Also saw Doug Sennick - another local from Corfe

I watched the auction Large Eggs sold for only50 pence a dozen (12)
Medium Eggs were 40 pence a dozen and
Duck Eggs 75pence a dozen

I chatted to Mon. Williams from West Street, Corfe Castle who works at the market
During a walk around the stalls I bought Lamb Chops and Cheese for £3.90

I then walked into Wareham town where I met June Cross from Corfe and also
Den Simpson an old school mate.
Arrived back at home at 11 15am

Time to do some decorating before lunch - I gloss painted the landing window.

1 00pm had sausage roll and coffee for lunch

3 00pm Picked up Fred, my grandson, from school. Took him home and stayued until 4 30pm.
Dinner at 5.30pm - Beef stew and dumplings

Spent the evening watching the T V and went to bed at 10 00pm

Today's weather: **Cloudy and cold. N.E. wind**

Name PETER POPE.

House 11.SA.

Year of birth 14/4/28.

Street WEST STREET.

Friday March 31st

Friday, March 31st 2000,   The Congregational Church,

This day, Friday would not normally be a very interesting day in the life of the Congregational Minister here in Corfe Castle, although every day can be busy especially with the needful visiting regularly, and also such a day for hospital visiting. Also Friday morning is often my turn for School Assembly here in the Village School, and of course our own Young Peoples Club - Cameo Club, which meets on a Friday Evening.

But this year Friday the 31st is a very busy day, because tomorrow is a very important day for our church here, we are opening our New Extension, the new Hall on the end of our church, this was the completion of our own Millennium Project, just over 18 months earlier we had decided in our church business meeting that we ought to make a special effort for the Millennium which was coming upon us very quickly, and was receiving a lot of publicity, it had been several years since our church premises had received a facelift, so the discussions started, first, was to higher the approach path to the front door, and make access to our church wheelchair friendly, then to remove some pews in the front and back of the church, then to recarpet right through, to make a doorway into the New Hall which was going to be such a great asset to us. So our Millennium Project was to be our New Venture with the Grand opening on April 1st Tea in Village Hall.

So, Friday the 31st was a busy day preparing for a huge festival!

Today's weather:

Name   Pastor David M. Foot.   Year of birth   1931

House   44 East St. Corfe Castle   Street

April 1st – April Fools day. Well hopefully not in my case! I work in the library but I live in Wool, which is a village about ten miles away.

The library, which was built more than **twenty-five** years ago, is open for two and a half-hours, four times a week. Saturday mornings are my favourite times here. Everyone seems happy and relaxed and on this particular day, which is the first Saturday of the month, a coffee morning is being held in the village hall, which is situated behind the library. The day is unfortunately wet but does not detract from the feeling that spring has arrived, especially when you see all the beautiful daffodils out and the gorse in full bloom everywhere. The library is quite small but is well used by the villagers and as well as choosing books is much used for greetings, gossip and information.

Lil Gibb is first through the door at half past nine. She is an avid crime reader as many are in Corfe – I wonder why! Lil is closely followed by Pat Buckley and her mum Mrs. Reid. All three come in at least once a week, as do many people. We even have one lady who takes out twelve books at a time, which is wonderful for library issues and reflects on the amount of choice that is available.

Back to this morning! No time for coffee – It's so busy! The new doctor calls in to join the library with his wife and son. I wonder if they will have time to read! Jeff Edwards, who is a lovely gentleman, is here to find some thrillers and pass the time of day. Barbara and Reg Illings, who travel from Swanage to see friends and choose books.

There have been so many people in this morning – it would be nice to mention them all! The time is five to twelve and Mr. Western rushes in and announces that I have got him out of bed! " What! " I reply. " At five to twelve?! " He quickly renews his books and pays his fines (I hope that the rest of the day goes better for him!) before I shut the library doors at twelve o'clock – or there abouts!

Today's weather: WET.

Name SUSAN ARNOLD

House CORFE CASTLE LIBRARIAN

Year of birth 15TH JANUARY 1949

Street GYLST,

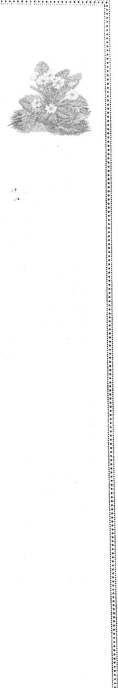

Today is Mothering Sunday, one of the children's favourite celebrations in St. Edward's Church. On the Saturday morning, we gather with the children of the Sunday School in the Robing Room to make small posies of flowers to be taken into the church on Sunday for the morning service. The children give the posies firstly to the mothers, and then to family members and friends. We also make a large card and a Mothering Sunday cake, which the older children decorate. The cake is cut and given to the congregation at the end of the service with coffee and squash for the children. Everyone enjoys this celebration, as it is a very happy and friendly way for family and friends to join together and celebrate in a very informal way, a very special day.

Today's weather: Spring-like – sunshine and showers

Name	Barbara Cannings and Betty Groves	Year of birth	
	Sunday School teachers since the 1960s		
House	St. Edward's Church Sunday School	Street	Meeting in the Robing Room

Monday April 3rd

I chose this date as it is a special anniversary for me in the village. Eight years ago to the day I started working as Clerk to the Corfe Castle Charity. As I walk around the village I am aware of how much the Charity has done in the village since 1992. The obvious example is the building of Abbots Cottages, a group of 9 houses for local people to rent in East Street. They won the Civic Trust Rural Housing Award in 1997 and were officially opened by HRH The Prince of Wales in April 1998.

As usual, after getting up I walked to the Paper Shop & bought The Times (35p). After breakfast I completed college work for my Association of Accounting Technician Course + took it into the College at Landsdowne in Bournemouth. As usual, it was very difficult to find a place to park! In Wareham, on my way home, I did some banking for myself + the Charity & stopped for lunch.

In the afternoon I dealt with urgent letters and phone calls for the Charity. I then changed into more formal wear for a Primary Care Group Board meeting at the Springfield Hotel in Stoborough (As I work from home I am fortunate enough to be able to dress as I please; but jeans are too informal for Board meetings!) Returned from meeting at 7pm, had tea + then went out for a drink at the Stoke ford Inn, on the road to Wool. (Lager - £2.20 a pint). Home + bed!

Today's weather: Heavy rain + thick cloud and very cold all day.

Name Beatrice Clarke

House 58 East Street

Year of birth 1953

Street

Tuesday April 4th

A.M.

The day dawned with airports closed and snowploughs in action —
luckily not in this particular area. 'Blackthorn winter' is here with
a vengeance! When the hedgerows are wreathed with the white flowers
of the Prunus Spinosa (Sloe) we can be assured of a very cold spell of
weather. It is an old fashioned prediction that is proven to be true
year after year, without fail. So the first task is to make some
soup for the picnic which Brenda and I share on our regular Tuesday
outings. This afternoon we shall take an audio/visual presentation
to the ladies of Langton Matravers W.I. They have chosen one entitled
'The Valley of the Giant'.

P.M.

Rain and sleet was encountered en route to Langton Matravers, and
there was no way we could have followed our usual Tuesday occupation
of wandering around various locations in Dorset, with our cameras,
in search of pictures and information for the compilation of our
programmes. The chosen programme this afternoon was well received;
the Village Hall at Langton was pleasantly warm and it was good to
see on the screen images we took a few summers ago of the Cerne
Valley.
After tea and biscuits, and some friendly conversation, we loaded
our equipment back into the car and drove to Swanage, where we noted
with wry amusement that the car parking was at 'summer' rates.
We had to visit both supermarkets to obtain the food items we
required, and then decided to park the car on the seafront where
we could watch the sea while we enjoyed our picnic. It was still
raining, and a strong cold wind was blowing, but a few brave people
were walking their dogs on the beach.
The soup was most welcome!

Today's weather: Blackthorn winter

Name CYNTHIA SANSOM   Year of birth 1928

House CUNNS   Street 7. WEST STREET.

I got up, washed and had my breakfast. I then brushed my dog Tess before taking her out into the garden. This the plot adjacent to the garden immediately at the back of my house.

I then went into the greenhouse and planted out my pot marigolds into a tray.

Then I went in and changed my clothes and took my friend to see her sister who is in hospital.

I did my shopping in Wareham then went back to my friend house for fish and chip dinner.

I went home and gave Tess her dinner then took her out into the garden while I washed the car, she played with her ring bringing it back to me to throw. I felt a few spots of rain and put the car into the garage and went indoors to finish making my Simnel Cake also a Chunky Top Cake.

I had a boiled egg for tea.

I had a restful evening then went to bed.

Today's weather:

Name SUSAN COOPER

House 58 WEST ST.

Year of birth

Street

Womens Institute entry for year 2000 Diary.   6th April 2000

Today the Womens Institute celebrated the 58th anniversary of its
founding in Corfe Castle in April 1942. Regular monthly meetings
are held in the Village Hall: today's followed the usual format of
reporting and discussing current WI business matters, followed by
tea then probably a talk or demonstration given by a guest speaker.

For tea we had buttered scones and an iced Birthday Cake made
specially for the occasion by Miss Margaret Stannett. Margaret's
cake, as always was praised and enjoyed by everyone present.

After tea Mr Parry Jones gave a talk about "The History of English
Gardens" accompanied by some interesting colour slides. A vote of
thanks to Parry was given by Mrs Rosemary Apsey.

Every year County needs to find ways of raising extra funding.
This year Dorset Institutes were asked to do something innovative
with £5.00, themed as "Fun with a Fiver." For this, our President,
Mrs Elizabeth Crabbe,baked and decorated a traditional Simnel
Cake. The cake was raffled at today's meeting and was won by
Mrs Kathleen Murphy. The £21.00 raised by the raffle will be sent
to DFWI Headquarters at Dorchester.

Two important features of our WI meetings are the Trading Table
and "Flowers of the Month"display. The Trading Table raised £12.50
for our own Funds. All the items sold were donated by members and
included many plants. A charming display of seasonal spring
flowers was exhibited by Mrs Winifred Whitby. Members showed their
appreciation by placing small coins around the flowers. The money
will be included in our annual contribution to Associated Country
Women of the World (ACWW).

The meeting closed at about 4.30 pm.

                                                K J Murphy.

Today's weather: Sunny with blue skies. Strong N.E Wind and very cold.

Name Mrs K J Murphy   for and on behalf   Year of birth
     10 Battle Mead   of Corfe Castle
House   C.C.   Womens Institute. Street

Friday April 7th

This morning dawned bright and sunny. Let us hope this is the foretaste of a lovely summer. I am High Sheriff of Dorset. Amazing. For this one year I will important – or more accurately people will think I am important.

Yesterday, also a lovely bright sunny day, I "made my declaration" and assumed the office. I did this at home, which was a scramble as the builders have only just left. Anne had a very busy time rearranging the house. For the occasion I had to wear "Court Dress" for the first time. This is based on what a prosperous 18th Century gentleman would have worn – stockings (actually tights), knee breeches, velvet waistcoat, cutaway tailcoat. Strictly I believe there should be a Court sword and sort of tricorn hat, but I intend to follow recent example and dispense with these. Not wearing proper trousers is a bit disconcerting. I found myself looking down in case I had forgotten to put them on. There were 38 guests, who arrived around midday. We showed them into the drawing room and offered drinks. Lewis Parkyn, the Under Sheriff, called everyone to order. Anthony Yeatman, last year's High Sheriff, read out his piece, and I read out my Declaration, which is the equivalent of an oath of office, doing so with some difficulty as I forgot to put on my glasses before I started and then couldn't get them out of my pocket. Brian Ruff, as my Chaplain, read a formal prayer. Brian then said grace and we went into lunch, split between the dining room and an "L" shaped table in the sitting room – lunch cooked by Anne and served by Helen and Karen with Viv and Beryl behind the scenes. For me possibly the best bit about the ceremony was that Alexander was there; High Sheriffs don't normally have 9-year-old sons.

The office of High Sheriff is the oldest secular appointment in the country after the sovereign. In the very early middle ages the King would appoint a "shire-reeve" to govern each shire or county on his behalf. I believe that the word "reeve" means something like "manager". I remember a few years ago my cousin Hugh Irvin in Aberdeenshire referring to someone who in England we would call a farm manager as a "reeve". As I understand it the "shire-reeve" or sheriff was responsible in the King's name for maintaining law and order, arranging and presiding over courts (later when the King's judges started travelling on "circuit" round the country the sheriff looked after them when they visited his county), raising levies to take up arms for the King (no standing army in those days), collecting taxes, and generally governing the county for the King. The office was well established by the time the earliest High Sheriff of Dorset of whom there is a record, someone called Beaduherd, was in office. He came to his end one day in about the year 892 when he saw some ships off Weymouth. He dutifully went out to collect taxes due from them. Unfortunately they turned out to be a Viking raiding party who didn't believe in paying taxes, so they killed him instead. Over the centuries other posts have been created to take on various of the High Sheriff's original responsibilities: the Lord Lieutenant to raise armed forces for the King (he is still responsible for the Territorial Army) and generally represent the sovereign; magistrates (Justices of the Peace) to preside over the lower courts and to do what is now done by local government, which they continued to do until 1888; professional judges to deal with more serious crime; the police; and the Inland Revenue. On the one hand the High Sheriff was potentially so powerful that he was not allowed to hold office for more than one year at a time, and then could not be re-appointed for three years. On the other hand, if the High Sheriff didn't manage to collect as much tax in his county as the King's officials thought he should have collected he had to make up the shortfall himself, so county worthies sometimes used to go to a lot of trouble to try to avoid being appointed.

So far as I can discover I am the first member of my branch of the family to be High Sheriff of Dorset in nearly 200 years. General Mark Bond and his sister Elizabeth Williams were both High Sheriff in the 1970's, but they are from the Tyneham branch of the family. My great-great grandfather's elder brother, John Bond, was High Sheriff of Dorset in 1830. His father, also John Bond, was High Sheriff of Cardigan in about 1800 on the strength of some property there which was his wife's dowry. To be High Sheriff of Cardigan was apparently less expensive than to be High Sheriff of Dorset.

Yesterday afternoon someone from the local press telephoned and after a few pleasantries asked the usual fatuous question: "How do you feel now that you are High Sheriff?" Before I could stop myself he got the truthful answer which was that I felt just the same as I did the day before. I then had to back track frantically and I managed to say that I hoped I could do something useful for Dorset during my year, which is also true. One area in which I would like to try to make a difference is that of youngsters, mostly boys, coming out of care or custody and having nowhere to live. Whatever happens it will be an interesting and enjoyable challenge, particularly in the Millennium Year.

Today's weather:

Name M.J.A. Bond   Year of birth 1942

House PUZZLEMANS HOUSE   Street WEST STREET

Saturday April 8th

I travel daily from Swanage to Corfe Castle to work. I am employed by the National Trust and my main duties are dealing with the general public.

People visit Corfe from not only our own country but from all over the world. Today we had visitors from Australia, New Zealand and students from Japan, Korea, and South America. We also had a large group on a pre arranged booking from France.

The bell ringers were practising during the morning (Saturday morning appears to be a practice morning) and the sound carries all over the village.

Today was also the day the Grand National was run at Aintree what a pity we don't have a bookmakers shop here to put on our bets.

Towards the end of the day I met a lady who was last here 38 years ago and enquired if the fish & chip shop was still here that she remembered.

Today's weather: Brilliant sunshine with a cloudless blue sky tempered with a mild breeze

Name DAVID NEWMAN

Year of birth 1941

House (Townsend Road Swanage)

CORFE CASTLE
NATIONAL TRUST Staff.

A Day With My Daughters.

Today was my daughter Jennifer's Birthday. So I went up to East Ewell where she lives to spend the week end with her and the family.

Jenny wanted to go to a cat show at East Grinstead, so we met my other daughter Carol there to see all those exotic cats.

The year 2001 will be a very important one for them both, as on Shrove Tuesday the Ancient Order of Purbeck Marblers celebrate the 350th anniversary of the signing of the Articles in 1651.

On Shrove Tuesday in the year 2000 , It was agreed by the Order, that as from Shrove Tuesday 2001, the 350th anniversary of the signing of the original Articles, Daughters of Freemen would have automatic right of membership as well as Sons.

So next year Carol & Jenny will be there with a quart of beer a penny loaf, and six shilling and eightpence (37 1/2P) standing at the Fox Inn, waiting to be escorted across to the Town Hall by Dave Glassock our Steward.

There they will receive a certificate of their membership and be among the first Ladies of the Order. (The girls can trace their ancestry through the Burt line back to to a Robert Burt Born in Swanage 1578).

Today's weather: It was a nice mild but cloudy day in Kent.

Name	Albert John Burt
House	Stonecroft.

Year of birth	12th January 1925.
Street	4 Colletts Close.

Monday April 10th

The usual Monday - get the washing done and out on the line to blow - a good day if it remains fine. I had a West Purbeck Group Women's Institute Committee meeting at Studland at Diane Vine's house at Manor Farm. I had a lift from Valerie Smith, our secretary, coming through from Church Knowle.

An energetic meeting with contributions from W.I. group members from Church Knowle, Corfe Castle, Harman's Cross, Studland and Stoborough. Among other social events we are trying to put forward a resolution, eventually perhaps to go forward to the national Federation *:to withdraw the concession for owners of second homes which allows them to pay only half of the Council Tax.*

All our villages feel that we are loosing the communities when there are more and more second homes used only at weekends, giving little or no input to village life.

Returning home, I was almost late for lunch but Tom had the vegetables cooking so all was well.

The afternoon remained fine so the washing dried and we talk the dog for a walk in Rempstone woods. We don't often see more than one Roe deer down there but this afternoon there was a magnificent stag with eight hinds - they were curious but not frightened.

Home to tea and a quiet evening - only two phone-calls!

The television was <u>not</u> particularly interesting.

Weather Cold, dry and very blowy.

Today's weather:

Name PEGGY HUNT   Year of birth 1924

House 71   EAST   Street

Tuesday April 11th

Not very good weather, my sons Tim & Bob have left for work, one to Sturminster Marshall, and one to Wareham. I am left to do all the jobs a 'Mum' does.

Tuesday mornings its Coffee at the 'Springwell Close' community room, together with those who live at 'Uvedale', St Edwards Close, Jubilee House and other friends. Ann the resident Warden joins in the general chat, and a very pleasant hour is spent.

Home now to wait for the fishman, my neighbour joins me, we know when the van is coming as the cat appears. We are able to buy really fresh fish and shell fish.

The afternoon is spent preparing for a Committee meeting of our Poole & District Parkinson's Branch. We have a membership of 300, the largest Branch in England. We have a good committee and we work hard but well together.

Now to the Post office to pay the Bills and to collect my pension, 75p extra this week, a pity that the community charge and gas payments went up by £5.00 a month.

The boys are home, the meal finished, off to the meeting at Canford Heath, home about 10.00 p.m, enough for today – GOODNIGHT.

Today's weather: OVERCAST – DAMP.

Name PAT STOCKLEY

Year of birth 1933

House 50

Street WEST STREET

Well the usual "beep-beep" wakes me up again, 6.00 am, at least it's light now. Doesn't seem so bad getting up when you can see what you are doing. I like getting up before the rest of the house as I can potter around tidying last nights coke can and crisp packets. Also after the kettle has boiled I can sit, coffee by my side, and surf the Internet a wonderful thing that is, the world at my fingertips. This being the year 2000, I check my emails. Years ago we all just looked forward to the postman, now we check our emails.

Goodness, it's finally getting up time, let's get them all off to school and work. Like many households in Corfe it's frantic here in the morning – arguments over the bathroom, whose toast is this, etc., but it all works out well in the end. The short drive into Halves to drop the youngest two at the bus stop is always fun – "have you got everything, lunch money, PE kit". After they pile out of the car I drive into the Square to collect my magazines. It's always busy in the Square someone always coming and going, deliveries going on – until you actually stop and look and watch you don't realise how busy Corfe Square gets. Then I realise a large piece of Corfe, to me personally, has gone. Mum and Dad are no longer at Brook Cottage, no more popping down to say hi to Mum as she cooks breakfast for her B&B. That's when, just for a moment, Corfe is empty for me. All the rest is not important, Mum and Dad are gone – living it up in retirement in France.

Well now it's punishment time – swimming – trying to get this wreck of a body fit, so Vista Bar here I come. Forty minutes of attempted breast stroke and that's enough. "What now?" - my mind is thinking of all I've got to do but first the dream – a lottery ticket – but I expect that's all it will be. It's a shame that we have no lottery outlet in Corfe.

10.45 and some pottering around the house sorts out two bedrooms, one blitzed bathroom and least it looks tidy. Looking out of Pippa's bedroom window the Castle looks so grey, so cold and unwelcoming. It's nice to know that the village itself and its people are not like that.

I'm, or rather my stomach, is thinking lunch time, but first I'd better pick up my Echo so I've got something to read as I'm chewing my turkey roll. I decide to drive into Corfe via Sandyhill Lane. It's lovely with lots to see and if you ever get the chance to walk the route try it. I half expect to see Mum walking down the lane but no reality kicks in – she is not here. Reality takes a back seat again as I pass Brook Cottage, expecting to see the door open or B&B knocking. I wonder how many of you have come up round that corner on a sunny summers afternoon and seen the door open. Anyway the poor staff in the paper shop are inundated with walkers and school kids so it's 32p thrust into the hand and off with the rolled up newspaper. Driving up East Street I can hear the kids in Corfe school. I miss dropping Robbie off at the school as it was always nice to chat with other parents. Robbie always asks Grandad Trevor what it was like 100's of years ago at Corfe school and Grandad Trevor has to explain that it was only 55 years ago he was there. Dad for all his rolling gait, Dorset accent and few beers in the Fox misses Corfe and the Parish Council. His few years on there were good for him and I think good for Corfe and it also enabled him to escape Mum's watchful eye for an extra hour or an extra pint or two.

After lunch just doing paperwork keeps me busy. Do you know how many companies want you to buy gas/electric from them? It takes me two hours to work out the cheapest one. Then the SAS come through the door, sorry it's Robert with the immortal kids cry of "I'm hungry when's tea – can I have a biscuit?" Well before I start tea I take a few minutes to watch 15-1 – must try and sharpen my brain!!!! Tea done and dusted and a quiet evening in. It gives me time to reflect on the day and how different days can be.

It's been an honour to be asked to do this and I hope everyone finds something of interest.

Weather – sunny spells, slight cloud, cold breeze.

Name TIM CATTLE   Year of birth 1957

House OAKLEIGH.   Street PARENTS' –
SPRING BROOK CLOSE   LATE OF
HARMANS CROSS   BROOK COTTAGE
                                          EAST ST.

Only had one number on the lottery so the dream goes on!!!

Thursday April 13th

It's 7.30 am. time to get-up. As I draw my curtains back and contemplate my lovely view of the Purbeck hills and most of the castle - in recent years foliage has obscured a little of the view - but no matter its still a wonderful sight and once again think how luckly I am to live in this region.

This is a three generation household, my daughter is back from university for the Easter break - my father is 88 this year and very active for his age. Breakfast is staggered and help-yourself. This suits me as I try to avoid all discussion - never was very good in the mornings!

After a few chores its now 9 o'clock and I must leave for work in Swanage. I may not have queues of traffic to cope with but I do have a few obstacles to get past to get out of the village - first task is to get round the corner from West Street into the Square, the problem being the parked cars and brewery vans at this hour. Nevermind, I have time and gives me the chance to waive to a few people on their way to collect their daily newspapers.

I skim into work dead-on-time for 9.30. I work in the public library in Swanage - I hope the public is in a good mood to-day, since I am. Its a very busy but small library, well used by a cross-section of the community which makes it interesting and enjoyable. I wonder how long libraries will continue to exist in our ever changing world of technology.

At five I finish for the day. Must remember to get some petrol on the way home, 78 pence a litre now. Public transport would be more sensible but our steam train runs for the tourist season only and the buses hourly. Just time for quick change as I'm off to my yoga class at the Purbeck School in Wareham - then its back home to get a quick supper for us all. My father has just got back from his bridge session at the British Legion - he's lost again, three pence down!.

Time to put my feet up and catch up with the newspaper.

Today's weather: Fine, but I'm looking forward to seeing Geert's rainfall count.

Name Sarah Dupuy

Year of birth 1952

House Kerilee

Street West Street

Dry and cold - splendid sunrise for my 69th birthday - the first in this house. Here the postman comes by 7.30 am (more like mid-day where we lived in Devon!) - cards, parcels, and of course the usual 'junk mail' - that went straight in the bin - the SITA refuse lorry backs down this narrow road each week and collects the rubbish in black plastic sacks provided by the council. Walked down to the village to pay a cheque in at Ian's sub-post-office - amazed to find minimum deposit is now £10 - whatever happened to small savers? Bought a copy of *What's on TV* (40p) - seem to be about twenty TV channels, but we rarely watch other than the news - there's so much pernicious, tasteless and mindless rubbish. Bought doughnuts (30p each) for the building gang who are well on with a small extension at the rear of the house - a cheerful and hard-working crew, though we could do without Two Counties Radio- and the so-called music, or the advertisements which lately all seem to end with a breathless, shouted and oft-repeated exhortation to '*visit our website on dublyewdublyewdublyewdotcom...*'.

Well, it was just one year ago that Yvonne and I visited Combe Keynes and Lulworth, and made up our minds, literally on the spot, to move to Dorset - and here we are, very happily. A village with PO, general store, bakery, butcher's, newspapers, National Trust restaurant, buses, train - what a contrast from our Devon village, with the nearest facility 4 miles away and no buses. Also we are now nearer our family - our grandchild Becky Murton can come 'to the seaside' for the day, and we see more of our son Tim who is an actor with a company at the Millenium Dome in London. Becky's parents, Phil and Wendy, are flying to New York today - our son-in-law is in the motor trade and this visit is some kind of reward for success. (Will Becky be reading this 50 years on, aged 53?)

Partly to escape the sounds of the building operation, partly to celebrate The Day, we drove to Swanage for a bite of lunch in the little cafe on the sea-front, by the brook outfall. But first, the splendidly bracing smell of the sea - how lucky we are to live so close to such a fine and varied coast-line, even if some of it is inaccessible on account of military occupation. An unexpected and most generous gesture by the cafe proprietor - Yvonne must have mentioned, as the waitress cleared away, that it was my birthday lunch - and as we left I was presented with two cream cakes to take home for our tea!

To the highlight of the day - the second performance, in St. Edward's Church, of *Thy Kingdom Come*, a celebration of 2000 years of Christian service and self-sacrifice. Yvonne sings in the choir, and I take a few little parts in the scenes depicting various great lives such as St. Martin, Gladys Aylward and Cecil Pugh. Maurice our Rector, and Ann Gaudin, have worked so hard at this presentation, and we, the cast, have been rehearsing for months - so good to see the church well filled with ?audience - ?congregation (!), who were kind enough to applaud generously tonight especially for the dance by children from the village First School. One more performance to go.

And so into my 70th year - pronounced fighting fit by our very agreeable new gp Steve Horsnell, practising in a suite of 'porta-cabins' while he negotiates for new surgery premises - possibly in West Street. This, after eight moves, is our final final move! Yvonne is a great gardener, we have a most pleasant little house, with a stile at the end of the garden into a field where, each morning, I climb over to give a Polo Mint to each of the two in-foal mares grazing there. And I look out over the hills, and the common, under this great sky, and think how lucky I am.

Today's weather: bracing !

Name Roger Free   Year of birth 1931

House 12, Townsend Road   Street

Saturday April 15th

I was still on the train coming back from London as Friday changed into Saturday. I had been to visit the British Airways London Eye and the Millennium Dome with my Gran, Linda Applin who lives in Corfe Castle.. The Eye is a giant Ferris Wheel (I mean **really big**) on the banks of the River Thames near to Waterloo Station opposite the Houses of Parliament. It has 32 pods in which people can ride to view the sights of London. It cost us **£11.90** (1Senior Citizen & 1Child) for a ½ hour ride but it was well worth it.

After our ride we returned to Waterloo and took the Jubilee Underground Line to North Greenwich to the Millennium Dome. It is a huge circular building made of steels struts covered in Teflon. We were in it for 8 ½ hours, leaving in time to catch the 9.55pm (21.55hrs) slow train, stopping at every station, to Poole. Gran then had to drive to Corfe Castle.

The Dome was really interesting and fascinating. I enjoyed the 'Home Planet' and 'Work and Learning' where there were lots of 'hands on' activities. In the 'Talk' zone we learnt all about the ways of communication in the future and also sent lots of free emails to friends and to my Dad and Granddad. It cost **£37** for the two of us.

We had lunch in Harry Ramsden's fish restaurant in the Dome, I had sausages and chips and Gran had Fish and Chips.

The show in the centre of the arena lasted for ¾ hour and was amazing with lots of acrobats and dancing.

We arrived back at Corfe Castle at 1.00am, very tired but we had enjoyed the day.

I was up at 9.30am to help Gran and the other members of the village Millennium Association at their fund raising coffee morning. I helped Gran with the raffle - we made £83 profit. I was given a rugby ball from the bric-a-brac stall.

> *A fund raising Coffee Morning is held in the Village Hall most Saturdays. The Millennium Association hold one every two or three months to raise money for our Millennium Celebrations throughout the year and also to raise money to build a sports pavillion off West Street, Car Park.*
> *The stalls were- bric-a-brac (Stephen DruDrury & Jim Rosewarn); Cakes (Joan Marshallsay);Raffle (Linda Applin &Diana DruDrury);Celebration Mugs and Millennium Bug Game (Mary Rosewarn);Clothes (Peggy Hunt);Teas &Coffee (Mary Wills, Jan Harriott & Eileen Van Lelyveld);Books (Angelica Seik) The total sum raised was £195.00 which was not as much as we have made in the past.* Linda

For lunch we had Pasta Bolognaise followed by yogurt

We were planning on taking out Mary's dog in the afternoon but unfortunately it was raining and as I had only brought one pair of shoes I didn't want to get them dirty so we watched the television and played on Gran's computer.

After tea we went to the Church to see a Millennium Play - 'Thy Kingdom Come' which was about the people who had made a difference to society over the last 2000 years. Although Gran thought I might be bored, I enjoyed it especially the second half. It was 10.30pm when we got home so I watched 'Match of the Day' on the Television where Manchester United had won 4-0 against Sunderland. Gran read the paper. I was very tired when I went to bed.

The weather was sunny in the morning but rained all afternoon- dry by evening.

Name ANDREW APPLIN   Year of birth 1987
CHELTENHAM
House STAYING AT   64. WEST ST Street
                  CORFE CASTLE

Today is Palm Sunday. The weather is dry and sunny. The children from St. Edward's Sunday School walked with the Rector, choir and friends, a donkey and palms, along West Street to the Church. This procession takes place every year on Palm Sunday. During the service, each member of the congregation is given a palm cross.

Today's weather:

Name ST. EDWARD'S CHURCH SUNDAY SCHOOL Year of birth PALM SUNDAY

House ROBING ROOM : WITH TEACHERS Street & CHILDREN
BETTY GROVES ; BARBARA CANNING and TARA MAURIELLO

Monday April 17th

The day broke with the sun shining, I was getting ready to go with Carol to Cash & Carry to price items for the refreshments for the May Fayre. The phone rang, it was a Rainbow mum checking on the right date for our visit to Farmer Palmers. I had given everyone the date of Tuesday 17th April. I hastily rang Farmer Palmer and arranged for our visit for the 18th then rang all the mums who actually realised I meant Tuesday 18th April. Which is why I am writing this for Monday and not as I was anticipating Tuesday. What a muddle.

Any way eventually Carol and I set off stopping briefly at Farmer Palmers to give confirmation of our visit, then on to Winton to buy some sandwiches for lunch, before arriving at Cash & Carry.

Most of the afternoon was spent traipsing backwards and forwards up and down the aisles getting provisions we all take for granted when buying in the shop. How Carol manages on her own I don't know, by the end of the afternoon I was shattered. We eventually arrive back home around 5pm, me to a cup of tea, but Carol still had to unload the car, then start working in the shop. A quiet evening was spent at home arranging with the children when to do a bedroom swap, and checking I had everything organised for the trip to Farmer Palmer.

Today's weather: Fine all day

Name Judith Jenkins   Year of birth 1951

House 14   Street East Street

Tuesday April 18th

My day started as usual at 6.30 AM. after my routine chores, I prepared the tins for a baking session later today. Then into Wareham to help an old client to bath. Before retiring last September I worked part-time in Wareham with the Community Nurses as a Health Care Assistant.

On my return home I continued with my baking. I wanted to make a Simnel Cake which is traditional Easter Fare though I believe it first appeared on Mothering Sunday. also a Rhubarb Cake which is similar to apple Cake though a couple of extra's.

We are having a visitor for Easter so any baking done in advance is is beneficial.

This afternoon I went to see my sisters, I am very lucky I have two and we live within 5 miles of each other. We usually try to meet each week to catch up on family news.

On returning home I prepared our evening meal, and spent the evening doing some cross stitch. I am doing one of Corfe Castle for my niece.

Today's weather: Cold Cloudy and a little rain

Name June Cross.
Year of birth 1937.

House Seven Townsend Road.
Street

Wednesday April 19th

I live on Lempstone Estate, 'in the sticks'. Life here is alot different to living in the metropolis that is Corfe! We wake up to a lovely spring morning, sun shining and all the birds singing. While I let our two dogs out and the cats come in, I watch the buzzard in the fields at the bottom of the garden, on the lookout for his breakfast. After feeding the chickens some corn, I hang out some washing. Our two boys aged eleven and eight are on school holiday, so they go out to play after breakfast. A couple more loads of washing goes on seeing as its such a lovely day. The garden is very soggy after all the rain that we've had, you tend to spend alot of time in wellies out here! I normally work in The Sweet Shop in Corfe, but I'm off today. The chicken house gets its weekly clean out and then I get three loads of logs from the wood shed and take them indoors to stack next to the rayburn so that it dries nicely for fires. Our relations turn up and take the boys out for a few hours, oh the peace! After a quick bit of housework, vegetable peelings go on to boil up for chicken food, and more washing gets hung out. I meet the new postman, nice chap. Lunch time arrives and Paul comes home for an hour. Taking advantage of having time to myself after lunch, I do a bit of decorating and paint a door and window frame. Veg peelings cooked, I chop them up and mix with layers mash and feed chickens, checking for eggs that have been laid so far, retrieved from under a broody hen who's turned very stroppy and pecks any hand that goes near her! The boys come back. Clouds are starting to roll in, late afternoon, turning to rain, so take the washing in. Time to lay a fire, as it's still chilly in the evenings at this time of year. After cooking dinner and feeding the menagerie, I shut the birds away for the night, watch some telly for the evening, enjoy a nice bath and so to bed.

Today's weather:
  Sunny morning, rain afternoon.

Name RHAINE DRUITT

House THE SCHOOL HOUSE

Year of birth 1963

Street BUSHEY.

Thursday April 20th

8.00

I was woken up by my Mum because my brother and I had to go and see the dentist in Upton for my appointment at 9.05. On the way to Upton we stopped at the bakers in Corfe Castle.

9.05

Arrived at the dentists. I had one of my teeth drilled and filled with a white filling.

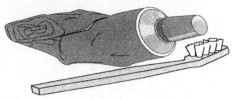

9.30

Left the dentists and drove in to Poole where I bought a magazine and some paper in W.H. Smiths. My brother then bought a cricket ball as a birthday present for his friend and we went home, stopping to change our tyres at a garage.

1.00

I had some bread rolls from the bakery for lunch and my Granny came to stay. I then went outside to play football with my brother and a friend.

7.00

I had pizza for supper, followed by an ice lolly and then sat down and watched various programmes on the T.V.

10.30

Went to bed.

Today's weather: Drizzle and cloudy – rivers flooding because of the rain

Name	Toby Young	Year of birth	1986
House	Lynch Farm	Street	

Friday April 21st

Nigel was up and out on the farm by 6.30 this morning to milk the cows, clean the yards and do the feeding with his dad. We came out on the farm at 8.30 after we'd fed our chickens. I fed & strawed the calves, heifers & bulls while the kids helped their gran feed the cattle lambs, fat lambs and check all the ewes and lambs.

We came in for breakfast at 10.30 and as it was Good Friday, I drove into the village and bought Hot Cross buns from (49) Dragons. Then we decided to let the heifers out to grass. They had been in the barn for the last 5 months so it was really nice to see them running around and they did a few laps of the field before they calmed down. Nigels parents then went to Encombe to check and feed the 1000 sheep we have there, while we moved 150 sheep about ½ mile to Blashenwell. It went quite smoothly, the 2 dogs worked well the kids were on the quad bike and Nigel and I walked.

It was about 3.00pm before we had our lunch, then it was back to the routine work of milking cleaning the yards and feeding the cows. I fed the calves and bulls then I cooked the kids tea. The heifers weren't so lively so Nigel, Jed and I walked them on two more fields to where we wanted them. The milking was finished at 7.30 then we had our evening meal.

Today's weather: Sunny with heavy showers in afternoon.

Name Nigel, Sally, Tom, Evie & Jed Percy

Year of birth 1964, 1966, 1990 1992, 1996

House West Orchard Farm Cottage Bradle Nr. Corfe Castle

Street

Today is a busy bustling day. The start of another Easter weekend in "Marblers" the Gift Shop and Tea-room in West Street – the home of Buck and Julie Buckhurst since June 1990. Chatting with them, they told me that by the end of the year things will have changed..

After ten years in Corfe Castle, they are retiring, to live not far away, still in Dorset. Preparing for this move they are already planning for their closing down sale in September.

Looking forward to the:-

CLOSING DOWN SALE

AT

MARBLERS
CORFE CASTLE

(In West Street, where the three trees grow)

FRIDAY 15th SEPTEMBER
until
THURSDAY 21st SEPTEMBER

A good opportunity to acquire nice gifts at cheap prices.

At least **20%** off Biscuits, Jams, Books and old Poole Pottery

and

At least **40%** off everything else!

Buck & Julie Buckhurst - Tel: 01929 480326

Maybe the new family moving into No.5 in the Autumn will write a page for this Diary.

Good luck Julie and Buck. See you at the Sale of the (New) Century!

Today's weather: Sunny

Name	Julie and Buck Buckhurst	Year of birth	are retiring this year
House	from "Marblers"	Street	5 West Street

Sunday April 23rd

7.30 am. Parked the car with ladders, paints, new pots, pans etc and drove to Corfe Castle from Southampton to arrive about 10 am.

Lots to do to get the cottage ready for holiday visitors who start to arrive next Saturday.

The cottage roof has been completely rebuilt with Purbeck stone, using as many original stones as possible. To facilitate the scaffolding the kitchen had to be demolished and then rebuilt.

So - we unloaded the car and had a cup of coffee while we decided on a plan of action. The whole house is covered in dust from the stone cutting, so started cleaning, polishing and made up the beds in the top bedroom. Beautiful views of the castle in sunshine.

1 pm. ate pasty and super danish pastry from the bakery. Watched the British Grand Prix on TV. The race was won by David Coulthard in dry conditions - surprising, because in the two previous practice days there was heavy rain and hailstorms. Roads around the circuit had been closed off.

Discovered ants coming in by the front door.

Tidied the garden in the afternoon. A song thrush is nesting in the honeysuckle. Birds singing everywhere. Maybe we shall live here soon! Jackdaws nesting in the chimney - despite our efforts to dissuade them. 6.30. Had quick evening meal & started painting kitchen cupboards. (Quick break for Antiques Roadshow) & continued until 2 am.

Not the usual way to spend Easter Sunday!

Today's weather: Mostly sunny, light showers

Name Dawn Moriarty   Year of birth 1947

House Rose Cottage   Street West Street.

Nowadays, in the year 2000, public holidays mean staying at home and keeping one's head down to avoid New Britain - the day trippers, the "second homers" with their four-wheel drives and rubbish bags; and the "Margate Mob" from the steam railway.

A sultry, misty dawn with no apparent chorus for once - perhaps the neighbour's cat got them!

Down to the Square first thing to trade in a week's sheet of vouchers for the "Telegraph" at the Sweet Shop and to greet the ever cheerful Gertie Welsh wending her way around the village. Carefully avoiding the cars blocking the pavements and gutters and rushing through to Swanage with boat trailers and bicyles swaying in the slip-stream.

A sunny morning of gardening - cutting the grass, setting out shrubs and a first cut of the escallonia hedge which is growing like lightning this very wet year - so far this April 4¼ inches of rain says the jam jar rain gauge - and another ½ inch this afternoon and evening. Sowing seeds has been the stickiest we can remember in forty years - but they are all coming up.

Coffee - and phone calls to the Festivities Committee mob to find and arrange the loan of our PA equipment for village functions throughout the Summer. Shades of the old Father Christmas Committee set up by Stan Sheasby after WW2 and resurrected by his brother, Les, in the early 1960s. The voluntary Committee now provides the Christmas lights and decorations, tree and crib, children's party, OAP's (sorry Linda!) party, carol singing and the arrival of Father Christmas - and all for free.

A visit from Yvonne and Roger Free, recently moved into the Bennett's house in Townsend Road after a life-time of school-teaching travel, to deliver some letters, talk gardening and swap potted shrubs.

Lunch on the remains of Don Palfry's brisket of beef and probably far too much to drink.

Now raining hard - nearly ½ inch - an afternoon vanished in sleep and the papers.

Awake again and writing letters for the CPRE and then delivering them in Wareham. Driving in driving rain, tail-gated by light-flashing New Britain on its way back to Town to add to our overheads.

And so to bed.

Today's weather: Morning - sunny : afternoon/evening - rain (½")

Name	David KING	Year of birth 1928
House	Greyflete	Street Higher Filbank

Tuesday April 25th

As it turned out, not a good day for me - but that's what life's all about, isn't it. Sad days to balance out the happy days. 8.15 a.m I called a taxi to take one of my two Toy poodles, Lizzie, to the Vet in Wareham to be operated on for a growth in her mouth. The taxi driver kindly brought me back to Corfe for free as he was coming back anyway. I then went to the village shops and Post office to collect my Widow's Pension. At 12.00 noon - a phone call from the Vet :- Lizzie's tumour was much worse than suspected and was inoperable. He asked me if he should bring her round from the anaesthetic or let her slip away while she was asleep. He said she would only live another couple of months anyway. I felt there was no choice — I could not bear to see her suffer; such a dear little dog, so I sadly opted to let her go. Then went next door and sobbed all over my son, William (the postman). In the afternoon I had to put on a brave face as I was on duty at the Tithe Barn Museum in Swanage. Came home on the bus at 5.O'clock and William took me to fetch Lizzie from the Vet. She was in a lovely little coffin, ready to be buried in the little orchard behind my cottage, where pets seem to have been buried over 100's of years. Polly, my other poodle misses her terribly after 9 years, and so do I. But we'll get over it. Summer's coming — and tomorrow is another day.

Today's weather: Rain a.m, brighter p.m.

Name Mrs JAN BLIGHT

House Deep Thatch

Year of birth 1936

Street 72, East Street

Another birthday!

Started the day by opening cards and presents. This helps to soften the depressing thought of being a year older. Since it was school holidays, my sons were able to help, prior to going to their holiday jobs at the Fox Inn and Model Village respectively. My eldest son is at university and holiday employment is now a necessity.

I went to visit Eileen Allcock and walk her dog. I hope I am as fit when I am 91.

We have three dogs, our 11½ retriever, Jazz, has not been well, so I took him to the Vet in Wareham at 5 p.m. This short trip, however, took an hour. Road works in Sandford caused a tailback of traffic to the cross-roads in Wareham. The Wareham by-pass was also at a standstill

In the evening, my husband, Michael, and I took our sons, James and Charles, ten pin bowling in Bournemouth. It was great fun.

We then went for a meal at Pizza Hut. My daughter, Judy, was away on a residential riding holiday and was unable to join us.

Today's weather: Mild and grey

Name	Sheila Spinney	Year of birth	26th April 1949
House	Purbeck House	Street	East Street

10.13 a.m.	Woke to "Five" on the radio, which automatically put me in a bad mood! Clambered out of bed, had shower, two slices of toast and got dressed.
11.55 a.m.	Strolled up Colletts Close to catch the bus at 11.58 a.m.
11.59 a.m.	Bus arrived. Paid my fare to Stoborough, and got to Stoborough Green at 12.07 p.m. Met Fern and we walked into Wareham to get a train to Bournemouth with Melissa.
Afternoon	Spent in Bournemouth "shopping" which resulted in all three of us buying a can of diet Coke, a pasta salad and some strawberries each. A useful shopping trip!
3.15 p.m.	Became very wet in Bournemouth Park during a water fight. I successfully lost, whilst Melissa remained bone dry! Fern laughed!
7.01 p.m.	Arrived home after an eventful train and bus journey. Ran into the kitchen and cooked myself a risotto in 20 minutes — ate it and got changed.
7.24 p.m.	Noticed Jaffa's big eyes staring at me and realised he needed feeding. Oops!
7.26 p.m.	Fern arrived and as soon as my Dad got in he drove us to Swanage.
7.34 p.m.	Rang Lauren's doorbell. Paid appropriate attention to the cat. Walked with Lauren, Fern and Vicky to Courthill Wines and rented The Exorcist and Austin Powers 2.
8.16 p.m.	Sat in Lauren's lounge eating chocolate, pringles and a bottle of wine, watching a scary movie.
11.00 p.m.	Listened to Foo Fighters, Red Hot Chilli Peppers and then watched Austin Powers 2.
1.35 a.m.	Went on the Internet and chatted with various friends in Bere Regis, whilst eating chocolate, pringles and wine.
2.04 a.m.	Still chatting and watching TV
2.05 a.m.	zzzzzzzzzzzzzz.......

Today's weather: Cloudy but warm

Name   Jo Kemp

Year of birth   1984

House   7

Street   Colletts Close

Friday April 28th

Domestic morning for Joan and delivery of order from Cleall's, our local grocery shop. Richard went shopping for some fresh food and hardware, then fed the fish in the pond. We heard on the radio this morning that research shows that beer is good for you (we've known for a long time that wine is good for you) so after shopping Richard went to the Isle of Purbeck Golf Club for a pint (nothing new about that!).

Lit the fire to cheer us up on this dull wet day and had salad lunch. Although the bluebells are out and the apple blossom and clematis montana are coming out it feels more like winter.

Went to Upton Park to see an exhibition of local artists. Great pictures but as we have a house full of paintings we don't need any more. Treated ourselves to dinner at the Trottolina Italian restaurant in Wareham. Excellent meal with a bottle of their table wine. Gave our collie 'Janet' a last walk. Finally it's stopped raining.

Today's weather: WET, WET, WET.

'SUNSET' by Penny Wilton

Name Richard Piercy
      Joan Piercy

House The Mount

Year of birth 1929
              1929

Street West Street

My Birthday

This year we acted on the spur of the moment and for my birthday we went to France on the Barfleur, the ferry which runs from Poole to Cherbourg. We left at 0830 on Friday and had breakfast on the boat. We arrived at 2pm and drove to Vannes where we had a hotel booked. It is amazing how clear the French roads are compared to our own - but I suppose it is not really surprising when you realise that France is twice as big as this country, with the same population.

We booked into the hotel and then out to a fantastic restaurant called the Atlantique, which specialises in fish. Super meal, with excellent Muscadet, during which we chat to a girl from Paris, who is down for the weekend. Afterwards back to the hotel for cafe and Calvados.

On Saturday we visited the market; like St Lo it has a super range of products which are sold in a way which would be impossible in this country; beaurocracy has gone mad here, and we blame it on the EU, when in fact it is all the fault of our Civil Service. Then out to lunch on moules frites at a restaurant overlooking the Golf de Morbihan; again very good. A tour round in hot sunshine, ending sitting by the sea at a little penninsular watching the world go by.

Dinner again at the Restaurant Atlantique - too good to miss. When we get there it is full, but happily Madame recognises us and makes room at a table in the corner.

Next morning a visit to Quiberon and then back to Cherbourg for the return home. Overall a very memorable trip to France, all the better for being unexpected.

TRAVEL AND ACCOMMODATION ITINERARY

PLAN TOURISTIQUE DE VANNES

ÉDITÉ PAR
L'OFFICE DU TOURISME DU PAYS DE VANNES

7, rue Thiers - 56000 VANNES
Tél. : 02 97 47 24 34 - fax : 02 97 47 29 49

PLAN OFFERT PAR LES ADHÉRENTS DE L'OFFICE DE TOURISME

Pays de Vannes

Today's weather: _Sunny and warm in France_

Name Stephen Du Drury   Year of birth 1939

House Harris   Street Coast Street

Leaving London at about 10.30 pm we started our journey to Corfe Castle on Saturday 29 April. We usually travel late, to avoid the traffic on the North Circular road and the M3 motorway. Keeping the radio tuned to Magic FM and with the air blowing cold to stay awake, we arrived in Corfe at around 1.00 am on 30 April to celebrate our first anniversary as owners of September cottage. With the increase in petrol prices to 80 pence per litre we notice the cost of these trips a bit more, even though we only have a Ford Fiesta and the journey is no more than 150 miles.

Just like film stars arriving at the airport, we had our picture taken by a flash camera as we approached Wareham. We realised that we were in just too much of a hurry to see our dream home in the country. Although we expect to pay a few pounds for this picture, we really hope that there was no film in the camera, so that we won't have to pay the speeding fine.

Pushing the front door open against the weight of the junk mail, advertising leaflets and free newspapers we are home again! Time to unpack and a quick cup of tea before bed, at around 2 am.

We hadn't planned anything for our diary day. We were just going to let things happen. A chat with Allen, next door, about the blocked drains led to a decision to sort them out properly sometime this year before the occasional inconvenience of an overflow becomes a real problem. The lawn received a trim during the 'Eastenders' Omnibus on BBC1. Eastenders is a very popular TV soap opera chronicling the lives of ordinary people living in east London and has been running for 15 years.

The land line in the cottage is just for incoming calls and emergencies, so we called Pat (a local handyman, whose number we had taken from one of the advertising leaflets) using our mobile phone. We wanted him to quote for some work that needed to be done at the back of the garden. Pat arrived at 4 pm but meanwhile, Marta had gone to investigate the cost of parking in West Street car park as we were expecting some visitors next day. Compared to London, the prices at 20 pence for an hour and £2.20 for over 4 hours seemed very reasonable. On her way back, Marta noticed that The Fox Inn had an attractive menu and we decided to go out for dinner in the evening.

Pat did a thorough job of assessing the work required and also told us that council permission was required to cut down trees more than 3 inches in diameter, with a £2,000 penalty for failure to comply. The Corfe steam train went by twice whilst we were discussing the gardening project. Billowing white smoke, and with its characteristic puffing and whistling it made a thought-provoking 19th century backcloth at the beginning of the 21st century.

We arrived at The Fox Inn for dinner at 7pm only to find that we should have booked in advance, as all the tables were reserved. The landlord took pity on us and said that we could use a table in the corner which was not booked until 8 o'clock. We ordered 2 pints of Young's Special at £2.30 per pint and 2 steak and guiness pies with chips and salad at £5.45 each. We followed with Dorset Apple cake and custard, and a banana split for dessert for a further £4.90 and were very pleased with our choices. Although, we didn't finish until 8.15 pm the people waiting for the table were very amiable.

Curious about the Medieval Weekend being held in the castle grounds, we strolled up to the gate to take a look. Seeing that a number of tents and displays had been set up we decided to take a closer look the next day. Walking back, we noticed that the lawn in the National Trust tea garden had been extended and that a new stone wall had been constructed.

We continued our walk around the side of the castle following the Corfe river as the light began to fade. We stopped near the old mill to listen to the soothing sound of the river and to look at the many wild flowers growing along the riverbank. It was getting dark by about 9 pm and so we headed for home. Pat rang the doorbell at about 9.30 pm to deliver his estimate for the gardening. We then settled down to watch TV including a documentary about the rock'n'roll group Status Quo, which was popular in the 1970's and 1980's. At about midnight, it was time to reflect on our diary day before going to bed.

Today's weather: Beautiful sunny day, temperature 18 ° C.

Name *Marta & Rob Reynolds*   Year of birth *1958 & 1949*

House *September cottage*   Street *East Street (no. 29)*

I woke up at 0930 it was a very bright and sunny day. I had my
breakfast and got on with some studying to do with my City Guilds
part 3 welding fabrication exams in June. At about 1130 I made
myself a coffee and had a break. It being a dry and pleasant day I took
myself down to the pub where I met a few friends and we got chatting
about one thing and another. At about closing time I went home and
made myself some lunch and went out into the garden shed to make a
pair of hanging baskets and brackets for a customer in the village.
Early in the evening istarted doing drawing of wrought iron gate for a
family friend of ours for Christmas. Then later on that evening the
power supply went off due to a bad connection outside. When the
power came back on we all watch a bank holiday film on BBC one.
And got every thing ready for work the following morning

JUSTIN CROSS   1973
7 TOWNSEND ROAD   EAST STREET

Today's weather:

Name   Year of birth

House   Street

Tuesday May 2nd

GOOD MORNING,

THE ALARM RINGS AT 6 30 AM, THE DAY HAS BEGUN. AFTER THE USUAL WASH, DRESSING AND BREAKFAST, IT'S A QUICK LOOK AT THE CROSS WORD TO GET THE BRAIN CELLS WORKING. AT 7.15AM TIME TO FEED THE CAT AND DOG, SORT OUT A NEW FACE, AND HEAD FOR WORK.

A SHORT WALK DOWN WEST ST, THROUGH THE ALLEY BY THE BUTCHER'S ON OUT TO THE ROAD, TURNING LEFT, WISHING BARBARA'S DOG, BESS, "GOOD MORNIN" (ONE DAY SHE WILL ANSWER,) CROSS THE ROAD AND HERE WE ARE AT MORTON'S HOUSE HOTEL, WHERE TODAY I AM BREAKFAST WAITRESS AND IT'S NOW 7 35AM

FIRST JOB IS MAKE TEA OR COFFEE FOR THE CHEF THEN FINISH LAYING THE BREAKFAST TABLES FOR THE HOTEL GUESTS, TODAY WE HAVE ELEVEN AND THE FIRST TWO ARRIVE AND 7.55AM. FOR THE NEXT TWO HOURS ITS ALL RUSH TO SERVE EVERYONE, CLEAR THEIR TABLES WHEN THEY DEPART AND DO THE DREADED WASHING-UP. AT 9.30AM THE WAITER FOR TODAY ARRIVES, MORE COFFEE, AND HE STRIPS ALL THE TABLE CLOTHS AND TAKES ANY ORDERS FOR MORNING COFFEE VISITORS. A GROUP OF TWELVE AND THEN TWO SMALLER GROUPS OF FOUR AND TWO MEANWHILE THE RESTURANT IS HOOVERED AND DUSTED THEN LAID UP FOR A BUFFET LUNCH. AT 12.15PM THE FIRST VISITORS ARRIVE FOR A BAR LUNCH. DURING THE TWO NEXT HOURS WE COVER EIGHT BAR MEALS AND TWELVE FOR THE BUFFET. AS USUAL I'M LEFT THE WASHING-UP (I KNOW WE HAVE A MACHINE BUT SOMEONE HAS TO FEED IT AND WIPE-UP AFTER) 2·45PM AND IT'S TIME FOR HOME AT LAST I ENJOY MY WORK WITH THE YOUNGER CROWD, BUT ITS GOOD TO GET HOME. SHOES OFF, COAT HUNG UP, GREET THE DOG AND A HOT CUP OF TEA- BLISS. 3 30PM TIME TO START OUR OWN MEAL, MY SON AND HUSBAND ARE ALWAYS HUNGRY BY FIVE O'CLOCK. ROLL ON BED TIME.   GOOD-NIGHT

Today's weather CLOUDY, DRY WITH N.E WIND, BRIGHTENING LATER TO WARM AND SUNNY

Name SALLY-ANN WELLMAN   Year of birth 1945

House 72   WEST Street

I woke this morning pleased to see that the good weather seems to be holding, compared with the miserable wet conditions that have lasted since mid March. At last, after a lengthy delay the cattle can have their freedom in the field.

My first task each morning is to feed and check the pigs in the fattening unit, thankfully everything went well and the animals were enjoying the sun.

After a quick breakfast, the moment had arrived to let the cattle out, a moment, as a farmer, I thoroughly enjoy. My father, Pete, had the honour of opening the gate, but as always the cattle seem to suffer a moment's shock - can it be true that the gate is open! Once a couple of them realise that freedom beckons they take tentative steps towards the gateway and as they reach the lush spring grass, excitement takes over and playtime takes hold, more cattle realise what is happening and out they charge, feet kicking in the air, leaping and bounding, bellowing out noises of absolute joy.

With the cattle out and daylight hours getting longer, it gives me the chance to enjoy working in the fields again, watching nature thrive again after her delayed rest.

The weekend just gone, myself and Jayne, my wife, enjoyed a double celebration with family and friends. Firstly, our eldest daughter, Lisa was four and secondly our youngest, Chloe was christened in the village.

If the rest of the year can continue like this last week, it will be a good one.

Today's weather: Sunny, with a light easterly breeze

| Name | Robert Green | Year of birth | 1965 |
| House | Little Woolgarston Farm | Street | Sandy Hill Lane |

I chose today's date at random, actually Ian at the post office did !
When I enquired about the diary he asked me to choose a date? It was October 1999 I didn't know what I would be doing on any particular day in the year 2000! He opened the page on the 4th of May I duly paid my £2.00 and thought no more of it......

Some months later when I spoke to friends about the diary they told me that they bought pages specifically to coincide with an event or anniversary of some kind! I felt guilty! I hadn't put so much thought into it, I just asked Ian to just open a page! So I racked my brains and then I realised that without thinking about it I had picked a special day after all. On the 4th of May 1986 I met my husband Mark, while we where both on holiday in the Canary Islands! Now I could tell people why I chose that day, even if it was by luck and good fortune rather than any conscious decision on my part (Hooray).

When Mark and I sat down to write what you see before you now, I explained that it was for the "Diary". I decided to look up the word diary in the dictionary, it describes a diary as "a daily record of events or thoughts". That is, it was to be a record of events that happened that day, a normal everyday day in Corfe Castle Dorset. As you will see below the day was quite normal (well at least for me), so much, for specific events or anniversaries.

Today Mark got up early to go to Plymouth, he left the house at 6:30 am. I stayed in bed until 7:30, George is awake but as usual Zak is still asleep. It is raining. We have breakfast and head to school for 8:45, by car. This is George's 1st year at school and he seems to be settling now, arrive back home 9:05. Zak plays with Duplo, while I fill the dishwasher with aftermath of breakfast. I put on children's TV for Zak, Tellytubies and Tweenies are his favourites. I go upstairs to move mine and Mark's clothes from our old bedroom into the one I just finished decorating, it's looking good, no clutter (give me a week!) my next job will be to decorate old bedroom for the boys, as it is the biggest and they have so many toys. Zak comes up stairs to help !*!*!

He is still in a cot at night and does not like the idea of sleeping in a different room. He doesn't like change even at nearly three; he knows what he wants. We both have lunch, cheese on rye bread from Sweden which Mark had bought on previous business trip.

The phone rings! Why does it always do that when you have just started eating?, It's my sister from Ireland, reminding me of my godson's birthday (tomorrow!). It's a bit late to send a card now. My mother would usually have reminded me of these family events, as she knew that I always forgot them, I now have to rely on others to remind me as my mother died just over four months ago.

After the call I rush to Wareham to buy card to post to Ireland, no hope of getting there by tomorrow!)!* I Went to the library to return books, fortunately Zak has fallen asleep so I am able to leisurely look at books, rather than rushing while Zak tears around the library saying he wants every book and video with "Thomas the tank engine" on it. I left library with books for the children and myself, Mark doesn't like fiction much, in fact he hardly reads at all, except for astronomy or computing books.

I Rushed back from Wareham to collect George from school, once home we start the usual battle of getting George to change out of his uniform and hang it up before watching CITV. Eventually he reappears changed, they both sit with a drink and a biscuit.

Mark arrives home early, I wasn't expecting him until 8 or 9 tonight. I prepare pasta for dinner for the boys and me as Mark has already eaten!!!!! Of course he has! a three course meal paid for by his company, while we eat pasta with cheese washed down with apple juice! At least Zak enjoyed it he had two more helpings, after having ice-cream for pudding, Mark takes the boys into the garden to play football (it might work off some of that three course meal), actually it should be called retrieve the ball from your next door neighbours, as that is what they do most of the time!!. I cleared the table and told the football hooligans I am going to lie down on the bed. The next thing I know it is 11 o'clock !

I get up, get changed and wash, and go straight back to bed --- well there is nothing else to do at that time of night is there?

Today's Weather : Rain

Name : Olivia Hawthorne   Year of birth : MDCDLXVI

House: Harry Carter's old house . No. 6 .   Street : Halves Cottages

The first thing I see out of the window from my bed in the morning is a very large yew tree, during the winter, the berries are prolific and every sort of bird feeds and shelters in it's branches, this morning however there was only a pair of pigeons.

Friday is the day I don't have to be at work until 11.15 so today it was down to a couple of hours of housework and hanging out the washing before settling down to half an hour on the computer typing out some invoices. No exciting "E Mails" for me. Only one from my son at university telling me how hard he is working! Let's hope this is true.

About 10.30 I walk down East Street post some letters and go to the library.
In the car park I see my father so I have a chat to him before he goes into the doctor's surgery to collect his tablets. He gave me a black bow tie, which he is lending to Geoffrey for tomorrow when we are waiting at the "Christmas Festivities" old peoples party. The trouble is. How do you tie a bow tie? In the village square in the National Trust Office I see Robin and ask for a lesson.
An impressive demonstration but I shall never remember how to tell Geoffrey.

The garden we go to this morning is in West Street and it runs down to the "God's Acre Cemetery. It is very colourful this time of year a real spring garden with daffodils, bluebells, apple blossom and two beautiful "pulsatilla vulgaris" Geoffrey mowed the lawn and I did some weeding. We went home at lunchtime our much loved family pet "Abby" was pleased to see us.

The afternoon was spent mowing grass. The first garden I was working in is a holiday Let. Today I met the couple staying they had spent a good morning walking on the commmon and were much appreciative of this beautiful part of Dorset.
While Geoffrey was still working in Calcroft Road I went on to another garden in Collettes Close – the grass needed mowing!!
The next garden I went to was in Colletts Close too this lawn needed a mow as well!

After a welcome cup of tea I walked the short distance home and you'll never guess – yes I mowed the grass and had just finished when Geoffrey returned at about 7'clock. After having eaten supper and showered all the grass mowings out of my hair! We settled down to an evening of watching television or maybe sleeping in front of the television . What was on? <u>Gardener's World!.</u>

Today's weather: A LOVELY DAY.

Name	JANE WINDSOR & GEOFFREY WINDSOR (WINDSOR GARDEN SERVICES)	Year of birth 7TH MAY 1952 12TH JULY 1947
House	HATTON'S RIDGE	Street 117 EAST STREET

Saturday May 6th

On the first Saturday of every month the Village Hall Committee stages a coffee-morning to raise funds or to help a good cause. This Saturday (May 6th) the profits were for our Brownies and Rainbows. At present we have 16 Brownies and 7 or 8 impatient under 8 year olds called Rainbows. Over £180 was added to their funds! The Brownies had fun helping and had a stall of their own selling gifts and toys.

In the evening about 70 of us "oldies" (or, to be more polite "village elders") were guests of the Christmas Festivities Committee. A few years ago it was suggested that a Spring Party would suit better than a cold dark December evening and it proved very popular. The Hall was cheerfully decked out and very welcoming. The hosts wore black + white, — men in black bowties + women in white head bands. We were cossetted and treated to an excellent supper and wine. Beside each place were some raffle tickets and about half the guests were lucky to draw a prize. Afterwards a pianist soon had us singing old songs and our hosts provided an impromptu cabaret.

Today's weather
Warm by day. Wet + thundery at night.

Name MRS JOAN BRACHI

Year of birth 1921

House JUBILEE HOUSE

Street EAST STREET.

Sunday May 7th

I am standing outside the Church of Lady St. Mary in Wareham with a group of excited children and a sprinkling of adults. We are waiting for the start of the service that will see us all confirmed into the Church of England. Its strange to find myself here, I am fifty four years old and have finally decided to join the Church. I have been to many church services in the past but have never felt part of it. I loved the story of Jesus but the Church seemed full of ritual that excluded me.

Today will be different because this time I am going to publicly declare my belief in God and be confirmed into his church. Today I will feel welcome and confident that I know enough of what is going on to help me to be part of it. I thank my friend Rector Maurice Strike for helping me to change my attitude to the Church. The Bishop of Salisbury arrives outside the church dressed in his splendid robes and mitre, and my friend Sid whispers with reverence "I think that's the Bishop". What was it that gave him away I enquired of Sid with a chuckle. I wonder if I shall have to give up sarcasm in my new role ? I could not help but notice that the Bishop looked a lot like the late comedian Larry Grayson - oh dear another impure thought. We all followed the Bishop into the packed Church and down the aisle, and took up our reserved seats at the front - after all we were starring in this production ! I waited for the Bishop to say "shut that door" - disappointing.

The Church is full and the service very moving and there are about thirty of us all individually confirmed by the Bishop. One by one we kneel in front of the Bishop and then follow him down the aisle out of the church - sent into the world holding a single lighted candle. The whole church is inspired, happy, joyous something special is taking place - just like the family get together you might have in your good dreams. The congregation pours out of the church and mills around in an excited flap of chatter and acknowledgments. We all make our way to a nearby hall where there are speeches and strawberry cake. It is all very English and I like that.

We cannot face getting our own lunch so we pop into the Fox to have a drink with Graham. We have one of his special chicken and chips dishes and then saunter home in the sunshine, only to be accosted by Linda waving a page from her "diary".

Name DAVID WALKER   Year of birth 1945

House 55   Street WEST.

Today is my birthday; Trevor, Neal, Paula, Carla all come into the bedroom at 7:30, dressed ready for school to wish me Happy Birthday. I open my cards and presents and give them all a kiss.

Ray takes Trevor to school with all his luggage as he is away for the week, going to Wales for a field trip as part of his 'A-level' geography. The builders have arrived as we are converting the garage to form part of the lounge. We have never put a car in the garage as it is just full of rubbish!!

Pat next door shouts over the fence, "Happy Birthday", and gives me a card. She then comes around for a cup of tea. The washing machine finishes its first load of the day, and as the mist is lifting and the sun is trying to break through, the washing is hung out on the line.

The phone then rings, and its my friend Pat Weller from 95 East St. wishing me Happy Birthday, and she invites me around for lunch and wine!

After this excursion, its back home to prepare tea as the girls and I are out early this evening. During the tea making, Gill Hole arrives from Bradle Farm with a card and present. She stays for orange juice and a chat, but shortly after she arrives, Di Gregory from Knaveswell Farm arrives with yet another card and present, (not doing bad am i!!!!). " Can't stop, I have been working all day teaching in Poole, and have to get home to feed Harold and the children. See you Friday night for our 'girls night out'"

As my friends filter out, Paula, Carla and I are off on our Monday night jaunt. Carla has her gymnastics at Olga Kemp Welch, and Paula has her Sea Rangers at Whitecliff, which I stay and help with. We varnish a boat ready for the boating season. We arrive back at home around 9:50. Neal has been out playing football with the local lads and the team in the car park. Ray is busy tapping away on the computer, as he works night shift from home. We find time for a cup of tea and a quick chat, then I say 'goodnight' and go off to bed. I have to be up early to go to Lulworth Castle in the morning, to advise a lady about wedding reception and flowers.

Today's weather:

Name   YVONNE HENDER   Year of birth   1957

House   88   Street   WEST STREET

This was a glorious May day, beginning in light mist and reaching temperatures of over 20° by lunch time. Our crab apple tree is in blossom for the first year, planted to replace the large ash tree that was cut down two years ago. The circle of bluebells are flowering in the "wild" area of the garden with forget-me-nots every where. We have put out the green plastic dining table and umbrella on the patio, expecting months of al fresco meals this summer. The blue tits have forsaken our bird-box this year, but the blackbirds have returned to their usual spot in the hedge, near the central-heating vent, and are rearing the second batch of chicks.

My husband went to the dentist in Bournemouth this morning. He reluctantly gave up his old Subaru car recently and we are adapting to sharing the Citroen,, so I had to beg a lift to Yoga class in Wareham. Someone remarked how fortunate women are these days to be able to spare a morning for exercises and relaxation instead of staying home to do the washing and cooking.. However, my washing and cooking were waiting for me when I got back!

In the afternoon I decided to tackle the curtains that have been hanging in the lounge since we retired here four years ago. They needed shortening before I washed them. But they shouldn't need doing again for a while because we have regretfully given up our wood fire and are waiting for a gas coal-effect fire to be fitted. Then I made a tray of sage and onion stuffing (with fresh sage from my herb garden) for tonight's barbecue at the British Legion for members of the Twinning Association. Forty people bought tickets and baps were ordered from Dragon's Bakery. There was apple sauce too, to eat with the slices of pork roasted on the BBQ by Mike Davies from Swanage. Mike put up his gazebo shelter in the grounds of the Legion because he has been caught before trying to cater in heavy rain. This evening remained warm and fine. We had and enjoyable time playing Boules on the special pitch, some in a very amateur fashion. Barry Wilson organised the teams, Richard Piercy poured the wine, and Herman and I served the food.

Today's weather: Hot & dry

Name

    Ruth Nuttall

Year of birth   1936

House

Street

    22 Colletts Close

Wednesday May 10th

Young family – **Jane**: housewife   **John**: Finance Director, working in London during the week   **Emily** (19): at university   **Charlotte** (18): at boarding school   **Toby** (13): at boarding school   **Jack** (12): attends prep school – day boy
7 cats; 5 kittens; 2 guinea pigs

7.25	Woken by Jack (overslept). It's usually the other way round. Slept through two alarm clocks!
8.00	Drive Jack to school at Langton Matravers (The Old Malthouse)
8.15	Collect newspaper in Corfe Castle
8.30	Have breakfast – tea and toast
8.45	Feed animals. Look for lost kittens (5) three days old. Give Mum special breakfast. Rescue kittens from under sofa.
9.00	Housework – washing, ironing, tidying etc.
10.30	Write letter to Toby. My mother, who lives in Cornwall phones.
11.00	Sunny day so decide to plant some wild flower plants I've grown from seed in my newly grass-seeded area of "wild garden". Try to stop cats digging them up. Put sticks around seedlings.
12.45	Lunch – salad – feta cheese – pitta bread
1.15	Friend arrives – another Mum from school – we are going together to watch our sons at Clayesmore School, Iwerne Minster, take part in an Athletics Match.
2.00	Watch our sons and support other Old Malthouse boys – weather hot and sunny – then sudden down pour – shelter under trees but get wet! Lots of schools taking part – boys and girls 8-13 years old. Had welcome tea at the school. Sandwiches and cake.
5.00	Drive Jack, four friends and other Mum back to Old Malthouse School, stopping briefly at home so boys can see kittens. Feed cats
6.00	Jack does homework till 8 o'clock. I listen to his violin practice and test his French for exam tomorrow.
8.00	Supper – salad. Play cards with Jack. He goes to bed at 10.00.
10 - 12	Speak to my husband on phone. Do some tapestry – kneeler for Church at Steeple. Watch TV
Midnight	Go to bed

Today's weather: Sunny/rain

Name   Jane Young   Year of birth   1953

House   Lynch Farm, Kingston   Street

Got up around 6.30 in the morning and made a cup of tea. At 7.00 I went to wake my daughter whose name is Chloe. She attends the Purbeck School and is 15 years old.

Left for work at 7.30 a.m. I work at Daler-Rowney (art materials) in Wareham. Had a pleasant day with the girls (working hard of course) and finished work at 4.15. Came home and made the tea.

In the evening went to the local Bingo which is in the Village Hall. I had a nice evening playing Bingo and talking to friends, catching up on the latest news of what is happening in Corfe over a nice cup of tea. The evening was all the nicer because I won a prize!

After Bingo I went to see Graham and Annette in the Fox. Had a glass of red wine (or two) and then made my way home and went to bed at about 11.30.

Today's weather: Misty and some rain but very warm

Name	Susan Robson	Year of birth	1950 - ·
House	24	Street	East Street

Some examples of prices in May 2000

1 pint Semi-skimmed milk 26p (Supermarket)

42p (local shop)

Large wholemeal loaf of bread form39p

to 80p depending on shop.

Eating Apples 99p Kg.

Pears £1.79 Kg.

Tomatoes £1.08 Kg.

Mushrooms £2.40 Kg.

Independent Daily Paper 45p

Local Daily Echo 32p

Unleaded petrol 78p per Litre

£699 (EXC. VAT)
£856.58 (INC. VAT & DELIVERY)

Prosignia 330 PC (speakers optional extra)

Compaq Prosignia 330

- Intel® Pentium® III Processor 650MHz
- 64MB high performance 100MHz SDRAM
- 8.4GB (5400rpm) hard drive
- Compaq S510 15" colour monitor (13.8" viewable screen area)
- 40 x CDROM
- Compaq 56k V90 fax modem + FREE CompaqNet internet access
- **FREE HP610C colour printer†**
- Microsoft Windows 98 & Microsoft Word 2000, Norton AntiVirus V5.0

£699 EXC. VAT   £856.58 INC. VAT + DELIVERY
£5.93 PER WEEK EXC. VAT + DELIVERY

Power up your Prosignia

Upgrade your spec as above
- CD rewritable 4x/8x/32x: £129 exc. VAT, £151.58 inc. VAT
- 128MB high performance 100MHz SDRAM: £65 exc. VAT, £76.38 inc. VAT
- Creative labs SBS52 speakers: £30 exc. VAT, £35.25 inc. VAT

The free printer is available on selected Compaq Prosignia 330 desktop models. Call us for details of other PCs included in the offer.

☞ NEW INSTRUCTIONS £135,000
- ☞ Attractive renovated cottage in Corfe Castle
- ☞ Lounge/dining room, kitchen, 2 bedrooms, large bathroom.

L8 WEST. ST.   **SOLE AGENTS**

ST. MICHAELS GARAGE

Valley Road Swanage Telephone 01929 480221

Ford QUALITY USED CARS **Ford**

OO (W) FORD Focus 1.8 Ghia 5 dr, pacific green metallic, alloy wheels, air conditioning. Our demonstrator under 2,000 miles £13,495
99 (V) FORD Fiesta 1.25 "Zetec" 5 dr, Moondust Silver, new shape. Our demonstrator. Air conditioning, very low mileage............£8,995
99 (T) FORD Focus 1.6 LX 5 dr, 10,000 miles only. Air conditioning, sun roof, moondust silver. Excellent condition and value............£9,995
98 (S) PEUGEOT 1.6 1.1 "Zest 3", blue metallic, only 16,000 miles, one owner from new, excellent condition, power steering, sunroof............£6,695
97 (R) FORD "KA" 1.3 Efi 3 dr, supplied and maintained from new by us. One lady owner, 11,000 miles, radiant red, must be seen............£4,995
98 (R) FORD Escort 1.8 Si Estate, one local owner from new, alloy wheels, roof rails, air conditioning, sunroof, power steering............£7,595
97 (P) FORD Mondeo 1.8 LX 5 dr, new shape, radiant red, power steering, electric windows & locking, excellent value............£5,995
96 (N) HONDA Prelude 2.3i 4ws Automatic, one owner from new, low mileage, excellent example of this rare coupe, has to be seen............£9,995
95 (N) FORD Escort 1.6 LX 5 dr, locally owned, full service history by us, excellent value, sunroof, electric windows, air bag............£4,495
94 (M) PEUGEOT 306 SL 4 dr, one local owner from new, 40,000 miles only, hosts of features, must be seen and driven, great value............£4,995
89 (F) RENAULT 21 Turbo, very low mileage, locally owned & driven by one lady, excellent condition, leather seats, power steering............£2,575
94 (L) VAUXHALL Cavalier 1.6 "Envoy" 5 dr, locally owned, power steering, sun roof, central locking, excellent condition............£3,495
93 (L) FORD Mondeo 1.8 LX Auto Estate, good condition, power steering, sun roof, ABS Brakes, 73,000 miles only excellent value............£3,995
90 (G) ROVER Montego 1.6L Estate, 7 seat conversion, roof rails, a good value for money workhorse, try an offer?............£1,795
1999 "T" registered Channel Island Cars available for delivery Fiesta or Focus many Models & Colours FROM £7,350

"THE PURBECK FORD CENTRE"

Today's weather:
Humid and overcast

Name " *MARKET PRICES* " . . . . . Year of birth . . *TODAY!*

House   Street

Saturday May 13th

Today is my 29th Birthday. I woke at 7.30am to the sounds of the birds singing. My wife Corrinne brought me breakfast in bed, bacon, eggs, toast + a cup of coffee. I opened my cards, they were from my mum + dad in France, my wife Corrinne, our 4 cats - Willow, Barley, Asha and Bramble, my mum + dad in law - Gill + Dave, my brother + sister in law David + Karen and their children Rosie + Jamie, my other brother and sister in law Nicky + Julie and daughter Joanne + 'Bump' (one on the way) + my sister Helen + family. My other sister Becca phoned to wish me happy birthday. I got up and went to play golf at the Isle of Purbeck Golf Club near Studland, I played quite well + enjoyed the spectacular views overlooking Studland Bay, Brownsea Island and Poole. I came home about to 2pm + had a bite to eat. We then went shopping in Poole were I bought some golf balls + a golf glove. At 5.30pm I had an appointment booked at Dr Feelgoods Tattoo Studio in Poole High Street. I had a mermaid tattoed on my left inner arm. It took about an hour, a bit uncomfortable but bearable!! We got back to Corfe at 7.30pm + went to a BBQ at Corrinnes Brothers (David). It was a joint BBQ with their neighbours Carly and Ian. We all had a great time with plenty of food + drink. Later on we had a go on Jamies scrambler with only one slight casualty, nothing serious We came home at 10.15 and went for a nightcap up at the Greyhound. We got home about 11 and collapsed into bed. I had a great day, Corrinne paid for my tattoo as a birthday present, also she gave me a waterproof golfing jacket. Also I had money from mums + dads and family.

THANK YOU ALL
GOODNIGHT!!!

Today's weather HAZY START. CLEARING MID MORNING VERY HOT AND SUNNY. MISTY EVENING.

Name PATRICK CATTRE   Year of birth 1971

House 6   Street EAST STREET.

Sunday May 14th

The first barbecue of the year

My favourite season is early summer which arrives about May in Japan, possibly a little later here. It is warm and sunny and the trees have soft pale green leaves.

It's lovely and warm today, almost summer. The children have already pulled their paddling pool out and have filled it with water. Amazing! paddling in May; summer must have arrived! We'll have a barbeque this evening.

The children love eating outside, but there is always more to do.

We'll have yakitori, Japanese chicken kebabs. The chicken is chopped into little pieces and pushed onto bamboo skewers. Some are mixed with onion or pepper pieces. The are marinated with yakitori sauce made from Japanese soya sauce (shioyu), sugar and sake, with a clove of garlic and ginger for extra flavour. Mmm, smells nice!

Mariko wants to make some sushi so I cook the rice and season it with rice vinegar, sugar and salt. She spreads the rice on sheets of nori (seaweed) and places cucumber sticks, crab sticks or thin slices of omelette on top before rolling it up. She is very good at making it!

Canna and Shuna will be looking after the fire. It will be a lovely evening. I wonder whether Doug will be back in time to enjoy it. Too bad if he isn't!

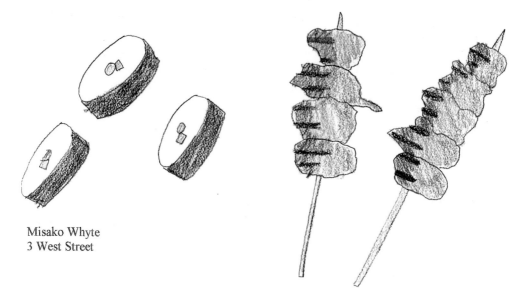

Misako Whyte
3 West Street

Monday May 15th

(In the News: Trouble in Sierra Leone as the rebel forces attack; Air Traffic Controllers under investigation after a near-miss at Heathrow; Northern Ireland situation still delicately poised.)

(Note: Christopher and Helena are no longer residents of Corfe Castle, having moved from there to Swanage in March this year. However, they continue to work in Corfe, and have many links with people and activities there.)

Monday, 15th May, 2000 dawned bright and sunny (in fact, it was officially the hottest day of the year so far). After the usual morning chores, we packed our things into our red Citroen van and headed off for Corfe Castle, driving via Langton and Kingston to see the lovely views across the valley.

It being Monday, and hot, we found it difficult to get going with work. (Chris is an Internet researcher and software writer, and Helena is a professional artist working in the traditional style of the Old Masters.) Nevertheless, we both managed to get a few things done before we had to jump into the van again and drive over to Wareham for our six-monthly dental check-up. (Helena got a clean bill of health but Chris needed a filling redone.)

Back in Corfe we had lunch in the garden (we should mention that our "office" is in fact Chris' parents' house in East Street). We were joined by Chris' sister Catherine, whose one-year-old son, George, spends mornings at East Street, being looked after by his grandparents. As it was so lovely and warm, George had the fun of playing in a makeshift paddling pool - a little green plastic box!

We had planned to try and book some travel insurance today for our upcoming visit to the USA in June. However we ran out of time and ended up doing this a few days later. As with our air tickets and our coach tickets, we did this online using the Internet.

It was Helena's birthday on the following day, Tuesday 16th, and one of her presents was some new plants from the garden centre at Norden. Gillian, Chris, Helena and George made the journey there soon after lunch. Gillian and Helena had fun choosing plants, and Chris and George had fun exploring (with George in his push-chair). There was a turkey and a peacock to see, which was exciting. Helena came away with Geraniums, Calendulers and Lobelias.

Back home again there was just time to unpack everything and race off to catch the Post Office before it closed. Nigel, Chris and Helena made the trip, accompanied by Nigel and Gillian's two dogs, Harriet and Bobby. After this trip, we made another trip out, this time for a walk on the common. Helena was keen to photograph the bluebells before they vanished again for another year.

We did finally settle down to some work after all these planned and unplanned excursions; Chris getting back to his computer work and Helena repotting her new plants (after finding that the light in the loft studio was no longer suitable for painting).

Back at home in Swanage in the evening we decided to have a go at making a Birthday Cake for Helena. Although a cook of many savoury dishes, Chris had never made a cake before; and Helena, although being an excellent cook, did not have much experience in the field of cake-making either. The resulting scenes can only be described as hilarious (unless you were a great cake-maker, in which case they were horrendous!) Nevertheless, a chocolate cake was duly baked, and on the following day, after being liberally iced, it was found to be wholly palatable (which was both a joy and a relief).

At the end of the evening, as part of our church's 50-day Bible-reading plan, we sat down and read Chapter 5 and 6 of Luke's Gospel (with lots of help from William Barclay's guide to explain the parts we found difficult to understand).

Today's weather: Bright, sunny and warm (the hottest day of the year so far)

Name   **Name: Christopher and Helena Humphries**   Year of birth   1966, 1969 respectively

House   at 142   Street East Street.

Tuesday May 16th

It's a beautiful May day, the cool easterly breeze blows our pink cherry blossom into the garden like summer's confetti. The cuckoo calls from blue distances and the great tit's song soars and speaks of days to follow.

Hardy wrote of trees speaking as the wind blows through them, and it's like that today. Butterflies are flitting from bloom to bloom in our garden and bees hum in the columbine---how sweet is life.

I think of my dear departed parents and of a previous May day when they were still with me; a part, so much a part of my life. One of mother's favourite old songs was "Here we go a-maying, through the meadows straying, you and I".

What I would give to see their dear familiar faces on such a lovely day. I'm thankful my brother Michael is within hailing distance as we have much in common. He's such a gentle fellow.

My husband William has today taken the steam train from Corfe Castle station, something he loves doing, into Swanage to do some quiet shopping---before the visitors appear from far and wide.

As I write I can see three lovely horses in the meadows beyond, and the hills an evergreen backcloth against the clear blue sky. The scene is all so familiar to me, and is like a familiar beloved face that one never tires of seeing. Across the road from our home is a small orchard, where sheep are feeding.

As I write a chicken has begun clucking busily, the usual sound it makes having successfully laid an egg. All the peaceful summer sounds of living in this part of England "far from the madding crowd's ignoble strife ".

Hawthorn blossom clothes our trees like clotted cream, and the hedgerows of hawthorn have a particular scent which pervades the warm May air. I can think of nowhere else on this day I would rather be. Home is where the heart is and my heart has found it's resting place.

My only sadness is that I can't see those dear departed faces, and can't put my arms around all those I love. My comfort is that I'm living still where past days have been shared with these folk. The hills, trees, returning swallows, flowers and sounds are still here and come again, and for that I'm so thankful.

I think of my first wedding day ,which was 16th May years ago; surrounded then by my relatives, and relatives of the man I had married. I was so blissfully unaware of what life held, having grown up in such a protected household. It was then a beautifully sunny day,and from the hotel the sea sparkled in the sunlight as the champagne sparkled in the glasses! I have no regrets about my life thus far. All experiences enrich and enlarge one, and help one to grow and learn that human life has many facets. One can benefit and come to terms with all experiences, and use them to shape our present, the future and what it can hold.

We eat, we sleep, we are surrounded by Nature's beauty; we love, we are loved---- who could ask for more?

" There's night and day, Brother, both sweet things;
sun, moon and stars, Brother, all sweet things.
There's likewise a wind on the heath,
Life is very sweet, Brother-----

Who would wish to die ?"

Today's weather: *A beautiful May day.*

Name MARION ORMEROD   Year of birth

House THE GREY HOUSE   Street WEST STREET.

Wednesday May 17th

The day starts as usual by getting up at 7am, letting my two dogs out in the garden where they chase one another around. (One is a Golden Retriever called Bonnie and the other a Lhasa Apso called Poppy) whilst I get on making breakfast and preparing packed lunches for work, the rest of the household is in a rush to see who can get into the bathroom first. By 8.30am everyone has departed in their different directions. My husband Stanley to Southampton where he works for Southampton Freight Services – my daughter Victoria to Poole where she works for Barclays International Bank. I have a few more minutes before I leave, I work in the village. The last thing I have to do before leaving for work is to give Bonnie and Poppy their breakfasts.

I work for Corfe Castle Holidays which is owned and run by Mr Michael Bond we let holiday cottages for self-catering holidays in and around the Corfe Castle area. This year is a very busy one for Michael as he is High Sheriff of Dorset for the year. Part of my job is to keep the High Sheriff's diary and to make sure that he knows when he has to attend official duties, where he has to be, and at what time, what he has to wear at it might be his Court Dress, and to liase with the Under Sheriff's office in Poole. Being the Millennium Year a luncheon party has been arranged today, for the present and past High Sheriff's of Dorset, Michael and his wife Anne are due to attend. It is to be held at Plumber Manor, Sturminster Newton.

Whilst Michael is performing his High Sheriff duties, I am left to ensure that Corfe Castle Holidays runs smoothly and to deal with any problems that may arise, or queries that holidaymakers may have before they book one of our cottages. I then deal with the post, bookings, accounts, High Sheriff events, telephone enquiries, appointments, etc. It is a very busy day. Home for a quick lunch and again to let Bonnie and Poppy out, then back for the afternoon.

After a hard day it is home to prepare dinner for everyone. Victoria is first home, with Stanley later. Then watch some television, off to bed, ready to start all over again tomorrow.

Today's weather: DRY BUT CUOLER THAN PAST FEW DAYS

Name: MRS HELEN LAYTON   Year of birth 1951.

House MOONFLEET   Street HIGHER FILBANK

· Today was a special day for me. I took part in the RDA (Riding for the Disabled Association.) Dressage day in Kingston Maurward

I was riding a pony called Jodie. Jodie belongs to the Southfields RDA Group in Langham where I ride every Saturday. It was Jodie's and my first ever Dressage Competition. We were both very nervous, although we had been practicing for this event for weeks.

My parents and even my grandma had come to watch me.

There were 16 competitors in all, children and adults. I felt I had done pretty well and Jodie had been a good pony, too, but I was still surprised when I came first in my category and was awarded a blue rosette.

ME ON JODIE ——>

Today's weather Sunny with showers

Name Zoe Squirrell. (10 years old)   Year of birth 19·12·89

House The Drey   Street 6A Halves Cottages

Friday May 19th

So far, so good. It is a stunningly beautiful day of sunshine and showers, spring green leaves, an abundance of flowers on hedges and verges and birdsong everywhere. It's just past 2.00 p.m. and I have finished my meals on wheels round and had my lunch. I bought one of Joan Dragon's 'Chicken Mayo in Brown' rolls because I knew I wouldn't have time to make lunch for myself. Richard, my husband, keeps telling me I should eat properly.

There were nine meals to be delivered today of which seven were Shepherds' Pies and two were Beany Shepherds' Pies for the vegetarians. Everyone had Vanilla Sponge with Custard for pudding which was fine for all, including diabetics. Usually I do meals on wheels with Linda Applin but occasionally we do it on our own. I had collected the frozen meals from the freezer in Corfe yesterday, ready for de-frosting and cooking today. This morning was the usual busy scamper. Richard set off just before eight with our two children, heading for work and school. Having sorted the chickens, the house and the telephone calls, I nipped into Wareham to do the shopping and came home again in time to put the foil wrapped lunches into my none-too-large ancient Rayburn.

At five to twelve I set off for Corfe, three miles east along the twisty valley road. The hot meals were in foil containers, aircraft-style, packed into polystyrene boxes on the back seat of the car. My first stop was at Jill Foley's house to pick up the list of recipients. Jill does the mind-boggling task of co-ordinating all the volunteers, meals and money. The price of a lunch today was £2. Jill's list is produced on her computer, complete with adorable illustrations. Today there was an otter. I worried about being late for Mrs. White in case she was fretting but all was well. Everybody was so friendly. Mrs. Gibb in Colletts Close reminisced about the days when she too had delivered meals on wheels. Mrs. Welchman, sitting upstairs with a lovely view over the Halves, looked sad and tired but perked up when I arrived and was so very gracious. Mrs. Hyde had laid the table for herself and her husband and we chatted about wind and weather. Mr. and Mrs. Stockley were their usual cheery selves. I miss Mr. Pond who died not long ago and I felt sad as I passed his empty house. There was always beautiful classical music playing on the radio when Mr. Pond's lunch was delivered and sometimes he would be humming. Mrs. Churchill is new to the list and I delivered her lunch to her daughter, Shirley Lardner's house. It was lovely to see Shirley again. She was a brilliant Playgroup leader when our children were small. There was not much time to stop and chat because the last lunch was cooling down inside its polystyrene box and my car was probably causing a minor obstruction.

My final delivery was to Mr. Marshall at Gaulter Cottages, Kimmeridge, five or six miles from Corfe, back along the valley road and past my home at Whiteway Farm. Mr. Marshall has not been long on our list so this was my first visit to him. Gaulter Cottages are perched on the cliffs above Kimmeridge Bay and as I walked along the narrow path towards the last cottage in the row, clutching the lunch wrapped up in cloths, I was accosted by a snarling, barking dog. The further I went the fiercer the dog became. I was so afraid that I turned back, fearful both for the lunch and myself The dog lost interest and went into his house. I returned, nervously, and tiptoed past. Mr. Marshall seemed pleased with his lunch and asked me how long I had lived at Whiteway. 'Not long' I replied 'about thirteen years'. We chatted a little and then it was time for him to eat his Shepherds' Pie and for me to go home. The list and the cash were returned to Jill and the polystyrene boxes were ready for Monday's deliveries. The moment had come when I could tuck into that delicious Chicken Mayo in Brown.

Today's weather: Beautiful

Name Susie Bond

House Whiteway Farm

Year of birth

Street

Today is my Daddy's birthday.

Nick and I gave him a "supersoaker" water pistol. This may have been a bad idea. He filled it up and chased us with it.

Mummy asked Mr Miller to make Daddy an owl carved from wood that came from the old bell frame in the church. He was really pleased with it.

Daddy went to Sandroyd to watch Nick play cricket while Mummy and I went to church for the wedding of Elizabeth Strike. Elizabeth looked really beautiful and the church was packed full. Afterwards I gave Elizabeth a horse shoe that had come from the Forge in the village, and I had my picture taken. Mummy and I went into the churchyard to wave Elizabeth and Sam goodbye. She was driven away in a carriage drawn by two horses.

On the way home we stopped at the Forge so that I could buy a horseshoe to keep. It will remind me of today and hopefully bring me luck in my exams.

Daddy and Nick came home and they were both very happy as Nick had had a great innings and then taken the wicket that won the match.

Today's weather: *A very pleasant sunny day.*

Name JULIA SPOONER   Year of birth 28-11-1990

House MEADOWSIDE   Street 129 EAST ST

Sunday May 21st

Sunday at the Rectory - but not the usual Sunday routine - because this is the day after the day before - our daughter's wedding day; Elizabeth's marriage to Sam Fuller. And here, on the croquet lawn, stands the marquee dressesd as a Palm Court, for yesterday's tea dance reception, for what was the first wedding for decades (ever?) at the Rectory.

After yesterday's reception for families and close friends, today a lunchtime gathering for local friends from the village and valley (we wish we could have invited everyone)- arriving in a sudden burst of rain for 'bubly an canapes to celebrate the marriage. The marquee tidied and re-arranged, Sam's best man and ushers tend the bar whilst Elizabeth and Sam greet the guests.

All of us - Strikes and Fullers -are still on a 'high' after yesterday, remembering the marriage service taken by Maurice (after a quick change from morning dress to cassock albe); the splendour of the music with our own organist and choir augmented by trumpet and violin and the boys of the Old Malthouse School; the church itself so beautifully decorated by Diana, Betty and their talented team; the lovely surprise to find so many people gathered in the square to greet bride and groom as they left the church in horse and carriage; the warmth and love from village and friends surrounding us throughout the day.

The plum on the cake, today's merry gathering of more friends in the marquee, people meeting and greeting, awash with conviviality, all in celebration of this happy occasion and again, we're overwhelmed by love, kindness and generosity. What a glorious weekend it's been for all of us at the Rectory!

Ending quietly with a family dinner, one of those rare occasions that brings together various strands of family from both sides of the Atlantic. And a new branch is added to the tree!

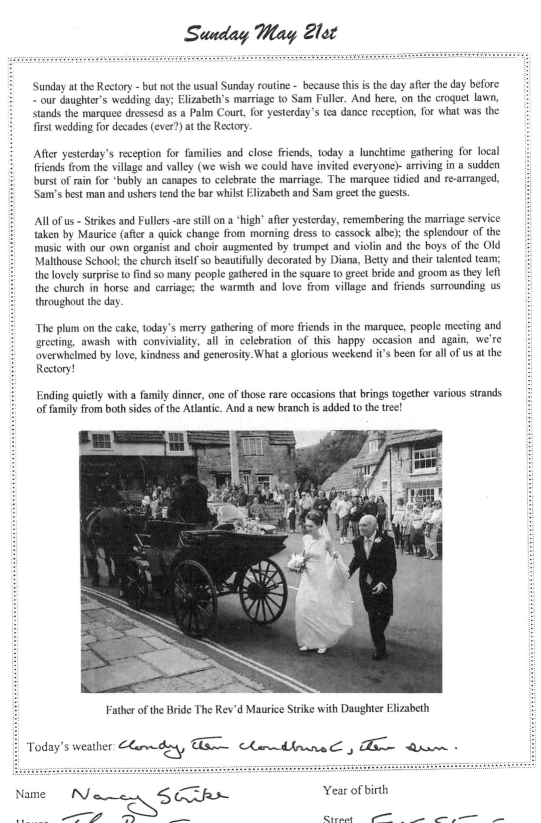

Father of the Bride The Rev'd Maurice Strike with Daughter Elizabeth

Today's weather: Cloudy, then cloudburst, then sun.

Name   Nancy Strike   Year of birth

House   The Rectory   Street   East Street

Monday May 22nd

It's Monday - I wake up to the sound of the traffic going by - the empty lorries make such a noise rattling up the road.

Just before 7 a.m. my husband brings me a cup of tea. I get up and wash, then we have breakfast - fruit juice, cereal and coffee. Bess our dog is already out in the garden.

I start getting ready for work, and at 8.30 I cross the road to go to Morton's House. I look after the bedrooms and the laundry, it's a very busy day.

I get back home, have a sandwich and a coffee, then do my housework. At 3.30 Oliver, my grandson, arrives back from school. He calls in every day on his way home.

It's time to make my daily trip to the paper shop for the Daily Echo, then to the Post Office and Clealls Stores.

 Now it's time for my big walk of the day with Bess, up through the Halves - the buttercups, daisies and clover are a picture today! We then go on to the Common and back via Webber's Close.

Time now to start getting our evening meal, fish and new potatoes.

On the evening news we heard that Sir John Gielgud has died.

Today's weather: Dry and sunny, but windy

Name   Barbara Cannings   Year of birth   1935

House   42   Street   East Street

IT'S A MATERIAL WORLD

PURBECK
DISTRICT COUNCIL

Every year in the United Kingdom over half a million tonnes of textiles are thrown away, adding to the country's already burgeoning landfill sites. Unbelievably, textiles account for up to 3.5% of our national domestic waste stream

But of course, just because we have grown tired of or outgrown an item of clothing and no longer have any use for it doesn't mean the end of its useful life. There are more options than to simply put the item out with the refuse where it will not be of use to anybody. Unwanted clothes, bedding, curtains, linens and pairs of shoes can all be taken along to your favourite high street charity shop or sold at a car boot sale. Everybody loves something "new" to wear without spending a small fortune!

Purbeck District Council provides Oxfam textile collection banks at most of the recycling centres throughout the District. If you do choose to place your unwanted textiles in the Oxfam banks, please remember to place them in a plastic bag first - this prevents moisture getting into the textiles before the bank is emptied. Remember even fabrics that are worn or damaged can be reused as industrial wipes or wadding.

Over 30 tonnes of textiles were recovered from Purbeck's Oxfam banks during 1999/2000. Please help to make this year's figure even higher...

For further information about textile recycling and other recycling schemes in Purbeck please telephone Susan Pitt, Environmental Services Officer, on 01929 557281.

Today's weather: WET : WET : WET !

Name   *Historical facts...*   Year of birth

House   *.. "recycled" from the*   Street
             Local Press .

Wednesday May 24th

My alarm goes at 6.30 and I hit the "snooze" button once before getting myself ready to start work at 8.00. I am employed by Dorset County Council, Social Services, as a Home Care Assistant. Home Care is the service which enables elderly, sick and disabled people to maintain their independence and remain in their own homes by providing them with essential care. I make several calls, helping people to wash and dress, making their beds and preparing breakfast. My last call this morning is in Springwell Close, a small council owned estate of 21 bungalows for elderly people who have a Warden who visits daily to check that all is well.

From Springwell, I walk home through The Halves, the remains of the village's medieval field system. The area closest to the village centre is mown to make a recreation ground but in the other sections the grass is long and full of seed-eating birds. One section is golden all over with buttercups and pink clover is growing up between. Six horses are grazing in the buttercup field.

At 11.45 I walk to the village School where I work as one of two lunchtime Supervisory Assistants — generally known as "Dinner Ladies". Between us we set out enough tables in the hall to seat the whole school - currently about 75 children aged 4½ to 9 who live in Corfe Castle and the outlying area. We supervise them as they eat their packed lunches brought from home and then watch over them as they play in the playground to see that they don't hurt themselves or each other, to wash grazed knees and settle little squabbles. In the summer, when the weather is warm and dry, we take the children onto the playing field to eat lunch picnic style and then we can wave to the steam trains as they pass by.

I arrive home about 1.15 and after a bread and cheese lunch take the dogs walking. We take the underhill path from Chetlow to Woolgarston and come back along the top of the hill. It begins to drizzle as we set out and then rains quite hard, so we have a drying off session with a fan heater and lots of old towels when we get home. Despite the rain we enjoy the walk —lots of wild flowers and birds along the underhill path but no small blue butterflies today.

Once a week I do an evening shift for Home Care, so after dinner I make 5 visits, getting people changed into their night clothes, helping some into bed, making bedtime drinks. I arrive home about 10 pm by which time I am ready for supper and bed myself!

Today's weather   Warm sunny morning. Persistent rain in afternoon

Name   MARY GREEN   Year of birth   1948

House   5   Street   MEAD ROAD

My friend Mrs. Spinney arrived about 9 a.m. to see if I was still here, as I am very ancient!!! I then took my dog, Gaby, for her morning walk.

Later, I drove down to our Doctor's temporary surgery, it cannot be faulted, but I feel sorry for Dr. Horsnell (our new doctor) as he has not yet found a house for himself and his wife and son. Rumours are flying around:
(1) about a surgery being purpose-built here in Corfe as a permanency for any medical practitioner who comes to work here in the future
(2) that there is a possibility of Dr. Selwyn's former surgery being bought for us all to use again.

I then drove to Foley's in Valley road for petrol – by then the sun was coming out and as usual I thought how lucky we are to have such a beautiful county and to have such a caring and happy village. I went to our shops – we have a very good selection and all excellent :- newsagent, grocer, a butcher, a baker, a National trust shop, two cafes and a superb Post Office with a very kind and helpful Postmaster – also four pubs! Long may they all last!

I managed to do a little pottering in the garden while someone was painting my front door and another friend came to see me at about 5.30.

Today's weather: Sunny, one short shower, but strong wind and cool

Name	Eileen Allcock	Year of birth	1908
House	Troutbeck	Street	17 Colletts Close

A day with Postie.

At 5.50 am. my alarm goes off. I don't get up. At 6.15 my second alarm goes off and I do get up. This makes me think I get a 25 minute 'lie in' every morning!

Having got ready and had my breakfast listening to a radio station with more adverts than music, I wheel my Royal Mail cycle out of the front door. I cycle round to the Post Office at 7.15 in time to receive the sacks of post brought from Wareham. So I thought. It actually arrives at 7.30, so we're 15 minutes late before we start sorting. I think it's going to be a long morning, because the telephone bills have come so we'll be delivering to virtually every house today. Thanks B.T.

Finishing sorting at 8.35, my colleague, Kathy, and I bundle up the sorted mail and put it in order, in our cycle pouches. I start my delivery round, or 'Walk' as it's properly called, and notice it's starting to rain slightly. Having completed East Street up to the Castle Inn and back to the square, I collect the full pouch for West Street at the P.O. in the steadily increasing rain. Up West Street I go, delivering (yes, you guessed it) in the rain. I don't know about a bicycle, I'm going to need a submarine if this keeps up!

I'm late finishing by an hour! It's now 11.15 and I cycle home to have my second breakfast. At home I look down at my wet Royal Mail uniform and think to myself, I've got to get out of these ridiculous clothes and into my ridiculous clothes. One thing I must do before 12.00 (when the library shuts) is photocopy a sheet which advertises my model exhibition at the N/T Castle View Visitor Centre on Monday, for the May Fair. Once that is done I run down to the Square to distribute them, trying not to notice it's still raining.

Back home, I do some financial calculations on how our Wedding plans are doing (the church is booked for the 17th of June). Fairly satisfied with the result, I make some sandwiches and sit with a video over lunch. It's called 'Car Wars 9' and......is probably best left at that!

Since my model collection will be on display at the May Fair, I think it's a good idea to finish the 4 new ones I've been working on. Actually the battle-damaged USS Enterprise NCC-1701 is finished, the new NCC-1701-A only needs it's decals applying, the smaller NCC-107 (made from spare kit parts) just needs a name painted on, so I think I'll concentrate on the one that needs the most work. A conversion kit for making a ship that was only seen in the last episode of Star Trek - The Next Generation, the triple engined NCC-1701-D, a nice model.

Suddenly the afternoon's over (where'd it go?) and Jo's back with the shopping, which we put away. We have dinner watching Sliders (I think it's getting better), Top of the Pops (I think it's getting worse) and go on to watch several gardening programmes (I think I like watching other people work).

But the most unusual aspect of the day: I didn't spend any of it in the pub!

Today's weather: I think it might have rained. A bit.

Name William Blight (Postie)   Year of birth 01/01/70

House Brushwood Cottage   Street East Street No: 74

Saturday May 27th

6am.Wake to music and news from bedside radio.Draw curtains to greet
a wonderfully bright and sunny dawn,so welcome after two very dull days
of non stop rain.The garden is now glistening with freshness in the
bright yet watery sunshine. 6.30am After getting out of bed as carefully as possible in order to avoid my back pain which is always at
its worst after a nughts sleep,I go down stairs to make our usual
morning pot of tea,which I dutifully take into my wife who pretends
to be still asleep,even for a kiss and a mug of hot sweet tea! I then
go back to my bed to enjoy my tea while listening to radio 4 weather
forcast(awful) Then world news(depressing) boy shoots teacher(America)
Then sports desk followed by the very pleasant Open Country program,
sanity at last! 7am. Shave wash and dress,which due to back problem,
takes nearly an hour. 8am. Down to make my six part porridge,consis-
ting of a tablespoon of oat flakes,wheatgerm,oat bran,wheat bran ,
saltanas,sunflower and pumpkin seeds.All mixed with skimmed milk and
cooked for half an hour in a double saucepan,then served with clear
honey or soft brown sugar.Needless to say my wife won't have anything
to do with it! While waiting for my breakfast to cook I run through
an exercise routine that helps to relieve my painfull back.
  10am. Take car back to Stoborough garage for new battery,as it decli-
ned to start yesterday on their forcourt in the pouring rain,after
filling up with petrol.An ideal place to breakdown as they soon found
some jump leads and a battery to get me going!
11am. Continued into Wareham to shop,then to Bovington and Wool.Back
at Corfe Castle at 1.30pm,for lunch of boiled bacon ,hard boiled eggs
and salad,followed by fresh raspberrys and ice cream.
Afternoon Listen to Archers,put feet up and rest.Later heard radio
4's profile of the life of Catherine Booth,founder of the Salvation
Army.A really amazing woman,
Late Evening. Very heavy rain at present time.Had light supper.Enjoy
pint can of Boddingtons beer,
11pm Hot shower,mug of hot cocoa well laced with whisky,and so to bed.

Today's weather:

Name JOHN DIXON   Year of birth

House 3 THE DOLLINGS   OFF   Street EAST

TODAY IS MY FATHER'S " WELL OVER 70 AND JUST UNDER 80th
BIRTHDAY " !!

WE CELEBRATED THE OCCASION WITH A FERRY TRIP...FROM
SHELL BAY TO SANDBANKS AND SAT IN THE CAR PARK BY THE
HAVEN HOTEL AND BREAKFASTED ON SMOKED SALMON SANDWICHES
AND CRISPS !

WE THEN WENT TO HAM COMMON, NEAR HAMWORTHY MARINES BASE,
AND WATCHED THE LOCAL CANOE CLUB'S HARBOUR RACE.

HAVING WATCHED THEIR ANTICS FOR A COUPLE OF HOURS WE
DEPARTED FOR A DRIVE THROUGH THE BEAUTIFUL DORSET COUNTRY-
SIDE, TAKING IN CORFE MULLEN, BERE REGIS AND WOOL, RETURN-
ING VIA LULWORTH AND CHURCH KNOWLE.

WE SPENT THE REST OF THE DAY BASKING IN THE SUNSHINE
IN THE HAVEN OF OUR GARDEN SIPPING THE OCCASIONAL LEMON-
ADE !!

FATHER AND I FINISHED THE DAY WITH THE TRADITIONAL DINNER
OF ROAST BEEF, YORKSHIRE PUDDING, ROAST POTATOES AND THE
USUAL VEGETABLES, THEN BREAD PUDDING AND CUSTARD FOLLOWED
BY A COLLAPSE INTO THE ARMCHAIRS FOR THE REST OF THE EVE-
NING !!

SO TO BED, ENDING FATHER'S XXth BIRTHDAY !!

Today's weather: WARM, SUNNY AND DRY.

Name JEREMY MARTIN FIGGINS

Year of birth   2nd JULY 19XX

House WESTCOTT

Street   WEST STREET

Monday May 29th

Good May Fair weather, not too sunny and no rain, not much sleep either the night before, cooking for today, loading car and van to save time.

Left home in West Street for the Castle armed with plenty of plants and produce, red, white and blue ribbon to decorate stall.

The grass in the Castle was wet from last night's rain, feet a bit soggy!

Gates opened at 10 a.m., mainly locals first of all, grockles not awake yet. A brisk trade 'til lunchtime, by now we're a bit hungry even though we had sampled sticky jam doughnuts from Nigel Dragon's bakery in The Square. I had ordered lunch the day before for Betty Crackle and myself from our local, 'The Fox'. Lunch was lovely, cheese ploughmans with all the trimmings washed down with mugs of tea from the Youth Club stall.

We sat for a bit listening to Dave Ford's organ. The visitors had arrived by now and all stalls were busy. Bouncy Castle always popular, games galore and a small play set the scene for an enjoyable afternoon.

Transport arrived about 4.30 p.m. to ferry the weary home.

Packed away all the equipment, or nearly all, ate tea which some kind person had prepared earlier. Day is nearly over, always a good one seeing people you know and having a natter.

Poured myself a whisky, a final weary stroll around the garden before dark.

Today's weather: Remained fine with sunny spells.

Name: Monica Williams   Year of birth 26/10/52

House: 94.   Street: West.

On this wet chilly day let's hope June will soon bloom.

Many villages have an annual Flower Show and for a number of years Corfe Castle was no exception. However, gradually public interest waned and no amount of cajoling by the organisers could persuade more than a few people to enter. Eventually the expense and hard work involved could no longer be justified and the Garden Club who were responsible for the show dropped the event.

As an experiment, the Flower Show was replaced by a much more limited Club Show. This was open to club members only and had a smaller schedule. No advance notice of entries was needed, members simply wandered around their gardens on the day of the show and harvested what was available. This informality paid off and the number of entries was not far short of what used to be achieved after weeks of hard work. This year's show will be on 18th July.

Although a registered Flower Show judge, I have never judged at the Corfe Castle Show as rules state that members of a club should not judge at their own show. This makes sense and avoids accusations of favouritism. When judging at other shows outside the area I like to do the judging and then make a quick getaway before the public are allowed in to see the results. There is always the odd person who disagrees with the judge's decision. "My marrow is bigger than all the others, why didn't I get a prize." The fact that the marrow was as tough as old boots and completely inedible never seems to occur to the proud owner.

Freshness is an important factor in deciding the best entry. With runner beans it is common practice to snap one in half to see if it is "stringy" and therefore tough. I did this at one show and the bean bent double without breaking. Obviously this bean had been picked some days earlier and allowed to dry out.

The first thing I do when judging a class is to check that it is "as schedule". It is surprising how many green-fingered entrants cannot use those fingers to count up to ten. If a class is for six rose blooms then that is what the judge expects. All other numbers should be disqualified but if seven blooms appear in the vase I would turn a blind eye while the steward removes one. If there are only five roses then there is no alternative and I have to write N.A.S. on the card. These cryptic letters are an abbreviation for "Not as Schedule" and the entry is disqualified.

Footnote: Sadly, the Garden Club's Treasurer, Arthur Millington, died this year. He was largely responsible for organising past shows.

Today's weather: Wet and chilly

Name — Harry "Bob" Bowler — Year of birth

House — 20 — Street — Townsend Road

The last day of May started with beautiful sunshine — a lovely morning for walking the dogs on the common, which is a carpet of colour at this time of year. The blue-bells have not been quite as good as usual, but the patch of deep red-purple dactylorhizas is very good. There is an abundance of flowers that you can see at every step you take; two or three different blue speedwells, and bugle; yellow potentilla, vetches and birds foot trefoil; pink clover and lousewort; masses of daisies and buttercups especially on the area that was cultivated during the World War II. Some of the rarer things you have to hunt for and I am eagerly awaiting the time to look for the bee orchid and the little butterwort, both of which have been missing from their usual places for the past two years and I am hoping they will reappear.

My passionate love for the Common is not just a love of the flowers that grow there, but stems from childhood days when the common was everything to me and my family. There were picnics on Sunday afternoons, when I made daisy chains for myself and my doll, and if we had visitors the outing was always a walk on the common; if it was a family gathering we had enough people for a game of cricket, with Eiffel Tower lemonade to quench our thirsts. It was the play-ground for all the children of my own age, and we made 'dens' in the fern and played hide-and-seek — and never got tired of it. Most important of all was the fact that we lived from the common, and my generation will be the last to remember how we collected the furze for the bread-ovens, kitchen ranges and coppers, and fern for bedding for any animals we had — and to cover up the rhubarb and any tender plants. My father swept the chimney with a gorse bush tied to the garden broom; and there were rabbits to be caught with the help of a ferret. Anything and everything that was edible was gathered to make jam, wine, medicines, pies and puddings; it was all very pleasurable to a child, and only in later years did I realise what hard work it was for my parents and ancestors. Nevertheless, they didn't starve, and there was fuel for the taking — so they were much better off than the villagers in other areas who had lost their commons. Fortunately I am still able to do many of the things that my ancestors did, and my daily visits to the common are by choice and not necessity; and I hope that the traditional use of the Common will be remembered for future generations.

Today's weather:

Name Brenda Chappell   Year of birth 1931

House 60 East Street   Street

Had a busy morning - took my Himalayan and Neatherland Dwarf rabbit for a check up and injection for myxomatosis to our vet in Bovington.

Made investigation into two stray cats which had been abandoned in this village. Hoping someone will give them a home.

We ate our first strawberries this season and they were delicious.

Also started to build our rabbit a lovely hutch for outdoors for his run. He will be a house rabbit.

Hoping the weather will cheer up - maybe we will get a good June.

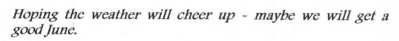

Today's weather: Cloudy with drizzle - and cold

Name	Mrs. Evelyn Harley	Year of birth	1934
House	The Triangle	Street	103 East Street

Friday June 2nd

I am sitting in our lovely cottage garden and will allow my thoughts to flow. For I do believe that a diary should include secrets as well as facts.

A certain sadness is in my mind, now that the lush, green, sappy freshness of May has passed. But soon will come the warmth of high summer dog days, Wimbledon and Adalstrop steamy heat of June.

One year ago my life hung in the balance. Major heart surgery had left me seriously ill and weakened. Twelve hours to live our own troubled doctor gave me; telling my wife Marion within my hearing. However, I have pulled through to realise first hand that illness, especially proximity to death, does help to prioritise one's time and interests.

Too many to list here but I will make a start. Top of the list is Marion. Closely followed by my 3 children and 4 grandchildren who I would love to see grow up. As I sit, Marion, looking youthful, is walking around the garden with the insouciant swinging grace of perfect health; beside her trots our old Norfolk Terrier, Tigger. Marion today wears a green golf shirt and blue trousers.

I can see Corfe Castle ruins from our garden. Fortunately the beauty of West Street, and our friends and acquaintances in this living community enable, on a sunny day, the castle's history to fade. But I do think about those folk involved in the tragedies and murders of more brutal times in the last millennium,

Earlier today I was sorting, little by little, through reams of Lionel Simpson's music; an attempt, at his widow Bettine's request, to catalogue his largely unpublished but hugely talented work. Lionel died in 1998 aged 97 yrs and was our village organist and composer for 30 years.

Music for me is an especially powerful component of life and I have wide tastes. This morning I heard a song-thrush and a blackbird's song soar above the traffic noise of East Street. What a triumph! Similarly I love to hear our sensitively played organ voluntary; perhaps our finest weekly live music. The organ notes shine through the noisy clearing of microphones and chairs and can rise above the chink and chatter of coffee. Likewise, the truly wonderful notes of our church bells ring out above the roar of traffic.

I used to have a firm religious faith; my grandfather, Professor W. P. Patterson was moderator of the Church of Scotland and our family includes 7 generations of clergy. The fragility of my faith is exposed by new styles of worship and the uncritical acceptance by the Church of England of the rise of charismatic fundamentalism; dangerous and ultimately self-destructive I believe.

How I would like all clergy to have the charm, warmth and humility, like our Rector Maurice Strike; but also posses Biblical scholarship.

It is mild but cloudy now in the garden at noon. A blackbird still sings out at the top of our brown birch tree. I am still quite tired after 4 long days and late nights in Sussex; competing in a team of six for Dorset at croquet against 22 other counties.

On Wednesday 31st May I was working all day at Southampton, sitting with a barrister and a nurse on an Appeal Tribunal Panel. We were required to determine whether over £9,000 of attendance allowance money should be backdated and awarded to an 81 year old widow. She had sold her beloved house to pay for private nursing home fees but, pending the sale of the house, she had been state funded. We decided to award her the money.

At 5pm today Marion and I are making a husband & wife team for the Douglas Bader Trophy. This is a golf match Stableford at the lovely Isle of Purbeck Golf Club where we both belong. Bader was a wonderful example of determined humanity; despite losing both legs in the war, as a fighter pilot, he continued to lead his squadron and later played golf with artificial legs, playing to a 12 handicap. A croquet player I new well in Parkstone, Monty Spencer-Ell, had lost both his arms in the Great War. Amazingly he played to scratch with a mallet screwed into his shoulder!

Today's weather:

Name DR WILLIAM ORMEROD   Year of birth 1937

House 102   Street WEST

My 26th birthday. Over the past few years life has changed somewhat: I grew up in Corfe, got married in Corfe Church (June 19th 1999) and now live in South London. I have also just started my own catering business, so unfortunately I did not have much time to celebrate. Although working from home does allow some luxuries – I opened my cards over breakfast before making the long trek to the 'office', the kitchen...

My birthday actually started at about 12.30am when Stuart (my husband) arrived back from work bearing a gift – red poppies. He had acquired them from an unspecified railway station platform edge on his way back from Victoria Station. The only flowers he gives me are poppies (one reason is they don't cost anything!), as we first met on the canals where poppies were prevalent, so they have always meant alot.

Anyway, back to work; the day's cooking involved preparing the menu I have for the deliveries. I deliver pre-ordered food to actors on matinée days (twice a week). Today it is *La Cava* at the Victoria Palace Theatre, where Stuart is working as assistant musical director. Today's food includes caramelised onion tart, rosemary chicken, treacle tart, fruit salad, pasta salad, chocolate brownies etc.. As they are all cooked fresh in my little kitchen, the order of the day was cooking, washing up, clearing up, more cooking and finally the packaging of the food. Labels for each of the dishes then have to be printed and stuck on each individual container before they are placed in paper bags for delivery to the theatre. As soon as all that is done, I managed a quick cup of tea and a celebratory chocolate brownie (I imagined the candles and a chorus of singers!) before quickly vacuuming and washing the kitchen floor.

It was then time to leave for Victoria to deliver the food. Driving to the theatre takes about 40 mins depending on traffic so I arrived at 5.10 pm – half an hour before the end of the matinée. I wanted to arrive early so that I could sneak into the back of the auditorium to watch Stuart conduct the show – his West End début, conducting once a week. I was so proud of him – he looked fabulous although all you can see is his head and his hands! Once the show had finished, I dashed around to the stage door with the food for the cast. I waited for them to collect the food and to pay me. This is always the best bit when I get out to say hello to those buying my food – it makes the job worth while.

Stuart's brother and his girlfriend were also at the matinée, so we went to St James' Park for a picnic (some of my food!). Luckily the weather held off. The evening performance started again at 7.30 pm, so Stuart had to be back at the theatre in time. Leaving him there, I drove home. Not wanting to cook myself any supper having been cooking all day, I had fish and chips – a birthday treat! The evening then consisted of relaxing and watching the television whilst waiting for my husband to return home at 11.30pm with a birthday kiss.

Today's weather: CLOUDY

Name SARAH BARR (née PRESTON)   Year of birth 1974

House PATCHFIELD   Street VALLEY ROAD

Sunday June 4th

Setting the scene

My wife (Belinda) and I live at Scoles Manor, half way up Kingston Hill and along a half mile track looking back over the common to the Castle and hills. We have been here 12 years and run a self-catering business in the converted barns next to our house. Scoles Manor is reputed to be the oldest continuously inhabited dwelling in the parish. We have 4 grown up children and 2 grandchildren. This weekend we have staying with us our younger daughter Carrie (a doctor in Hammersmith) with her two, Rebecca (2) and Sam (1) together with Andrew our eldest son, an IT expert. We all had a busy day yesterday helping Liz, our eldest (a police officer in Poole), moving into a new flat in Lower Parkstone.

Here's my day

4.30am I notice the lights on in Andrew's bedroom and think he's fallen asleep without turning them off. I find he's wide awake working on the computer, and has spent the night revising our web site.

4.45am Listen to wonderful dawn chorus before going back to sleep.

7.00am Bring Belinda and Carrie a cup of tea. The grandchildren sleep on. Belinda goes to early church at Corfe and I work in the kitchen garden.

8.00am Carrie has got Rebecca and Sam up and wants to me to open up and feed our animals with them - Black Sumatra game fowl and Indian Runners with lots of babies, together with three calves. A great thrill for them.

9.00am Belinda back from church with croissants from the Dragon Bakery, milk from Cleall's and a Sunday Telegraph, collected from Margaret Dennis in Kingston.

10.30am Carrie and I drive down to the village. I'd seen that Nancy Grace, the NT archaeologist, is giving a guided tour of the castle entitled 'Digging up the Dirt'. We both enjoyed it a lot – very interesting and well put across.

12.30pm Back for lunch. Granny has coped well (as always) but Rebecca more than ready for food. The three calves had escaped into the garden but luckily two of our guests had spotted them before any damage was done. Andrew is up and gone for a run.

3.00pm Belinda and Carrie take the children to the beach at Studland. I plant spinach and lettuces. Andrew finishes his work on our web site (www.scoles.co.uk) - I'm thrilled with what he's done.

4.30pm I drive Andrew to Wareham station. He has to be back in London this evening.

6.00pm Children's supper for all of us – bangers and mash.

6.45pm Watch news on ITV. Not much of interest.

7.00pm I pick a basket of elderflowers - to make into cordial tomorrow

7.30pm Phone call from Will our youngest who is in the middle of his Finals at Oxford. He'll be finished next Saturday – what a relief.

10.00pm Bed

Today's weather: SUNNY MOST OF THE DAY

Name PETER BELL   Year of birth 1938

House SCOLES MANOR   Street KINGSTON HILL

Monday June 5th

7 a.m.   Staying at my fiend's house. Get up and have breakfast. Breakfast was fried eggs.

8 a.m.   We went to school. My school is called The Old Malthouse and it is in Langton Matravers.

9.a.m.   I had lessons

12.40 p.m.   Had lunch which was spaghetti, followed by rice pudding.

1.10 p.m.   Rest, read a book

2.10 p.m.   Cricket match. I got 15 runs and we won!

5.00 p.m.   Prep, which is two subjects

6.00 p.m.   Tea - which was tomato soup

6.30 p.m.   Activities - I played squash

7.30 p.m.   Go home

8.00 p.m.   Played on computer

9.30 p.m.   Went to bed

Today's weather: Sunny

Name   Jack Young   Year of birth   1988

House   Lynch Farm, Kingston   Street

Tuesday June 6th

This is what Class 1 did at Corfe Castle First School today. School starts at 8.45am.

Fred

I shared a book with Lauren.

The whole school went into the hall for prayers and a story.

Mrs. Coe took our picture.

Alex

We said some rhymes. Andrew

We wrote all the words that rhymed

Will

Some of us have milk at playtime.

We played a counting game.

Jossi

We worked out sums in our heads.

Michael

We eat lunch in the hall. Everyone brings a lunch box to school. Mrs. Hathaway and Mrs. Green look after us. We played on the field.

We went to our swimming pool.

Lauren

We listened to a story.

Laurie

We went home at 3 o'clock and Mrs. Coe had a cup of tea !

Today's weather It was a warm dry day. In the morning it was dull and cloudy but by lunch time the sun was shining.

Name Children of Class 1   Year of birth 1993 —— 1995

House Corfe Castle c. of E   Street East Street.
V.C. First School

Class 1 Corfe Castle First School Tuesday 6th. June 2000

Class 1 in front of the newly installed "Quiet Area" – roofed table and benches, trellis and planters (yet to be filled). The school's Millennium Committee raised over £1500 to present every child with an illustrated Bible and set up this area in the playground..

Gabriel Fry	George Hawthorne	Oliver Oddy	William Young	Fred Pope	Andrew Fry
Joss Venning	Elizabeth Hole	George Goodall		Lyndsey O'Brien	Michael Morris
Adam Fry	Sam Christopher	Lauren Davis		Laurie Beardmore	Alexander Rainbird
Sam Lightowler	Scott Dando	Fenja Squirrell		Tim Harrison	

Age range : 4 – 6 years

Children absent on Tuesday 6th June 2000 : Shaun Simpson and Daniel Lloyd

Picture taken by class teacher Mrs. Lesley Coe , using the Digital Camera bought for the school by the Douglas Strickland Bursary (Purbeck Arts Club) . Printed on school computer.

Name Class 1 – children

House Corfe Castle First School

Year of birth Ages 4 – 6 years Born 1993 – 1995

Street East

I woke up at 7.30 a.m. listening to the whining of the alarm clock. The birds were having a good sing-song, which indicated a nice day. This was confirmed when I opened my curtains to reveal a bright shining sun creeping from behind the hills.

I tuned into 2CR fm to help wake me up, had Kelloggs Rice Krispies for breakfast. I then did my usual bathroom routine, regularly interrupted by "hurry up" from my younger brother and sister! I then got dressed for work in a fairly relaxed outfit, which consisted of my burgundy skirt and black shirt.

I left at 8.25 a.m., fifteen minutes after Kayleigh and Callum (my sister and brother) left to catch their bus to Wareham Middle School. I met my friend, Cara, who I work with to have a lift to Swanage. We arrive at the Swanage branch of Humphries Kirk, Solicitors in Station Road at 8.55 a.m. I work as an office junior/assistant legal secretary and am soon to be promoted (August) to a full time assistant legal secretary in the litigation department. This week I am covering Jo (a litigation secretary) who is on holiday. My day has consequently gone very quickly indeed. My job today involved:

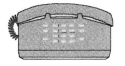

- Hand deliveries
- typing letters etc.
- Attending clients in person and by telephone
- banking
- Sorting post

Today was a refreshing change and I enjoyed it.

I arrived home at 5.20 p.m. to watch the remainder of "Home and Away".

Kayleigh had brought our horses, Jake and Maddy, down from Corfe Common to ride. We groomed them and then tacked up. We jumped them in the plot next to our house and then went for an enjoyable fast ride and jump around the Common.

We had finished about 7.30 p.m. in time for bacon sandwiches in front of "Coronation Street"!

For the remainder of the daylight, I went with Mum and Jumbo to check horses.

I went to bed at 10.30 p.m., read Wilbur Smith's "A Time to Die" for half an hour and then went to sleep.

Today's weather: Sunny, clear blue sky, little bit of wind, approx 13°C

Name	Natasha Potter	Year of birth	1982
House	9	Street	Webbers Close

My first connection with Corfe Castle began in 1950 when I first met my wife Anne who was born in Corfe in 1922. Her father Mr. Rupert Matthews was the headmaster of the local school. We were married in 1952 and until 1969 were in business in Swanage. We came to live in Corfe in 1969 quite by chance having spent some time looking for a house in this area, I took a sneak view of the property "Hillside" not thinking that it would be for sale, as luck would have it, within 3 weeks it was put up for sale and we purchased the property. It is situated at the southern end of West Street with uninterrupted views of the Castle, Village, East & West Hill and looking westwards towards Church Knowle. The house was built in the 1950s for a Miss Vera Collins a friend who originated from Swanage. There are two separate gardens, north - with a lawn and flower beds, south - with a Thyme lawn and shrubs. The property is surrounded by a Beech hedge. Latter we purchased the Orchard on the south side of "Hillside". My wife spent many hours tending the garden adding much ground cover and new shrubs. Anne died in 1997 and I have tried to keep the garden in reasonable order, but not being a gardener I have relied on my neighbours for their help and assistance.

My involvement with the village started with The Corfe Castle Town Trust, as its Chairman and Curator of the small Museum in 1987. Mr. Tony Brown created the Museum in the 1970s, during the past 13 years we have updated the display area and added further items of interest and there are some 280 items on display reflecting life in the village during the past four hundred years. I have also set up an archival collection of Photographs 456, Postcards 144 and Literary works 191 relating to Corfe, and I hope future generations will continue to add to this collection. These archives are available for viewing on request to the Curator.

I open and close the museum at weekends during the winter months and daily during the summer months plus the general cleaning. We have an average 122,000 visitors a year.

Today I have opened the Museum at 1000. The rest of the day has been spent cutting the grass and weeding in the orchard, trimming the hedges and two bonfires.

Closing the museum at 1730

At 1900 with my neighbour we visit the New Inn, Church Knowle for an evening meal, their fish menu is extremely good, and the wine and beer selection is first class.
After the meal we drive down to Kimmeridge and found there was only one other car there. We meet a very old friend Tony Marshall whose family have lived at Gaulter Gap, adjacent the cliff top for many years. Tony is in a rather poor health, and we stop to hear all his problems, and then walk as far as the oil compound. The whole valley was quiet, the sea calm and the sheep were grazing on the high ground, we both remark how fortunate we are to live in this lovely part of Dorset, returning home at 2130.

Today's weather: - Sunshine all day with a few clouds and wind S/E 3.

Name W.J. CARTER

House HILLSIDE

Year of birth 1925.

Street WEST St.

Friday June 9th

At 8 a.m. I saw a young deer in the garden, this is bad news, they eat everything! This bungalow is on the edge of Corfe Common and wildlife of all kinds come in foxes, badgers, rabbits, deer, moles and plenty of birds.

My father, a retired architect from The Public Trustee Office in London, bought the site and designed the bungalow. It was built of local stone by George Brinton in the fifties. The views are spectacular, the Common and Kingston to the south west, Corfe village, Castle and hills to the east - unrestricted countryside where cows, horses and sheep graze and people ramble.

Today I will feed the birds, walk to the village to buy my paper and do some shopping at Clealls, the local store, that stocks everything I need. I must go to the Post Office, then on to the library to return books. After that I will go by bus to Swanage. It is misty and inclined to rain so my work in my garden must wait. I could go on the steam railway, but that is rather slow. There will not be too many cars or tourists about, they do not come in poor weather. We grumble about the tourists, but we might not have our good shops and transport without them. A bus every hour to Swanage and Wareham is useful. I do not have a car.

This afternoon I have a friend coming. We will have tea looking out at the garden which is full of roses. Later I shall cook fish and chips and watch the television. There are gardening programmes tonight and of course the news. That does not leave much time to read the novel that I shall get from the library.

Today's weather: Dull, drizzly but warm.

Name Barbara Goodwin   Year of birth 2-8-19

House COMMON WELL   Street WEST STREET.

Saturday June 10th

I have loved Corfe Castle ever since I first visited when on holiday in the fifties. I would dearly love to live in the village but the price of property prohibits that and I must be content with visiting as often as I can. I live at Holmebridge, seven miles from Corfe and the scene of one of the last battles of the Civil War. The house is on the busy A352 but the country surroundings and the views make that bearable. My greatest delight is waking in the mornings and seeing Corfe Castle on its mound in the distance.

My first visit to the Village Hall was for a Bangers 'n Mash lunch put on by the local WI. What a wonderful meal, with tasty sausages, creamy mash and beans, followed by apple pie and cream, and coffee. A wonderful initiation to the activities of the Village Hall. Since then, three years ago, I have been to every coffee morning. I have met many friends at these functions and there is not a room in my home that does not display at least one item bought from the various stalls. The lamp-shade in the bathroom was 20 pence, a little candle holder was 10 pence. There are ornaments scattered about, even cushion covers and clothes. My winter raincoat cost the grand sum of 40 pence! But it is not just finding things so cheaply. It is the fun of looking through the various items on the stalls, of meeting friends and chatting over coffee.

I always arrive early and spend some time choosing books in the little Library. This morning I was extra early so I walked down into the Village. It was a beautiful morning and I was hoping to have a coffee and a toasted crumpet in the gardens of the National Trust Tea-rooms but found they did not open until 10 o'clock. The National Trust shop was also closed until ten but I went into the newsagents next to the National Trust. This little shop is like stepping back into the past with its rows of sweets in jars on shelves. I bought a magazine (64p for a thin magazine: that would no doubt have kept someone in food for a week when this shop first opened). Then I walked down to the Station, passing the appetising smell of bread issuing forth from the Dragon bakery where the assistants bring a feel of the past in their frilly mop caps and aprons. I sat on one of the seats on the station platform for a while. The sound and smell of the steam trains always takes me back to the days when we used to wait on Wareham Station for the steam train to Corfe or Swanage. The line was finally axed in 1972 but volunteers have gradually been working their way back from Swanage so that Corfe Castle station is alive once more. Finishing the line to Wareham is said to be quite close now.

On my way back to the Village Hall I looked into the Castle View florist and crafts shop with its Pottery Men plant pots, rows of jams and mustards, tins of Corfe Castle biscuits, carved wooden bowls and many plants and flowers including a beautiful bridal bouquet and a lovely arrangement of flowers on a stand, all in white with shades of lavender. These were ready for a wedding in St Edwards this afternoon.

No great treasures to be had at the coffee morning today and none of my usual friends were there. I had a cup of coffee and a biscuit, sitting on my own for the first time. However, there were still lots of friendly faces around and I consider myself very fortunate to be able to join the friendly people of Corfe Castle on their coffee mornings.

Today's weather: *Beautiful sunshine with a light breeeze.*

Name   Barbara Charles   Year of birth   1929

House   Regular visitor to   Street
coffee mornings in Corfe castle village Hall.

As a 'local', that is born and bred in the village, I write now a snapshot of my life in Corfe Castle, beginning with the highlight of this day. My wife Aileen and I were treated to a gorgeous lunch at the Ship Inn at Wool. I am a hearty eater and love meat. Our grandson, Martin, made this outing possible. Martin is one of our nine grandchildren born to our three daughters, all of whom live within a radius of ten miles from our home. It is being with Martin today that makes me think back to my youth.

My life began at what is now 40 West Street where I was brought into the world under the supervision of Dr. Dru Drury. I had two brothers the elder, Arthur, was ten years my senior who, when he left school began as a labourer on a farm at Tyneham until the war began. My father was employed at Pike's Clay Pits and walked across the Creech Hill to work daily. I attended school in what is now the British Legion building and progressed to 'big school' which is where our present 1st School stands. I had always wanted to work in a shop so began young, aged ten years, working after school hours at Clealls Stores in the same building as present day. My job was to weigh butter from 56lb boxes, lard from 28lb lumps and sugar from 2 cwt. sacks in 2, 3, 4 and 6 pound bags. At Clealls my younger brother, Charlie, assisted by carrying the heavy loads into the loft.

Having left school at fourteen and until I was twenty, I continued full time work at Clealls. I was taught to drive by George Moss when I became sixteen. With no obligitory test I was let loose in the delivery van – a Dodge. By my own admission I was not a natural driver then and there were incidents I do remember like the occasion when I braked sharply going up Blackmanston Hill towards Kimmeridge and all the boxes of groceries shot backwards in the van resulting in the need for some reorganisation! Despite my rocky start at driving I still drive seventy years on. As a teenager my only real pleasure was to travel on the train to Swanage - 9d return - to go to the Grand Cinema and then to the pub for half an hour to drink a pint of bitter. Today's lunchtime drink was a refreshing lager and lime.

I began my trade in 1934 when I worked for Stevens, the butcher at Swanage. In 1937, Sid Paine, a friend, who worked at Coopers Stores, one of the three grocery shops in the village, told me a job was going at the butchers. I went along and was taken on. Little did I know this would be my work until 1989 when at seventy-five I eventually hung up the choppers and knives. Ted Moss who owned the shop was called up to fight for his country in 1939 and I was left in charge receiving an exemption from call-up for two years to manage the shop. 1942 brought some major changes for me. I married Aileen, a 'local' girl, who had always lived at 95 East Street with her mum and grandmother. I became a member of the Royal Artillery based at Devonport and soon found myself in Germany as a cook for an officer and nine 'look-out' men overseeing Hill 112. War was cruel.

On my return, Aileen and I lived with her mum until we moved into one of the new houses in Webbers Close in the late 1940's. In 1948, Ted Moss went to farm at Challow and Gerald Cooper became the owner of the shop. Back on the job I did deliveries and sold meat from the van on Tuesday and Friday mornings to the residents of Church Knowle, Steeple, Blackmanston, Kimmeridge and district. We sold all good quality meat, mainly fresh, but also some pies and cooked ham. I was often able to take home some tasty off-cuts. My least favourite job was having to pluck feathers from pheasants. It was not so much the process as the smell - the birds had been hung well and the ripe odour of aged flesh was horrid. At Christmas I also plucked chickens, turkeys and geese, approximately 140 in total, in the slaughter- house buildings which were on the now Springwell site. Jack, Ted's brother, owned the abattoir and employed five men. We thought nothing of having to kill a hundred pigs on a Sunday morning and my pay for those hard few hours was £1.00.

They were busy years but now, although I keep active, my days pass at a steadier pace. I am a villager and have never travelled far. My only holidays to Teignmouth and Longleat have been courtesy of my daughters since they have been grown up. My greatest joy is the garden. Self taught, I had two allotments for many years but now I spend a couple of hours a day tending our flowers. Aileen is the digger and I am the planter. On this day though I only pottered for a short while before our trip out and this evening I rested with Dougal our two year old Shihtzu who is our wonderful guard dog and companion.

Today's weather: SUNNY AND WINDY

Name BILL STOCKLEY   Year of birth 1914

House 8 Webbers Close   Street West Street

I started my life in Corfe and have lived here on and off over the last 30 years. At present, I live in a two-bedroomed flat in Battersea South London with a flat mate (33 year old single sales-woman.)

My day started at 7.30am by my radio alarm. The builders came at 8am to redo some external decorations to the property, that had been poorly done 6 months ago by Wandsworth Council the freehold owners. After a quick breakfast of Kelloggs cereal, fresh fruit and Earl Grey tea, I set off on my pedal-bike to work, with a rucksack and helmet on board.

I work every Monday as a Research nurse for Battersea Research Group, at present looking into risk factors that are relevant to patients in the Wandsworth Primary Care Group who have Ischaemic Heart Disease. Today, this involved cycling to St George's Hospital in Tooting via my office in Battersea. I had a rather daunting prospect of finding 400 listed patients' blood cholesterol readings, if they had ever had one. I spent all morning in the Biochemistry laboratory, sitting at a computer searching each individual name for their latest readings. At 1.30pm I had finished and sat outside in the sunshine on a hospital bench among various visitors and patients and employees of the hospital, enjoying the fresh air. I ate a home-made cottage cheese and marmite and cucumber sandwich, a fresh nectarine and a banana. I then set off on my bike back up Tooting High Street. I stopped off at the local street market and bought a pound of red cherries and two mangoes for £2.00.

I then arrived back in the Research office and caught up with other work. I work the rest of the week in a busy General Practice surgery as a Practice Nurse. We have a huge diversity of multi-cultural patients, many of them who could not visualise this beautiful part of the world as they never get the opportunity to leave their high-rise council blocks for long. I normally run general clinics seeing patients for 10 minute appointments in the morning and afternoon. I give travel advice and vaccinations, ear syringing, four layer compression bandaging, asthma and diabetes advice, family planning advice and certain basic drug prescribing as well as advising for many other health care problems.

I finished work today at 5.30pm and rushed home to prepare a picnic supper for five people. My boyfriend had driven up from Datchet, Berkshire after work and we had a mad dash driving to the Royal Albert Hall to meet friends and go to the ballet 'Sleeping Beauty' performed by the English National Ballet. We have a box that has been in the family since the the Albert Hall was built and most members of our large family enjoy going to the wide variety of performances on offer throughout the year.

I normally play tennis every Monday in Battersea Park on the outdoor courts with friends and we then go for a drink in the pub afterwards. Tonight was a treat and a change to my normal Monday routine. After the performance we headed back to Battersea to go to bed, ready for another day in busy London.

Today's weather: Warm and Sunny

Name SUSANNA JANE PRESTON   Year of birth 1970

House PATCHFIELD   Street Valley Road.

The 13th – and I feel very lucky that on 13th June 1966 (it was a Monday) my mother (the late Elizabeth Crone) and I came to live at the Old Forge (For record purposes I mention that the cottage was then called "Derrycreeven" and nobody can explain its origin). Bought form the Bond Estate by a developer in 1964, we purchased from Miles Estate Agent in Swanage for £5,500 (a lot of money then) in joint ownership.

The Old Forge is the only known medieval house to have survived in the village. The north section of it was converted into a forge during the 19th century.

The Old Forge, 38 East Street, home of Eileen and Lucas van Lelyveld

Although it is 34 years ago our "arrival" memory is as clear as if it were today! We had travelled from Yorkshire in my snazzy turquoise and white metropolitan sports car (it has been said even Noddy would sneer and as a point of interest was voted amongst the 100 worst cars of the century by the Daily Telegraph poll on December 31st 1999!) I loved it! The rendezvous with the removal van was arranged for 9 a.m. No problem parking outside; no yellow lines and cars on East Street were nothing like today's fast end steady flow.

From that moment on we experienced the welcome and hospitality of Corfe Castle's real community spirit. Betty Groves had the shop (now Y Jewellers), almost "next door", as a home made cake shop and came round with a big jug of steaming hot coffee; quickly followed by Mrs. Laura de Beaufort Welchman (the Rector's wife) with a delicious strawberry tart. Life in Corfe Castle has been "sweet" ever since.

My husband, Lucas, has travelled to London today on the 7.15 a.m. National Express bus to meet his brother, Peter Paul, who is on a brief visit from Holland; I write my diary page, a task which is bringing back many happy memories.

Today's weather: Rain and clouds turn to sun

Name	Eileen Van Lelyveld	Year of birth	1932
House	The Old Forge	Street	East Street

14th. June 2000

I got up at 7a.m. to a foggy chilly morning. Took Daisy out into the woods and field, (now cut and cleared).

9.30a.m. Left for R.D.A. (Riding for the Disabled). When I arrived at the stables the 5 ponies that we need were already in the stables. I set up the school while the other helpers groomed and tacked up the ponies.

10.30a.m. The children arrived. 10 of them today. One new little girl loved stroking the ponies but screamed the place down when we tried to put a hat on her. She went rigid and screamed even louder when we tried to put her on the pony. We let her 'pet' the pony for a while before taking her back to the school 'bus. (Better luck next time). Otherwise the class went very well and was enjoyed by children and helpers.

12.30p.m. Arrived home to find Terry cleaning the conservatory roof. No sun today, but it will improve things when it does come out (the sun I mean).

The Hibiscus, which I bought yesterday has come into flower already, it is a lovely salmon pink.

2.15p.m. Julian (son-in-law) rang to say that his mother has been taken into hospital. He is not sure what is wrong, but thinks it is her heart again.

4.00p.m. Took Daisy out again. To the hay field this time. She went mad chasing rooks.

5.00p.m. The farmer has just let a herd of heffers into the field at the back. They are charging around like mad things and have started all of the village dogs barking.

Did duck a l'orange for supper tonight – treat for a week night but it was on special offer at the Co-op.

Not much on Telly tonight except football.(Euro 2000).

8.35p.m. Found a play on ITV called 'Rhinoceros' about a handicapped boy, and this was very enjoyable. Some lovely views of the Welsh countryside.

10.45p.m. and so to bed with my book.

Today's weather: Foggy chilly start, clearing to sunshine later then mist again in the evening.

Name   GRETA HARDY

House   BADGERS

Year of birth   1932

Street   SOUTH STREET KINGSTON.

Thursday June 15th

Awoken at 5:30 am by the alarm clock. A cloudy start to the day, really rather gloomy for the start of an adventure! Little traffic on East Street apart from the occasional delivery lorry going to Swanage. My bags are packed with the bare essentials for my trip to the Le Mans 24 hour race which will take place this weekend on June 17th & June 18th. Feed the cat. Leave the house, family still sleeping, at 7:00 am and drive to catch the ferry to Cherbourg from Poole.

For the rest of the family, it is a normal day - all school-based. My wife works at the school helping out with literacy. Our eldest son is taking his 'A' levels in Maths, Physics and Geography. For our second son, the main event of any importance is the EURO 2000 football tournament currently underway. Literacy, Art, RE, Maths & Science await our daughter at Wareham Middle School.

Today's weather: Overcast, cool, windy later in the day

Name P. Sellen   Year of birth 1954

House 140 East St.   Street

We awoke to a nice summer's day - quite a relief as the Corfe Castle Festivities Committee was as usual holding their annual Cheese and Wine Party at the Model Village tonight. The gardens are looking particularly beautiful at the moment so everyone was able to enjoy them at their best.

It is hard to believe that this is our third season running the business. It is a particular labour of love for me as the Model Village was the brainchild of my father, Eddie Holland. He came up with the idea at the beginning of the 1960s, and when the house now known as Drury's came up for sale, its gardens seemed to him the ideal site to fulfil his dream. With enthusiastic support from my mother, and the help of an architect friend, the model was painstakingly constructed by a local firm of builders, and was finally opened to the public in 1966. Since then it has been visited by many thousands of people from all over the world. My parents. gave up running the business twenty years ago, due to ill health, and it was let out to tenants. However following a winter of extensive building works and the complete re-planting and restoration of the gardens, my husband and I took over the running of the Model Village in April 1998. We have a very supportive little team of helpers (two of us have lived here all our lives - a rare thing these days!), and we all much enjoy meeting the wide variety of people who walk through our doors each day.

We had a busy day, with three school parties, and the Cheese and Wine in the evening was a very jolly, well attended affair, and it being a lovely summer's night everyone was able to sit out on the terrace or in the courtyard, which added to the enjoyment.

Today's weather:

Name   LIZ AGNEW   Year of birth

House   MERRYFIELDS   Street WEST STREET

Carol's Birthday.

Carol aged 3

Today is my eldest Daughter's birthday, and I went to visit her in her home in Gravesend, Kent.

Carol is now a little older and the Head of the Infant's Department of Higham School Kent.

In the afternoon we went to the Chatham Dockyard to see the H.M.S. Cavalier. with her son Tim.

The Cavalier is the only preserved Destroyer from the Second World War.

In the evening we went to a party to celebrate the wedding of Grant & Jana. Grant is the son of Gordon, my deceased wife Muriel's brother).
Jana is a girl from the Czech Republic, & like many Europeans, Multi Lingual.

Today's weather: Nice and sunny and dry, very hot, 90F.

Name Albert John Burt.	Year of birth 12th January 1925.
House Stonecroft.	Street 4 Colletts Close.

Memories of Dave Ford I came into this life in August 4th 1916 at Woodyhyde Farm, about 1 1/2 Miles from Corfe Castle. My early recollections are of early cars, Model T Fords and playing with mud and water, an old Albion lorry, solid tyres and chain drive, left to decay on the Farm, a relic of the First World War.

I almost drowned in the pond having overbalanced and landed face down in mud and water. Brother Gerald saved me from drowning. I was only 3 years old.

The Corfe – Swanage train at 9.5am. Our old clock in the kitchen invariably adjusted to the train, which was always on time. We had no wireless until 1924. Then a crystal set & headphones (very numb ears)

In 1925, my father (George Ford) was approached by Bankes Estate to make something of the very derelict old tannery by the millpond & stream. It had not been used for years. A.Moss, the Corfe builder, put up 4 lock up garages & a large side entrance & a pit inside of main building. This was Purbeck Garage and a shell petrol pump was installed, first in Corfe.

A Buick taxi was purchased in 1926. My sister Ivy (Burridge) & older brother Victor (V & I Ford) ran the business but later owing to serious recession things did not go very well. I remember well, we always went fire lighting on Challow Hill and in Corfe Common which was permitted in those days during winter months.

Mr Ralph Mitchell the smithy (now No 8 my shop) was one of the Corfe blacksmiths. Unfortunate circumstances caused my father to take over the business in 1929, and Mr Mitchell was employed by him then.

Back at Woodyhyde, us lads Bill & Bert Bishop & my younger brother Ron, built a shack, tent like, down in "plot" and we installed a crystal set & headphones, used to listen to Radio Normandy. We had "cook ups" with sausages we got for 4d a pound from Ted Moss, Butcher in West Street and a tin of bully beef from Tom Coopers for 4d a large tin.

I was sent to Swanage Grammar School when it opened in 1929, but was never a great success. Latin, french, algebra, floored me completely so I left school at 16, helped milk the cows in morning and at 17 with Austin 10 (blue) van conveyed milk in churns to the Corfe Castle United Dairies. It was tipped into a large tank and then pasteurised. Churns steam cleaned (upside down on special pad) in van and mechaniced all day at the Purbeck Garage. Mr Mitchell, apart from being the smith also mechaniced in the garage workshop. I can remember working on Dr Dru Drury's 1910 De Dion Bouton.

My Father also started a bus service in 1929. Commencing from Woodyhyde Farm via Corfe – Kingston – Worth - Langton - Swanage and back to Corfe via the Valley Road, i.e. Harmans Cross. This started in 1929 and built up to 5 coaches by 1935 when the whole system was sold to Southern National. Our busses were the only ones to run a service via the Valley Road to Swanage.

I went into the RAF in July 30th 1940. What a story that is. But I married by only love, Clara, on 24th July 1940 and I received my call up papers that morning. In March 1946 was demobbed and restarted the Purbeck Garage & Store at No 9 East Street.

At the 2000 May Fayre Ursula and her father Dave Ford, selected a diary page for 18th June, partly becuase it was the birthday of Daves late wife Clara. Unfortunately Dave died on 7th December. Steve Ford (Daves son at the garage) found the notes for this page in his fathers effects and his wife completed the page. She also read out the page at Dave's funeral which was the last one conducted at the Methodist chapel. The funeral was conducted by The Rev Sylvia Garrett.. Fittingly Daves Grandfather laid the foundation stone to the Chapel two generations earlier.

Today's weather: *A real Summer Day.*

Name DAVID (DAVE) FORD   Year of birth 1916

House TOWNSEND RD   Street EAST

Monday June 19th

We were not in Corfe Castle, but had gone to Exford, on the edge of Exmoor, for a long weekend. We left the hotel about 10am after breakfast, and drove to the Tarr Steps. These are large stone steps, about 1 metre wide, across the river Exe. It was a very pretty spot and there was a 1½ mile circular walk which went along the river bank, across a bridge, and back the other side. It was a lovely walk and took us about an hour. The weather was very hot and sunny, we were dressed in T-shirt and shorts and it was still warm in the shade of the trees.

After the walk we drove into Dulverton, which is a pretty village, where we stopped for a cup of tea. We then walked down to the river and sat in the shade for a while. It was very pleasant. We set off for home about 12:30pm and the traffic was not too bad. Once we got to Dorchester the sea-mist came in and obliterated the sun, but we went to B&Q in Poole and the sun was out there. They didn't have what we wanted and so we had a sandwich and then came home.

The conservatory was very hot and the garden looked dry. After unpacking the case I watered the garden and we spent the evening in the conservatory until it got dark.

Today's weather Hot and Sunny

Name Heather Taunsh   Year of birth 1943

House 10 West Street   Street

Tuesday June 20th

HELLO! MY NAME IS TINA HOLLISTER & I LIVE IN HARMANS CROSS, WHICH IS A LITTLE VILLAGE ABOUT 2½ MILES FROM CORFE CASTLE. I WAS BORN IN 1942 (GO ON YOU WORK IT OUT!) & CAME TO SWANAGE FROM DERBY TO WORK IN 1965, SO I AM NOW ALMOST A LOCAL. I MET MY HUSBAND, DAVID IN 1975. HE IS AN ACCOUNTANT & WORKS FROM HOME. WE HAVE A SON, JAMES, WHO IS 22 & HAS JUST FINISHED AN ACCOUNTANCY DEGREE AT SOUTHAMPTON & IS EAGERLY AWAITING (MAYBE!) THE RESULTS. HE LIVES WITH HIS GIRLFRIEND OF 4 YRS, SARAH, IN SWANAGE.

TUESDAY JUNE 20th BEGAN AS MOST OF MY DAYS DO. AT ABOUT 7.30 A.M. ALARM, TEAS MADE, SHOWER, FEED CATS, I HAVE FOUR. & THEN BREAKFAST WITH DAVID. FAIRLY GLOOMY DAY. WISH THE SUMMER WOULD COME, AS EVERYONE IS SO MUCH HAPPIER WHEN THE SUN SHINES. JAMES CALLED IN ABOUT 10.00 A.M ON HIS WAY TO HIM SUMMER JOB. WHY ARE THESE CHILDREN? ALWAYS TIRED? DID A BIT OF HOUSEWORK (BORING) & THEN WENT TO SEE MY GIRLFRIEND, WHO HAS JUST TAKEN OVER AN HOTEL IN SWANAGE, BITTERLY REGRETING IT, IT CAN ONLY GET BETTER. ARRIVED AT OUR SHOP (I WILL EXPLAIN) ABOUT 12.00 P.M. MYSELF & MY FRIEND JAN. RUN A TINY SHOP IN CORFE CASTLE SQUARE SELLING MAINLY ICE CREAM, & LOTS OF PRETTY THINGS AS WELL. IT HAS BEEN FAIRLY QUIET SO FAR THIS SUMMER, & TODAY WAS NO EXCEPTION. JAN CAME IN ABOUT 2.30 P.M. & WE CHATTED ABOUT THING MANY & VARIOUS. I DECIDED TO CALL IT A DAY ABOUT 5.30 P.M.

HOME TO HUSBAND & CATS, ALL OF WHOM NEEDED FEEDING. TONIGHT IS AN IMPORTANT NIGHT BECAUSE OF THE EUROPEAN 2000 FOOTBALL COMPETITION. ENGLAND NEED TO BEAT ROMANIA TO CONTINUE IN THE COMPETITION. BOTH DAVID & I ARE GREAT FOOTBALL SUPPORTERS. WE HAVE OUR DINNER IN GREAT SPIRITS, THEN I DRIVE US TO CORFE TO THE GREYHOUND INN, TO WATCH THE MATCH WITH FRIENDS. WE LOSE, DESPAIR! HOW COULD THIS HAPPEN? WE COME HOME DEJECTED. WE WATCH THE HIGHLIGHTS? ON THE TELEVISION, WE STILL LOSE! WE FINISHED OUR DAY WITH A LARGE SCOTCH & RETIRE TO BED TO DREAM OF BETTER THINGS. GOODNIGHT

Today's weather: GLOOMY AT FIRST, A LITTLE BRIGHTER LATER

Name TINA HOLLISTER.

House 'BOX OF DELIGHTS, CORFE CASTLE.

Year of birth 1942.

Street The Square

A stunning "Hollywood" type of sunset with shafts of pink light projecting over the hills to the west of the village at the end of this, the longest day of the year.

Oh, and yes it's also my fifty fifth birthday although according to my Mother who was there, I really arrived in the early hours of the following day!

I am delighted to report that it has been a beautifully warm, bright, clear and sunny June day. The attached photographs show a back garden gathering at 124 East Street to celebrate the afore mentioned birthday. Arranged, as it was in unguarded haste in the wake of a good evening in the Fox Inn, it proved a happy get together.

The "party people" were primarily village residents and in the main, members of the Corfe Castle Festivities, an enthusiastic team responsible for the Christmas illuminations, which enhance the village at the end of each year. In addition, they give a good deal of their free time running numerous other events including children's and elder's parties, cheese and wine evenings, discos, Christmas Carols and many fund raising functions. Today started well with a meeting with the Swanage Branch of the Royal British Legion where we set out the plan for a Summer Open Day. There followed a little light shopping before we returned to 124 East Street.

Our homecoming coincided with the arrival of Jane and Geoff Windsor. As always good company. They kindly assisted us in clearing a large quantity of chocolate birthday cake and some sparkling wine. Complex garden planning followed and fired with imagination and slice of enthusiasm, Anne and I then set off fully intending to buy a small wooden sunshine room for the garden. We returned from our garden quest with two terra-cotta plant pots but on the plus side, they did match!

The winning No's :-
F. 10, 24, 33, 37
THE NATIONAL
LOTTERY 46
THE ESTIMATED JACKPOT FOR
WED 21 JUN 2000 IS £4 MILLION
173-08911025-16328
F. 01 12 13 32 34 39
G. 09 11 19 32 39 41
WED21 JUN 00
FOR 01 WED DRAW
010022   £ 2.00
RET NO 187349
173-08911025-16328
FILL BOX TO VOID
HE DID HIS BEST !!

Today's weather:

Telephone chats with offspring -Matthew who lives in Bath and Luke and our daughter in law, Claire and grandson, Sam living in Steyning, Sussex. Then a quick call to Mums - Anne's in Okehampton, Devon and mine in New Milton.

For general interest also included in this little missive, the winning numbers for today's National Lottery recorded in pencil at the top of an unsuccessful ticket. If my crystal ball had been working, we would have been £4 million better off (a third conditional?). Please do feel free to use the numbers for any future games of chance with my blessing.

An inspiring television documentary programme on channel 4 this evening. It was the incredible account of Sir Ernest Henry Shackleton's epic journey across the Southern Oceans in 1916 including the subsequent rescue of his men. I would have no hesitation in recommending this remarkable, inspiring tale of endeavour, leadership and amazing courage.

Name *Robin and Anne Swaine*   Year of birth *1945*

House *Kenneswitta*   Street *East Street*

Thursday 22nd June - my 61st birthday.

I looked out of the window and it is blowing a gale and there is no sun - not a bit like a lovely warm June day!

I live in Church Terrace and the builders have our roof off and the plastic has been flapping all night with the wind so we have not had much sleep!

The Terrace was built to commemorate Mr. Bankes' birth almost 100 years ago. Alan and I have lived here for 42 years.

Sarah and my two grandchildren Amy and Chloe rang me before they went to school and sang "Happy Birthday".

Brenda Chappell and a friend, Pat Cherrit came in for their "hair do's" and we were talking about Corfe and how many of us born and bred and over 50 still lived in the village and we could only count 15 in East Street and 13 in West Street, very sad.

I wonder how many of us will be living here in 20 year's time? My father and Grandfather were both born in the village.

Today's weather:
Very windy and a lot of cloud - cold

Name	Jill Beavis	Year of birth	1939
House	22	Street	East Street

Friday June 23rd

After breakfast I set out on a long walk to collect our newspaper. It is a tiring walk but an attractive one; especially on a sunny day. It contains many memories for me.(I should mention that I was once the Headmaster of the local Primary School, catering for children from Corfe and outlying villages from the age of 5 to 11. I will probably be the last Headteacher to live and be involved in the village.

I served from that cold and snowbound Winter of 1962/63 until 1977 when the School became a 'First School' for children aged 5 to 9.)

My wife, Dorothy, began the Playgroup in the Village Hall in 1964 and ran it for nine years. She also assisted me with many School Visits, sometimes under canvas. We both got to know the children well and created a kind of partnership.

Beginning my walk to the Square, I first passed from a small lane in East Street into the far end of the Halves (three fields dividing East Street from West Street). From this vantage point I was to see one of the most agreeable views of Corfe Castle Village and its Castle. Continuing my walk through the Halves my memories were stirred when I reached the field near the swings. During my time this was used as a School Field - for football and Annual Sports Days. (It was not until 1968 that the School was fortunate in acquiring its present School Field.) Soon I arrived in the picturesque West Street and collected my newpaper in the Square. Here stood the Parish Church with its link with the local School and children.

I recalled the imaginative efforts made to transform the Square ready for Christmas - with its coloured lights and Father Christmas. Sometimes members of the School Choir performed near the Crib and Christmas Tree. It was here that I had once organised the Annual Church Bazaars on the Church Lawns. Inside the Church the school-children had performed their Nativity Plays and Carol Services. Looking out from the Church, I recalled that the "Dragon Village Bakery" opposite was devised and is operated by a former pupil - Nigel Dragon. Now leaving the Square, I turn right into East Street and soon espy on my left the Village War Memorial which commemorates the village lads of two World Wars who never returned. Many had, no doubt, attended the local Schools in Corfe and outer villages. Here I cannot escape my personal memories of lost family members (Father, Grandfather and Uncle). Also fellow RAF comrades who did not "make it".

Now I approach familiar territory. On my right, the original local School opened in 1834 - the year the Tolpuddle Martyrs were transported to Australia. This was still in use as a Dining Hall until purchased by the British Legion in 1976. Across the road is the current School, opened in 1896. Here my memories are naturally most abundant. I always have very affectionate memories for all the wonderful children I had the privilege to have in my care. I am always really delighted to meet them again in our mature years - although I cannot always recognise them at first. Then, passing the new Village Hall, I still have much to remember - happy Social Functions, Entertainments, Coffee Mornings, Meetings and many other gatherings. Soon I was back home in Mead Road, glad to rest my weary feet! However, a very wet Winter and Spring had resulted in vastly overgrown trees and shrubs in our garden. We spent a long afternoon cutting down what we could and placing them in black bags ready for the "Tip". During the evening we watched Television.

Today's weather: CLOUDY, DRY   .... And so to bed...

Name   TED HOPKINS   Year of birth 1916

House " CHILBECK "   Street 16 MEAD ROAD

Midsummer's Day and as usual a busy one on my allotment, where I took a break from my ceaseless war against weeds to cut the first Cos and Lollo Rosso lettuces.

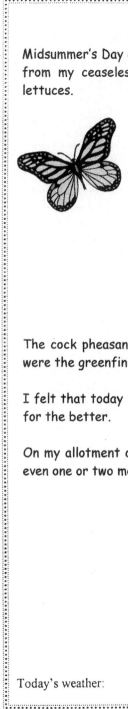

I was pleased to notice a good selection of butterflies during the morning - the usual Meadow Browns and Red Admirals of course, and also the first Painted Lady of the year and a couple of Clouded Yellows, not usual this early.

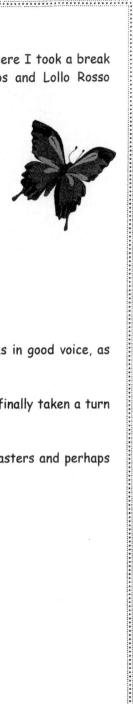

The cock pheasant who has his home around East Street was in good voice, as were the greenfinches and chaffinches.

I felt that today for the first time, the gardening year had finally taken a turn for the better.

On my allotment at least there have been no horrendous disasters and perhaps even one or two modest successes!

Today's weather: Dry. Breezy. Sunny spells

Name	Richard Pearson		Year of birth	1940
House	18		Street	Halves Cottages

What is it that is so special? Corfe had observed another Millennium in 1978, one thousand years after the young King of England, Edward, was murdered by Elfrida, as she hoped her own son, Aethelred would become King

'the north of the Castle   from a sketch by Derek Matthews

On this early summer's day, where are the jackdaws that were a feature of the ruined keep of the castle? Their 'cawing' was music to our ears. What has happened to the fragrant wild thyme that used to grow on the castle hill, a relic of plants in the kitchen gardens of the castle? Where are the wild orchids and myriads of small butterflies on the Purbeck Hills? What has happened to the sky-larks which soared high into the sky with their song? Where are so many bats which vanished after the elm trees at the top of West Street succumbed to elm disease?

Purbeck is still unique. Once a "Royal Warren", so described in *Picturesque Rambles in the Isle of Purbeck* 1882, by C.E.Robinson, with etchings by Alfred Dawson, it maintained its quaint and half-medieval atmosphere; this raffish character is under threat from urban-minded people, aiming to 'tidy it up'. It must be questioned whether the National Trust are going too far in cleaning up the ruins and village. It must not become another "disney-land". Weeds must remain; they are only plants unwanted by some.

My Aunt Winifred (Winnie), was locally known and loved as "Miss Matthews", the teacher. She knew (I was also so fortunate), a very different village, although most of the buildings were the same superficially as today. Early in the morning the clay workers used to set off on their bicycles with their 'dinner' to go to the clay pits on the other side of the hills. I remember how Eddie Holland (then one of my heroes) opened a newsagent shop in The Square; and he never looked back!

Miss Matthews, the teacher, walked from Corfe to Church Knowle School via the Common and the Copper Bridge, in all weathers carrying an umbrella, not so much against rain, as to shoo away over-friendly heifers and bullocks. Some of the children came from Creech, walking over the hill; she dried their wet clothes, keeping a dry supply in the school. There were no "school buses". She used to take them on 'nature walks' at different seasons. They all left school with a good grounding in the "3 R's". Today's children are "bussed" to Wareham, becoming urbanized, believing milk only comes out of supermarkets, and food out of tins.

When Winnie first lodged with Mrs Cleall opposite the Town Hall, next door lived someone affectionately known as "Old Lou", and her brother Henry, who kept bees. On the death of King George V in 1936, Henry put the hives into mourning with black cloth, talking to the bees, telling them of the death of the King; otherwise, he claimed, they would fly away. Old Lou brewed beer every Thursday, even though the "Fox Inn" was only a few doors away.

Between the two wars, Corfe was a cultural attraction, and every Summer Exhibition at the Royal Academy would include several paintings and etchings of Purbeck. A number of practising artists lived here. The sculptor, Mary Spencer-Watson is still active at Downshay. The group at Little Woolgarston was well known. The local G.P., Dr Dru Drury, who looked after everyone, must not be forgotten, as well as the Rector, the families Bankes and Bond, and the farmers, as well as the pre-historic people, whose tumuli are everywhere and should also be remembered; Generations of quarrymen and marblers have contributed to the unique atmosphere of this place.

Purbeck people have never been bothered with "political correctness". Chapman's Pool was the scene of the import of "brandy for the parson, baccy for the clerk". The landlord of the "Fox" ("no names, no pack drill") never hesitated to welcome those of whom he approved to stay on after closing hours, in the back parlour. I am sure I must have had a glass of cider when below age at the "New Inn" after a visit to Creech Barrow, paid for out of the sixpence in my pocket.

The local economy was supported by sustainability (now lacking!), fuel from the numerous coppices, at Sandy Hills, Woolgarston, Tabbit's, Cow Leaze, Rickett's, Harman's, Parsonage, Scoles Lane, Willwood, Bucknowle, Wadhill, Horseground, to mention only a few.

Food was local, so no plastics and wrappers from supermarkets, no non-compostable dustbin refuse. However, we have some consolation today, in that the prevailing wind is from the south-west, blowing away from Purbeck the pollution that emanates from the megalopolis to the east.

Today's weather: CLEAR SUNNY and DRY

Name   Derek Howard Matthews   Year of birth

House   92   Street   West Street

Monday June 26th

I got up at around 7am, which is pretty early for me. I then had a hot shower. After eating my breakfast, getting dressed and ready for the day ahead I got into the car. My mum drove me to my singing tutor's house in Studland. My tutor's name is Joanne Moore. After some of her other pupils arrived we drove to Bournemouth via the toll ferry. We arrived a little later than planned. We were competeing in the Bournemouth Music Festival, so we were all very nervous. I was shaking all over when my name was called and it was my turn to sing. I did my song "I could have danced all night." from the musical "My Fair Lady." I made a mistake at the beginning but I came 4th out of 24. I got a merit certificate. I had my lunch and then was driven back to my mum's office in Wareham. I stayed there for a while and then went to school in the lunch hour. My friends were all surprised to see me as they thought I was ill. After lunch we played rounders in P.E. Then we had a talk on contreception in P.S.E (Personal and social education). At 3.25pm I went home on the school bus. When I got in I watched television and played on my playstation. I went to bed at around 10pm.

Today's weather: Hot & Sunny.

Name Becky Eady

House Shiralea

Year of birth 1986

Street Higher gardens

My Birthday

My birthday was going to be a relaxed day with my husband. We planned a lunch out and a quiet day together. Perhaps working in the garden, perhaps a bit of light shopping............

Happy Birthday...

All started well; lots of cards and presents, which was really nice and an extended breakfast. However during the morning things started to go wrong! There were several phone calls during which it became clear that the Millennium dinner menu card had some problems with it's formatting at the printers. I should explain here that the millennium dinner was due to be held in the Castle on the evening of the 1st July and the Committee had been working on it for months. It was important that it was a memorable evening and there was great attention to detail, so

something had to be done when it was realised that the cards had mistakes. In the end it was down to the Chairman - himself - to sort it out!!

All of this meant that he had to spend time on the phone talking and negotiating with the printer. The cards had to be delivered in draft by fax and then a car journey to Verwood to collect the finished product. By the time he got back it was too late to do anything, so we had supper in. Ah, the things we do for the Millennium!!!

Today's weather: DRY

Name Diana Dudkin   Year of birth 1943

House HERONS   Street East Street

Wednesday June 28th

Awoke to the sound of my wrist watch alarm at 7.30am. Turned over to cuddle my wife Sheena only to remember that she was house sitting for her mother who lives nearby in West Street. I washed and dressed and started my job as subpostmaster by visiting our sorting office. Actually a small room at the end of the house which doubles as a sorting office from 7.0am - 9.30am and as a laundry cum store room for the rest of the day. Our cat "Scampi" also lives in here most of the time since we have no garden. We have 2 part time posties who sort and deliver the mail to most of the village.

I dealt with the special delivery mail and solved a few problems before taking my pile of personal mail, missorts, gone aways and redirections into my office to sort through.

Wednesday is the day that all subpostmasters have to produce a cash account. To report the weekly transactions and balance the cash and stamps etc, so I made a start on the preparations for that. 8.20am breakfast of bran flakes and fruitibix, and the morning BBC news, weather and sport. A quick shave and wash then open the post office doors at 9.00am prompt.

A busy morning it being near the end of the month, lots of car licence discs and council tax bills.

My wife phoned mid morning to say she had hurt her back, again, and couldn't move. I closed the post office at 1.0pm and went to see how she was. Unfortunately she couldn't get up so I phoned the doctor for advice and eventually went to collect some strong pain killers for her from the surgery.

I returned home and finally finished my cash account at about 5.0pm by which time most of my family had arrived to help celebrate my 46th birthday. Instead of the barbecue which we had planned we had fish and chips, a few cans of beer and a bottle of wine as they left at about 10.0pm I went to make sure that my wife was comfortable and returned home at 11.0pm. Having tidied up I secured the shop and house and went to bed. I read for an hour or so before sleep.

Today's weather   Cloudy start   Sunny afternoon   Cloudy night

Name Ian Tarbotton

Year of birth 1954

House The Post Office and
      The Town House

Street The Square

Today Michael has his big party for his year as High Sheriff of Dorset. Doug Whyte, as Constable of the Castle, has very kindly allowed us to hold it in the castle grounds, in the marquee that has been erected for the village Millennium Weekend celebrations. We have been given an official list by the Shrievalty Office of various people who must be asked by virtue of the posts they hold within the County, and Michael has also asked everybody with whom he has special contact, particularly within the village, as well as our closest family and friends. In all it comes to almost 400 people, a real cross-section of local life from the Lollipop Lady to the Lord Lieutenant! Because it is Millennium Year, Michael felt he wanted to make it special, so as well as red and white wine, real ale, local cider and soft drinks, there is to be a Hog Roast, which seems particularly appropriate as the party is being held in a medieval castle. Three enormous roasting spits have arrived and been set up beside the marquee, each containing a whole pig. There are big baskets of flowers decorating the outside of the marquee, and from inside we can hear the music of a quintet from Michael's regiment, The Light Infantry. The entrance to the Castle looks magnificent with banners and lights; it is a beautiful, hot June evening, and people are eating and drinking outside, with the magnificent back-drop of the castle against the setting sun. The Hog is delicious, with stuffing, crackling and several different relishes, served in a bun. There is a hum of conversation, and people are wandering up the castle to explore. Terry and Trish, in costume for the occasion, are at the castle gates to repel gatecrashers. Our twins, Edward and Charlie, have given up their wheelchair-duty – nobody has needed them – and are sitting on the top of the Outer Bailey bank, surrounded by the available teenage glamour and beer bottles. People keep coming up to me and saying "Isn't it a glorious evening – and what a wonderful setting". So far I have only managed to take one mouthful of my bun, there is no time for eating. The quintet, no doubt boiling inside their dark green uniforms with the silver epaulettes and shiny patent leather cross belts, are having their supper, and the pigs are now mere skeletons. The sun has gone down, the castle is flood-lit, and people are saying "Isn't it beautiful ... isn't it romantic ..." Stragglers are meandering down the path from the castle heights, slowly people are leaving. The twins are racing each other in the Red Cross wheelchairs down West Street. The Bankes Arms – who have organised the drink – are collecting glasses, the Hog Roast chefs have gone. The party is over. We wander home, happy and slightly tipsy in the warm summer darkness, hoping our guests enjoyed it as much as we did, and profoundly grateful to everyone who made it possible.

Today's weather: Hot Summer, Cloudless blue Sky

Name Anne Bond   Year of birth 1944

House Furzemans   Street WEST

51 West St

I woke up at 6.00am, earlier than usual, with a surprisingly clear head. Last night there had been a pig-roast in the castle which was held by Michael Bond who in the High Sheriff of Dorset for the year 2000. It was his 'Sheriff's Party' and the wine was flowing freely - hence my surprise at having a clear head.

Knowing I had a busy day ahead I got up immediately - I usually go to aqua-fit on Fridays but not this week. My biggest job was to write names on all the menus (220) for Saturday night's Millennium Ball. I should have had all week to do this but there were spelling mistakes on the menus so they had to go back to the printer and only arrived back late Thursday night. This is not a job that can be done quickly nor for long periods so I knew I had to pace myself and have frequent breaks. I did the first batch before breakfast and continued all day breaking off to do other things at regular intervals such as fetching my paper (The Independent 45p) from the Sweet Shop in the square, putting washing in the machine, hanging it out, filling bird feeders with sunflower seeds and peanuts etc.

At 2.00pm I went to the Castle to meet with other members of the Millennium Association Committee. We had hired a very large marquee for our weekend of celebrations (£3,713) and we were there to make the final arrangements for the first event which was a Family Disco Dance that evening. Steve Haw ran the disco and Jim Etherington and his band a very popular local band also contributed. Steve Haw is also one of the proprietors of Cameo Event Hire who supplied the marquee. It was pavilion style with opening windows and doors along one side and with very smart internal drapes in white and blue.

Once we were satisfied all was ready I went home to continue writing the names on the menus. At 5.30pm I suddenly realised that I had not eaten since breakfast and quickly cooked and ate some pasta as I was due back at the castle by 6.00pm!

My job for the evening was to be on the gate - I was very happy with this arrangement as although I like the music, being in the marquee it would have been too loud. I was helped first of all by Angelica Ford then by Jan Harriott. It cost £4 for each adult with concessions for families. We stamped everyone's hand as they entered so that they could be identified if they needed to leave the castle and return. Unfortunately the only toilets were near the square.

This was an extremely successful event, we took well over £1000.00 on the gate. The bar was organised by Mike Perry from the Bankes Hotel in the square and run by Sam Hill and others - the takings were also considerable.

We received nothing but praise from everyone except one village couple who refused to pay and claimed their 'village rights' to come into the castle free. They were very angry when we explained that the castle was closed except for our event and they went away.

The dance was due to finish at 12 midnight but continued later. Together with other members of the committee present we cleared away the debris inside the marquee and as much as we could see in the dark outside.

Very tired committee members made their way home and I certainly was tired and fell into bed at about 2.00am.

Fortunately the weather remained dry, although overcast, all day and throughout the evening.

Name Linda Applin
Vice Chairman, Millennium Association Committee
House
64, West St.

Year of birth

Street

Today is the second of three days of celebrations being held beneath a marquee in the Castle. In fact, as the church clock struck midnight to welcome the new day, the old one was still in full swing. We were trying to persuade Jim Etherington to close his act and allow us to go home to our beds. The Family Disco, together with the live music of Jim and his band, had been well received with many more people than expected turning out to enjoy the entertainment on a calm, warm evening. After some general clearing up we went home for some sleep before preparing for the Grand Ball later today.

7.30am soon came round and back to the Castle for a litter pick around the grounds, before going inside the marquee to erect the tables. Tickets for the Ball were sold out long ago and extra tables were squeezed in to accommodate the great demand. Soon they were in place complete with fresh, white, linen tablecloths. Marita, the local florist, was on site arranging the pedestal flowers and placing them on the stage and in the corners of the marquee. These, together with the table decorations, were in blue and yellow, the adopted colours of the Association, and looked magnificent against the linings of the marquee and the white of the table linen. The effect was further enhanced by balloons on ribbons in identical colours. By mid afternoon the caterers were busy preparing the meal. Their staff had finished the table settings thereby completing this magical picture. On my return home to dress, I was welcomed by the news from my wife that the band leader had broken down. However, a later report suggested he would arrive by the time dancing was due to start, so, panic over!

7pm saw the first guests arrive. The ladies were in fine dresses and the men in dinner jackets and bow ties. They were greeted at the Castle gate by Barney Bay walking on stilts, and with some comical exchanges he directed them towards Bob Richardson, a local photographer, who was ready to take their picture. This he did beneath a floral arch with the Castle as a backdrop. Mike Perry, the licensee of the Bankes Arms, and his staff were soon busy serving drinks at the bar and taking table wine orders, while Linda Applin and others sold tickets for the raffle. The two hundred and twenty guests assembled in the marquee and with an atmosphere of expectation were called to their places for dinner.

Rev. Strike said grace before a meal of Deux Mille Rillettes (hot smoked salmon rillettes), followed by Centennial Chicken (breast of chicken stuffed with Ricotta cheese and spinach, fresh tarragon and cream sauce) with vegetables and new potatoes with chive butter and a dessert of fresh berries with walnut shortbread and whipped cream, was served. The delicious meal, superbly prepared and presented, was rounded off with coffee and mints. During the meal, guests were entertained by Barney Bay who visited the tables twisting balloons into all sorts of shapes whilst engaging the patrons in some banter. Jack Stephens worked at other tables deceiving guests with close-up conjuring tricks.

Following the meal, Stephen Dru Drury the Chairman, said a few words of thanks and then presided over the two raffles. The first, for a Fortnum and Mason hamper donated by Sam Chalmers, was won by Sarah Jarvis who held the lucky ticket number drawn from the drum. The £100 note raffle was won by Simon Robinson while Mary Rosewarn collected the second prize of a magnum of champagne. Comedian Phil Lowen then provided entertainment which he concluded with a remarkable Pavarotti impersonation.

The Tony Crane Band started the dancing with guests jigging and jiving, wiggling and waltzing and twisting and tangoing the evening away. Others, less energetic, looked on with a drink or two, or chatted with friends. Two o'clock soon came round. The band had finished an hour earlier and Steve Haw concluded the festivities playing music from his disco. By two thirty we had said farewell to the last of the revellers. We collapsed the tables and gathered the chairs to assist the early morning cleaners and then headed for home reflecting on a simply wonderful evening which had joined the community in celebration. This was, after all, our aim and we could not have wished for a better result.

Two down, but we still had the religious service and children's party to go, so sleep was going to be short again.

Today's weather: Rain at first but fine later. A perfect summer evening for the Ball.

Name   Jim Rosewarn   Year of birth   1945

House   April Cottage   Street   West Street   7

Millennium Weekend Children's Party

A party for all children in the village was held in the Castle on Sunday afternoon, 2 July 2000. Everyone enjoyed a delicious tea and entertainment by Barney Bay. Later the High Sheriff of Dorset presented a mug to each of those present.
The names of all those who received a mug are on this page.

Enjoying the tea

Lauren Vinney
Owen Haskins
Sam Lightowler
Michael Morris
Tom Oddy
Ryan Holcoop
Ollie Oddy
Joss Venning
Lauren Davis
Lizzie Hole
Joanne Ford
Luke Reynolds
Lindsey O'Brian
Max Girkins
Poppy Atwell
Shuna Whyte

Alexander Wilson
Robert Fretwell
Poppy Davis
Emily Nelson
Tanya Davis
Holly Smith
Jason Simpson
Josh Davis
Geogina Atwell
Rosie Davis
Zoe Squirrell
Kieron Reynolds
Emily Girkins
Tom Davis

Ryan Vinney
Hallum Stuckey
Venja Squirrell
Sam Christopher
Callum Morgan
Shaun Holcoop
Alex Rainbird
Lottie Anstey
Shaun Simpson
Carys Ellison
Katie Hole
Lorrie Beardmore
Emily Ward
William Wilson
Chloe Morgan
Canna Whyte
Laura Ailwood

James Drane
Anastasia Beaumont
Melanie Western
Harriett Simpson
Esther Brett
Ben Jarvis
Geoffrey Dragon
Victoria Parsons
Bryony Ireland
Sherradon Maud
Alexander Bond
Anna Philps
Mariko Whyte
Rosie Ford
Eddie Stuckey
Tom Davis

Barney Bay entertains

Chelsea Haskins
Eddis Suckling
Stuart Vinney

Brian Dragon
Christopher Bray
Spike Davis

Bethany Somers
Craig Viney
Tim Harrison

Beckey Varney
Chloe Ellison
Evie Beardmore
James Western
Catherine Atwell
Joe Freeman

Hayley Ailwood
Benedict Girkins
Amber Nelson
Cherry Smith
Kerry Hathaway
Mariel Harrison
Pete Morris
Fred Pope
Julia Spooner
Matthew Davis
Alec Harrison
Lawrence Restarick
Jamie Ford
Nick Spooner

The High Sheriff presents Mugs

Today's weather:

Warm, dry, & fine

Name Millennium Association

House Various

Year of birth

Street

Today, my last day in Corfe, turned out to be most fruitful. My parents and I, having toured the castle a few days earlier, finally made it to the Castle View interactive center. The displays were interesting, but I really enjoyed chatting with Nancy Grace, the local archaeologist for the National Trust. I had a look around upstairs and saw the cannon balls and some leading from the glass windows in the guardroom. That Lady Bankes gave the guards the pleasure of glass gives some clue to her generous personality. She must have treated her tenants and servants well to have generated such loyalty in hostile times.

The people at the center provided me with much appreciated sources, pointing me in the right direction, to re-enactment societies and the like. It means a lot, being a 9x's great-granddaughter of the brave Dame Mary myself! I love learning about the past, and having family involved makes it all the more interesting. It seems funny, but in the States we think something old if it has 100 years of history, let alone 300 - 400 years!

I hope to come back one day, maybe with more research into the American side of the Bankes family.

I believe we're related through Mary's youngest son, William, though these family trees say he died young and unmarried. I'll have to dig a little deeper.

Also drove to Swanage and Studland. Beautiful beaches, though the water is a bit colder than that in the Gulf of Mexico! The weather here is much nicer than in Texas right now. I'll hate going back. Thank you for all of your help in my quest for siege information. Best wishes to you all.

Today's weather: Sunny and warm

Name	Megan Elizabeth Edwards	Year of birth	1982
House	While in Corfe, The Ragged Cat At home: Houston, Texas	Street	West Street

We are on our fourth day of a camping trip to France. Today we planned a canoe adventure for our boys..... myself, husband Steve, Joe (4½) and Charlie (2½) are the "expedition members!" A small tributary of the River Loire at Anjou Loisirs is the waterway to explore. This place is gorgeous, an ideal wide, calm river – with a shady parking spot for our bright red Landrover!

We pumped up our bright yellow, full whitewater spec Canadian canoe, fixed in the seats, found paddles and carried our craft to the water's edge. The canoe was then filled with dry-bags holding other essentials – first aid kit, repair kit, suncreams, spare clothes, camera, a picnic and the boys' water pistols.

Steve and Joe

Joe and Charlie were already very hot, the weather was in the 90's; they were covered in sunscreen, wearing buoyancy aids and proudly holding their very own wooden paddles, with pirates faces painted on the blades .. we were all set to paddle the river L'Eure.

Charlie with his pirate paddle

The first hour or so of the journey was through beautiful green scenery, thick wooded banks and open meadows – we passed an old Citroen car being used as some kind of pump-house – it looked like a scene from 'Allo 'Allo. We paddles through huge, rubbery lily pads – the boys were disappointed not to see a frog sunning itself on one of these! But we did spot other wildlife – herons, dippers, moorhens, ducks, buzzards and kingfishers. The turquoise kingfishers shone so brightly in the sunlight! Joe and Charlie were both expert at spotting these amazing little birds.

Soon the sun became too much and we all needed a break off the water. The section of bank we landed on was gorgeous – there was a little ruined fort type building – while exploring this Joe spotted a lizard in the rocks – this was then his mission. Between us we found so many gorgeous small rock/stone coloured lizards – they were extremely fast and all attempts by Steve to catch one failed miserably!! Joe was in his element, pretending he was Australian, Steve Irwin. Charlie let out squeals of joy each time he saw any movement and was really happy when we found a little frog. We finally ate our picnic – although the dry-bag will never be the same again after camembert, brie and bananas had melted in the 90° heat inside! Yuk! The return journey was fun – we saw some lovely rocky gorges. Charlie slept in the bow of the boat for the last hour back – complete peace and contentment on his face!

Me, Joe and Charlie (asleep in canoe) at the finish of our journey

We returned to the campsite on the banks of the river Loire, where we showered, fed and watered, then we watched the sun set over the river. The boys took minutes to fall into a deep sleep, snuggled in their sleeping bags. We then sat under the stars with a bottle of local red wine! A wonderful day!

Today's weather: Very sunny and hot - 90°F + all day!

Name	Gina Gynes and Steve, Joe and Charlie	Year of birth	1965
House	Myrtle Cottage, Bushey	Street	

My carer arrived at 9 00am to help me get up, to wash and get dressed. She also got my breakfast of toast and marmalade. The hairdresser came at about 9.30am, I was just about ready for her After my hair was done at 10am, I had time to sit down and get my breath back. My son Handel and daughter-in-law Lynda were coming to take me out for a surprise.

They arrived with my granddaughter, Laura, at 11am I opened my presents. I had a long silk scarf, from my friends Rene and Frank in Wales, a begonia from my friend Betty, an African violet from Laura, slippers from Handel and Lynda. From my other son, Hugh and daughter-in law, Susan who live in Malta, I had a Tom Jones CD double album We went out into the garden, which was looking beautiful with my lilies in full flower, to take some photos.

We drove to the Bank's Arms at Studland for our lunch. I had a lovely prawn salad, but it was really too much for me to eat. Then we drove down to Swanage and parked along the sea front using my disabled badge, because I can't walk far. Handel and Laura went off to look round the shops Lynda stayed with me and we watched the people on the beach and in the sea When Handel and Laura returned we drove back to Corfe Castle and it was time for them to leave me

The family had tired me out and I think I had a snooze in the chair. At about 5pm, David the Pastor from the Congregational Church arrived with a card, signed by all my friends at the 'Happy Hour' and Pam, his wife, sent some cakes and scones from the tea they had after the service We had a lovely chat

Later, another carer came to help me get undressed and ready for bed, but I don't go to bed that early I then had another lovely surprise Carol, my daughter-in-law Susan's daughter arrived at 9pm with a card and present. It was a CD of Welsh songs which reminded me of my childhood in Mountain Ash.

It was a lovely way to spend my 84th birthday I have been very happy, since I moved to live here in Corfe

Today's weather   Sunny, then cloudy with a few spots of rain, then brightened up

Name	Mrs Queenie Delphine Hurrell (Widow)	Year of birth	5th July 1916
House	21	Street	Springwell Close

Thursday July 6th

A beautiful summer's day which helped me to make the quick decision to catch the boat from Swanage Pier for a day in Bournemouth. Something new to us and also to a brother from Kenilworth, Warwickshire, and sister-in-law, who were staying with us for the week.

A glorious crossing, with a short stop at Brownsea Island to off-load a few of the passengers, then soon afterwards Bournemouth Pier became visible.

A far more interesting way to travel compared to the usual way by car along overcrowded "A" roads. So very peaceful! No "smog" of exhaust fumes either!

After some five hours in Bournemouth it was again a smooth crossing back to the peaceful Purbecks. Our visitors marvelled at the spectacular coastline which we so enjoy each and every day.

Today's weather. Warm and sunny, some haze around 4 p.m.

Name	R. Williams	Year of birth	Pensioner!!
House	5 The Dollings	Street	Off East Street

Friday July 7th

This walk starts for me in the Square in Corfe.

I walk down Oliver Vyes Lane. At the first rock from the Castle I see a tree creeper, a blue tit and a tree creeper. A little further along I see a brown trout in the river, well camouflaged by the bank. A shrill cry makes me look up. I see a peregrine falcon being mobbed by a raven, both residents of the Castle.

I reach the Kimmeridge Road and cross to the wooden bridge and lean over to watch a pied wagtail on the rocks by West Mill, catching insects hovering over the water.

I turn left and take the bridleway towards Church Knowle. I noticed earlier in the year a lot of bee orchids growing here.

I saw a yellow hammer on a fence post and watched it for a while before it flew into the bushes. A bit further on I saw a male Dartford Warbler and a couple of white throat.

I reach the lime kiln and see a couple of walkers sheltering. From their attire I instantly recognise the infamous grockle!

I carried on down to the Church Knowle Road and I saw a dog fox slink into the bushes by Glebe Campsite. I crossed the road and walked into the field containing the Bucknowle Villa.

The rain had stopped by the time I had reached Copper Bridge. I saw a wren by the bridge. I walked through West Halves where a few horses graze.

The car park has quite a few cars here now. I suppose the good weather's brought the visitors out. I turn right at the end of the car park and into the quieter part of the village, but also probably the most picturesque part of the village.

One last gaze up the road and home - until another walk – another day!

Today's weather   Rain turning to fine. Wind moderate N/NE

Name	Lee White		Year of birth	1969
House	7 Webbers Close		Street	West Street

I moved from North Dorset to Hatchards in West Street with my husband 13 years ago today: we'd both been artists most of our lives — the light which is so special in the Purbecks attracts many artists to this area. Hatchards has been a shop for many years and in the early 1900's Mr. & Mrs. Hatchard ran it for boot repairs and sold sweets to the local children — gob stoppers as they were called.

WET DAY, CORFE CASTLE
From a watercolour by © Pamela Russell

I have kept the shop and gallery open for the past twelve years selling gifts together with our paintings, prints and postcards of our work. The shop has been manned by local volunteers and the profits have gone to various charities, the past four years we've supported Holton Lee, a local respite centre for the disabled and their carers.

Hatchard's exterior and interior has been used many times by film companies — the best known film being "The Mayor of Casterbridge".

Since my husband died, I have run art groups in the Purbecks, helping others to enjoy their leisure painting, by giving instruction and also visit a number of established art clubs in the area helping them develop their talents. Doing this helps me, as I now find without my husband, being an artist all the time and working alone far too solitary.

The weather is beautiful today — my friend and I took our dogs down to Winspit — the fields were covered with clover and the smell was quite intoxicating. We admired the beauty of the sea breaking against the cliff rocks with the spraying foam hit by the sunlight forming into little sparkles of light. We sat for ages mesmerised before heading back to Worth Matravers and a café lunch at the Barn Café. How lucky we are to be surrounded by the sea!

VIEW FROM THE ARTIST'S STUDIO, CORFE CASTLE
From a watercolour by © Pamela Russell

I did a short spell looking after the shop and in the evening had supper with friends and watched the tennis from Wimbledon on TV.

Today's weather   Beautiful!

Name	Pamela Russell	Year of birth	1934
House	Hatchards	Street	West Street

the Castle and the Square
from a linocut by Derek Matthews

Early today, Sunday papers were being collected by residents and visitors, as well as real bread, hot from the oven of the Village Bakery (not "bread", so-called, from supermarket shelves). Perhaps we should be thankful that there is also in Corfe one grocer. Earlier in the previous century there were four grocers: Cleall, Cooper, Driscoll, and Whoadden, all able to make a living for themselves. Today, only Cleall is left, as well as Don Palfrey, a first class butcher selling many local products. His predecessor had the slaughterhouse, now closed.

There used to be two bakers; now Nigel Dragon is the only one. One of his predecessors, Battrick, baked from wood fired ovens in the old mill near the mill-pond, burning faggots gathered from the many coppices in the district. The other baker was Hibbs in West Street. Battrick's firewood was stacked on beams across the Corfe River, outside the bakery. I shall never forget the fragrancy in the air as they burned, before being raked out and the bread put in to bake. That was real bread.

Corfe was once locally self-sufficient in food; corn was grown on top of West Hill, and ground in one of the water mills along the Corfe River; fresh crabs were landed along the coast at Winspit. There were dairy and beef cattle, and every farmer's wife kept chicken free-ranging near the barns, for their brown eggs.

Other essentials were readily available (quarrying needs a separate chapter); lime was burned in the kilns at the foot of West Hill for use of farmers and also local builders expert in the traditional vernacular. There were three blacksmiths, and Ford's Garage, where vehicles could be repaired, and springs mended; Sheasby ran a coach and taxi service; Wilts and Dorset buses had regular schedules; as did the Southern Railway. All this has largely vanished; we have "nodding donkeys" at Wytch oil field and Kimmeridge. Quarrying has changed. A main industry now is tourism.

Today the parking bays in the Square were too narrow to accommodate the immaculate Range Rovers and "People carriers" of the visitors arriving from the Megalopolis, becoming country people for the day. Although before the main summer holidays, Corfe village was choked by traffic looking for the West Street car park, which is sited on the wrong side of the village, causing extraneous traffic to negotiate the Square and winding narrow West Street, which cannot absorb the extra traffic.

By 9 o'clock the traffic was streaming in from Wareham, through the village as the main life-line to Swanage. It is even worse on weekdays, when lorries go through to Swanage; however, we can put up with those which keep Dragon's Village Bakery supplied with flour, and the brewery drays for our four pubs.

After more than twenty years no agreement has been reached on the problem of traffic in the village, which needs a relief road to keep out extraneous through traffic, as well as a properly sited car park for visitors. Corfe is being devastated; will such an outrageous situation be repaired before the end of this new century?

This morning, the steam "fun railway" was already in action between Swanage and Corfe. But no longer can we get into a compartment in Waterloo, and alight on Corfe Castle station. Southern Railway used to carry stocks of coal to Corfe Castle goods yard. It also took the full milk churns from the Milk Factory each day. Now there are no dairy cows, and the rural economy hardly exists. Even Wareham Market does not deal in livestock any more. Governments hate rural people because they do not earn enough to pay the stealth taxes, so rural life seems expendable.

On a more cheerful note, by 9.45 could be heard "Plain Bob Doubles", on the newly installed Millennium Bells, being rung by David Langford, Jill Foley, Lyn Higgens, Ken Lees, Betty Crackle, Carole and Brian Dean, and with two visitors, in the Church tower of St Edward The Martyr. There is also a Congregational, and a Methodist Church, and Weslyan Chapels occur in unexpected places.

The bells are reminders that there is something intangibly special about this place, which may be one reason why people come here in droves; and why the residents value it so much. What is it that is so special? We used affectionately to call the tourists "grockles". Those of today on their brief visit have little time to discover the underlying magic.

Today's weather: OVERCAST _ DRY

Name   Derek Howard Matthews   Year of birth

House   92   Street   West Street

Bees…..what? Where? Ouch!

On arriving in Corfe Castle in September 1998, I decided that I would like to try my hand at bee-keeping. I had long been interested in bees and their product – HONEY!

Fortunately, within a few weeks I met East Street beekeeper, Bob Carter, who told me that there was another person interested in taking up bee-keeping in the village, none other than Joe Williams, our local West Street plumber.

As bee keeping is not as easy as it looks, or in Joe' s words 'I thought it was just a matter of turning the tap at the bottom of the hive and filling a jar!', we agreed we would enter this big unknown together.

Under the guidance of Bob Carter and attending meetings of the East Dorset Beekeepers Association we acquired couple of our own colonies.

We have had a laugh or two along the way, with incidents of being chased by our own bees and running the 100 yards in 7.6 seconds to get away, discovering that bees don't like blue vans and that bees trapped in beards get upset, finding out that there is always one bee that won't give up the chase until, 'thwack!', it causes its irritated keeper to commit the unthinkable.

In our first year, 1999, our honey crop amounted to just a few pounds despite hours of work being put in cleaning equipment and looking after them. A pretty poor show, but things can only get better or can they? 2000 was bound to be a better year, after all it is the end of the Millennium.

As it turned out, the winter wasn't kind to us and we lost one or two colonies and the strong hive swarmed in the Spring after a period of poor weather leaving us with a very depleted stock. Fortunately, an Association beekeeper was giving up bee keeping, and I managed to acquire a couple of colonies, one of which, I was told, could be a bit tetchy. The colonies were transferred to a site at Bucknowle Farm late one evening.

Within a day or two, and keen to show off my new bees to Joe, we went to have a look at them to ensure that they were OK. Within seconds of opening up the hive, we were amidst a dark cloud of agitated bees. A few seconds later, we could hardly see through our veils. Unfortunately Joe had failed to put on a second pair of trousers; perhaps I should have warned him that the bees might be a bit highly strung.

The first hit was just above Joe's knee, but being cool Joe took this in his stride and didn't flinch. The second and third hits were inches higher up his legs resulting in a couple of yelps and muttered expletives. The bees, now on the rampage, saw Joe as an easy target and the upward attack continued towards… well, you know where. By this time Joe was getting a little agitated as one sting after another found their mark. I muttered something about finishing our work quickly and getting away, but by this time Joe was jumping up and down before suddenly haring off towards the safety of his van and shouting over his shoulder, 'they're your ****** bees, I'm off'.

A few days later, I received a message to say that farmer Rodney Parker had been stung , and son Ian and their dog had been stung, and the cattle were jumping up and down. Something had to be done quickly! That evening when the bees were quietly in bed, we loaded the hive into Joe's van and took them to a field in the middle of nowhere where they stayed for the rest of the summer.

We have learned a few lessons and had a lot of fun from bee keeping. Ever wondered why Joe now drives a white van?

Douglas Whyte
3 West Street

11TH JULY 2000

MY 54TH BIRTHDAY.

I Awoke at 6:30 and had my breakfast and opened cards and presents from Helen and Vicky.

Took the dogs, Poppy and Bonny, for a short walk let the Guinea pig, Wilbert, out of his hutch and left for work just after 8am.

Arrived in Totton, near Southampton, at 9:20, normally the journey takes about an hour but for some reason there was an awful lot of traffic around today.

Arranged shipments to Poland, Ireland, New Zealand and Canada for a number of my customers, had to speak to my agent in India about one of our shipments that had not been delivered although the vessel arrived 2 week ago. It would appear that the receiver had only paid the duty on the 7th and the shipment is being delivered tomorrow. He will email me if things change.

Had an interesting enquiry to ship a Hovercraft to Kingston, Jamaica, this will take some looking into. We will have to load from the water, must check weight that the ship's derricks can take. The hovercraft weighs approx. 100 tonnes.

A firm in Bristol rang about sending some modified Range Rovers to Saudi Arabia, I understand that they have been lengthened and have 6 wheels, he is sending photos and drawings. 2 may have to go by air and the rest by sea.

Lunchtime bought cakes for colleagues at work, seems a strange tradition.
Left Totton at about 6pm and arrived home at 7pm.

Sam and her fiancé, Mike, arrived with a present and card after I had opened these we all sat down to a birthday dinner that Helen had cooked. At about 10 Sam and Mike left.
I went to bed about 11.

Today's weather: Sunny with Showers

Name STAN LAYTON   Year of birth 1946

House MOONFLEET   Street HIGHER FILBATIK

CORFE CASTLE MILLENNIUM DIARY

WEDNESDAY, 12TH JULY 2000

My name is Sam Brett and I live in Townsend Mead at the Kingston end of Corfe Castle. I am nearly 14 years old and I attend Poole Grammar School. This morning I woke up at 7 am and had breakfast (cereal and toast) with my Mum. My Dad is up in Yorkshire on business, staying at our holiday cottage near Settle in the Dales. He has a couple of clients near there and sometimes goes up for a few days at a time.

Esther, my sister, gets up half an hour later than me because her school is nearer and she doesn't need to be up so early. I left the house at around 7.45 to catch the bus to school (my Dad usually takes me because he works in Bournemouth and it is on his way). The bus journey takes about 45 minutes.

Registration is supposed to start at 8.45 but our form teacher Mrs Mallace-Gouldbourne never arrives until five to nine so my class is always late for assembly! My first lesson was double English (a double lesson lasts one and a quarter hours); our English teacher is called Ms Burgoyne and she is not bad.

Our next lesson was art and my last art lesson ever! I have chosen my options for GCSE and art is one of the subjects I will be dropping. Our teacher is Mr Mouzer, he seems a bit strange and he walks like a fat penguin but he is not a teacher you would like to cross. All we did in that lesson was to watch a video about a "psycho" painter who was drawing people with mashed faces. I was glad when it was 11.40, time for break.

I went back up to the classroom and ate most of my packed lunch before the bell went again at 12 noon for the start of Chemistry. Dr Smith started "having a go" at one of the class in her Birmingham accent. I found it difficult to concentrate throughout the lesson, even though I usually quite enjoy science subjects.

Our lunch break started at 1.15 and I went out to play football on the field with the rest of my class. We all came back in at 2.15 and after registration we headed off to maths on the floor below our form room. Our Welsh maths teacher Dr Noble took us into the computer room and we worked out how to plot quadratics on a program called Omnigraph. At the end of the lesson I went down to catch the bus and arrived at home at 4.30.

I ate an early dinner and then went out again to play cricket for Wareham Cricket Club. I made fourteen off the bat, but I didn't bowl very well and in the end we lost by thirty runs to Bere Regis. I came home and had some supper before going off to bed. School again tomorrow, I can't wait for the holidays, only another 9 days to go!

Today's weather:

Cloudy with sunny intervals

Name   SAMUEL BRETT   Year of birth   1986

House   THE DREY   Street   TOWNSEND MEAD

我做梦也没有想到会嫁到英国的一个小镇.

我是一九九六年夏天在中国成都遇到我先生的.

中国有一句古语说得好"千里姻缘一线牵".

一九九九年十一月六日我穿上了白色嫁衣做了这

个小镇的第一位中国新娘. 并在这个传统的

小镇上住了三个月.

小镇山青水秀. 异常清新、并以古老残缺的

古堡闻名. 晴朗的夏日每天总是吸引来不少游

客. 当地人悠闲地带着自己的狗去后山散步. 人

们生活在平静有如世外桃源的环境里. 与我在

中国忙碌的生活形成鲜明的对比. 这美好的

记忆将会永远印在我的脑海中……

I'd never truly imagined that one day I would marry into a family living in the village of Corfe Castle. I first met my husband-to-be in the city of Chengdu during the summer of 1996 and on Saturday November 6th 1999 became Corfe's first Chinese Bride!

This beautiful village attracts plenty of holidaymakers all year round. Locals regularly walk their dogs on the Common and in the surrounding countryside. Life is peaceful and relaxed - in direct contrast to my busy and hectic lifestyle in China.... These are just some of the memories of Corfe which I will always cherish!

Anna Hui Dru Drury

The Transmission Tower Run!

<< Fast pace down through St Edwards Close, leaving the Castle Inn to my right. A light is on in the Rectory and I slide on the wet and waterlogged pitch. The hoot of the steam train as I cross the bridge (the wooden gate needs fixing!). No deer in the fields and Sandy Lane is silent but there are several walkers descending the path enroute for the village.

Hard slog up to the Tower where the view of the Purbeck Hills and Tynham always impresses. Over the gate and down the chalky cutting to the Lane once again. It is muddy and treacherous underfoot but regain a good pace on the road. Final dash along the edge of the fields above Sandy Lane, over the stile and finally view the lights of the village hall. I line them up with the bottom of the field and push on for the railway line. No train so head straight over the tracks and up to the main road. The last 100 metres are tough but a final turn down the drive and I'm home..... >>

Time: 14:00 minutes

Elevation: 100 M

Weather: Wet, Cloudy, NW 4-5

Today's weather:

Guy Dru Drury

Name

Year of birth 1966

House Staying at Herons

Street East Street

We both were born and brought up in this part of Dorset and returned here in April 1999, having lived in the Portsmouth area for almost thirty years. We met people by walking down across the Halves every day to buy a newspaper at The Sweet Shop in the Square, and we have kept the habit going. It is unusual not to meet someone to talk to on the way and the trip, which can take as little as twenty-five minutes, might take an hour or more. Today we met Joan Marshallsay in West Street. She told us about her flourishing garden, growing mostly in gro-bags and buckets, and her mini-bus holiday coming up in a few weeks time. On the walk back we talked to another lady whom we had not met before. We left her at the track beside Robin and Anne Swaine's house, where we turn off to rejoin East Street. We saw our milkman, Dennis, collecting money on his second round of the day. We wonder how long we will continue to get milk delivered to our door.

At this time of year there are often school groups walking around the village, armed with clip boards and questionnaires. Sometimes we are asked to answer questions for their geography projects. The questions, and our answers, are usually the same - "How long have you lived here?" (somehow they can distinguish residents from visitors, we are not sure how) - "Where do you do your shopping?" ("We buy all our bread in Dragon's Bakery - our favourites are a wholemeal sandwich loaf for breakfast toast and a Marathon at the weekend. We go to Dorchester every fortnight") - "What is the biggest advantage of living in Corfe?" ("It is just a wonderful place to live") - and "What is the main disadvantage of living here?" ("There aren't any disadvantages for us").

We particularly like the variety of footpaths that stretch away from the village in all directions. Although East Hill might be busy on summer days we can walk on West Hill for an hour and meet fewer than a dozen people, even in mid-summer. Our favourite stroll starts at the Common behind Halves Cottages and goes up to Monkey Hill, with its view of the valley. We turn west along the ridge and cross the road leading to Blashenwell Farm, on to Copper Bridge and round towards West Street car park. We take the wooden footbridge over Corfe River and continue up to the Church Knowle road, then head across the field to the green track up to West Hill. Although we are the only people on that part of the hill there are often signs of recent visitors - children's names marked out on the slope with white chalk stones. Finally we scramble down the steep slope to the bridge by the old West Mill and along Ollie Vye's Lane back to the Square.

Today's weather: Early shower - cloudy morning - bright later. Very breezy.

Name	Brian and Carole Dean	Year of birth	1945/46
House	2 The Dollings; East Street	Street	

This is the last day before my 80th birthday.

My family of four have arrived and most of the day has been spent in preparation for a buffet supper for family and friends this evening.

The fine dry evening was a bonus enabling us to spill out into the garden.

A very happy occasion.

Today's weather: Warm and sunny

Name	Betty W. Rowles		Year of birth	1920
House	Falconwood		Street	Townsend Road

Sunday July 16th

TWENTY-ONE AGAIN!

I woke up to the sun streaming through the window this morning, which was lovely, as the weather has been awful lately.

Then I remembered - 31 Today - the years are flying by far too quickly for my liking! 'Halfway to 62'.

I soon cheered up when I heard the rustle of wrapping paper & my husband Pat handed me a lovingly wrapped gift, a really nice watch. My cats - Willow, Barley, Asha & Bramble gave me a cup with "only my cats understand me" written on it. They wrapped it very well! I had many other gifts and money from my family, in-laws and friends and lots of cards and flowers, and lots of visitors! I've had a lazy day today - lovely! Pat & I went ten-pin bowling in the afternoon & then we went on to 'The City Bay View' chinese restaurant on Poole Marina. Had a great meal - totally pigged out!

Another year gone, another year older. I've had a lovely day. Many thanks to my husband & cats, all my family & friends.
I love you all dearly x

Today's weather:

Name CORRINNE JAYNE CATTLE   Year of birth 1969

House No 6   Street EAST ST

As on most mornings I woke at about 7.30 and Patricia my wife made a cup of coffee and toast for our breakfast while we watched the BBC news on the television.

As usual I drove Patricia to work in Swanage. We left home at about 8.30 and we took the main road to Swanage which was very quiet and we only passed one tractor en route!!

Patricia works for Browns opticians and today she was working as a receptionist for one optician and one dispensing optician. They were fully booked which means 13 patients per day, and she was kept fairly busy booking in clients and processing the orders for lenses. The majority of the patients are over 60 and are entitled to a free sight test,. Private patients are charged £18.50 for a sight test. At lunch time she bought a sandwich (£1.20) and sat on the beach to sunbathe for an hour before returning to work The price for Single Vision lenses at this time is about £48, Bi-focals £88 and Varifocal lenses £150. Frames start at £29.50. The most expensive are the Flexon (bendy)frames which are about £150. It takes from 3 days to 2 weeks to process the specs depending on the prescription and type of lens.

I had a busy day getting quotations from various suppliers for the Xmas Festivities Committee which I joined last year. The committee want to upgrade the lights in the village and square for the Xmas and New Year period and I have got involved helping on the technical implementation. The rest of the day I spent building retaining walls for the flower borders in the garden. This needed to be done following the building of a natural stone wall to enclose the garden. (known locally as the 'The Great Wall of China')

At 5.30 I collected Patricia from work and returned home for a BBQ meal in the garden. On the way home we filled the car with diesel (£32.50). A tank of diesel normally lasts about 2 weeks doing local journeys.

In the evening our daughter Melissa (21) who is studying for a teaching degree at Chichester, telephoned from Ascot where she has a holiday job at Ascot Racecourse (£8 per hour!!) She needs to earn some money to pay off her overdraft!

Our son Jonathan (24) also phoned from work (Scott Arms at Kingston) where he works as a chef

About 9 pm. We walked to our local pub, The Fox Inn, for a few drinks!!!! Annette and Graham were running the bar and quite a few of our friends were there. We intended to have a quick drink but stayed till closing time

Today's weather: A lovely sunny summers day

Name Roger White

Year of birth 1944

House Wayside Cottage

Street 46 West Street

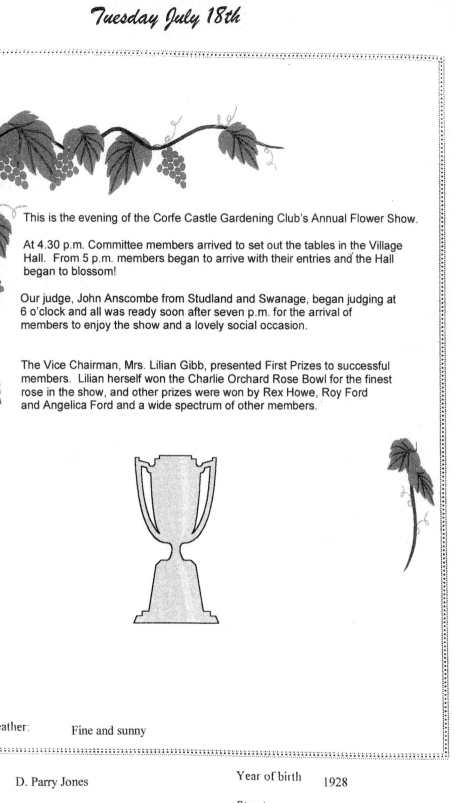

This is the evening of the Corfe Castle Gardening Club's Annual Flower Show.

At 4.30 p.m. Committee members arrived to set out the tables in the Village Hall. From 5 p.m. members began to arrive with their entries and the Hall began to blossom!

Our judge, John Anscombe from Studland and Swanage, began judging at 6 o'clock and all was ready soon after seven p.m. for the arrival of members to enjoy the show and a lovely social occasion.

The Vice Chairman, Mrs. Lilian Gibb, presented First Prizes to successful members. Lilian herself won the Charlie Orchard Rose Bowl for the finest rose in the show, and other prizes were won by Rex Howe, Roy Ford and Angelica Ford and a wide spectrum of other members.

Today's weather: Fine and sunny

Name D. Parry Jones Year of birth 1928

House Corfe Castle Village Hall Street

Today we are starting our summer holiday — one week cruising on the rivers Rhine and Mosel in Germany, which will be our first cruise.

We are also travelling by Eurostar train through the Channel Tunnel — another first for my husband and I.

We left Corfe Castle at 6 a.m., the sun was just coming up so I think it will be a sunny day in Corfe.

We were at Wareham Station in time to catch the 6.35 a.m. to Waterloo. After a comfortable journey we arrived at about 9 a.m. but our next transport (Eurostar) was not due to leave until 10.30 a.m. Time for a welcome coffee and sandwich (no time for breakfast).

We boarded our train to Brussels, found our seats and settled back to enjoy our first experience, which was a bit of a let down really, just 20 minutes in the tunnel and then surfacing to a sunny day in France.

After arriving in Brussels we had a three hour coach journey to Cologne. We arrived at our cruise boat at about 6 o'clock. The cabins were a bit small but we were hoping to spend little time in them!

We were early to bed after a long , tiring journey and thinking of our next few days cruising.

Today's weather: Sunny when we left Corfe

Name   Winifred Whitby   Year of birth   1923

House   19   Street   Colletts Close

The Millennium Flower Festival

Held in St Edwards church 20th to 24th July.

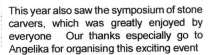

The Flower Festival and Robing Room Refreshments, this year raised £3,593.75 towards the church running expenses This could not have been achieved without the hard work of arrangers, husbands, stewards, the scone maker, cake makers, robing room helpers and the assistance of Jan & Tina at the Box of Delights. Carole and all at Clealls and Ian at the Post Office.

Diana, Betty, Lynn and Chris

This year also saw the symposium of stone carvers, which was greatly enjoyed by everyone   Our thanks especially go to Angelika for organising this exciting event

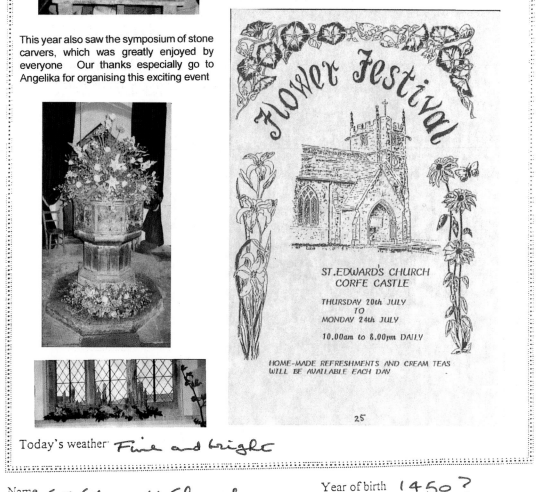

Flower Festival

ST. EDWARD'S CHURCH
CORFE CASTLE

THURSDAY 20th JULY
TO
MONDAY 24th JULY

10.00am to 8.00pm DAILY

HOME-MADE REFRESHMENTS AND CREAM TEAS
WILL BE AVAILABLE EACH DAY

25

Today's weather: *Fine and bright*

Name St Edwards Church   Year of birth 1450 ?

House The Square   Street

Friday July 21st

Today I woke up at my friend Catherine's house in Blandford. Mum came to fetch me on her way back from London. We got home in time for lunch, which was a jacket potato and baked beans. As it was a lovely sunny day I went outside and played with my bunny. Her name is Sugar and she is mostly white with a little brown. She is so, so, so fluffy, especially on the bottom of her back feet. She is two months old and I got her for a birthday present. My birthday is in February but I had to wait until she was born in May. She was born at my school, The Yarrells in Upton, because one of our teachers breeds rabbits at school. When you are in year six you are allowed to look after the rabbits. Then you are called a 'Rabbit Monitor'. There are seven rabbits to look after, three males and four females. They are all mini-lops like Sugar. When my Mum was little and she lived in Corfe, she went to The Yarrells, but in those days it was called St. Monica's, and it had no rabbits and no boys.

Later this afternoon I am going to go to the last ballet class of the term in Swanage. My teacher is called Mrs. Ranger who is very nice but strict, and I am doing Grade 4. There are about fourteen girls in my class including Julia Spooner who is my friend and lives in Corfe. All the Mums are coming to watch us dance because it's the end of term.

Later tonight our cousins are coming round for a BBQ in our garden, before they catch the ferry to France. By the end of today I shall be ready to curl up and go to sleep like my hamster.

Today's weather: Hot and sunny.

Name: Annabel Bond

Year of birth: 1990

House: Whiteway Farm

Street:

Today I've been thinking about my mother (Annie Wills, nee Paine, always known as "Nancy"), as she died exactly ten years ago on 22nd July 1990, aged 86. All who met her knew she was remarkable: competent at all she did - running a home on a very small budget, with skills in all the domestic arts; green-fingered gardening; exquisitely fine embroidery; leatherwork; making Dorset buttons; reading in authentic Dorset dialect; taking a lead in the various organisations she belonged to, e.g. the Methodist Church, the W.E.A., the W.I. and particularly the Parish Council.

She was the first woman on Corfe Castle P.C., and regaled us with the goings-on after Meetings, when the men deliberately left no space for her on the old benches (before the fine chairs used now), but she worked hard on the various committees, including the Corfe Castle Charities, God's Acre, School Governors, etc. She was involved in numbering the houses in the parish when this was made compulsory, and in planning new street lighting, but the task she set herself - her "manifesto pledge" - was to get Corfe put on Mains Drainage, and she was so proud when this was achieved!

She had a clear memory of the village from her childhood before the First World War. NOW I wish I had written down all the anecdotes about family and neighbours. As I walk around Corfe I remember some of the tales she told over the years.

Along West Street I hear her telling of collecting the house-cows from various cottages before going to school in the morning, and taking them up to the Common for the day, then fetching them in the afternoon - each cow knowing and walking through her own front doorway - the low, wide doors and passages through the cottages led to the gardens and cowsheds at the back of each place; of the local wives taking meat in their own dishes to be roasted in the ovens at Hibbs's Bakehouse - my mother's mother had been a Hibbs, and Uncle Tom Hibbs was the baker until he sold out to his brother Albert (father of Jack & Harry). As I walk in Middle Halves I remember being told that Albert paid Tom for the business in gold sovereigns, which Tom pursuaded his workmen to push on a small-wheeled hand-cart in the mud up through Middle Halves in the dark to his house (now Halves House, East Street).

I walk through The Square - and Mum tells of mischievously tipping over the buckets of water laboriously hand-pumped by the old women from the pump by the Cross and laboriously carried, two buckets at a time, using a yoke across the shoulders. The luckier villagers had their own wells or pumps in the yard, but most had to collect every drop from the public pumps; and she tells me of the annual Fair in The Square before the Great War, and Rosie Day making toffee and stretching it over the old rusty nail on the wall by the (present) Post Office; and the first Moving Pictures, showing a man climbing the wall outside a pretty lady's bedroom, - and at this point Mum (aged about 6) being shooed out of the canvas fairground booth alongside the Greyhound. As I walk my dog down Ollie Vye's Lane, I remember being told of the way the fairground showmen's horses were "stabled" under the Castle Bridge and washed and watered in the river close by. Looking at the railings round the Castle, she tells me of her forebears tearing the newly-installed rails down each night until the Bankes of the day agreed to allow the villagers their centuries-old rights to roam freely among the ruins. And of a schoolboy in her childhood who regularly climbed to the top of the Keep and retrieved bits of lead shot from the stonework - I still have a piece of it which she was given! As I walk up Challow Lane I hear her tales of the little children taking their "nammet's" in the school lunch hour up on Challow Hill and running back to school when the bell was rung. And so many more tales!!

Mother's father Joseph Paine was a coal-merchant before WWI, but in 1918 he took the tenancy of Bucknowle Farm. Mum was the 3rd girl (the only boy came after her), and she was the cleverest in the family, gaining a Scholarship to Parkstone Grammar School at 14.

As I see the new Room at the Congregational Chapel I can hear Mum telling how she would walk from Bucknowle in time to get her Granny up & dressed for the day - the old lady lived in the one-roomed dwelling which used to stand on that site - and then catch the train for Parkstone, returning after school to make sure her gran was all right, before walking back home, to do homework as well as farm and household chores.

She gained another scholarship to Poole Art School at 16, but was forced to forget formal further education, being sent into "service", first at Manor Farm, East Stoke, then in Dorchester. After that, she returned to Bucknowle to help her parents, before getting married. In the traditional way she then devoted all her talents to the local and domestic sphere.

Her life almost spanned the 20th Century - born 1904 died 1990 - and was fairly typical of a village girl/woman of her age: a child living in a close community of family and neighbours; attending the village school; gaining limited access to secondary education; going into domestic service before marriage; an adult continuing her education in the "school of life". If she had been born 50 years later she would have gone on to university and a career - maybe in politics- but ~~she~~ within her own sphere she demonstrated the drive of many unsung women of the 20th Century to break the monopoly of men in running local and national affairs, and in her own small way she achieved quite a bit!

Today's weather: CLOUDY START, BUT THEN A LOVELY HOT, SUNNY DAY.

Name (HELEN) MARY WILLS   Year of birth 1938

House 56A   Street East Street

As the Church Flower Festival was in progress, I went down to see the arrangements. It was lovely.

After lunch I decided to go for a walk on the Common: 53 years ago, just after the War, when we came to live in Corfe, Corfe Common was not so overgrown. I started on our side, known as Brickyard Common because of the pockets of clay by the stream on the south side which was used to make bricks and land drains. It is now overgrown with Reedmace (bulrush) and other water plants.

There was an ancient grey poplar which has now fallen down. Dwarf willow was in seed, and Chamomile was just starting to flower, later there will be a pink mass of Saw-wort and the blue of Devil's-bit Scabious.

At the pond on the side of the Common next to the road to Swanage were pink Bog Pimpernel, Cross-leaved Heath and various St. John's Worts including the remains of Marsh St. John's Wort. The Lousewort which covers the drier parts of the Common has gone over, but the Marsh Lousewort was flowering. The Pond still has the invasive Crassula Helmsii (from New Zealand) and rampant Parrot's Feather. Plenty of Lesser Water Plantain was growing nearby. Also near the Pond there appeared to be dozens of Marbled White butterflies, Skippers and Wall butterflies, also a Yellowhammer was singing nearby.

Over the Kingston Road on the other part of West Common there were numerous Sedges and Rushes by the Corfe River, also remains of Bogbean and Yellow Iris. Thistles included Dwarf Thistle and earlier, Meadow Thistle. On the drier parts were some Harebells, Knapweed and yellow Cat's-ear. There are even patches of Bell Heather on the top of the hill towards the barrows.

The National Trust had cut the Bracken, Brambles and Gorse recently so there was little sign of Ragwort but masses of Fleabane in the damper spots.

Today's weather: Fine

Name Joan Bowyer   Year of birth 1919

House Peake House   Street Valley Rd.

CORFE CASTLE STONE CARVING SYMPOSIUM 2000

Wednesday 19th of July - Wednesday 26th of July
VENUE: St. Edward's Churchyard, in the centre of the village

Participating Artists: Carlotta Barrow, Swanage
Tony Birks-Hay, Yeovil
Christopher Burke, Swanage
Michael Grevatte, Glastonbury
Paul Davis, Corfe Castle
Jean Hartley, Studland

Warren Molloy, Wareham
Angelika Seik, Corfe Castle
Jonathan Sells, Corfe Castle
Jigger Stockley, Worth Matravers
Mary Spencer Watson, Dunshay

Sponsored by Local Quarries; H.F. Bonfield & Son, W.J. Haysom & Landers, Keates, Lovell, Suttle.

Today's weather: Dry, warm, sunny Intervals

Name Angelika Seik -Ford

Year of birth 1949

House 8

Street Halves Cottages

We are the residents of Lower Scoles Farm!

Peter Hartle aged 45
Hazel Hartle aged 39
Tim Hartle aged 15
Joe Hartle aged 13 (14 on Sunday)
Ben Hartle aged 12

We make high quality ice cream on the farm with local milk and cream, all natural flavours and no artificial additives. Also we run a herd of 19 ostriches – the residue of a larger herd waiting to go their new homes!

Our day starts with a hectic rush to get the boys off to school catching the bus at the end of our lane. A chicken was stolen by a thieving fox last night so we're all a bit cross this morning.

Peter and I start on ice cream work with me in the office taking orders and generally tending to business. Peter manages the production with Sandy Stockley from Kimmeridge (today they are making 1000 litres of coffee liqueur!) Pete Rowle from Corfe goes off on his deliveries starting from Puddletown, Sherborne, Gillingham, Shaftesbury and Blandford and back to base having manoeuvred through the "grockles" at 5 p.m.

Peter heads off to Sydling St. Nicholas with a pallet of ice cream for the cash and carry (Sandy still beavering away!) and I'm busy getting orders for tomorrow.

<u>Break for food!</u> Dogs, cats, hens, ostriches, fish and of course us!

Fill washing machine, attempt to tidy house in 5 minutes (impossible task and pointless too). Hector, (one of our flatcoats) has found an old, flat dead bunny and is chewing it under my desk!

4p.m. Boys back from last day at school as they have now broken up for the summer holidays.

Embark on tea, more washing and attacking the garden and fall into bed at 11 p.m.

Today's weather.　　Bright and dry

Name　　Hazel Hartle

Year of birth　　1961

House　　Lower Scoles Farm

Street　Kingston (in the Civic Parish
of Corfe Castle

Sidelines - News from the Railway

The Swanage Railway is now operating its full high season timetable for the summer. with two trains running every 35 minutes from 10.30am from both Swanage and Norden. There is also an evening diesel service which leaves Swanage at 19.10, 20.20, 22.00 & 23.00 and Corfe Castle at 19.45, 21.10, 22.30, 23.25. The fare for this is £2 return and so it a good way to visit Swanage for an evening out.

There will be a Fireworks Specials service for the Swanage Carnival weekends when Norden Park & Ride will be open until midnight. There will be no Wessex Belle Dining Trains but there will be an intensive 30 minute diesel shuttle service between Norden and Swanage departing on the hour and half hour. The first train will leave Swanage at 19.00 (Norden 19.30) and the last train from Swanage will be the 23.00 returning from Norden at 23.30. There will be plenty of time to have a meal before the fireworks or a drink afterwards.

Residents of Purbeck can purchase a community card for £5 which entitles them to half price travel on the Swanage Railway for a year. With this the cost of the diesel fare is only £1 return, very good value.

The Wessex Belle Dining Train is operating on both Friday and Saturday evenings throughout the summer. As the evenings are now lighter it is a lovely way to enjoy a sumptuous 5 course meal and watch the Purbeck country side go by. Booking is essential on 01929 425800.

The Railway could always use more volunteers, in the shop, the buffet or on the Wine & Dine train as well as renovating the carriages. Please telephone Swanage Railway on 01929 425800 if you would like more information.

Heather Tainsh

Today's weather:

Name   **From "The Corfe Valley News"**   Year of birth

House   Street

This week we are on holiday in the Loire valley staying near Thouars south of Saumur. Julia is very keen on riding and all things horsey, so I was really pleased to find that we are near the Ecole Nationale d'Equitation. This is a prestigious school for riding and the training of riding instructors, and it's also home to the Cadre Noir, who hold demonstrations of classical French riding techniques and jumping skills. We watched one of their training sessions (the climax is when the horses jump straight up in the air with all four feet off the ground), and visited the stable blocks and tack rooms. Julia especially was delighted with the horses, which are huge and beautifully groomed.

The rain started again and we set off for lunch. One of the pleasures of our holidays is stumbling on nice unexpected places to eat, and we found a lovely little restaurant in a place called Gennes, which seemed otherwise to be quite unprepossessing, especially in the rain.

Fortified by lunch we set off for the Caves of Gratien Meyer for a tour, and to buy some wine to bring home. The children were fascinated by the way the caves were cut deep into the cliff side. One of the men encouraged them to try their hand at 'turning' the bottles in the sediment racks, and they found out how hard that is to do! By the time we emerged the rain had stopped and the sun had come out. When we got back Nick was changed and out in the pool in seconds, closely followed by his sister. Not me - even at their age I would never have got into such cold water!

Today's weather

Name KAREN SPOONER   Year of birth 19 — 4 — 1954

House MEADOWSIDE   Street 129 EAST STREET

Friday July 28th

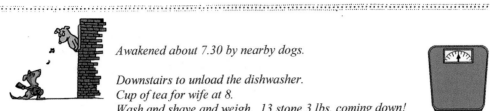

Awakened about 7.30 by nearby dogs.

Downstairs to unload the dishwasher.
Cup of tea for wife at 8.
Wash and shave and weigh. 13 stone 3 lbs, coming down!

Breakfast 08.30. ½ grapefruit, one slice of toast and tea (no sugar – voluntary diet)

Wait for morning post. Literature requested from Zeneca on genetic engineering delivered.

Next into garden to see if fine crop of apricots had been attacked by pests. Probably pick weekend and freeze. Transplanted 3 tomato plants. Plant number of blackcurrant cuttings. Watered needy plants. Wife out shopping in Swanage.

Lunch 13.30. Sausage rolls, salad and Edam cheese. Tea and fruit. Attempted crossword. Started to read material for my MSc degree, which has to be finished by September 30th.

Mended vacuum cleaner which smelt of burning. Cause not established. Now the cordless/mobile phone kaput for the 2nd time, still in guarantee. Will take it back to Argos in Dorchester for replacement.

Cut marrow from garden. Prepared it with cabbage, garlic and onion for dinner. Not enough water in pressure cooker – horrid mess in bottom of it. Potatoes not ruined – any longer and they would have been. Tropical fruit (tinned) for dessert!

Cleaned it all up, loaded dishwasher. Will run off peak electricity tonight/early morning.

Checked e-mail for news of my son in Wellington, New Zealand. No news.

20.00 hours. Writing this up. Will pursue MSc. work until 23.00 hours, then watched news. Decaff coffee.

23.30 hours bed. A tiring exasperating day.

Today's weather: Warm (70°F), cloudy and clear. Wind SW. Slight shower mid-day

Name	Mr. A. J. Ide	Year of birth	1925
House	8	Street	Colletts Close

During the year St Edward's Church staged a review of 2000 years of Christianity as seen at the end of the 20th Century: here is what many people missed - "Thy Kingdom Come"

In this year of celebration there are parties, balls, 'the eye and the dome' but little focus on Christianity. As part of our millennium celebration we give this presentation in thanksgiving for the many who have followed in the light of Christ.

It is a presentation with a difference, informal in style, some lines learnt - others not, scripts visible and properties to an absolute minimum.

With thanks to all taking part and our production team who have given so much care and time.

Maurice Strike

The Company

Mary Rose Bray	and with the children
Betty Carter	Hayley Aylward
Roger Free	Geoffrey Dragon
Ann Gaudin	Jamie Ford
Judith Jenkins	Ellie Ford
Eileen Van Lelyveld	Jade Hedges
Pamela Russell	Emily Nelson
Peter Smith	Alexandra Salt-Jenkins
Michael Spinney	Cherry Smith
Judy Spinney	Holly Smith
Maurice Strike	Eleanor Wallace
Nancy Strike	
Joanna Watson	
Matthew Watson	
Mary Wills	

The Programme

Martin of Tours (316-397)
A Roman soldier who took pity on a beggar and became a Christian
Columba (521-597)
Left Ireland to found a monastery on Iona
Aiden (d. 561)
Was sent to Northumberland to convert the Vikings
Cuthbert *(d. 687)*
After a life as a missionary, Cuthbert was able to retire to Farne Island, near Lindisfarne
Bede (673-735)
A great writer and teacher who lived all his life at the monastery at Jarrow
Hildegard (1098-1179)
A poet, musician and missionary
Francis of Assisi (1182-1226).
Who was very conscious of the balance between God, man and the natural world
Julian of Norwich (1342-circa 1413)
A calm and stable influence during the turbulent time in England
Cranmer (1489-1556)
Archbishop of Canterbury who was caught between Tudor politics and Christian reform
Herbert (1593-1633)
A priest, a poet and a musician
The Wesleys: John (1703-1791)
Founder of the Methodist movement
Charles (1707-1783) *'The most gifted and indefatigable hymn-writer England has ever known'*

Elizabeth Fry (1780-1845)
Quaker prison reformer
William Wilberforce (1759-1833)
Philanthropist and advocate of the abolition of the slave trade
Shaftesbury (1801-1885)
Social reformer and factory legislator
Joseph Bamien (1840-1889)
Leper missionary who ministered single-handed to the spiritual and physical needs of 600 lepers
William Booth (1829-1912)
Founder and first General of the Salvation Army
Gladys Aylward (1902-1970)
Missionary in China, with Jeannie Lawson she founded the Inn of the Sixth Happiness in an outpost at Yangcheng
Cecil Pugh (d. 1941)
Squadron Leader and Padre who gave his life for his men
Dietrich Bonhoeffer (1906-1945) *Lutheran Pastor who denounced Nazi ideology Executed*
Martin Luther King (1929-1968)
Baptist minister and champion of civil rights in the USA. Assassinated
Janani Luwum (1922-1977)
Archbishop of Uganda, who was murdered because he stood up to President Amin

Today's weather:
SUN & HEAVY SHOWERS --- (FOR APRIL 13, 14, 15 MOSTLY COLD & WET)

Name VENUE - THE PARISH CHURCH OF
ST EDWARD KING AND MARTYR
House CORFE CASTLE

Year of birth PERFORMANCES: 8P
THURSDAY 13 APRIL
Street FRIDAY 14 APRIL
SATURDAY 15 APRIL

A lovely summer's day and the friends and relatives that came to lunch were able to eat and sit in the garden, after which several of us walked to Swyre Head. We took a car as far as Kingston, but when I was a child we had to walk all the way, and a visit to Swyre Head was one of our regular days out during the summer holidays.

I was born 73 years ago today, in the cottage next door to where I live now at 160 East Street. My parents moved into 158 East Street (then numbered 92 East Street) in 1923, at a rent of 2s. 5½d a week, and lived there for the 55 years of their married life. My husband and I moved into 160 East Street in 1952; our weekly rent at the time was 8s. 0d. a week, and we have lived here now for nearly 50 years. The two cottages belonged to the Bankes Estate.

The history of the cottage where I was born has always interested me. Originally there was a small dwelling on the site, illustrated below by Mr. I Gumbrell, whose precise drawing shows the east side of the building, which is the side facing the present A351 road. The dwelling had one room downstairs, in which an open fireplace occupied 7ft. of space on the N. side, and one room upstairs. On the S. side there was a lean-to of some kind. Many cottages in the village were built with stone from the slighted castle, but the Royal Commission on Historical Monuments say this dwelling was built in the late 16th. cent., so it predates the Civil War. It would also appear to be something other than a labourer's cottage because the west wall has a chamfered stone doorway with a two-centred head, alongside which is an opening which the RCHM describe as a blocked loop-light, but which an old stone-mason in my childhood days called a 'leper's squint'. The building was well away from the centre of the village and I have always wondered if it was in fact a lazar-house — the village isolation hospital where the poor victims could be segregated from the rest of the community.

The RCHM say that the west wall is the only visible work from the 16th. cent, but when carrying out alterations we uncovered the original south wall with the doorway through to the lean-to, and the present owners have uncovered the large open fireplace. When I was a child this had been partially enclosed and my parents had a kitchen range standing in the space. My father used to sweep the chimney by attaching a gorse bush to the garden broom and then climbing up inside as far as possible with it.

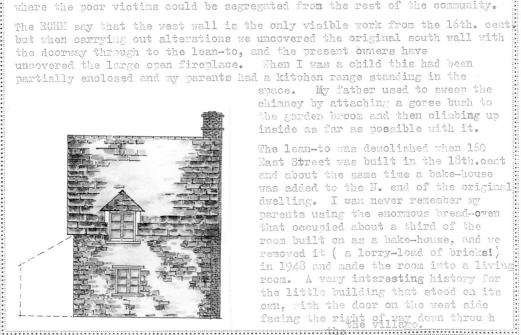

The lean-to was demolished when 160 East Street was built in the 18th.cent and about the same time a bake-house was added to the N. end of the original dwelling. I can never remember my parents using the enormous bread-oven that occupied about a third of the room built on as a bake-house, and we removed it (a lorry-load of bricks!) in 1948 and made the room into a living room. A very interesting history for the little building that stood on its own, with the door on the west side facing the right of way down through the village.

Name Brenda M Chappell   Year of birth 1927

House 160   Street East Street.

My walk started at Copper Bridge. I walked up past Common Well. saw a male bullfinch fly by into the hedgerow. I looked towards Bucknowle and noticed a pair of spotted flycatchers using a dead alder as a perch.

My grandfather would bring my mother and her sister here to cut rushes to use as thatching material for his hayrick.

I walked along the hedgerow towards West Common gate, noticing on the way a flock of blue tits, great tits and chaffinch mobbing a male tawny owl sat in the oak tree in the hedge. I noticed a lot of selfheal and harebell in the grass as I reached the West Street gate.

I turned to the right and went down the hill on the road. As I neared the pond I saw a flock of long-tailed tit come from the blackthorn on the left and go into the hawthorn on the right of the road.

The pond has a little water but not a lot.

I walked up the hill a bit and turned off to the right and headed towards the marsh. I went past a pair of yellow hammer on the gorse to the right of the track.

When I got to the marsh I saw a female roe deer and a fawn feeding in the marsh. She saw me and took flight towards Great Knowles.

I saw a heron lazily fly over the marsh and head for Frog Hole, I noticed a female sparrow-hawk weaving in and out the trees on the edge of the marsh.

I walked across the road and up to the sand-pit, listening to the skylarks singing all the way to the top. I stopped for a moment and looked at the castle - one of the best views in Corfe. I came up here last year and watched the eclipse. As I stood for a while I saw a male wheatear, a few meadow pipit and a skylark around the mound I was stood on.

I walked along the top of the common heading for Kingston Road. Most Septembers at dusk if you come here you will hear the strange chirring call of a nightjar. If you are lucky you may even see one. This is also a good stargazing spot.

I saw a buzzard over Lynch and a few more skylark.

I came down to Widdicombe Bottom - the black-berries are getting red now. There was a dartford warbler and a whitethroat in the gorse.

I walked back to West Street Common gate noticing a male kestrel heading for Speckle Bird.

As I reached the gate I turned for one last look and wondered what the small-holders that made a living off this land in times gone by would make of it now or the village of Corfe Castle for that matter.

Today's weather: FOG FIRST THING - HOT LATER

Name CHRIS WHITE   Year of birth 1969

House 7 WEBBERS CLOSE   Street WEST

Tuesday August 1st

7 a.m. Radio comes on – news headlines on Radio 4. People being urged to boycott petrol pumps because of price – 82.9p per litre! 70% of which is tax. Milk 74p a litre and bottled water 80p per litre. How daft can this world get. Farmers get 14p a litre for milk.

7.30 get up. Make cup of tea. Take one up to Peggy. Get dressed. Go to fishing lake to collect fishing fees. Nice shower of rain last night. No rain for over a week so it freshened things up a lot. Only three people fishing for £5 per rod per day.

8.30 Breakfast. Cornflakes, two cups of tea. Feed goldfish in garden pond.

9.30 Go to garage. £20 worth of petrol. Check tyre pressure.

Odd jobs most of morning.

1.00 Lunch. Cold beef and salad. Melon for sweet.

2.30 Olive miller's funeral. Peg, Jean King and Mrs. Welsh in car. Lovely old lady. Never complained!

Told Wareham by-pass blocked with smoke. Took dog for a walk at Scotland Heath. Could not see anything.

Supper – bread and cheese and lettuce.

Nothing on TV

Bed 10.30

Today's weather: Hot - 25°C (80°F)

Name	Tom Hunt	Year of birth	1922
House	Castle Cottage	Street	71 East Street

Today we received some lovely photographs of the splendid event, held just a month ago: The Millennium Ball, July 1st.

That super sunny, summer weekend, Valerie, my wife, and I stayed in our cottage in Corfe Castle, which is popularly rented to holiday guests. This time we felt quite privileged to enjoy the facilities with good friends from Norfolk, Pat and Philip Bray.

Since 1975 Valerie and I have worked in Dubai in the United Arab Emirates, with our home base in Berkshire. However, since 1995 we seem to have adopted Dorset (or vice versa!) with property in Lulworth Cove and here in Corfe Castle. Friends, Eileen and Lucas (Van Lelyveld) of "The Old Forge",

FARRIERS LODGE

38 East Street, persuasively encouraged me to purchase Farriers Lodge, No.36 which was in much need of attention. The cottage was fully restored and refurbished in 1997/8 by Cyril Witherington and family (H.A. Stockley Builders). The first holiday guests were welcomed on Saturday 1st August 1998. Now two years later we can see why they all enjoy their holidays in Corfe Castle so much.

We were delighted to be associated with the Millennium Ball by being able to donate the Fortnum and Mason hamper as the prize for the free draw for the holder of the lucky ticket number.

Oh, yes, and here's to the success of this "Diary 2000". A great idea.

Valerie Chalmers and Stephen Dru Drury, Chairman of the Millennium Association, congratulating the winner of the hamper, Sarah Jarvis

Today's weather: Cooler with storms (hopefully only a temporary break in the brief late summer)

Name	Valerie and Sam Chalmers	Year of birth	1943
House	Farriers Lodge	Street	36 East Street

THE CORFE CASTLE W.I. CELEBRATE THE QUEEN MOTHER'S 100TH BIRTHDAY.

IN 1572 THE FIRST QUEEN ELIZABETH SOLD THE CASTLE AT CORFE TO SIR CHRISTOPHER HATTON. FOUR HUNDRED AND TWENTY EIGHT YEARS LATER, UNDER THE SHADOW OF THE CASTLE RUINS, CORFE CASTLE W.I. CELEBRATED THE 100TH BIRTHDAY OF HER MAJESTY ELIZABETH THE QUEEN MOTHER BY INVITING ONE HUNDRED PEOPLE OF THE VILLAGE TO A FREE CREAM TEA IN THE VILLAGE HALL.

THE HALL WAS DECORATED IN RED, WHITE AND BLUE STREAMERS, FLAGS & BALLOONS, WITH A LARGE COLOURED PHOTOGRAPH OF HER MAJESTY AS A CENTREPIECE IN THE HALL ALONGSIDE OF WHICH WAS PLACED A HIGHLY ATTRACTICE FLOWER ARRANGEMENT, OVER ALL OF WHICH WAS A HAND PAINTED BANNER DECLARING 'HAPPY BIRTHDAY'.

PRESIDENT ELIZABETH CRABBE WELCOMED ALL OUR VISITORS AND HOPED THEY WOULD ENJOY THIS TEA ON SUCH A VERY SPECIAL OCCASION.

IT WAS A SPLENDID AFTERNOON THOROUGHLY BEFITTING THE ANNIVERSARY.

oday's weather:

BETTY CARTER.   Year of birth

se   Street

Friday August 4th

I arrived home at 4.20am as the sky was just getting light. I work at the oilfield at Wytch Farm. The plant that processes the crude oil before it is sent to Hamble by pipeline had shut down and I had been waiting for the re-start. I work in the laboratory and was needed to test the quality of the oil and gas.

I awoke and got up from my bed at 10.20am to find that my teenage daughters were typically still asleep.

Today is the Queen Mother's 100th birthday and a peal of bells is being rung in the village but the effect is rather spoilt by the noise of building works from a house in the next road.

I went into the garden to feed my pets and immediately caught the smell of yet another bonfire, a real problem in Corfe where one thoughtless person can pollute the whole village.

After lunch I took my daughter Rebecca to Studland to rehearse for the Summer Show and I then went on to Swanage to do some shopping. I later collected Rebecca and went home to start preparing dinner before my wife Sue, an Environmental Health Officer, returned home from work at 5pm.

My other daughter Jennifer returned at 6.30pm from her summer job at the Model Village and we had dinner.

The rest of the evening was spent preparing to travel to London to celebrate my mother's birthday with the rest of my family.

-oOo-

Today's weather: warm and sunny with occasional dark clouds.

Name   Terry Eady.   DOB 29.06.48
            Shiralea, Higher Gardens
House

Saturday August 5th

Woke quite early after dreaming as to how I was going to beat James Kirkwood and Laurie Malt by after they thrashed me at golf on the on the Dene Course yesterday - some cunning scheme involving club handles and superglue!

It will be our 45th Wedding Anniversary tomorrow, and I am hoping that the flowers that I ordered from Forget-me-not will turn up before too long. We have got the grandchildren coming down next week, so Tescos was hit pretty heavily yesterday, and we have been busy organising beds as there will be nine of us by next weekend.

Went down to get a paper and have a joke with Oil and Julie Dixon in the Sweet Shop, warning them of the impending horde and that they will be cleaned out of sweets by Friday.

Over to the Village Hall Coffee Morning. We took some runner beans over, as we have got a problem here of over-production, the freezer already being full. Quite a number of friends there, and the beans hardly touched the table! Walked back, and were followed up our drive by Woppy, the black stray cat that lives in a shed opposite. Woppy is a friend to all who pass, a cat with a lovely disposition, a model resident of Corfe Castle. However, unlike other residents, he does like to rollover and have his tummy tickled.

The flowers have not arrived yet, and anxiety is setting in -did I give the right date, or the right address? Sat down to have a quick bite of lunch, and relief- the flowers arrived.

Went up to Church Knowle Fete. As it was fine there was a huge crowd and the car park field was very full. A great atmosphere with Wareham Town Band and lots of games and activities for the children. Bought some plants and met and chatted to a number of people from Corfe, including William and Marion Ormerod.

It's all go! We have been invited to our neighbours Ken and Mary Wollaston for a drink and to meet the couple who have just moved into the cottage nearby. Looks as though the evening will stay fine, as we are going for an Anniversary Meal at La Trattoria in Swanage, and I have booked a table on the terrace. Bit worried about parking, as it is the last night of the Regatta, and there are going to be fireworks.

Lucky , just managed to squeeze into a small place opposite, which tested my reversing skills to the utmost. As always, they made us most welcome at the restaurant, and our table was excellent. They were extremely busy, and we had to wait a bit, but as the fireworks were coming soon, it was not a problem. Also, there was a friendly crowd on the terrace, so we had a chat and a really good laugh.

The fireworks started at 9.45 and were truly spectacular and we could not have had a better seat. Everyone in the restaurant had crowded onto the stairs and terrace to watch it all. We have booked our table for next year! All in all a great day.

Today's weather: A lovely fine day

Name	Roger and Doreen Frost	Year of birth	1934
House	Springwood	Street	85 West Street

Who killed Wulfric?

There he lay, face down, a fatal stab wound in his back, on Corfe Common near the end of West Street. Nearly 90 would-be Cadfaels from the year 2000 stood round the 'body' - the central prop for a Mediaeval Murder Mystery Walk set in 988. The Shire Reeve, John Truman, accompanied by the trouvere Johan D'evreux, the Abbess Gunnwold, and Lady Matilda of Queen Aelfthryth's household, opened up an intriguing web of past secrets and possible motives as the throng witnessed the discovery of a bloody knife, a leathern wine bottle, and heathen ritual evidence, whilst following the trail past Copper Bridge to The Rings (alias the Tumuli) and West Mill. Royal indiscretions, tensions between Christianity and older religions, unexpected family links between characters, all kept the multitude absorbed. It all revolved round the murder of King Edward by - probably - his step mother Aelfthryth at Corfe in 978, but could it have been Wulfric who did the deed? Is his recent death a revenge killing? Has he been silenced to protect the real killer?

The complex tale unfolded, revealing many twists and turns, until finally the Shire Reeve called on the modern followers to vote on the identity of the killer. A clear majority accused the diminutive Abbess Gunnwold - she had met Wulfric earlier in the day when she had plied him with drugged wine; she could thus strike the fatal blow without fear of retaliation from the strong young man.

This was a great way to spend a sunny summer afternoon!

'**Double Act!**' presented the Mediaeval Murder Mystery Walk on four Sundays in the summer as part of the Millennium Celebrations in the Village. The plot was devised and written by Peter Smith of Townsend Mead who was also the Shire Reeve. D'evreux was Leigh Skene of Swanage, the Abbess was Judith Jenkins of East Street, and Matilda was Anne Gaudin of Wareham. Linda Peters of Wareham collected the ticket money, Margaret England of East Street was prompter, Martin Smith of Townsend Mead was Stage Manager. Other Double Act Members who came along were Eric and Chris Cannicott, Dawn Newell (Wardrobe mistress, a Home Care Assistant for many Corfe residents), Penny Smith of Townsend Mead, and David Kemp of Colletts Close.

Double Act! is the amalgamation of Purbeck Community Theatre and the Corfe Valley Drama Group, and is based in the Village Hall. See the Diary Date for early December to read about this year's major production of '1066 - And All That'.

Today's weather:

Name	'Double Act!'	Year of birth	PCT 1990, CVDG 1994, DA 1997
House	Corfe Castle Village Hall	Street	East Street

Monday August 7th

I am sitting in my study from where I can see a beautiful photograph of my grandparents, taken about 1900. On the 15 July, I visited my grandparents' cottage, then called "Derrycreveen". Eileen and Lucas van Helyveld kindly showed my sister and I and my husband around the property, which they have sympathetically restored and extended. On entering the front door, the memories of my regular Saturday visits to them started to flood back. I was 16 then and studying at the Poole Commercial College. I recalled my grandad watching for me at the window (he knew which train I would be on from Swanage). "The maid's 'ere" he would say to granny. I always thrilled at his eager welcome. Granny was in her late 70's and very restricted by her advancing arthritis, for which there was little relief. Grandad gave me the shopping list which included a bag of sweets for me. This done, I cooked our lunch on the old coke stove in the front room. Then to granny's needs; foot care, hair wash and sometimes a trim. Once I went too far, kept getting it uneven and she finished up with a short hair cut (it was beyond her shoulders at the start). She didn't complain but said it would probably be better short. In the afternoon, I would take her out onto the Valley Road in her wheelchair, so that she could gaze on the Castle. She loved these outings and always marvelled that I had the strength to push her up the hill. My grandad was a real character; he loved his pint or two! He tried unsuccessfully to fool granny into believing he hadn't called in at "The Fox" on his way home from fetching the morning can of milk from the dairy. "I can smell it on your breath George" she would say.

My granny died in Christmas Close, Wareham aged 89. Grandad died a few months later, of a broken heart it was said, also aged 89.
Gandhi wrote "love is the greatest and humblest strength the world has."

Today's weather: Fine and sunny, not even a breeze

Name MRS. JANE BURT (née (MARY ISA) JANE WILLIAMS Year of birth 1936

House 38 East Street "THE OLD FORGE" REVISED Street

(now living in Kingsdown, Kent)

Tuesday August 8th

Not exactly your typical day, selected some months ago, but it does highlight the kind of busy community and private life that our generation experience here in Corfe Castle.

It began as usual, feeding our young cats, cup of tea to Rosa, my wife, breakfast, then a walk down to the village for the papers. But in recent days the morning village trips have included visits to our local shops for donations and gifts to help our Church Bazaar, which will be held next Saturday, 12th August. It was a low cloud, humid drizzly morning, which brought crowds of tourists into Corfe.

After a quick lunch I walked to the Model Village to carry out my afternoon shift in the gift shop/garden and model village counter. Rosa and our neighbour, June practised their watercolour techniques in the conservatory as the weather had improved rapidly and bright sunshine brought many people to see the Model Village. I met visitors from Germany, France and Mexico among others and returned home at 6.30 for a late tea.

Our daughter Sara, in East Grinstead was due to have a routine operation at 6.00pm, so we were pleased to hear from her husband, Tom at 8.00 pm that everything was fine and she was in the Recovery Ward.. We phoned the hospital at 9.00pm and by that time she was in her room asleep. We telephoned our daughter in Baltimore, Maryland - five hours behind our time - to give her the good news, then emailed both daughters to express our delight at the safe outcome.

Some relaxing celebration seemed in order so we opened a bottle of Chilean Red wine and I wrapped up a nice book of Poems by John Keats called 'When the Night doth Meet the Noon', illustrated by reproductions of landscapes by Turner, Constable and others, to send to Sara, who writes poetry and has a successful poetry web page on the internet.

As ever, the day ended as it began, with the ritual of the feeding of the cats. And so to bed.

Today's weather:

Name GEOFF MARSHALL   Year of birth 1924

House RYCHANCE,   Street HIGHER GARDENS

Wednesday August 9th

There has been much debate as to when the new millennium actually starts, 1st of January 2000 or 1st of January 2001!!

As far as Corfe Castle Post Office is concerned the 21st century arrived today in the shape of the "Horizon" computer system. After centuries with the same paper book accounting system the post office finally realised it would have to automate or get left behind by its competitors.

Developed and tested over several years, the Horizon system has a flat, touch sensitive screen, barcode and magnetic card readers and the latest technology smartcard reader. An ISDN line keeps Horizon in constant communication with centralized computers to transfer up to date information and data at the touch of a button. When the whole 19,000 post offices are on line during 2001 it is hoped that Horizon will be used to develop new products and services especially in the financial sector.

Today's weather: Fine All Day

Name Ian Tarbotton   Year of birth 1954

House The Post Office   Street The Square

Today is our 43rd wedding anniversary. In 1957 we had £45 in savings, our weekly combined income was £20 and the rent for our flat near Hampton Court was £3. After a lifetime of travel and 26 moves we feel fortunate today to have three happily married children, eight grandchildren and a house at the top end of West Street – Russet Cottage.

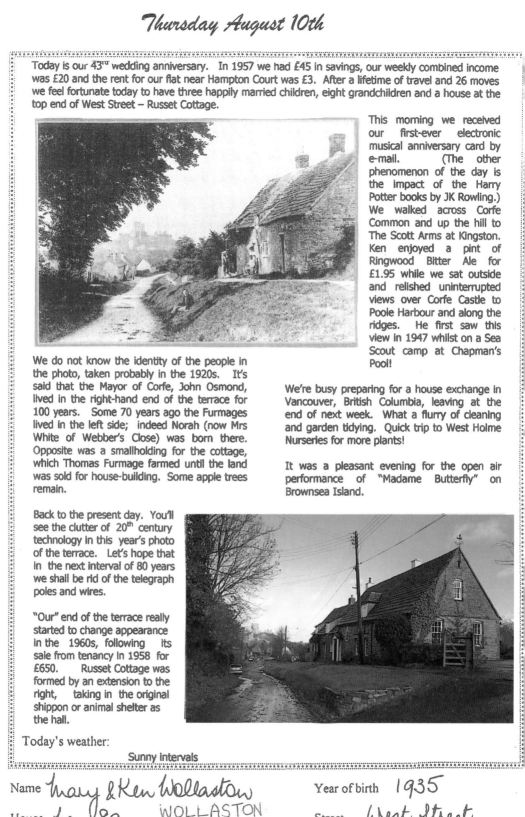

This morning we received our first-ever electronic musical anniversary card by e-mail. (The other phenomenon of the day is the impact of the Harry Potter books by JK Rowling.) We walked across Corfe Common and up the hill to The Scott Arms at Kingston. Ken enjoyed a pint of Ringwood Bitter Ale for £1.95 while we sat outside and relished uninterrupted views over Corfe Castle to Poole Harbour and along the ridges. He first saw this view in 1947 whilst on a Sea Scout camp at Chapman's Pool!

We do not know the identity of the people in the photo, taken probably in the 1920s. It's said that the Mayor of Corfe, John Osmond, lived in the right-hand end of the terrace for 100 years. Some 70 years ago the Furmages lived in the left side; indeed Norah (now Mrs White of Webber's Close) was born there. Opposite was a smallholding for the cottage, which Thomas Furmage farmed until the land was sold for house-building. Some apple trees remain.

We're busy preparing for a house exchange in Vancouver, British Columbia, leaving at the end of next week. What a flurry of cleaning and garden tidying. Quick trip to West Holme Nurseries for more plants!

It was a pleasant evening for the open air performance of "Madame Butterfly" on Brownsea Island.

Back to the present day. You'll see the clutter of 20th century technology in this year's photo of the terrace. Let's hope that in the next interval of 80 years we shall be rid of the telegraph poles and wires.

"Our" end of the terrace really started to change appearance in the 1960s, following its sale from tenancy in 1958 for £650. Russet Cottage was formed by an extension to the right, taking in the original shippon or animal shelter as the hall.

Today's weather:
Sunny intervals

Name Mary & Ken Wollaston
WOLLASTON
House no 89

Year of birth 1935
Street West Street

Today is the second Friday in August! From Weymouth I am visiting my sister Eileen and brother-in-law Lucas at The Old Forge. We are recalling how for many years during the mid 1960s and 1970s we were often together on "this Friday" in Corfe Castle when everyone seemed to be very secretly preparing their floats and fancy dress for the Carnival, always held on the second Saturday in August.

One year, our children entered on a float as characters from "Alice in Wonderland" and were so excited when they won first prize in their category. After the Parade, all down East Street and through the Square to West Street, there was lots of fun and dancing and wonderful refreshments, including a pig roast.

Neil, Paul and Karen Glaister – Corfe Castle Carnival 1967

I could say that if it wasn't for me, Eileen wouldn't be in Corfe. Eileen and my widowed mother, Elizabeth Crone followed us from Yorkshire in June 1966 in order that Mum could be near our young family; our oldest sister, Sybil and her family were living in Australia. My husband, Donald, and I with our three children Neil, Paul and Karen, came to Poole in the summer of 1965. Donald had transferred from the Yorkshire Police to the Dorset Police. It seemed in those days that the summers were long and sunny – many times we boarded the steam train at Wareham to visit Mum and Eileen. To us it was all so new, different and exciting. At that time we lived at a Police house near Poole Quay, now the site of the Headquarters of the RNLI (Royal National Lifeboat Institution).

It's amazing how a particular day or date starts you thinking. Now, in Corfe Castle, the Carnival is over and no more second Fridays and Saturdays in August on the calendar of highlights – but the memories linger on. Our children still talk excitedly about happy days in Corfe Castle and now bring their own children to the village.

Today's weather: Brilliant sunshine

Name	Babs Glaister	Year of birth	1934 (Neil 1960 Paul '62, Karen '64)
House	At: The Old Forge	Street	38 East Street

DRAGON'S VILLAGE BAKERY

Opened April 1992

Present Staff.   Nigel and Joan Dragon

Mark Hathaway (Baker)

Harry Brierley (Weekend Baker)

Liz Finney (Full-time Sales Assistant)

Sue Legg (Part-Time Sales Assistant)

Hannah Gregory }
Rosy Smith   }   Saturdays and School Holidays
Jess Tearle   }
Joanna Watson }

Alison Kemp (Roll Filler)

Debbie Reynolds

Annual Turnover approximately £150,000

Saturday takings in August £1,560

Opening Hours Easter to Christmas 7 day per week 8 a.m − 5 30 p.m.

Christmas to Easter: Closed on Wednesdays

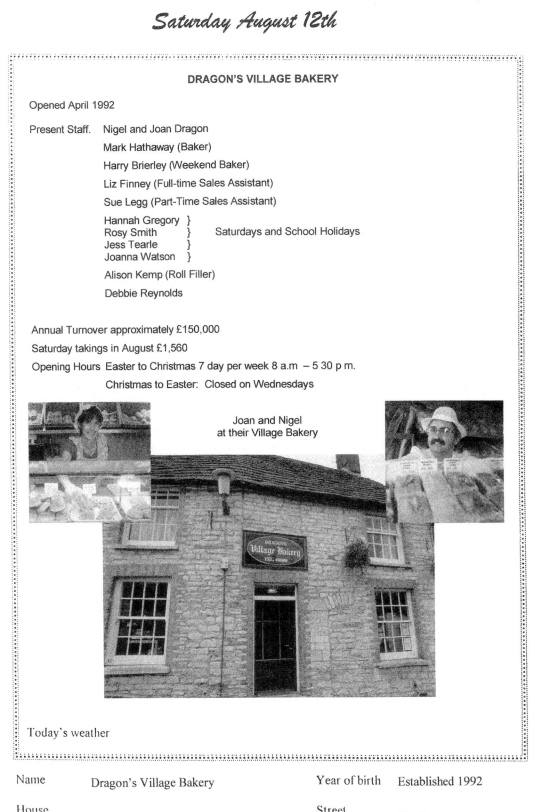

Joan and Nigel
at their Village Bakery

Today's weather

Name	Dragon's Village Bakery	Year of birth	Established 1992
House		Street	The Square

Sunday August 13th

This was a quiet day of rest and anticlimax amidst the general rush and excitement of August holiday-events. Our teenage grandchildren, Emma and Julia, had gone home after ten days of sun spent in afternoons on the beach at Studland, Weymouth and Canford Cliffs, and evening meals outdoors on the patio. The next batch of younger granchildren, Amy, James and Athena, were expected today but delayed their arrival so that they can go to the Millennium Dome in London tomorrow. Sigh of relief! We were gathering our strength after the Annual Church Fete yesterday. My part had been to sell gifts of perfume, soap, scarves, trinkets,tea-towels, china ornaments, glass vases, etc. Most of the gifts were new and we made over £100. Penelope Smith helped with the sales, showing a good head for business! Everyone expects a bargain, especially the ladies of the village who come back to look several times to see if there are any reductions. I bought a Book Lovers Notebook to record the monthly meeting of the Reading Group who meet at my house.

Herman went to Steeple Church at 10.30 a.m. to take the Family Service, a lively affair, after which Julian Cotterrel invited the congregation of 28 to look round his garden at Steeple Manor. I sang in the Choir at St/Edwards and afterwards had drinks with Joan and Rex Howe.

The misty rain didn't inspire us to be active in the afternoon, so we had no knowledge of ~~had no knowldege of~~ how the tourists were spending a wet Sunday in Corfe Castle. A great contrast to last Thursday when we took friends from Devon to walk round the Castle and the Tea Rooms were so busy that we left our table and came home to have tea and eat my home made raspberry jam sponge cake.

When I walked down to Church for Songs of Praise at six o'clock the traffic returning from Swanage was not heavy. Very few of us turned out for the service, and those who had got caught in a shower of rain on the way home.

I hope the weather is fine next Saturday evening when Colletts Close holds its Millennium Get-Together in the cul-de-sac.

Today's weather: Warm and misty. Wet in the evening.

Name   Ruth Nuttall

House   Crowestones

Year of birth   31/10/36

Street   22 Colletts Close

Monday August 14th

07:00 The alarm heralding the first day back to the routine of caring for our fifteen month old grandson George, after a week's break. As Christians we always start the day with a 'quiet time' when we read the Bible together, follow the 'Every Day with Jesus' notes by Selwyn Hughes and pray together.

Christopher our son and his wife Helena had stayed over night in order to make an early start. (They have their office & studio at our house). Chris searches the internet for pharmaceutical companies and Helena is an artist.

08:00 I drove with our dog Bobby on the back seat of the car from Corfe to Godlingston Manor collecting a newspaper at St Michael's Garage on the way. Our daughter Catherine was waiting with George for his morning at Corfe with his grand-parents while she works as a solicitor with Humphries Kirk in Swanage.

08:45 Feed the dogs and walk them around the Halves - have breakfast and help Gillie look after George. Load the car for a shopping trip to Swanage taking George with us.

10:41. Purchase parking ticket in Co-op car park. Unload buggy: Gillie and I wheel grandson down a very busy Station Road and into Bath Travel. Sign for our Autumn break in Malta to be shared with Robin and Ann Swaine our neighbours in East Street, Corfe. To Boots with holiday photos for processing and purchase several items. Into pet shop, purchase fish food for the Koi carp and discover that we were fifty pence short. Our friend Robin passed by, saw us in the shop and promptly came to our rescue. Into Co-op, place George into the seat of a shopping trolley and victual the Humphries household.

11.42 Depart for Corfe - George falls asleep before reaching Harmans Cross. It had remained dry all morning but the wind had become very strong. On our arrival we notice that Christopher had removed the gazebo cover because it had been taking off in the high winds. Very carefully carry George into the house and lay him down on the settee so that he could continue his morning sleep.

12.00 Nigel calls on Michael Spinney opposite and arranges sailing trip in Poole Harbour for the next day.

12.15 Go on line to check our bank balance and spend some time ascertaining several of the payments and work out which pension payments had come in.

12.30 Write a letter to a firm of solicitors in London for A.C.T.S. (Association of Churches Together in Swanage and District) for which I am secretary.

13.00 Walk dogs over Halves - call in on Robin Swaine and pay back the fifty pence - consider various ideas for paving around his summer house.

13.30 Catherine returns from work in Swanage and the family sits down to lunch in the kitchen.

Towards the end of the meal Gillie sounds the 'alarm' as water pours through the ceiling. The cistern of the upstairs toilet leaking. Gillie summons the plumber. Nigel ties up the ballcock. Mop up.

14.30. Nigel prepares boat for trip planned with Michael Spinney - sort waterproofs, life jackets and check outboard motor.

16.00. Plumber calls - discover the cistern is cracked - cut off water to unit and discuss the purchase of a new suite. Discuss other building jobs including taking an electrical cable through the garden from the garage for a permanent line down to the pond. Make arrangements for having the living room decorated whilst we are on holiday in October.

17.00 Chris & Helena take dogs for a walk over the Common.

19.30 Watch Coronation Street

20.30 Gillie and I walk the common with the dogs, to the 'Top of the World' (the burial mound at the east end of the main common), along the ridge and back via the lower route towards the Halves Cottages stile.

21.00 Watch Prime Suspect V

22.30 Take the dogs for a last walk in the dark half way down the Halves and back

23.00 And so to bed.

Today's weather: Dull and damp with strong winds by midday.

Name - Nigel Humphries

House - 142

Year of birth - 1937

Street - East Street

Tuesday August 15th

August 15th 2000 - just 100 years ago today my mother Gertrude Hoare neè Campbell was born at Charlton Mackrell in Somerset. She came to Corfe Castle in 1929 after her marriage to my father who was transferred from the Blandford area into Purbeck by the then Dorset Roads & Bridges Department.

At birth she was not expected to live yet she survived and lived into her 90th year. The youngest of seven children (she had 6 brothers) she claimed to have been spoilt but was also fortunate in that her parents believed that girls should be as well educated as boys. Yet on leaving school she went into service as did many of her contemporaries. She travelled quite extensively with her employers and talked of a Lady Hawley with whom she spent summers at Sandbanks. Latterly she lived and worked at Lytchett Matravers.

During this time (the 1920's) she led a very interesting life - riding both horses and a motor bicycle also dancing (she met my father at a dance at Lytchett Minster!)

She was an accomplished seamstress and after coming to Corfe Castle continued dressmaking - she used to make Barbara Cannings' skating dresses *(and her knickers during the war years!!!)* Her experience in service became very useful after my father died whilst I was still at school - she worked for the Sheasby and Moss families and continued to do so until well into her eighties.

She continued to live in the house in which I now live - I returned to Corfe Castle in 1991.

Unfortunately her latter years were marred by arthritis but her mind was always active - she enjoyed reading and took an interest in current affairs.

****

Today being the 15th of the month is the copy date for the Corfe Valley News of which I am the current editor. This is a monthly magazine which has a circulation of 900 copies covering Corfe Castle, Church Knowle, Kingston, Kimmeridge, Steeple and all the surrounding farms and hamlets.

My first task this morning was to start to type up the hand-written copy which I have been sent.Many regular entries and advertisements are on floppy disc and just need any amendments before printing..

When that is done it is a case of waiting until the end of the day for any further contributions and also to check for any that have been left at the post office. Most people who have computers or typewriters are very good and send their copy ready printed in A5 format This is a big help.

Lunch time - time go round to Mary Wills and to meet our friend Pearl Wakelin from Portway Farm, Winfrith Newborough. We meet for lunch every 3 or 4 weeks and have been doing so now for several years. We try to find somewhere different every time and as yet we have managed to do that. Today we are going to the National Trust Tearooms in the village.

It is such a lovely day we opt for a table in the garden overlooking the castle - all the tables are full. Unfortunately the hot sun has brought out the wasps which are a bit of a nuisance. We enjoy our meal - Sally Audrain is the manager and chef and produces some very tasty dishes. It is my turn to pay today; Martin Smith is in charge of the cash desk. He is the young man who, a couple of years ago designed the Millennium Association Logo and is working here in the school holiday.

After a short walk around the village we go our separate ways.

Linda Applin   64, West Street

Wednesday August 16th

Mrs. Selby:

It's a very dull morning. I let the dog out at 7.20 and then went back to bed and had a nice cup of tea made by my dear husband Alex. Had a nice bath and dressed with Alex help. Then I had breakfast of cornflakes. My next job was to feed the birds after which I started to prepare the lunch. It was chicken casserole, followed by fruit tart and cream.

I did some washing then had coffee and read the paper. Lunch was at 12.15.

I spent the afternoon with my friend Vera. Went back home at 4 o'clock for tea and watched TV.

At 6.30 went to the whist drive in the community room which we all enjoy.

Mrs. Beavis:

I got up this morning at 6.30. Had my usual wash and dressed. Made the bed and had breakfast, then fed the birds. I collect a few papers and deliver them and have a chat on the way.

 My next job is to make a cake for my sister who is coming tomorrow and will take it home with her.

Now it's time for lunch. I am having salmon salad and apple and custard for pudding.

I usually go for a walk with my friend Alice and her little dog.

I am going to the whist drive this evening and am looking forward to it.

Today's weather   Dull to start with. Warm and sunny later

Name	S. Selby and V. J. Beavis	Year of birth	1915 and 1918
House	18 and 20 Springwell Close	Street	West Street

Thursday August 17th

Thursday 17th August dawned fine and misty. Victoria and I picked up our luggage at 6 a.m. and set off for our long-awaited trip to Romania. I had adopted Victoria almost 10 years ago from a hospital in Bucharest, Romania, and we had been planning to go back for some time.

When we left Corfe Castle it was looking very beautiful, half shrouded in morning mist.

We soon reached Gatwick Airport and a few hours later found ourselves in Bucharest, standing outside a very smart newly built airport in the boiling hot sun, the temperature about 30°C. The old airport was a quarter of the size, very bare and ugly, so this was a welcome change.

More changes greeted us as we drove to our hotel. Many, many more cars and shops filled with brightly packaged goods. When I had been here immediately post Caucesco cars were sparse and <u>very</u> old indeed, the shops appeared uninviting and the window dressing spartan. Victoria could hardly take it all in, she was so excited!

We both viewed the line upon line of high rise, dirty, poverty-stricken flats with dismay, trying to imagine how hard it must be to live in these, particularly in this intense heat.

As we stopped at each junction with traffic lights, little ragged children without shoes appeared at car windows with their hands stretched out for money. They looked so thin and emaciated, I could hardly believe that only a few hours earlier I had left c country so well supplied with food that it had become obsessed with fat, dieting and keeping fit. It had even started fat camps for children" the year before!

We soon arrived at the same hotel I had stayed in 1990 — looking exactly the same. The big difference was that you were greeted warmly instead of with suspicion, as had been the case in the Communist era.

All the friends I had made in 1990 came over to see us and were thrilled to see the 10 year old Victoria who had left Romania in a carry-cot at 3 months old!

What a reunion!   What a day!

Today's weather   Fine temperature in Corfe 19°C

Name   Mrs. Sally-Anne Parsons   Year of birth   1947

House   Townsend House   Street   123 East Street

Friday August 18th

My summer holiday

Two days ago I came back from Japan with my family. We were in the plane for 14 hours. I enjoyed looking of the window. We flew over Greenland and it was really icy we saw ice hills and mountains!

In Japan we went swimming every day. We walked to the pool which was in my Mum's old school in a village called Tamaniwa in northern Japan. One of the best things about the pool was our dad was allowed to stand in the water and throw us into the water. One of the reasons we went the pool everyday was because it is really hot and sticky in Japan at this time of year. In the summer in Japan there are an enormous number if different insects. Some of the more interesting ones are the Praying Mantis, all sorts of grasshoppers and cicadas and large black and yellow spiders!

We had a good time but it was nice to get back to Corfe Castle.

Name: Canna Whyte   Year of birth: 1992
       3 West Street

Saturday August 19th

Fete day dawned with sun and no rain. The Encombe Fete always seems to be blessed with good weather! Four of our family had come down to help. There are never too many helpers on Fete Day.

The craft stalls started rolling through the village from 8.30 a.m. on their way down to Encombe House.

By midday everyone was in position, the Wareham Town Band started to play, the Beer Tent and the Burger Van were open, people started to come in to picnic beside the lake in front of Encombe House.

It's difficult to imagine more idyllic surroundings! All this time, I was up and down from the village ferrying people and kit.

The crowds really started to mill around from 2 p.m., buying at craft stalls and village stalls, watching Punch and Judy, a stilt walker and a fire entertainer, eating local Purbeck ice cream and cream teas and listening to a trad jazz band. There were village games, a very successful coconut shy and a children's fair.

There was an unscheduled event too! A helicopter landed to take a young boy to hospital for urgent treatment to a bee sting.

At 4.30 the Grand Draw for the raffle signalled the end of a hectic afternoon. 3,500 people had visited the Fete. It was all made possible by the great number of helpers who came from all over Purbeck.

My job kept me in the Treasury giving out floats, changing money, looking after lost property, directing lost souls and, most important of all – counting the money!

On the day we took £13,000 and by 7 p.m. all was banked. Not a bad day's work! St. James PCC and Macmillan Cancer Relief as well as many other Purbeck charities will benefit from the profits.

Today's weather: Sunny

Name   George Pitman   Year of birth   1935

House   The Old Post Office   Street   Kingston

Today my mother is here again on her usual annual long summer holiday from Nottingham. I don't know how we manage in my tiny flat but it's great having her here. Mum always has a chirpy outlook on life. It's amazing to think it is 14 years this summer that I have lived in Dorset. Originally I came from Nottingham.

For those of you who don't know me, I'm quite "mutt 'n' jeff" (deaf) and have been all my life, although I didn't know till my last year at school. At age 25, after carving and sculpting stone and wood for eight years, I had the chance to study stone masonry and architectural carving. Studying was a whole new concept to me, as I'd never taken an exam before!

A course at Weymouth College armed me with considerable stone mason's knowledge. People are surprised to hear I had no art schooling and sculpturally I am self-taught. I have trained myself, since I was a kid, playing with plasticine and whatever else I could shape. I have undertaken hundreds of commissions and sell many sculptures, many hidden away in the nooks and crannies of Purbeck.

In 1994 I was Artist in Residence at Christchurch Priory, after winning the 900th Anniversary Sculpture Competition. It was my first opportunity to carve something larger than the normal (9' 6") in the Priory gardens. The scene on this sculpture depicts a human comedy of monks, bishop, normal soldier, Henry VIII's henchman, a medieval couple getting married and a modern day vicar along with little suggestive looks and hidden detail.

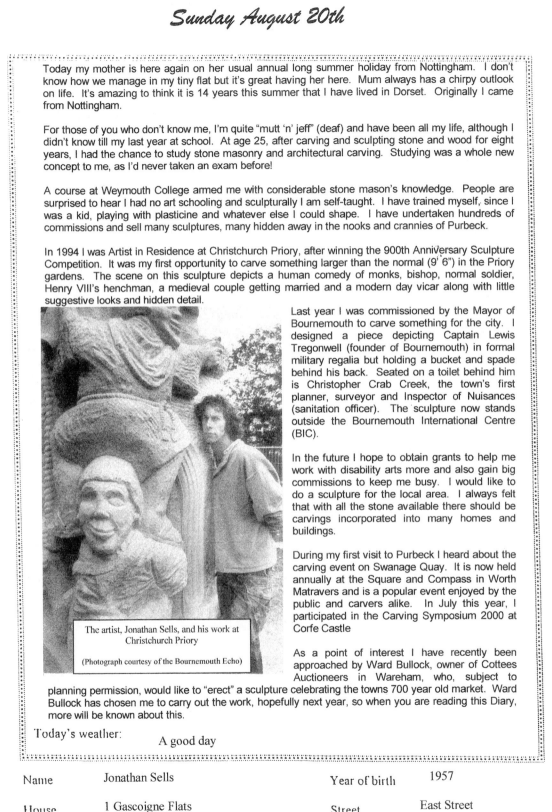

The artist, Jonathan Sells, and his work at
Christchurch Priory

(Photograph courtesy of the Bournemouth Echo)

Last year I was commissioned by the Mayor of Bournemouth to carve something for the city. I designed a piece depicting Captain Lewis Tregonwell (founder of Bournemouth) in formal military regalia but holding a bucket and spade behind his back. Seated on a toilet behind him is Christopher Crab Creek, the town's first planner, surveyor and Inspector of Nuisances (sanitation officer). The sculpture now stands outside the Bournemouth International Centre (BIC).

In the future I hope to obtain grants to help me work with disability arts more and also gain big commissions to keep me busy. I would like to do a sculpture for the local area. I always felt that with all the stone available there should be carvings incorporated into many homes and buildings.

During my first visit to Purbeck I heard about the carving event on Swanage Quay. It is now held annually at the Square and Compass in Worth Matravers and is a popular event enjoyed by the public and carvers alike. In July this year, I participated in the Carving Symposium 2000 at Corfe Castle

As a point of interest I have recently been approached by Ward Bullock, owner of Cottees Auctioneers in Wareham, who, subject to planning permission, would like to "erect" a sculpture celebrating the towns 700 year old market. Ward Bullock has chosen me to carry out the work, hopefully next year, so when you are reading this Diary, more will be known about this.

Today's weather: A good day

Name	Jonathan Sells	Year of birth	1957
House	1 Gascoigne Flats	Street	East Street

A busy day today. Start right after breakfast to make cakes for tomorrow's Bazaar at the Congregational Church. What cakes to make? Some fruit, one or two sponges, flapjacks, maybe rock cakes.

Must take out of the freezer the ones Christine brought down from Rugby, quite a variety.

Next get plants ready for the stall.
There are some begonia rex, thyme, marjoram, ground cover geraniums, also weigh up some tomatoes, runner beans and courgettes.

Tomorrow evening there is to be a Bingo in the Legion Club, which I will be running. Have to get the prizes for this, so take a trip to Swanage in the car.

We need 20 prizes in total for the Bingo, plus a raffle and a Special Raffle. 4 Bingo prizes will come from Don Palfrey, our local butcher and will be collected tomorrow. 4 more will come from Cleall's Stores and will kindly be delivered by them straight to the Club. This leaves me to find 12 more for the Bingo, plus 6 or 7 raffles such as chocolates, biscuits, fruit, toiletries, pot plants, wine or a cheese board.

The day finishes with a game of Whist at the Springwell Community room, always an enjoyable evening.

Today's weather: Sunny and fairly warm.

Name: Joan Marshallsay

Year of birth: 1921

House: 76

Street: West

Tuesday August 22nd

A CORFE CASTLE BEEKEEPER

Today I removed my honey crop. I keep at present eight hives of bees and have been beekeeping since 1946, when I took up the hobby after spending six years during WW2 in the Royal Navy.

So, down to business! I should perhaps explain that in beekeeping there is in the hive the brood rearing area where the queen lays eggs and young bees are reared through the egg, larva and insect stages, and above this the honey storing area. The two areas are separated by the beekeeper placing a perforated metal sheet between the two which prevents the queen from passing upwards and laying eggs in the honey storage area. Eggs and larvae mixed up with honey are not to our taste!

One's honey crop depends on a number of factors – the queen's laying ability to produce the strongest possible force of bees, the weather, the local flora, and the knowledge, skill and experience of the beekeeper. In a very good year one can obtain as much as a hundredweight of honey from one good hive; conversely, there are the occasional years when one obtains hardly any honey. Over a five year period in this country one hopes perhaps to average each year something like 35 – 40lb per colony.

In the Corfe Castle area, in addition to the nectar to be obtained from fruit trees and bushes and flowers in the village gardens, I rely for my crop mainly on blackberry which flowers from about the end of June for about a month, and is common enough in the hedgerows and alongside the railway cuttings and embankments, to produce a very pleasant medium coloured honey. It is at this time that one prays for at least a fortnight of settled good warm sunny weather.

By this day each year I know I have my crop for the year and now I have to remove it from each hive which will still contain a good many thousands of bees In the middle of summer a good hive will contain up to something like 70,000 bees which will reduce to 8.000 to 10,000 during the winter. A bee in summer, working day and night, lives for about six weeks; bees hatched in Autumn will live through to the following Spring.

A hive consists of boxes of combs placed one above the other. I have already two days ago been to my hives and placed what we call a 'clearer-board' between the honey crop boxes and the brood rearing chamber. The 'clearer-board' consists of a wooden board which fits exactly over the top of a box of combs. In the centre of this is a hole into which is placed a 'Porter bee-escape', so called after the name of the person who invented it This is a wire spring valve system which allows bees to pass down through the board and prevents them from passing upwards again. The bees when separated from the brood rearing area will always go down to join the queen and the brood.

I put this board in two days ago and by now, 22nd August, they will have passed down through the board and my honey crop in the boxes above will be clear of bees , though there may sometimes be the odd bee or two still left, but in general the system works extremely well.

I have left removing the crop until this evening when most bees have stopped flying, for like most creatures bees are born robbers and will quickly steal any honey that is easily obtainable. This evening, when they were quiet and resting in the hive, I have quietly removed the boxes of honey and taken them home, having left each hive sufficient stores of honey and pollen to last them through the winter. I am 'entitled' to the honey surplus to their needs as a result of my efforts through the season This year, despite it being cold and wet through much of May and June, has shewn us a dry warm spell through July and August and my crop is quite a good one. I now have to extract it, filter it and bottle it!

A honey crop is not obtained without some effort! But what an excellent hobby!

Today's weather

Today's weather Warm, sunny and dry.

Name BOB CARTER   Year of birth

House 51 EAST STREET   Street

I woke up, just before the 6 am alarm, to a beautiful sunny morning with a light Easterly breeze. The sun is rising noticeably later each morning. I got up when Graham had made the tea, and removed the first big spider of the season from the bedroom wall, with the aid of a glass and postcard. After showering and dressing I went down the garden to feed the hens and let them out into their larger run. They have a bowl of milk, corn and layers pellets. I collected the egg (only one so far) and, because they sleep in their nesting boxes, unlike normal hens which roost, I have to remove any pooh which would make other eggs dirty. After a second cup of tea, I got ready for work, washed and dried up the tea mugs (couldn't leave them to drip-dry, which is our usual practice, as we have two young adventurous kittens who are learning to climb!).

Graham went off to work at 7.20 am He works for Southern Electric Contracting, currently at Chase Manhattan. I left for work at 7.30 am I work full-time for the GP surgery in Wareham as the Personnel Manager. As well as being responsible for the staff, I am also involved in a lot of surgery administration. At the moment the only full-time receptionist is off sick and another receptionist is on holiday so I am helping out a lot on reception - a job which I used to do full time that can be very rewarding but occasionally quite unpleasant, depending on the patients! I "opened up" and dealt with the telephones in readiness for the onslaught Once there was enough staff in to deal with the 'phones and the front desk, I popped my head into the weekly GP meeting for an update. The morning was spent dealing with the usual daily work including registering new patients, checking the email for prescription requests, medical data entry, etc Lunch was "on the hoof", as usual - last night's leftover veggies, salad and cottage cheese (I cannot bear waste!). At 1 pm we had our fortnightly staff meeting. There were only two items to discuss this week, one of which was the Flu Clinics, which are taking place in October. Patients are already enquiring about this year's flu vaccine! The Government wants everyone over the age of 65 to have a flu vaccine this year (previously it was all over 75s) After an unusually quick meeting, I returned to my office which resembled an oven (even with the electric fan on!), to tackle my in-tray

I finished work at 4 pm in order to drive to Wool to visit Bev, the staff member who is off sick following an operation. After a cup of tea and exchange of news, I headed for home via the back road. Deciding this was a bad idea in view of the time of year and number of camp-sites along the way, I joined the main road at East Stoke and had to cross the railway line where the gates are manually operated I wonder if that man is always there - I suppose he (or somebody) must be - and what else he does He can't be *that* busy with the crossing. I'm going to ask him one day!

I arrived home (a self-contained flat attached to my parents' house) at about 5.15 pm after battling with the Summer traffic Jacqui, my sister, was just leaving after collecting her ten month old son, Adam Mum had been looking after him while Jac was looking at a job. My brother, Andrew, and his wife, Fizah, and five month old son, Raiyan, were also at home They are staying at Duck Cottage, Creech Grange, on holiday for three weeks from their home in Singapore. We had a cup of tea and then I got on with my chores. Mum had already put the chickens in and fed them. I cleaned out the kittens' litter tray (more pooh!), watered the flower pots and my small vegetable patch (which involved carrying watering cans from the water butt to the back of the flat - good exercise!), picked beans and cut courgettes.

It was then time to prepare the meal for Graham's homecoming at 7.15 pm After we had eaten and washed up, it was nearly 8 pm, so we took Jay (Mum's dog) for a walk, and Andy came along too It was a beautiful evening, still and warm We walked through the car park field, over Copper Bridge across the little wooden bridge and back down the water meadow We saw Elise Hewitt walking Kay's dog In the distance we could see David (from over the road) walking his dog Trixie, closely followed by Max, his cat! We stopped and chatted to Fiona and Kay, asking after Maggie, Fiona's mare who was due to give birth to her foal imminently

The day ended, after showering, watching Ally McBeal on the television in bed with our two affectionate kittens, Oz and India Life isn't half bad!

Today's weather· Beautiful, hot & sunny

Name Jenny Whittle

House 57A

Year of birth 1965

Street East Street

A fine day in the context of this otherwise dismal summer. I started work at The Model Village at 0930. Days such as this usually see visitors choose the beach over a day in the village – today was no exception.

In fact due to the lull in visitor numbers, I was able to read for much of the day. The book that I am currently reading is for my university course, a history of totalitarianism by Leonard Schapiro.

On returning from work I took the dog for a walk over at Arne, I was with some friends and we saw a number of deer and rabbits, both of which were of great interest to the dogs.

At 2030 a group of friends who were all at Forres prep. school in Swanage met up for a few drinks at 'The Pevril' near the town Pier – we have all been to school in different parts of the country but still found a wealth of subjects to talk about including two of our number becoming professional musicians and another having played rugby for Scotland U-19s.

Today's weather Warm and Sunny

Name James Spinney   Year of birth 1980

House Purbeck Haze   Street East St.

Friday August 25th

Today I got up at 8.30am as I had to be at work for 9 o'clock.
When the postman came at about 8.15am I opened my GCSE
results. I got 3 A*'s, 5 A's and 3 B's, so I was extremely pleased,
and it put me in a good mood. Although I was very relieved that
the waiting was finally over! I then got ready for work (I work at
Dragons Village Bakery) and walked there. It was quite a busy day
so I was exhausted by the time I got home! When I got home
there were a lot of strange men wandering about, (who I later
found out were electricians), who were working on our new
extension we are having built. I relaxed in the afternoon by
listening to music on Radio 1 and CD's. I also got ready for a
show I was performing in that evening. I then had tea which was
baked beans on toast with hotdog sausages. For pudding I had a
strawberry Cornetto. I finished getting ready for the performance
which was being put on by Studland Youth Music Theatre which
I am in and is run by Joanne Moore, with help from Ronnie and
Marleen who makes the costumes. The performance went really
well, although a thunderstorm started as we performed the last
number, a choreographed rendition of "Love Shine A Light" by
Katrina and the Waves (which was the winner of the Eurovision
Song Contest a couple of years earlier!). Despite the weather we
still managed to raise a lot of money for charity. I then went
home and got ready for bed which I finally crawled into at about
11.00pm thoroughly exhausted after a long tiring day.

Today's weather: Mixture of cloud, showers, sunshine and thunderstorm

Name Rosy Smith

House Larksgate

Year of birth 1984

Street Townsend Mead

This is what we saw the day we went to Longleet Safari Park. It was just like Africa.

A lion

A tiger

Sealion Boat

Today's weather: Very warm

Name Luke Reynolds   Year of birth 1996

House 17   Street West

On this Sunday, 27th August 2000, it is the 55th anniversary of our wedding day.

We are here in Corfe Castle with our daughter, Karen, son-in-law, Frank, grandson, Nick and granddaughter, Julia, celebrating the day.

Fifty five years ago the war was over and my husband was in England for the first time for nearly four years. We went to London for the three days we had together before he had to go back to Greece and I to my R.A.F. station.

We married in Cambridge during a heat wave and today, here in Corfe, it is just as hot!

Food was still rationed so the meals in our hotel were quite sparse, few vegetables and very little meat.

What a change from our anniversary meal today.

Today's weather: Hot

Name	Jean and Harold Churchman	Year of birth	
House	Meadowside	Street	129 East Street

Bank Holiday Monday.

The day dawned bright, sunny and warm with the promise of becoming very hot. Today felt different, as though a new era had begun. Don and I were starting the next 25 years of our life together.

Life had started 25 years ago when Don was a happy-go-lucky fisherman, who had finished one season free and fancy free and started the next almost married with 3 children. We were married 4 months later. Now Malcolm, David and Elspeth are all grown up, happy and we have our lovely grandchildren. We moved to Corfe Castle from nearby Wareham where Don was born and I lived for 13 years.

The first time I had seen Corfe Castle was one Christmas when Corfe takes on a magical tranquility with the beautiful subdued lighting in the Square, Church and the Castle. I fell in love with it.

So, back to today – up early as usual. Lots of cooking. Sandwiches and salads to prepare with much help from family and friends – all for our "Bit of a do" in our very attractive village hall in the evening. How exciting it all was. We had friends and family staying with us and many more coming later. Before that there was dog walking to fit in with Jess and Stella up on the common – Beware of the adders. So busy we didn't even notice the usual tourists who visit our "museum" village.

6 p.m. – would we be ready? 7 p.m. the same thoughts and doubts. Still like most "Bit of a do's" we just about made it. I know in the end everything went well and a good time was had by all. Eat drink and be merry and thank you everyone for coming and making our "Do" memorable.

Here's to the next 25. If they're as good as the last ones they will be pretty good.

Today's weather. Hot and Sunny.

Name Mrs Viv Godwin   Year of birth 1936

House 47   Street Halves Cottages

Today is the day after August Bank Holiday Monday.

My day starts at 6.45am which allows me time to give our dog
a short walk and to prepare myself for work.

I am a manager of one of the largest Holiday Parks in Dorset
and my day commences by ensuring the office is prepared and
ready to deal with all the day to day enquiries that such a
busy Park attracts at its busiest time. The booking system
is computerised which makes that aspect of the business
much easier and less time consuming. The weather is good
today, and with the Park full to capacity many of our guests
are staying on site and making the most of our facilities.

Most of the morning is taken up with our weekly managers
meeting and briefings, and the afternoon attending to new
arrivals and dealing with customer telephone calls and
enquiries.

I left the Park at about 7.00pm to drive home and even at
that time the queue of traffic stretched back from the
Holton Heath traffic lights to the Worgret roundabout, as
people returned home in cars and coaches from the beaches
at Studland and Swanage.

When I got home and as my wife prepared our evening meal,
I walked our elderly Golden Retriever on the Common. She
much prefers to walk in the evening when it is a little
cooler, and this evening is perfect. I could clearly
see someone launching a micro-light from East Hill, and
the train steaming its way back down to Swanage from Norden.

After our meal I attended to some correspondence and my
wife worked in the garden until it became too dark.

We then spoke on the telephone to our daughters, one at
her home in Bournemouth and the other on holiday in Spain,
before retiring to bed at about 11o'clock.

Today's weather: Dry and sunny.

Name Denzil Sluggett   Year of birth 1939

House 24   Street Colletts Close

Born in a mining village, I spent most of my working life underground in the mines. When I came to live in Corfe Castle my life was transformed. I am enjoying my life. I live in Springwell Close, it is great and so are the people who live here. We have a Coffee Morning on Tuesdays, a Whist Drive every Wednesday evening and out of the proceeds we have coach outings. The Village Hall is also a gathering place for us.

There are some lovely walks around Corfe Castle within a radius of a mile or two with a different view everytime you turn your head. The focal point, of course, is the Castle. It stands majestically in its ruined state, defying all the elements and steeped in history.

But, my favourite place is the Common, where I walk with my dog, Belle. Here I see the wildlife, the scenery, the horses and soak up the atmosphere generally. When I walk off the Common on to West Street in springtime one finds a profusion of snowdrops, primroses and daffodils nestling at the feet of thatched cottages or homes with roofs of Purbeck stone - it's a picture postcard image of 'Olde England'.

The only way to describe Corfe Castle, in my humble opinion, is that it is next door to Heaven.

Today's weather:
                    Warm and sunny.

Name   G EDWARDS   Year of birth   1916

House   9 SPRINGWELL CLOSE   Street   OFF WEST STREET

Some pictures of Corfe from 1913. I found these in an old chest and thought they were of interest as it was obviously a better summer than 2000.

Hay making near West Mill.

The Cricket Club playing on the old pitch near the Church Knowle road.

A Dru Drury family picnic at Kimmeridge.

Dr Dru Drury, my Grandfather, from whose photo album these pictures came; this picture was taken during the late 1930s.

The Square as never seen today - no traffic except the Doctors 1910 De Dion Bouton, which was serviced by Dave Ford - see the entry for June 18th.

Today's weather:

Name Stephen Dru Drury

House 55 East Street

Year of birth 1939

Street

Friday September 1st

Pull in at the junction to Sandy Hill Lane & heave out the blue sign advertising the pottery & other crafts from the back of the car, as I do every morning. It sits on the corner of the road, slightly lopsidedly, encouraging passers-by to wander down & take a look at what's going on. Back in the car, under the bridge & right down the bumpy track to the workshops. Grab some handfuls of grass which are eagerly munched by my bleating fleecy friends opposite the workshops. Give them both a scratch behind the ears. The nervous one's not so sure about this, the other one loves it!

Fumble with keys and padlock, & once in, I'm hit by a blast of heat from the kiln. Check the answering machine & synchronise my radio with my neighbour's. I'll stick to radio 4 most of the day but will put on a tape when I feel like a change. I'll often whistle while I work! Due to the heat from the kiln, the mugs I threw yesterday on the wheel are already drying out, some polythene over the top should slow down the process. Change into dirty, clay-splattered boots. It's not yet cold enough for the mice to move in as they do each winter. Last year, one of them seemed to think my boots would be a secure hiding-place for food reserves. No need to check for half-eaten biscuits or ends of the loaf today!

With the kiln now down to under 150, it's cool enough to open. It's a bisque firing, the first of the 2 firings. Everything's piled in there, pots balanced on top of each other. I love the pots when they're still warm from the kiln, like freshly laid eggs! With the aid of gloves, I start unloading & juggling boards of pots around, trying to find space on the racks to store everything. The workshop seemed so big when I moved in 1 1/2 years ago, but now I'm using every inch of space, and could do with more. Somehow I manage to get all the pots onto the shelves though.

A quick drink & I'd better get on with handling those mugs. Roll out clay 'sausages' that I flatten & pile up ready for the next stage. Apron & wrist band at the ready in the fight against mucky clothes & soggy sleeve, I set to. Each mug is scored with a knife & the 'sausage' is stuck on, dipped in water and pulled repeatedly. All being well, a respectable handle will emerge, providing it doesn't drop off, or I crack or distort the mug in the process. Inevitably, one or two will fall by the wayside! They will be consigned to the clay slops bin to be recycled in the long run. The morning passes and I work my way through a board of the mugs & my tummy's rumbling. Once I've reasonably clean hands, it's cheese & pickle sarnies for lunch, perched on one of Nick's driftwood chairs outside while it's still warm enough. I get engrossed in reading last Saturday's paper, almost finish it and tomorrow I'll have to start all over again!

Back to work, & handling out of the way, it's time to start glazing pots. Wipe each pot with a damp sponge to remove any dust prior to being dipped in the glaze, preventing any potential problems . A paint-stirrer attached to a drill does a good job of mixing up the glaze. Methodically dip boards of pots, sometimes using tongs, always trying to avoid fingerprints or dribbles which will show up later. The trains rumble on by marking the passing of time. I get the mid-afternoon munchies & putting on an orange vest nip over the tracks to Clealls or the bakery, enjoying the chance to stretch my legs too.

The afternoon rolls on, glazing combined with chatting to any passers-by who have discovered me or customers who have come in search of a present in my showroom upstairs. Always enjoy chatting to people and it's good to get feed back on my pots. As the nights draw in, my season of chilblains and thermals begins. With less people around in Corfe, weekends will see me rushing round the country with a carload of pots in the craft fair build-up to Christmas.

Glazing almost over, I start clearing up, thinking about what I'll decorate tomorrow . Then I'll pack the glaze firing next week but that's enough for today. Pick up the sign on the way, & I'm off for a good soak in the bath to try & get the last remnants of clay out of my hair for another day!

Today's weather: DRY and OVERCAST

Name frances Pollard

Year of birth 12·6·69

House Corfe Castle Pottery, Sandy Hill workshops

Street Sandy Hill lane

ANGELIKA SEIK

SCULPTURE STUDIO

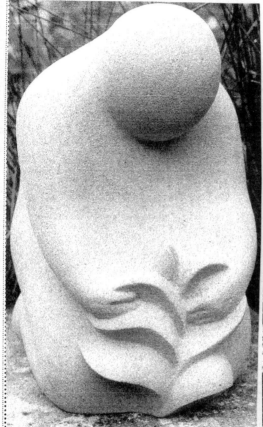

"GARDENER III - PLANT LOVER"
Bathstone

"PISCES"
Purbeck Marble

Today's weather: Misty Morning, Dry

Name Angelika Seik-Ford   Year of birth 1949

House 8   Street Halves Cottages

MORNING!!

IT'S A LOVELY SEPTEMBER MORNING AND IT LOOKS LIKE ITS GOING TO BE A NICE SUNNY DAY. HOPE SO, AS MY WIFE, JAN, AND I ARE OFF TO THE YEARLY STEAM FAIR.

I'M MIKE HARRIOTT, SELF-EMPLOYED PLUMBER, 53 YEARS OLD. HAVE LIVED IN CORFE FOR 11 YEARS NOW. IT'S A LOVELY LITTLE VILLAGE AND WE BOTH LOVE IT.

ANYWAY, BACK TO OUR DAY. THE STEAM FAIR IS AT BLANDFORD (STURMINSTER) AND IT'S A FIVE DAY EVENT – THE BIGGEST IN THE COUNTRY. YOU NEED AT LEAST THREE DAYS TO LOOK ROUND IT. LOADS OF STEAM ENGINES AND I'VE NEVER SEEN SO MANY HUGE FAIRGROUND RIDES, WOULDN'T GET ME ON ANY! IT COST US £10 EACH TO GET IN BUT IT WAS WELL WORTH IT. STAYED UNTIL ABOUT 7 O'CLOCK AND HAD DIFFERENT KINDS OF FOOD TO EAT AND THE ODD LAGER AND WE CAUGHT THE SUN AS, APART FROM ONE SHOWER, THE WEATHER WAS GOOD TO US.

POPPED IN THE BRITISH LEGION ON THE WAY HOME FOR A COUPLE OF DRINKS AND ALSO TO PAY OUR THRIFT CLUB, WHICH IS A CLUB YOU PAY INTO EVERY WEEK, OR WHENEVER YOU WISH, TO SAVE FOR CHRISTMAS.

WENT HOME AND WE WERE IN BED BY ABOUT 11 O'CLOCK AS WE WERE BOTH SHATTERED AFTER A TIRING BUT ENJOYABLE DAY.

GOODNIGHT!!!

Today's weather·   Dry and sunny, odd shower

Name	Michael Harriott	Year of birth	1947
House	Lagny Court, Jubilee Gardens	Street	Mead Road

Monday September 4th

6am.- the alarm goes off - I relax for a few minutes not really wanting to get up but today I am off to the Scilly Isles with my friend Charmian.

I get up wash my hair, have a shower and finish packing. The weather forecast for the next few days is not good with storms coming from the south-west so I need to be prepared for all weathers.

I also make some sandwiches for lunch, have some cereal (Crunchy Bran) and a cup of coffee. I make sure that all the doors and windows are securely locked and I am ready to leave at 07 30hrs I pick up my paper, the Independent (only 35p on Mondays 45p on other days), from the newsagents in the Square and also buy a bottle of Diet Coke (£1.00) for the journey.

I am travelling to the 'Scillies' by helicopter from Penzance some 200 miles away in Cornwall- the flight is due to leave there at 14.15hrs and we have to check in at 13.30hrs. The children are back at school this week so the traffic should not be too bad but I need to leave adequate time for the journey in case of traffic hold-ups.

I usually travel by an earlier flight at 09.15hrs. The means a <u>very early</u> start but with less chance of being delayed. The early flights were fully booked but the later one was also cheaper at £69 instead of £94. The is a considerable saving!

The journey was very slow as far as Dorchester with many people driving to work but from there it is mostly dual carriage-ways. I stop the service station at Exeter for coffee and a rest. I progress well as far as the A30 junction with the A391 near St. Austell where the A30 is completely blocked due to a serious accident. The diversion takes me southwards to the outskirts of St. Austell and then back to the A3 via the A3058. These roads were very congested with nose to tail traffic; the diversion added at least an extra hour to the journey. I was thankful that I had allowed myself some extra time! I later learned that some people had missed their flights due to this!

I arrived at the Heliport in Penzance at about 12.30hrs. I park the car and eat my lunch. Charmian arrives as I finish and we make our way into the Departure area and check in our luggage and catch up on each other's news. Charmian lives in North Devon but has spent Sunday night in Penzance with an elderly friend.

We travel by Sikorsky S61 helicopter which takes just 26 passengers for the 20 minute flight to St Mary's. The weather is good so we have an excellent view over Lands End and then the smaller islands of the 'Scillies' before we land on St. Mary's

After claiming our luggage we board the bus which is a shuttle service around the hotels on the island It costs just £3 for a return ticket

The journey to our hotel (The Godolphin) takes only 5 minutes. We have stayed there several times before - it is very comfortable with excellent food. Bed, breakfast and evening meal costs £62.00 per night - we are here for 4 nights. When we register we are surprised but also very pleased to see that the Owner/managers are still there. Last year they told us that the hotel was to be sold (£2.5 million) and they would be retiring.

After quickly unpacking and changing into shorts and T-shirt we set off for a walk around the Garrison at the western end of the island. There are wonderful views from here. On the way back we stop off for a cup of tea in 'The Corner House' where we met a very nice couple celebrating their wedding anniversary by visiting the Scilly isles for the first time. We also spent some time at a Craft Fair in the Town Hall.

We arrive back at the Hotel in time to investigate the options for entertainment this week. We then get changed and have a Gin & Tonic in the bar before dinner [Salmon Mouse with Anchovies; Apple juice; Trout with vegetables; Lemon Roulade accompanied by a bottle of wine and followed by coffee in the lounge] The hotel is full - most are from the same group from the Nottingham area who travelled to Penzance by coach and are accompanied by their driver/courier

Then off to The Parish Hall to a Slide Show (£3 each) of 'Underwater Animal and Plant Life'. Slide Shows are a feature of holidays in St. Mary's and are always well attended.

Back to the hotel, plan our activities for the next day, read a while then sleep!

Today's weather   Warm and Sunny

Name Linda Apple   Year of birth 1937

House 64   Street West

Awoke as usual at about 6.30 a.m. to car engines running and car doors being slammed, fell back to sleep until 9 a.m. Laid there wondering what to do with myself as I'm off sick with a back injury and cannot work.

Went downstairs, looked out of the lounge window and thought winter had arrived. I phoned my daughter, Cressida, in Cornwall and wished her a happy 22nd birthday, and truly missed her.

My sister, Karin, phoned and asked if I would like a trip to Swanage, so I put on waterproofs and wellies and off we went for a windswept walk along the beach.

We found shelter in a restaurant, had a light lunch and decided to go home.

I had a chat with Ian (my husband) who was very busy in the Post Office.

I thought it would be a good idea to go to bed for a rest, had a go at a crossword puzzle, continued with a book about the six wives of Henry VIII.

Cressida and Buster (my son) both phoned in the evening for a chat and to enquire how my back was and if I'd had a good day and all in all it wasn't bad.

Today's weather: Rain, cold

Name	Sheena Tarbotton	Year of birth	1955
House	The Town House	Street	The Square

Wednesday September 6th

I confess without shame that I am a day-dreamer. It is an Art.

Time & chance has brought me to this place which is a delight to one who wishes to re-capture those childling days of wonder & just float away with the wind driven clouds across these patchwork fields & awesome Purbeck Hills.

I have been dreaming to-day – drifting back, & would have liked you to come with me ——

Across the fields of Gold & Green
With hedgerows 'round & paths between.
Turned up ground in furrowed rows,
And straw made man to scare the Crows.
Black Rooks croaking in the trees,
Buttercups bugged around by Bees,
And for those with time to dream
Hypnotic Sunlight on the stream,
The stream that wanders down the glade
Thro' sculptured gullies by water made,
Where creatures toil o'er the land
To live their lives as Nature planned.
All these things I delight to see
And I wonder if there's a place for me.

It's Autumn now. What better time of the year to dream than these precious Autumn days?

Today's weather *Really warm – light showers*

Name *Arthur Ernest Ash*   Year of birth *2 ³⁄₃₆*

House *Becky Wobber Cottage*   Street *73 West St.*

Wonderful, sunny, early morning with a slight mist in the distance at 7am.

As I drove back from the village with the newspapers I realised that it was the first day back at school. There were clusters of school students waiting for the buses to Purbeck and the Middle Schools. I am always surprised how many teenagers there are the village. They all looked very smart . Many of the boys had some strikingly fashionable haircuts

The papers were all full of the latest fiasco with the Millennium Dome – yet more money being poured into it. People that have visited it seem to have mixed feelings – I want to go on the Wheel but the Dome doesn't attract.

Quiet day at home – I picked runner beans from the garden and found enough blackberries in the hedge for a pie. I harvested our damson tree – exactly ten damsons so they will become damson gin rather than the jam that I'd hoped.

In the evening we turned the heating on for the first time and it seemed that the autumn had come.

Looking at my favourite diarists – Samuel Pepys and James Woodford On 7 September 1660 in London Pepys had a quiet day too 'Putting my papers, books, and other things in order and writing of letters'. Woodford entertained eight guests at his parsonage 'I gave them for Dinner a Couple of Fowls and a Chop, and a Surloin of Beef rosted, and a plumb Pudding.'- this was in 1773 in Norfolk

Today's weather:

Name Nancy Logue   Year of birth 1941.

House 132   Street East Street

Today is my 85th birthday and I have received many cards including those from my 4 grown up married children .... John in Mandurrah and Patrick in Perth, both in Western Australia; Michael in Kent and Bridget in New Zealand. My 15 grandchildren and 5 great grand children also join in the "Happy Birthday" messages! The phone never seems to stop ringing with calls from friends and a lunch invitation to the Pines Hotel in Swanage from my friend, Jean Winter, who lives in Harmans Cross.

I am very happy living in Corfe Castle. Paul and I came to this cottage in 1973. AS a retired doctor (GP) with interesting connections, he often worked as a locum for the ship's doctor on the cruise liners and I travelled with him on many occasions. Sadly, Paul died in 1994 but we enjoyed very many happy years of retirement.

Over the years I have been an active member of the Corfe Castle W.I. with particular interest in floral art. As an Ikebana teacher, I was very privileged to have met ambassadors' wives from around the world as they were entertained at the Court of St. James.

Now I must start getting organised because I am about to travel to Australia for the 7th year running and today I've been to the bank for my travellers cheques. I drove there in my Mini City F registration car. I don't know what I'd do without my special little car, one of the most successful models of the last century and I think it was voted "Car of the Year 2000". I've had a quiet day really – too old for partying!

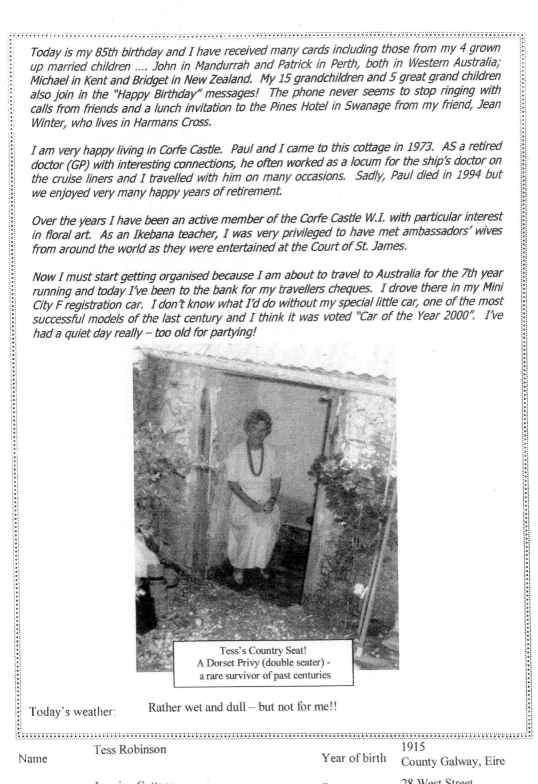

Tess's Country Seat!
A Dorset Privy (double seater) -
a rare survivor of past centuries

Today's weather: Rather wet and dull – but not for me!!

Name	Tess Robinson	Year of birth	1915 County Galway, Eire
House	Jasmine Cottage	Street	28 West Street

A misty, muggy morning - low clouds gently drifting up the valley from the sea. No time to lose today, up quickly to see the soldiers arriving at the gates of Corfe Castle, seeking rest and sustenance from Lady Bankes! Today members of the Civil War Society are at the Castle and everyone is in period costume

Pikemen, musketeers, pot makers building kilns using sawdust and bricks: piking/musketing demonstrations - lots of bangs! Christopher being recruited as a pikeman and practising his piking skills, then charging down the castle hill ready to spear the enemy with his pike. Checking on the new residents of the Castle - Phil's sheep - ensuring they were unperturbed by today's invasion; playing ghosts in the keep; watching the steam train and pretending it was a dragon blowing smoke. Firing the cannon. Digging in the archaelogical dig and finding bits of pottery, bones and flint. Couple of Romans wandering around too.

Took Shuna and Hallam home with Chris for lunch, then after lots of jumping on the beds and running round the garden, off to the Sweetie Shop (Saturday being Sweetie Day) for a 20p bag of loot. Then marched the gang across the Churchyard to Hallam's house to play.

Took Friendly for a long walk, across the Common, down to Blashenwell Water and across the back field to the Foxes Wood. Dragged Friendly out of the badger's set, which Brock has just cleaned again - he must be getting ready for Winter already.

Back through West Halves to drop Friendly at Mum's house. Fiona's mare has just had a foal, only 3 weeks old and very shy. Passed by the "It's a Knockout" Competition in the Football Field. We missed this event as we were too busy at the Castle playing soldiers. Loads of people there, playing tug-of-war with a tractor, football skills competitions and loads of other games.

Walked back to Hallam's house, for cups of lapsang souchong and then G&Ts with Lynne. Then back home with Christopher for a huge pasta supper; bath and bed for Christopher, with Peter Pan for the night-time story; and a cup of coffee for me.

Switched on the PC and found out what's going on in the world with all my friends. E-mail messages from Nova Scotia (enclosing pictures of a new baby), New York (info on new music to listen to from a friend), Saudia Arabia (message from my brother) and Barbados (a colleague requesting status on his next environmental project development mission).

Another full and exhausting day in Corfe Castle!

Today's weather: AN O.K DAY : The Rain just held off !

Name PARA MAURIELLO   Year of birth

House GARTH COTTAGE. THE SQUARE   Street

Sunday September 10th

We've been here 9 months now. As recent Berkshire residents, village life is new to us but its fast meeting expectations. We hope this is a 2-way perception! Today I went to church. We are so lucky to have a back gate which gives us direct access on to Corfe Common so I made this trip on foot. The state of my shoes betrayed my muddy route but the sound of the church bells calling as I walked on down West Street made every step worthwhile. On my way home, I thought about what I would cook later - funny how often I plan a mental meal rather than just enjoy the peace and quiet. Had it not been for the lorry drivers in France, I would have been alone today as Michael (husband) had a golfing week arranged near Bordeaux. The shortage of fuel and resulting strikes, however, have meant that his fellow golfers felt is irresponsible and foolhardy to head south. James (son) is partying with his old schoolfriends in Wokingham. As a university student, he finds Corfe life rather quiet. I did some gardening when I got home. Our large garden always needs some attention and now we are retired, I am hoping to develop some green fingers. In particular, some knowledge about plants that are unappetising to rabbits would be good. My houserabbit, Hercules, is working his way through the flower beds and we have a few bare patches. "If life's future problems and worries are all as appealing as this one, we shall be fine", I can remember thinking. Mum rang. She is going on holiday with Ray next week. The Olympic Games open in Sydney on Friday - I can't wait. Roll on tomorrow.

Today's weather: Patchy cloud. Warm

Name JULIET GLOVER   Year of birth 1950

House HALF ACRE   Street HIGHER FILBANK

Monday September 11th

This day's entry includes a little about my life and work here in Corfe Castle beginning with a typical Monday routine. As is quite normal, I rose from sleep at 6 am and made the first 'cuppa' of the day for Rene, my wife, and myself. Tea is the way to start the day for many and we are no exception. The morning was spent in the garden – today's jobs being digging out raspberry canes and gathering runner beans, the last of the season, for dinner. In the afternoon, we travelled by car to Wareham where we draw our old age pension. Collectively we receive £134 for the week, this is about £20 more than a married couple's allowance but I paid extra into a pension fund over the years so reap some benefit now.

On the journey to Wareham we noticed that at Stoborough there was a long queue of vehicles at the garage waiting to buy petrol. We later found out on the national news that the hauliers and farmers are picketing the refineries to prevent movement of petroleum etc in protest at the rise in price. The cost per litre at the garage is 81.9p.

My birth-place in East Street was opposite the Castle Inn in my granny's house, she was known by all as Granny Paine. My brother Peter, who is 7 years younger than me, lives in West Street. He worked for Budden, the butcher and my father worked at the cordite factory at Holton Heath then later became a harness maker. My schooling in Corfe was always enjoyable, I liked playing football and became a member of the school team. On leaving school at 14, Stan Sheasby offered me a job at his garage, sited opposite the War Memorial Cemetery, serving petrol to customers. The commercial grade of Regent cost 11d (old pence) a gallon and Shell (better quality) 1 shilling and 3d. I did this 7 days a week for 2½d per hour. Before work, for about six months I used also to deliver the newspapers for Eddie Holland, the newsagent, to the whole village. This would take up to 2 hours daily and a week's wage was 3s 6d. Stan was a good boss and it was he who gave me my first experience at driving a bus. We were on the highway near Upton in a Bedford, I was only 16 and keen to learn - we both lived to tell the tale and so did our fellow road users!

In 1939, I left Sheasby's to work at Tommy Cooper's grocery shop, just to try another job and this I also enjoyed. However, in August 1941 I was called-up for military service. This began near Weston-Super-Mare with 6 months training as a mechanic, working on aircraft. My base became Doncaster but I moved around during the 4 years. The lads and I went where we were needed - anywhere from Exeter to the Shetland Isles, which was a regular trip and for which we were given 1s a day flying pay. When in Purton, Wiltshire, in 1944, I met Rene who was from the East End of London and had seen more of the war than me. We married in Corfe church in 1947 and lived at Halves Cottages. By then I was back working for Stan as a bus driver. I used to do the local school run and also regular journeys to London, perhaps 5 times a week. The speed limit then for buses was 30 mph.

In 1954 I joined a small team at the Milk Factory at the eastern side of the railway station. My job was to unload the churns of milk brought there by a few local farmers as well as those that had been collected from other Purbeck farms. After pasteurisation and bottling, I delivered the crates to milkmen for delivery to households. I used to work a 7 day stretch and then have 2 days off. Here I stayed until the factory closed.

Whereas I had always been contented with my life and work, including my time during service, my next employment was a less pleasant 3 years working for the Atomic Energy Research Establishment at Winfrith. My home life meant a lot to me and never more so during this time. We had 2 children, Ian and Glenis. They each have 2 children. We are glad they all live close to our present home which Rene and I moved into in 1972. Wimborne Mead, off East Street, was built in 1934 for my parents.

My final employment was as a driver of milk tankers for Wincanton Transport collecting from farms mainly within Purbeck. I could tell lots of tales of my time as a tanker driver. Many of the farmers were real characters and brief exchanges of stories and jokes made this a happy end to my working life. I feel I must have pleased these men of the soil, because when I retired I was given, as a parting present, a Spanish holiday with spending money. This was in 1986, since when I have enjoyed good health and have taken pride in watching my grandchildren mature into adulthood.

Today's weather: Misty start then sunny and hot. 23 degrees Celsius

Name *Wilf Pope*

House *Wimborne Mead.*

Year of birth *Jan. 15TH 1921.*

Street *East Street*

THE SURPRISE

It was a fine sunny morning in early July in the year of our Lord two thousand. The sun had risen at just after 5 o'clock and by 6 I was up and dressed and enjoying the first cup of tea of the day. I hasten to add that though I am often up at 6 I am seldom dressed until a much later more reasonable hour. Despite the early hour the dew on the grass had evaporated so I took my second cup of tea into the back garden and started counting the corpses littering the lawn. The tally was high but I knew that tomorrow morning, and every morning at this time of year, the death toll would be similar. Under cover of darkness the armies of slugs would be back to ravage the plants in our back garden. They just cannot get the idea into their heads that our back garden is not a nice place to be.

I went back into the kitchen still wondering how I could fire the imagination of the local slug population with the idea of leaving our garden. As if on automatic pilot my hand reached for the teapot and poured another cup of tea. In my humble opinion tea provides a jolly good start to the day though, taking my children as being representative of the next generation, it seems that they prefer coffee. Still lost in my thoughts I picked up the half empty bottle of Chardonnay wine left over from last night's dinner, corked it and popped it into the fridge. It was then that a germ of an idea started growing in my thoughts. Why don't we go on a 'booze cruise' to France? I had heard the term bandied about but was not sure of the precise meaning. Was it getting 'legless' on a cruise or was it buying stocks of wine at a very reasonable price? Getting so drunk that one lost control of one's legs was not my idea of fun but the latter option certainly had its appeal. I decided to investigate the idea further but to keep my thoughts to myself for the time being. If I could organise the whole expedition it would be a nice surprise for my wife.

My first stroke of luck was to discover that cutting two coupons out of the local paper qualified one to purchase a return trip from Poole to Cherbourg on Brittany Ferries for the sum of £14.50. The time in France was limited to twenty-four hours; the fare covered two people and if we wanted to take our car there would be an additional cost of £14.50. This I subsequently learnt was what constituted a 'booze cruise' and on such cruises one could elect to get 'legless' or buy wine, do both or do neither. My mind was made up. The total fare at £29 was an absolute bargain when one considers that a return fare to London by bus would cost about the same for two passengers! A telephone call to Brittany Ferries revealed that we could leave Poole just after midday and arrive back at a little after midnight the next day. A two day holiday for the princely sum of £29.

On checking the family calendar, two-day blocks in which nothing had been entered were hard to come by but I eventually found one. With a great flourish I wrote across the two-day block in bold capital letters 'THE SURPRISE'. Within moments my wife was questioning me about the entry on the calendar but my resolve held firm to ensure my plan would be a surprise. I telephoned Brittany Ferries and made a reservation for the relevant dates.

Now that we had a firm date, the question of where we would spend the night in France had to be addressed. Snuggling down in the back of the car was no longer an option at my time of life. I telephoned a hotel that a friend had recommended to me and in a mixture of English and French reserved a room. The accuracy of my French was obviously in question as the hotel asked me to confirm in writing. Unfortunately to do this I had to obtain some advice from my wife. Needless to say it didn't take the brains of a Sherlock Holmes to work out the connection between the calendar entry, the Brittany Ferries envelope arriving on our door mat and the seeking of advice on how to make a hotel reservation in French. We were obviously going to France for a couple of days - what a surprise!

The only thing left that could now be a surprise was the hotel in France and that would be a surprise for both of us. Fortunately the hotel, situated within the ruins of a once fortified castle, was delightful and so our trip to France on 12 September 2000 proved to be a truly memorable occasion.

Today's weather: *Warm, sunny with light wind.*

Name THOMPSON

Year of birth 1938

House 9

Street Colletts Close

A Purbeck Visit

Arriving in Purbeck at the end of a six hour drive, the stars are bright silver against a black velvet sky. The air in Corfe is fresh and clear – we take great gulps revelling in the absence of the grime and pollution of London, our breath condensing into white clouds, miniature steam-trains. Another world, another time here. Silence. My great grandfather was the doctor in Corfe for years at the beginning of the 20th Century. London is my mission field. I am part of a dynamic young church – we are praying and believing that London will be transformed by the power of Jesus and His gospel, deeply convinced that Christ is the only hope for a lost world, that "all have sinned and fall short of the glory of God", that "God demonstrates His love toward us in this, that while we were still sinners Christ died for us", and that "if you confess with your mouth that Jesus is Lord and believe in your heart that God raised Him from the dead you will be saved". Our mission – the Great Commission. Coming home to Corfe gives me a sense of the eternal power of Jesus – things change slowly here...His Creation is more evident here. I love to go down to the sea at Kimmeridge, Worth, Studland – great windsufing down here when the wind's blowing..

This part of the country takes my breath away...purely the evidence of God the world's Creator. It's so different to the busy life we lead in London. Instead of being swept along in the pollution with the crowds of shoppers, commuters and tourists, there's the space to relax, walk the dogs, appreciate life and contemplate what it's really all about. The Dorset landscape always makes me think what a beautiful world we live in, if only we would bother to stop and take a good look at what surrounds us. The first time I came to Corfe Castle was an amazingly hot summers day and I will never forget it. We went for a walk on St Alban's Head and I longed to take those views back to the people of London who have never seen the sea. With this scenery in front of us I wondered how people can say that there is no God. Back in London, where things move fast and furiously, I know that not far away are peaceful scenes that add so much to our lives...seeing our God through the nature He has created. It is so peaceful!

Today's weather:

Name Jamie Drew Drury and Clare murchie

Year of birth 1971

House Herons

Street East Street

Thursday September 14th

CORFE CASTLE TOWN HALL AND MUSEUM.

The Town Hall was built before 1770. The original building was probably a single story structure with a thatch roof. The Town Council and now the Parish Council have held their monthly meetings in the Town Hall for over two hundred years.

The original museum was in existence from the mid 1880's until 1885, and occupied part of a house situated between the Bankes Arms and Clealls stores.

With the arrival of the railway from Wareham to Swanage this house was demolished in order to make way for the present Station Road. All museum exhibits were transferred to the Dorset County Museum.

The ground floor of the Corfe Castle Town Hall had been used for many purposes including a School, a Butchers shop, a Cobblers and a Carpenters workshop. Part of the south end was once the 'lock up' for lawbreakers.

The present museum was established here in 1962, by the Corfe Castle Town Trust under the direction of Mr Tony Brown, and the collection consisted mainly of his fossil and archaeological discoveries from the local area.

In 1988 the Trust decided to update the museum and extend the collection. During the last six years the collection has increased due to the generosity of many local residents.

The Town Hall building is at least 250 years old, and suffers from damp penetration. During the last year major renovation work has been carried out. The outside walls were injected and covered with silicone and the inner walls of the museum have been tanked. New shelving has been erected and the museum decorated.

The Trust's main source of income is derived from donations given by visitors to the Museum and is used to repair, maintain and restore the property and contents. For the recent work however, the Trust received additional financial aid from Corfe Castle Parish Council, Purbeck District Council, Dorset County Council and the Area Museum Council for the South West. The Trust acknowledges their support with gratitude.

The Corfe Castle Town Trust is a charity established in 1889 to maintain the property of the old Borough-The Town Hall, The Stone Cross in the Square, The Sign of Four in the Square, two old Water Pumps (Square & East Street), the two old Town Charters (1578 & 1661), the 15th Century Town Mace and Borough Seal.

The museum has been granted Full Registration by the Museum and Galleries Commission.

Opening hours-   Nov-March weekends only.
                 April-Oct daily 10am to 6pm.

Today's weather:

Name *The Town Trust*   Year of birth

House *Town Hall*   Street *West Street*

It's here again. It is September. My favourite month. Today began for me, as has almost every day for several years, with an eight o'clock walk on the Common with Daisy. I left Farthing Cottage, at the southern end of West Street and walked north towards the Castle, then turned right through Webbers Close and on to the Halves. On the left, just before the gate, the field is full of Jacob's sheep. Strange looking, brown-blobbed creatures. Their usual chorus of greeting followed me past half a dozen or so happily munching horses systematically partaking of breakfast, as their breath spurted rhythmically into the early morning air. Then across the next field, across the road and up the path through Halves Cottages and on to the Common. Then, while walking up the slope to the brow, meetings with other walkers; greetings, exchanges. Daisy, now joined by other four-footed friends, as I am by two-footed, introduce ourselves to the day: the beauty of it, and acknowledge the love of our inheritance. It really does promise to be a truly beautiful day. A drip on the nose and a nip on the fingers, but the mist slowly rising through the cobwebs towards the glowing orb in the sky.

But time passes. Commitments beckon. A hurried return, toast, tea and then into the car. An appointment in Wareham with someone in trouble, but no further. There is a petrol strike. We are all planning our lives very carefully. Not moving far unless necessary. A salutory lesson. What is necessary? Who - is necessary? I decided. I made my journey and returned. The village has changed atmosphere. Little, if any, traffic sound. Cars parked everywhere. The sound of voices instead. People talking to eachother. Bored perhaps. Standing at gates. Standing in the road. Just talking.

A quick bite, then to my feet again, this time to walk around the village. Something of which I never tire. As my feet walk, my mind travels too, around the houses in which I have lived and stayed. I go down West Street again, past Chaffeys this time, where I wintered three years ago, on towards the Square, past Lime Cottage, my first purchase in Corfe. Then on past Well Court, opposite the old Post Office, where I lived for such a short, sad time, round and through the Square, past Orchards Cottage on the left, where some happy summers were spent with my son and our dogs. The pavement ends and i cross just before Mortons House, and continue opposite the old Churchyard, The Castle Pub, on past East Hawes Cottage, another summer stop, then turn right through the five-bar gate, across the Halves and home again. 'Home' - but not home. Farthings took me in but it is not home in the real sense. Later, I make supper, relax but ultimately sleep evades me. I toss and turn and eventually go back to where my day began. The Common. My day becomes a circle. The world is a circle. Life is a circle. It is mild on the brow now: it is eerie, but not fearful. I am not alone. I can see through the darkness the outline of my next real home - High Standing. I am to be custodian of my own little piece of heaven. My life is a circle too. I have been coming to this beloved Isle since I was three years old. It has always been in my heart. Now it has taken me back. I am fortunate indeed. I belong in the hearts of its people. I belong in the heart of Purbeck.

A little day. A little life.

Today's weather: Dry and fine.

Name	Angela Reed	Year of birth	25.4.45
House	Farthing Cottage	Street	West

Today's weather: Sunny & breezy for the Choir Coffee Morning.

Name Sheila Doyle-Stevens

Year of birth 1925

House No. 8.

Street Springwell Close.

Sunday September 17th

House Sitting for a friend in Harmans Cross

Woke up to a pleasant sunny morning. Switched on Radio 2 and tuned into "Good Morning Sunday", one of my favourite programmes, presented by Don Mc Clean. Got up and fed four cats, Bonnie, Carlos, Bits and Bobs. Had breakfast: cornflakes, banana, orange juice and vitamin pills.

Washed pots, got washed and dressed ready for Church, but in between all this watched Olympics on TV from Australia.

Attended morning family service at St. Edward, King and Martyr Church in Corfe, which began at 10 30 After a very pleasant service we left Church at 11 15 a.m.

After Church off we drove to Wimborne Market, a very agreeable journey and bought pears and strawberries.

Arriving back in Corfe we called in the "Box of Delights" to see our daughter Jan. We then journeyed home for roast beef and mustard sandwiches followed by strawberries and double cream!

3.15 p.m. we went down to Swanage to sit by the sea to read and enjoy ourselves , which included an ice-cream Left there at 5 p.m due to rain clouds.

Called back home to collect a bottle of wine and feed the cats

Went back to Corfe, arriving 5.30 at the "Box of Delights" and waited for our daughter to close the shop at 6 p.m Went back to our daughter's home for the evening meal Roast lamb and roast veg, rhubarb crumble and cream. Looked at photograph of the Ball, taken in Corfe Castle grounds. Read the paper and chatted Left after a pleasant evening at 11.30 End of another day

Today's weather: Sunny and bright with threatened rain

Name	Willie Hartley (from Sheffield) (on holiday with daughter, Jan Harriott)	Year of birth	1922
House	Lagny Court, Jubilee Gardens	Street	Mead Road

Monday September 18th

I got up around 6.15 .m. It was fine then but it came on to rain about half an hour later. I did some cleaning, then had my breakfast, made my bed, tidied up my bedroom and bathroom. My granddaughter looked in on her way to work at St. Michael's Garage on the Valley Road. She had driven from Poole.

At 7.45 a.m. I went to see my neighbour who is an invalid. After I had warmed the porridge, washed up, watered the plants, emptied the waste paper baskets, took the milk stand out ready for next time and did the recycling bin. My neighbour has a carer to bathe and dress her and do as much for her as possible in a limited time.

At 9.15 my granddaughter rang to say there is still a fuel crisis and the garage has very little petrol. Doctors, nurses, firemen, carers and ambulances are priorities.

10.00 a.m. have lit the fire and tested the fire alarm (all well). Popped in to another neighbour who had a nasty migraine yesterday but is much better today. Her dog, Lesa, has turned out a lovely dog. She had it from a tiny puppy. Her helper, Rossie was there and Mary was much better today. Had a yarn.

11.00 Went to order my prescription from the doctor.

11.30 Getting dinner. The coal man has just been. It's £15.30 for 2 cwts. I store it all the summer while it's cheap. It goes up in price in a fortnight. Did some washing. Water meter man came to read the meter. Electricity man came to read meter.

3.30 My Grandson, Simon, came in. He is Chef at the Greyhound. Will have tea soon. Will knit, read and watch television for the evening.

Today's weather   Wet and windy

Name   Gertrude Maud Welsh   Year of birth   1920

House   54   Street   East Street

Today is the third anniversary of the move into our own building next to the First School, made possible by generous grants of money and a lot of hard work by local organisations and local people. The children love their Nursery and find it so much easier to start school in a place that is familiar.

Apart from blowing out the candles on our pretend cake and drawing some pictures for the diary, we had a normal day. It was a wet and dreary morning, but after we had finished our drink, biscuit and fruit, the sun came out and we went into the playground and played "What's the time Mr Wolf? ". Then there was just time for a few songs and nursery rhymes before it was time to go home.

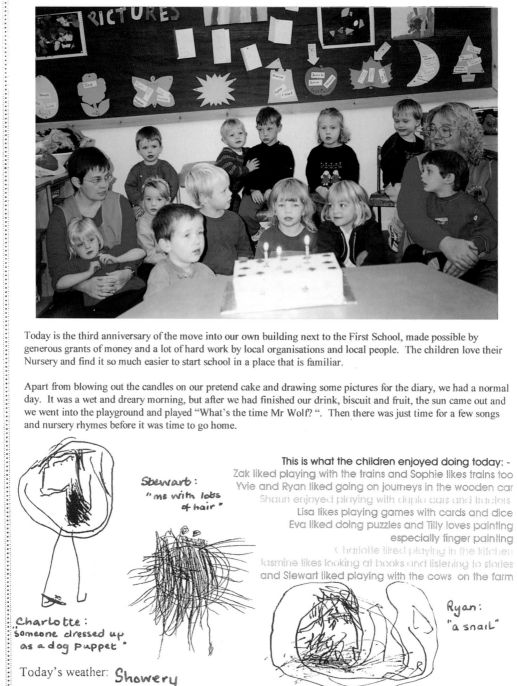

Stewart:
" me with lots of hair"

This is what the children enjoyed doing today: -
Zak liked playing with the trains and Sophie likes trains too
Yvie and Ryan liked going on journeys in the wooden car
Shaun enjoyed playing with duplo cars and tractors
Lisa likes playing games with cards and dice
Eva liked doing puzzles and Tilly loves painting
especially finger painting
Charlotte liked playing in the kitchen
Jasmine likes looking at books and listening to stories
and Stewart liked playing with the cows on the farm

Charlotte:
Someone dressed up as a dog puppet'

Ryan:
"a snail"

Today's weather: **Showery**

Name **Corfe Castle Community Nursery School** Year of birth **1997 (previously Corfe Playgroup)**

House **'Aunties' – Lisa Pierce, Monica Moss, Carol Pitman, Louise Aylward, Mandy Coward, Shirley Lardner, Marie Pope. Julie Fooks.**   Street **East Street next to the School in the garden of the Rectory**

A fairly average day for me!

Firstly seeing my daughter off to school, then my husband off to work, closely followed by me driving to Swanage Surgery to start my morning working as a community physiotherapist.

The first hour was typical. Dealing with phone calls, messages and paperwork and liaising with other professionals. Then I climbed in the car and drove around Swanage visiting four separate patients. Two of these were for the first time and two as follow-ups to previous visits. I combined seeing two patients at the helpful Day Centre.

Today was a little unusual as one person had an epileptic fit on me!

I rushed across the briny using the Sandbanks ferry at lunchtime – eating en route, to my second job as physio at St. Ann's Hospital. Most of this afternoon was spent with six patients from the Eating Disorder Unit. The Dietician and I work with them on an education programme. This day the topic was Exercise and Calories as many of these people use excessive amounts of exercise to lose weight.

I left St. Ann's at 4.30 p.m. and drove back through Studland to home – a very pleasant trip to and from work except in the height of summer.

Fortunately my daughter had started tea so I took over as we were rushing out for a 7 p.m. meeting at the Purbeck School about her trip in April. Back home at 9.30 p.m. and crash out with a glass of wine and catch up on my husband's days events.

Today's weather   Dull and damp

Name   Christine Kemp   Year of birth   1951

House   7   Street   Colletts Close

Thursday September 21st

I WOKE AT 7AM TO A GREY MISERABLE MORNING.
LAY IN BED & WATCHED TV-OLYMPIC REPORT FROM
SIDNEY AUSTRALIA - GREAT BRITIAN HAD JUST WON
A GOLD MEDAL FOR ROWING.

8AM - WENT DOWNSTAIRS TO PREPARE BREAKFAST
FOR OUR BED-BREAKFAST GUESTS & AFTERWARDS
ENJOYED TALKING TO THEM ABOUT THEIR WALK
IN THE PURBECKS THE PREVIOUS DAY.

10AM - DROVE TO POOLE TO TAKE PART IN A TENNIS
MATCH - FORTUNATELY THE VENUE WAS A CLUB
WITH INDOORS COURTS AS BY THIS TIME IT WAS
RAINING HEAVILY. STAYED ON AT THE CLUB FOR
LUNCH THEN DID THE WEEKLY SHOPPING FOR FOOD
& HOUSEHOLD SUPPLIES ON THE WAY HOME TO CORFE

ON REACHING HOME HAD TO QUICKLY CLEAN & TIDY
GUEST BEDROOMS READY FOR NEW ARRIVALS IN
THE EVENING

IT WAS NOW TIME TO PREPARE A MEAL FOR MY
HUSBAND & MYSELF WHICH WE ENJOYED WITH
A GLASS OF FRENCH WINE. THEN RELAXED-READ
THE DAILY PAPER & WATCHED TV - MORE FROM
OLYMPIC 2000

FINALLY RETIRED TO BED WITH AN INTERESTING
BOOK FROM CORFE LIBRARYS & READ UNTIL I
WAS READY TO FALL ASLEEP

Today's weather: WET

Name ANNEMARIE COLLINS   Year of birth 1942

House VERGERS MEAD   Street EAST STREET

A memorable day in the life of the Simanowitz family!

Anton exchanged contracts on his very first home, a one bedroomed flat in a well-constructed Regency building on the Brighton beach front.

Stefan had his stitches removed following reconstruction of his anterior cruciate ligament, a perfect wound, healing well, and he should be playing football again in eight months time.

And the log cabin went up at the end of the garden.

Today's weather: Wet and warm

Name	Milton and Elinor Simanowitz	Year of birth	1936 and 1942
House	Daisy Cottage	Street	West Street

TYPICAL SHOOT DAY

Waking up. Knowing what the day will bring, going through the routine – that now happens automatically – mind focussed on one thing only.

Out of the door, fighting with Aigles, Barbours, leads and whistles.

Greet the others and say, "Good morning Sirs".

We're off now, pile into the ex army wagon. It's a state, people on the floor, dogs on the benches, I always thought it was meant to be the other way round!

The wagon slams its brakes on ......"Quick, grab that dog", "Mind the flags", "Hold on I'm falling out". It's utter mayhem.

Finally we get there, get half pulled, half pushed out of the wagon. I started the day with a black labrador, why have I got a springer? "That's my dog, here's yours" – thankfully that's sorted. Send the dog away, he's gone away then sits down laughing at me ......

This carries on all day. It's completely hectic. At the end of the day get home and have to go through the routine backwards, fighting with whistles and leads, Barbours and Aigles.

The day has been organised chaos ..... why do I do it?

  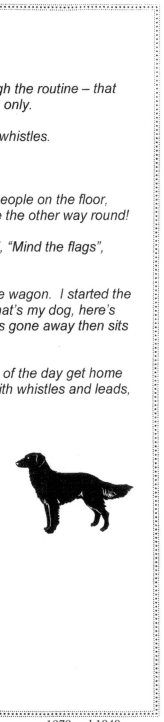

Today's weather:

Name	Carly Sorrell and Peter Manley	Year of birth	1979 and 1949
House	4 West Street, Kingston	Street	

This morning the Church bells of St. Edwards are ringing and bells are ringing in our heads on our 23rd wedding anniversary. Today we attend the 10.30 a.m. Communion Service conducted by the Reverend Herman Nuttall assisted by the Reverend Rex Howe, both retired clergymen resident in Corfe Castle. The Rector and his wife, Maurice and Nancy Strike, are away on holiday.

As we walk down the aisle to take our seats the most special and sacred memories of our marriage celebrations are rekindled, when the then Rector, the Reverend Gerald Squarey conducted the service. That weekend in 1977 was the Harvest Festival and the Church was aglow with blazing autumn colours; we were aglow too!

Today we are looking again at the wedding photographs and press cuttings of our Anglo-Dutch day. Marriage to Lucas after my long single life, including voyaging around the world as an officer on P & O's great white liners, was a wonderful new chapter in my life of adventure! I felt like a queen; in the year of her Majesty Queen Elizabeth's Silver Jubilee; now we look forward to sharing celebrations in the year 2002 – the Queen's 50th Anniversary of her Reign and our Silver Wedding Anniversary. Now back home from Church, we open our small shop, "The Blacksmith's Shop" (which we started in April 1999) and with weddings in mind, we sell amongst other unusual gifts – Lucky Horseshoes!

The Parish Church

ST. EDWARD KING & MARTYR

CORFE CASTLE

To Celebrate

The Marriage

of

EILEEN and LUCAS

SATURDAY, 24th SEPTEMBER, 1977

12 noon

Conducted by

The Reverend Gerald Squarey

Assisted by The Reverend Peter Paul van Lelyveld
(Minister of the Netherlands Reform Church)

Resident Organist: Mr. Lionel Simpson. .

Guest Organist: Mr. Maurice Turner
(Organist and Choirmaster, Westbourne Methodist Church)

Solo Chorister: Alison Seville

Children were amused

CHILDREN are an essential ingredient of a wedding. But they do tend to get bored at the reception after they've done their duty as bridesmaids, pageboys, flower girls, train bearers, or whatever. . .
So, what a splendid idea at the Corfe Castle marriage celebration of Miss Eileen Crone, when the 30 children were treated to a coach outing, complete with special food hamper. They missed all that handshaking and boring grown-up small talk — and returned just in time for the cutting of the cake.

Eileen's husband, the son of a Dutch Countess, is a member of the Royal Ocean Racing Club. He is also general manager of a shipping company in Sharjah, United Arab Emirates, which is where the couple will live — so Eileen has had to give up her work as secretary of Corfe's millenium and carnival committees.

Today's weather: Rainy morning sunny afternoon

Name	Eileen (née Crone) and Lucas Van Lelyveld	Year of birth	1932/1933
House	The Old Forge	Street	38 East Street

Monday September 25th

I awoke at 6.30 a.m to the sound of music from Classic FM on my radio-alarm, and gazed across at my bedroom window to view the sky trying to anticipate what type of weather I could expect today from this unpredictable British climate — so far, so good. I went downstairs, picked up the Daily Telegraph, read the headlines and the weather report whilst making my early-morning cuppa. After breakfast, I tackled the cryptic crossword, and then strolled down East Street to our friendly village store to buy some groceries and post my mail. On the way back I looked in at the National Trust gift shop to get ideas for presents to take to my family in Florida, with whom I shall be spending Christmas. Leaving the shop I greeted our famous village cat Rupert who spends most days curled up cosily in the window. On my return I decided to accompany my cousin on a visit to her Beach Hut in Swanage, travelling as usual by Steam Train from Corfe station. Alas, we had to return early, due to the weather, so I visited the Library next door to the Village Hall in order to renew my books. During the evening watched "University Challenge" and "Who wants to be a Millionaire" on TV, then read awhile whilst listening to Mozart on C.D.

Today's weather: Bright a.m. Rain p.m. 18°c

Name MRS KAY CHARVAT   Year of birth 1920

House DEEP THATCH   72, EAST Street

I chose today as my diary day because it is my Mother and Father's wedding anniversary. They were married on 26 September 1955. Of course without them I would not be here to appreciate the village of Corfe Castle and value the friendship of the people who live here.

The day starts at 8.30 a.m. with serving breakfast to our guests. Mike is in the kitchen ready with the bacon and eggs and also doing the Sun newspaper crossword at the same time. I'm not normally an early morning person but running in and out of the kitchen with full English breakfasts and pots of tea soon wakes me up. The telephone rings with people wanting to book rooms and Suppliers asking what vegetables, meat etc we need for the week.

Breakfast finished and guests begin to book out going their various way. Those going back to the city not really wanting to go back to the grime and hustle and bustle of city life. The times I have heard - 'Oh I wish we lived here'.

In comes Russell with the mop, bucket and Henry the Hoover to clean up from yesterday's visitors and with the help of Heidi make the bedrooms ready for tonight's guests.

Kevin the Chef is in the kitchen. The smell of steak and ale, chilli and chicken korma wafts through the kitchen doors being prepared for today's hungry people

At 11 a.m. people begin arriving for an early pint or morning coffee.

By 1 p.m. I'm running up and down the garden with ploughmans, sandwiches and various other meals. Warming up bottles of milk for hungry babies and mothers frantically trying to soothe them while they wait. Thank God for dummies!

Late afternoon weary travellers arrive with arms full of various bags and suitcases anxious to book into their room and get into country living mode. You can see the tension leave them as soon as they have freshened up and come back downstairs ready for their first drink.

My Mother and Father arrive in the evening for a celebratory meal and embarrass me in front of Mike by telling tales of when I was younger, some I remember, unfortunately? I don't remember being a difficult teenager?

What a great evening, probably too much red wine but wonderful to spend it with people you love and in a place where you love to live

Today's weather

Name Alison Wason   Year of birth

House Bankes Hotel   Street The Square

Today we have just realised that <u>this</u> is the day we promised to record for this special Village diary 2000! We have mistakenly already prepared notes for 19th September so, <u>today</u>, as we're spending a very quiet day at home, we're going to tell you about our very pleasant day a week last Tuesday, September 19th.

Jumped out of bed early this morning and, as is my wont, looked out of the window; firstly to take in the view of the Purbeck Hills, and then to see what the weather was like. Happy that we had a pleasant day ahead, I bathed, dressed and went downstairs ready to greet our two dear friends currently staying with us, Derek and Shirley Bull from Blisworth, the village where we lived until we moved to Corfe Castle six months ago. The Bulls have been on holiday in Cornwall and called in to see us on their way home.

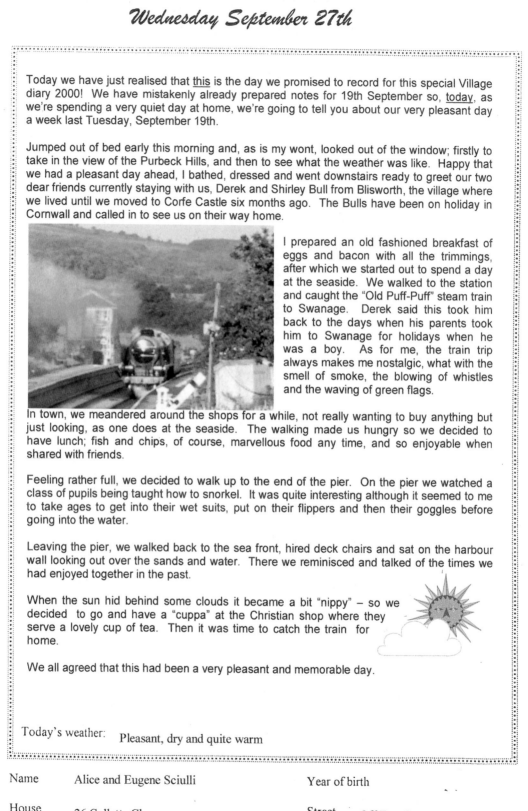

I prepared an old fashioned breakfast of eggs and bacon with all the trimmings, after which we started out to spend a day at the seaside. We walked to the station and caught the "Old Puff-Puff" steam train to Swanage. Derek said this took him back to the days when his parents took him to Swanage for holidays when he was a boy. As for me, the train trip always makes me nostalgic, what with the smell of smoke, the blowing of whistles and the waving of green flags.

In town, we meandered around the shops for a while, not really wanting to buy anything but just looking, as one does at the seaside. The walking made us hungry so we decided to have lunch; fish and chips, of course, marvellous food any time, and so enjoyable when shared with friends.

Feeling rather full, we decided to walk up to the end of the pier. On the pier we watched a class of pupils being taught how to snorkel. It was quite interesting although it seemed to me to take ages to get into their wet suits, put on their flippers and then their goggles before going into the water.

Leaving the pier, we walked back to the sea front, hired deck chairs and sat on the harbour wall looking out over the sands and water. There we reminisced and talked of the times we had enjoyed together in the past.

When the sun hid behind some clouds it became a bit "nippy" – so we decided to go and have a "cuppa" at the Christian shop where they serve a lovely cup of tea. Then it was time to catch the train for home.

We all agreed that this had been a very pleasant and memorable day.

Today's weather: Pleasant, dry and quite warm

Name   Alice and Eugene Sciulli   Year of birth

House   26 Colletts Close   Street   Off East Street

Thursday September 28th

I woke at 6-30 a.m. after a very wet & windy night. Here in Kimmeridge we experienced winds of gale force & more. The sea was running hard with lots of white water. I love to watch the sea in these conditions, but greatly respect it also. We are house-sitting in Kimmeridge for 3 weeks while friends are in Canada. It's a wonderful place, very beautiful in the summer & wild & dramatic during winter storms. It's a lovely house & we are enjoying it immensely. We have 2 dogs & 1 cat to care for, the 4 chicken were killed & eaten by a fox.

I take the dogs for a long walk each morning & today we went to the cliff-top. It was a little damp, but exhilarating. Timothy, our eldest son, & his wife Karen came for lunch. The weather improved during the day & by the afternoon was sunny, warm & breezy. We called to see friends at Church Knowle, who are on holiday from France.

I had a pleasant walk with the dogs. One is a black Labrador & the other a Jack Russell. Jack is keen to chase & kill all the pheasants around, so he stays on the lead. Will is more obedient & so can be free. We walked for about 2½ miles & I know it does me a lot of good.

Later, I drove to Corfe Castle to eat at the Castle Inn. It is now run by Alison, a friend from years ago. We ate a very tasty meal & then home. What a great way to spend a day in Purbeck.

Today's weather: Grey start, then warm sunshine.

Name JASMINE CATTLE
(formerly of Bridge Cottage)
on holiday from France
House House-sitting in Kimmeridge.
Year of birth 1938
Street East.

Friday 29th September 2000

At are Harvest Festival we had poems and a play. Everybody brought something we put them in boxes and sent them to the people in the village.

Today's weather:
15° C
Sun and Showers
Name
Class 2. Corfe Castle First School.
House
Year of birth 1993 (Age 7 children)
Street
East Street.

TWINNING ASSOCIATION MILLENNIUM PARTY

A record number of people (34) from Pont Hébert came to Corfe Castle for the weekend of 29th September – 1st October, staying with local families.

Over the past five years many friendships have been made through the Twinning Association but we were also very happy to see some new faces among the visiting group.. We started the weekend with a welcome reception at the Bankes Arms and after settling in, we met up again at the British Legion for a friendly Boules match – and needless to say the French won!

Saturday September 30th was the highlight of the weekend. Host families took their visitors out to see something of Dorset while a team of helpers prepared the Village Hall for a Millennium Party in honour of our French friends.

We were delighted that so many people of all ages from Corfe Castle joined in to make this a really memorable occasion. As it is Millennium Year we decided to have an entertainer, who kept us all amused with his card tricks stilt walking and trick cycling, all of which admirably bridged the language barrier.

After a splendid buffet dinner we danced to Steve Haw's disco and it was wonderful to see everyone mingling so happily.

Today's weather: A pleasant day

| Name | Ruth Nuttall Committee Member | Year of birth | Twinning Assn. founded 1995 |

House   Street

Sunday October 1st

Returned from Polly, enjoyed looking at the many maps of Tony's campaigns she is keeping for the Imperial War Museum. The garden falling back a bit I thought. Good trip back, the 70 miles took us 1¾ hours, traffic seemed thicker north of Salisbury than down here. Quick look round the garden as a few days away I always imagine something must have gone wrong but of course it hadn't.

Picked beans, calabrese, and sweet corn for supper, must have been pretty windy as the sweet corn was nearly flat. Tomatoes are now very nearly over but have had a marvellous lot this year, nearly all Gardeners Delight outside and Sweet Peppers in the G.H.

This evening forecast warns of strong wind and rain from the N.W. unusual quarter to come from. The trees still refuse to drop their leaves must be the rain last month about 4" This will give a long green autumn to look forward to.

Today's weather: Sun with blustery showers

Name Tim Hamilton Fletcher   Year of birth 1925

House Ormonde House   Street West Street

TODAY I WALKED ROUND THE VILLAGE

AND PICKED UP THIS LITTER. I WONDERED

IF IN THE FUTURE PEOPLE WOULD

STILL DROP THEIR RUBBISH IN THE STREETS.

Today's weather: A.M. CLOUDY/WINDY. P.M. SUNNY/WINDY

Name JANET PERRIOR   Year of birth 1950

House DOLLINGS BARN STUDIO   Street EAST STREET

The weather forecast was not good, so it was decided that after our morning's work Brenda and I would go to Dorchester, where we would look for potential locations, which, when the weather improved, we could photograph for the current audio/visual presentation we are compiling on William Barnes.

Dorchester is often our choice for an afternoon if the weather is poor. Apart from all the interesting buildings and places in the town, there are also various exhibitions at the County Museum throughout the year, and these exhibitions, along with all the other things in the Museum, are of a very high standard and always enjoyable. The current exhibition marks the 70th anniversary of Dennis Lowson as an artist of some originality, and the paintings on display were colourful, vibrant and meaningful, and we enjoyed them very much. We also recollected that William Barnes was one of the founders of the County Museum in 1845, when the exhibits occupied two rooms in Judge Jeffery's Lodging – so our visit was also connected to our present interest.

When we returned home we sat in the car outside "Culls", as it is known, and thought of the time when it was the first Post Office in Corfe village. Mrs. Bessie Honeybun, née Cull, told me that when her father bought the property in 1926 the door to the room on the left hand side of the front door still bore the sign that proclaimed "POST OFFICE", and mention is also made of this in the deeds of the property. The old postcard below shows that there were railings and a path to the door,

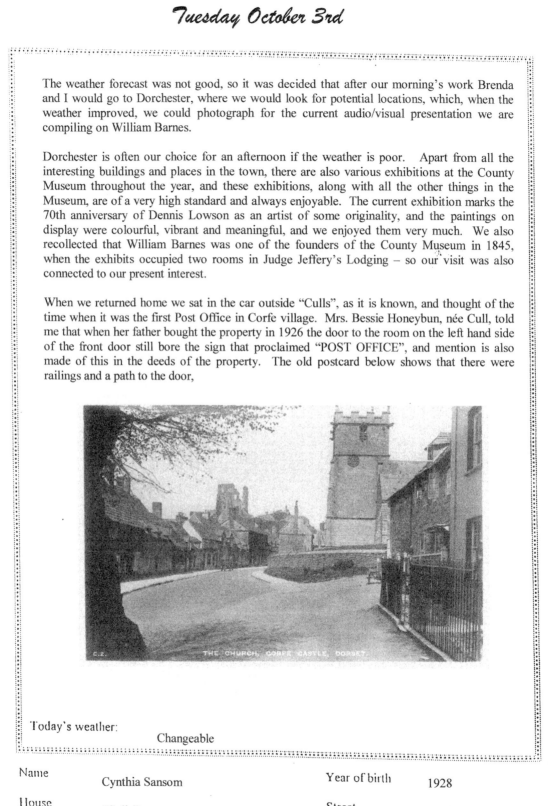

THE CHURCH, CORFE CASTLE, DORSET.

Today's weather:
              Changeable

| Name | Cynthia Sansom | Year of birth | 1928 |
| House | "Culls" | Street | 7 West Street |

Wednesday 4th October 2000 is like any school day; I say school day because our granddaughter Freya (age 3 ½) needs taking to Pre-School as she stayed with us overnight. Thankfully this is not too much of a daunting task, as a) she enjoys it and b) my wife is Chairman there. She will start what is now deemed as 'big school' next year.

I wonder just what schools will be like in say 100 years from now let alone by the end of the next millennium. I would imagine that 'knowledge' will eventually be transferred electronically direct to the brain – I know I have probably seen too many science fiction movies but I guess that at some stage be it 250 or 500 years from now it will happen. Anyone reading this and smiling is forgiven!

The route to Pre-school is today via the petrol station – yes in the year 2000 we still use petrol in our cars. The current price is 79.9p per litre – by the way did we ever sign up for the euro or is there now a new, world currency?
Question – In the year 3000 is there a world? (Not as we know it Jim – StarTrek films 1990's).

After Pre-school we all go to Swanage there are letters to post and food to purchase. Parking the car at the supermarket (Co-Op) incurs the following charge– 60p per hour but spend £5 with them and they refund the car park money.

There is a two tier system for postage, 27p for 1st class and 19p for 2nd class – off course we have email but not everyone has a computer. The laugh is that my first computer had only a 10 megabyte hard drive but my current one has a massive 10 gigabytes of memory. I can picture your face cracking up as you read this – 10 gigabytes, wow!!!

Trooping round the supermarket I can tell you that milk is 89p for 4 pints. Sorry 2.27 litres (we Brits never did get used to the metric system and certainly at the grand old age of 59 I am still thinking in pints and gallons) – what are they I can hear you say. Bread varies between 40p/60p a loaf and you can pick a mobile phone up for £39.95 – off course it's nothing like the telephones that you have but we are only just learning.

Back home just in time to see the Tory Party Conference – William Hague in full flow – did he ever become P.M..The previous week it was the turn of Tony Blair, both of them are promising the earth and with elections due probably next year things are running close.
After our evening meal and with Freya safely tucked up in bed my wife makes her regular telephone call to our two daughters (Fiona and Suzanne) and our other grandchildren (Ellie, Sophie and William). We then sit down and watch TV or read depending how the mood takes us. Life is hectic but never dull and we usually go to bed pretty tired.
Today's weather: Cloudy and dull

Name	Alan Blakey	Year of birth	1940
House	12	Street	South Street, Kingston

Thursday October 5th

I was born at Kimmeridge and moved to Corfe Castle when I was 7 years old. I moved to Ruislip permanently in 1945 when my husband came out of the army. Since then I have returned to Corfe every year on holiday.

We used to stay with my parents Jack & May Hoy who lived in what is now No. 66 West Street. But we now stay next door with Linda although my sister Joan (Marshallsay) still lives at No.76.

This year we are here for 8 days and today we went to West Bay. As we left Corfe we stopped in the square to post some letters and I reflected on how the village had changed since I was younger. We could buy almost anything in the village then - there were two bakers, several grocers, a gents outfitters, a drapers/ladies wear shop, three petrol stations, four butchers, a shoe shop, sweet-shops, a blacksmiths and several tea-rooms.

We drove to West Bay, stopping in Bridport for coffee and a walk around. Doug bought a pair of shoes which cost £20 but were reduced from £40 -**a good bargain!**

We had lunch at the famous Riverside Restaurant, Doug and I had Cod in Guinness Batter with Chips and Mushy Peas, Linda had Mackerel with Salad. Then Linda and I had Lime and Citrus Meringue. A carafe of wine accompanied the meal. The whole meal cost £50 for three.

We then walked around the harbour which has been made famous by the TV series called Harbour Lights starring Nick Berry as the harbourmaster. Doug found walking painful as he is recovering from an accident in which he broke his hip.

I bought a Christmas present for our next-door neighbour's daughter Rosie - it was a purse with her name on it - it cost only £2.99

We came home over the cliff top road through Abbotsbury - there were some fantastic views to be seen over the Chesil Bank and Portland as the weather was clear and sunny except for brief shower.

We arrived home in time to watch 'Countdown' on the TV at 4.30pm This is a letters and numbers quiz which we watch every day if possible - it helps to keep ones brain active!

We were all too full to need any tea so Linda & I attempted to do the crossword in the Independent while Doug had a snooze.

We then got talking about the village again and how things had changed.

I went to school initially in what is now the British Legion and afterwards to the 'big school' where we stayed until we left at 14. Mr. Mathews was the headmaster and Mrs. Rugby in charge of the infants. Children only moved to a different senior school if they went to the Grammar school. When I left school I worked at Hibb's the bakers helping Mrs. Hibbs in the house. I then went to London to work and came back to Corfe when the War started in September 1939 and then worked at the cordite factory at Holton Heath.

I met my husband when he was stationed at Glebe House - on the Church Knowle Road. We were married in Corfe in 1943 and my children were also christened in St. Edward's Church.

We watched some more television before having supper and a drink before bed.

Today's weather: warm & sunny

Name Eileen Weldon   Year of birth 1923

House Staying at 64   Street West

Friday October 6th

Hi, There,
My name is Janice Harriott, I am 46 years of age and live in Corfe with my husband Michael we have lived here for 11 years & really love it

At this moment in time we are on Holiday in Cyprus & it is our last Day so obviously it's not one of my typical days in Corfe

Cyprus is about 4½ hours on the Plane & it's in the Mediterranean, weather is very hot 88-92 & in England at the moment it's 50° so today it's Swimwear, tomorrow winter woolies. The Price of everything is so much Cheaper over here Meal for two with Drinks around £15, compared to around £30 in England, Petrol 38p Litre, England around 85p Litre.

Got up This morning & went sunbathing & swimming. Had a Spot of Lunch & had an Hour Relaxing on the Balcony. We then went for a long walk on the beach & stopped at a bar for a couple of drinks arrived back at the appartment & had a little Siesta (Hard life isn't it) then got ready to go out for another few drinks & a meal. Got back around 1130 and finished Packing as we have to leave at 4:30 in the morning & go back to reality, nice while it lasted though save now for next year.

Today's weather: Really Hot & Sunny... (in Cyprus!)

Name Mrs J Harriott   Year of birth 22.07.54
House Lagby Court   Street Jubilee Gardens

Saturday October 7th

What a lovely sunny morning.

I am welcomed first by "Abbey" our much loved dog who always has to make her presence known and then by my son with my early cup of tea.

As it is the village hall coffee morning I make scones and rock cakes for the cake stall before meeting up with friends for coffee, buying plants, Bric-a-brac, etc from the various stalls. This is a marvellous occasion with all the villagers participating and hoping for a lucky ticket with the raffle.

On returning home I find my sister and her son who have arrived for lunch.

In the afternoon we take Abbey for her usual walk on the halves and meet up with other "doggie walkers" who congregate at a very much-appreciated wooden seat for those with ailing legs.

The garden is somewhat taken over by leaves blown down by the gale so we spend time sweeping them up.

We have supper with my son and daughter in law after which we get great amusement from looking through the old family photos (*how time passes*) then it is upstairs to pack for our holiday to Sidmouth the next day.

Today's weather: DRY and SUNNY.

Name Sibyl M. Windsor   Year of birth 1920.

House "HATTON'S RIDGE"   Street EAST STREET. 11

October 8th 2000 is the 53rd anniversary of the day, in 1947, that changed the lives of my family forever. My father, Elias, my mother Phyllis and me, Brian Johnson, arrived at Steeple, Dorset. We were a Liverpool family, born and bred and had travelled by long distance coach to be met at the bus station, in Bournemouth Square, by Jimmy White, driving a Rover 12; what a difference from Liverpool. He was chauffeur for Mrs Holland-Swan. My father, Elias, usually known as Li or later as Ted, has a family line, in southwest Lancashire, going back to the 1500's as farmers and husbandmen. My mother, Phyllis, nee Kebby, has a family line that is Somerset\Devon, to the 1500's through her father and Gloucester, to the mid 1600's, through her mother. Mrs Holland-Swan, a recently widowed lady and chatelaine of Steeple Manor had engaged my parents as butler and cook. Although our time was brief at Steeple, due to her selling the Manor one year after our arrival, living there has made an impression upon me that will last until my dying day. Visits by the son, Ralph Swans and his wife Jocelyn, from London, the gardener Ted Elms and his wife Tressy, the house maid and her sister Beattie and Winnie Mintern who had been so cruelly denied returning to their birthplace, at Warbarrow Bay, Gerald White who worked on the farm and Jack Moss the farmer and his wife and, not least, the beantifiil Dorset countryside, had an everlasting effect on a 12 year old boy from Liverpool. Going to school by taxi and Sbeasby's coach, from Corfe, was a new experience and when the weather was fine cycling over Grange Hill to Wareham School. There wasn't enough room in the classroom and I was given an extra desk alongside Barbara Chaffey, now Canning's. Father bought an ex W.D Norton model 16H motorcycle and ex A.F.S single seat sidecar, for our transport. Petrol was still rationed and he bad an allowance of two gallons per month.

After the shock and sadness at leaving Steeple the family moved to Bishopstone, in Wiltshire. Unable to gain a place for me, at the local technical college, the family found itself, as though fate intended, back in Purbeck, this time at Morton's House, Corfe Castle, the home of Lt. Col. Ashley Bond and his wife Mary. We lived in the bungalow alongside the main house. Michael Bond was a small boy and Richard, not much more than 8 baby, were cared for by Nanny Berwick, in a wonderful nursery. At Christmas time, one year, I remember being invited to join the family, in the drawing room, for a puppet show. It was a time I remember of much happiness. Eventually we moved to Castle Cottage, in East Street, where I stayed until 1962, when I married, a Dorset girl, Gillian Ann Thomas from Corfe Mullen; with mother and father eventually moving to Springwell Close, when it was completed. Through my teenager years Howard Orchard was my best friend and his mother, a lovely old lady who was very long suffering with us boys. Howard and I enjoyed angling and music from the Big Band era. His elder brother Charlie tried to start a bicycle repair business in what became a ladies hairdresser salon just above Dave Ford's shop. Ernie Guy and I were keen motorcyclists and Old Time Dance enthusiasts. Norman Barnes lived on the farm at Aflhington, where we helped bring in the harvest, the old fashioned way. In the winter months the young men of the village frequented the Reading Room, in The Square. It was furnished with a small billiard table, board games, darts, some books and a table tennis table. The fireplace was small and made me think of Dickens Scrooge. When I was old enough I went to whist drives, very much a scene of the old style of country life. In the summer we had fun avoiding the village Bobby, Mr Morton, when we, under age, after football or cricket on the Halves, used to go to The Fox Inn and drink cider, illicitly passed to us through a small window down the side alley. Before we were of an age to get a driving licence many of us boys had old bicycles, which we stripped down and rode on the Common. Today they would be Mountain bikes. Visits to the cinema, at Swanage, were by steam train. Danny Macrae, with his Ford van and churns, served milk by ladle, into your jug or bowl. George Morris and Bill Nineham, were gardeners at Morton's House. Fred Churchill, for whom I worked on the farm at the bottom of the Castle. There are so many more about whom I could write but space prohibits. They were all part of a rural existence that had changed little since before the war. However one person merits special mention and she is Mrs Berwick, Nanny Berwick's mother. She told me of the days of the coming of the railway to Corfe and how that started changes to the old way of life. Mi, what interesting people and times they were. As a Scouse speaking lad of 12 years I must have been a strange phenomenon to be thrust into a rural way of life that had endured for centuries. I can remember only that I seemed to be accepted, without challenge or argument. Thank you, Dorset, for your hospitality and generosity.

I am only too well aware that things and people change with the passage of time and frequently not always for the better. Corfe Castle, in 1947, to a 12 year old, town boy, was a magic world. It will always remain so in my mind, whatever the ravages that have and are continuing to happen. Brian D. Johnson, born Liverpool, 1935 :-. Steeple Manor 1947-48, Morton's House and Castle Cottage, East Street, Corfe Castle, Dorset, 1948 to 1962
Phyllis Adelaide Susan Johnson, born Liverpool 1908 Steeple Manor; Morton's House; Castle Cottage, East Street and Springwell Close, Cotfe Castle, Dorset, 1947 to date.

Today's weather: *Raining again!*

Name BRIAN JOHNSON : writing for my Mother Year of birth 1908 : 1935
PHYLLIS JOHNSON (née Kerry)
House SPRINGWELL CLOSE   Street off WEST STREET

Monday 9th October, 2000

My 4½ year old son's cry for a cuddle starts the day at 5.30 a.m. - a fairly typical beginning. Monday is a work day for my wife and myself, the eldest boy goes to school, and the youngest (two years old) to the childminder. The early morning get-out-of-the-house routine accelerates, until I escape just before 8.00 a.m. for a very short commute to work just up the road.

I'm a warden for the National Trust, responsible for the practical maintenance of the Castle and other Trust properties around the village, including the Common. The first job of the day is unusual - I have to break into the tea room manageress' flat as she's locked herself out. The monthly staff meeting follows, lasting till 10.00 a.m.

Although every working day is different, one task that needs to be done regularly is feeding and checking up on the six Soay sheep that graze inside the Castle. As it's a Monday, the remainder of the day is taken up with the small tasks that have piled up over the weekend, e.g. replacing broken hurdles in the castle and litter picking. There is a small mountain of paperwork to tackle, and a meeting with a tree surgeon to discuss future work.

The end of the day sees me in bed at the same time as my sons, still a victim of the weekend's sick bug.

Today's weather: WET, COLD

Name PHILIP STUCKEY

House 15

Year of birth 1959

Street WEST STREET

Tuesday October 10th

Who am I? – I was born in Esher in Surrey in February1942. I was educated at boarding prep school in Suffolk and a day public school in Surrey. After 2 years training with the P&O shipping company, I joined the Army. In January 1964, after Sandhurst, I joined the 2nd Royal Tank Regiment. After 35 years service around Europe I retired and now work for the Army in Dorset. In 1967 I married an old school friend of my sister and we have 4 children.

Why do I live in Corfe Castle? Because we like it, but we arrived by chance. Tank training is done at Bovington, which is 12 miles from Corfe. In 1970 I was posted there and we spent 2 years in rented houses, first at Little Woolgarston House outside Corfe and then at Barneston Manor near Church Knowle. After a short break in B.A.O.R. we were posted back to Bovington and bought our own home. Apart from 6years of postings away from the area, we have lived in it ever since.

What work do I do? Since leaving the Army I have worked as a 'retired officer' in Bovington, responsible for the maintenance, conservation and running of the training areas in Bovington.

Our family is my main interest and although our children are all grown up and live in London, they still take much of our spare time – particularly our 3 grandchildren. Our elder son 32 is a property surveyor married with 3 children, our younger son 31 a chartered accountant, our elder daughter 30 a nurse and the younger daughter 26 runs a small catering business and is married to a professional musician, currently assistant director of a West End musical .

Our house is just outside the village and has 2+ acres of garden.Looking after both is a hobby but needs more of my time than I have available as I am active in several local organisations; I am a liveryman in the City of London and the treasurer of a local pheasant shoot.

What did I do today? I left home just before 8am, listened to the news in the car on the way to work, arrived about 8.15 at the forestry hut to discuss with the 3 foresters what was achieved yesterday, and what is possible today. I visited the garrison cashier with cheques for the shoot; authorised payment for the latest 7 tons of pheasant feed at £85 a ton. (How these poor farmers can pay their bills with such low prices I don't know.) Arrived at the office by 9.15, checked the post and answer machine. Discuss with E A the effects of yesterdays heavy rain (over 2 ins in 24 hours) on our SSSIs. Our silt filtration system seems to be holding up, thank goodness. 10.45 joined a meeting on possible rearrangement of Army training in Dorset. The meeting continued with a working lunch in the Officers Mess (1-1.45) No pre lunch drinks,quiche, carrots, runner beans, baked potato, followed by cheese and biscuits and coffee. By 2pm, we are in 2 land rovers on the training area visiting possible training sites. The training area covers some 2500 acres and we journey 29 miles! Back in the office soon after 4pm to prepare for meeting with Purbeck District Council in the morning.Finalise some draft letters and leave for home at 5.30(Another late day of unpaid overtime)! On my way home fill up with diesel at 83.9p a litre and arrive home soon after 6 for a cup of tea and piece of home made cake, read the paper, change and have a quiet evening at home with my wife, a rare treat for us both. A small gin before a delicious supper at 8pm of cold roast beef and salad, (left overs from a large joint we had at the weekend to feed all the children/spouses /partners and grandchildren who were here for the weekend). After supper checked my mail and collapsed in front of the TV news at 9pm, finished reading the paper with a glass of whisky and went to bed at 11.30pm having taken the dog for a last minute walk in the field.

Today's weather: WIND SW GUSTY SUNNY INTERVALS & LIGHT SHOWERS

Name GEORGE EDWARD PRETTON   Year of birth 1942

House PATCHFIELD   Street VALLEY ROAD
(GRID REFERENCE : OS SHEET 195 SY 968 807.)

Wednesday October 11th

An uneventful day. Awoken by our 4½ year old son (Hallam) at 5.30 a.m.. Not much sleep after that. The youngest (Edwin, 2yrs) was woken too late at around 7.00 a.m., so had hysterics when denied a third large bowl of cereal. Usual rush to get Hallam to Corfe Castle First School, which he attends three days a week as he's just joined the reception class (*not* keen). I also handed Eddie over to Lesley (childminder) at the school.

Finally off to work in East Lulworth (admin assistant in a job-share post at Butterfly Conservation, an insect conservation charity), posting parcels at Stoborough Post Office on the way. Work busier than usual as took sick leave on Monday (a bug doing the rounds in the family — and village) and the other admin assistant is off with a lung infection *and* laryngitis. A lot of catching up as well as the usual daily duties, and organising various aspects of the office's relocation to new premises up the road in November/December.

Finished my working week at 1.00 p.m., and picked up Eddie from Lesley's in Harman's Cross. Collected Hallam (and friend Shuna) from school at 3.00 pm, then to Wareham for 4.20pm with the boys for our six-monthly check up at the dentist's. H straight into the chair with his mouth open wide, E very reluctant. All three of us passed the check up. Poured with rain all the way home, and on/off for the rest of the day and night.

Usual routine of meals/baths/stories/bed etc disturbed by nuisance phone caller — a voiceless machine that occasionally tries to make contact with our telephone at all hours of the day or night (BT's helpful solution is to unplug our phone).

Now 11.00 p.m., about to switch out the light whilst listening to *very* heavy rain, and hoping there won't be a repeat of the flood we had in the kitchen last Christmas......................

Today's weather: WET!

Name MRS LYNNE STUCKEY   Year of birth 1961

House 15   Street WEST STREET

Off we go on another day at work. But we don't want to think about that, let's ask the audience. Not a bad show that! ("Who Wants to be a Millionaire"; a popular television game show).

It will soon be time to start putting up the new loom down East Street to Steve Ford's Garage. Being a member of the Christmas Festivities Committee is one of the most enjoyable things I have done, well just look at them!

Left to right
Back Row: Helene and Stan Layton; David King; Peter and Marie Pope; Joe Williams; Geoffrey Windsor
Front Row: Debbie Reynolds; Sam Layton; Monica Williams; Doug Whyte

Just part of a group of genuine enthusiastic, young at heart and 100% for the village, members of the Committee.

Ah, well here we are at work for another day at Coastal, Window Manufacturers, Holton Heath.

Today's weather:

Name	Kevin Reynolds	Year of birth	1963
House	17	Street	West Street

A typical term time day with each member of the family leaving Kingston, either to school or for work. My husband and our two children travel off the Isle of Purbeck with my husband usually working in Poole, but today he is much further north, flying from Heathrow to Edinburgh for a meeting. Meanwhile I go to work in Langton Matravers which means I can return home at lunch time and sometimes fit in a quick walk, which I do today.

I head off on a favourite, restorative, 'round', along The Lane, through the woods, down to Blashenwell and back up again past Willwood. Blashenwell, with its water wheel and duck pond, has its own very special, peaceful atmosphere and the views across to Corfe Castle from the footpath running above it are stunning. The hips and haws in the foreground gleam and a couple of buzzards circle overhead. The many pheasants and partridges scatter in alarm as I pass and there are often hares and deer by Willwood or in Kingston woods although I see none today.

Friday the 13th – unlucky for some perhaps, but in the evening all the family return home to roost, safe and sound.

Today's weather: Mainly dry

Name Edward, Fiona, Thomas + Eleanor Wake-Walker

House 5

Year of birth

Street West Street, Kingston

Friday October 13th

OUR DAY OUT

Our day out started early at Wareham Station with the promise of the day ahead. After arriving at Waterloo Station, there was only a short walk to the spectacular London Eye. The sun was warm and the large crowd was buzzing around its base. Having already booked I was most impressed with the instant issue of our tickets with one swipe of my visa card and no queue! The excellent queuing system shuffled us into our pod on time and we were soon elevated above London, which revealed itself to us as we gradually saw further afield. Our spacious capsule allowed about a dozen of us to wonder or sit, to take in the ever increasing vista or look down to other dangling pods, or the miniature crowds below. Misty green fields and trees finally emerged in the far distance as we reached the top, only to slowly vanish as we began our descent. With feet on the ground we took the filthy fumey Mayflower ferry to Greenwich and the Dome.

The covered ramp into the Dome area was lit by effective floor uplighters. We entered the Dome by the Work Zone where a busy conveyor belt moved documents, 'hamsters' turned in wheels and giant shredders and memos covered the walls.

Moving on, we found ourselves looking at giant puzzles and tests of skill, and a banqueting sized table football game where everyone could play!
We stopped by the Money Zone to buy Melanie and James their freshly minted £5 coins, before entering the Learning Zone where we found we had shrunk as we entered a giant school corridor! A strict schoolmaster ushered us into the school hall as the bell rang. Here we watched a non speaking film about a schoolgirl who was given a seed of inspiration by her teacher. As the film finished the girl beckoned us as the screen lifted, and we followed her into a darkened sparkly world of knowledge and wonder.
The experience of deep calm was not to be found in the Rest Zone though, not with children in tow anyway!

The Play Zone was interesting although Melanie and James were disappointed because there were queues for everything. We watched while a girl randomly played a 'piano' by using a mouse to break pulse light beams causing notes to play. Another fun area was in two parts. Each section had a video camera pointing at a settee, and behind each, a giant screen superimposed BOTH images together. This looked really funny as the screen showed the children pretending to fight or sit on top of each other!

But of all the zones, I think all our favourites was the Body Zone. The queuing here was long but well organised, as a juggler on a plinth entertained us using cricket sized glass balls -rather him than me! Then we really were inside the body! The ribcage framed a massive pulsating squelchy heart. James was most impressed except there was no blood!

By now, somewhat tired, we assembled in the central 'amphitheatre' where there wasn't a seat to be had! The Millennium Show was spectacular and very impressive - trapeze artists wearing stilts gracefully bungee jumped from the roof into the arena, columns rose up from nowhere, and wafty multicoloured fabric wrapped around a giant maypole. But what was it all about? We made our way out via the inevitable Gift Shop, then took a very pleasant boat trip back to Waterloo, watching the sun gently drift down behind that giant Dome.

Today's weather:

Name	Peter, Clare, Melanie and James Western	Year of birth	56, 59, 90 & 96
House	Stonewood	Street	Calcraft Road

Saturday October 14th

I got up & pulled my curtains to see a lovely sunny morning shining on my garden & the distant hills. It is mid October but there has been no frost. The garden, which gives me great pleasure, is still full of colour. The roses & annuals are still in flower, the leaves have yet to turn colour. The shrubs have grown to an exceptional height this year, due to so much rain ~~this year~~ I think.

I am looking forward to my day as I am going to the theatre in Poole this afternoon to see an Agatha Christie thriller. I am a member of the Dorset theatre goers Club. The coach picks me up at the end of my road in East Street & drops me off there on the return journey. We usually go to one show a month & go to various theatres in Southampton, Chichester & Salisbury among others.

Have just returned after a very enjoyable day & am now ready to fall asleep in my armchair!

Today's weather: ~~Sunny~~ & quite warm.

Name ~~Joyce Turnbull~~   Year of birth 18/12/1912

House ~~Stonewold~~   Street 1 Colletta Close

We are the Hunt family from "Marblers", 5 West Street. David and Fiona are both 38, Joanna is 13, Ben 11 and Millie is one year old. We have two dogs. They are black and white springer spaniels called Ebbie and Berry. , 3 guinea pigs called Fluffy, Pirate and Caramel and 4 horses called Shanty, Evie, Foxy and Chloe, who live at Thrashers Farm at Bushey.

David grew up at Bushey. His grandfather and father were farmers at Lower Bushey Farm. David still holds the tenancy for Thrashers Heath, which are the old clay pits where the clay for Wedgwood's Queensware Pottery came from.

Fiona grew up in Swanage. Her grandfather used to run Blight's Newsagents in Station Road.

We have been living in Wareham since we married in 1985 and have just moved into Marblers on 25th September 2000. So having just moved in we are still unpacking and sorting the house out.

We have a very busy day arranged today as Joanna is jumping her horse Evie in a competition at Bovington Stables in the morning and Ben is playing football against Portland for Wareham Rangers in the afternoon. The weather is fine and we all enjoyed supporting Joanna at showjumping. She did very well and came 2nd and 3rd in her two classes. We take her horse back to Bushey and leave to get Ben to football. They had a great match and won 5 - 4. Ben plays defender and is a very good player. His great grandfather was a professional footballer called James Boyd and he won a FA Cup medal in 1931 playing for Newcastle United.

We finished the day with a lovely roast beef dinner with Yorkshire pudding.

Today's weather:

Name	Hunt Family	Year of birth 1962
House	Marblers	Street 5 West Street

At the age of 88 years and being one of the oldest 'locals', I have a quiet home life which varies little from day to day. However, my lifestyle does give me time to reflect on days past. I spend much of my time watching television and reading the Sun newspaper particularly the football section. Southampton has been my team. My father was a supporter and at 12 years of age I went with him in Willy Blake's taxi to see the 'Saints'. Willy was the landlord at the Castle Inn but did some local taxiing mainly taking residents from Tyneham and other villages to the railway station in Corfe. We used him because he was cheaper than Sheasby's – my fare to Soton was five shillings and adults were ten shillings.

My first home was in Portland. I was about three when my father was to begin a job managing cows which were to supply milk for the Portland inhabitants. He was in the 'Reserve' but was posted to a remote island in Scotland during the war where he reported on enemy activity. My mother and I had to live with my grandfather at what is now Alpha, next to Dru Drury's in The Square. At 4 years I began school which I didn't take to. I was locked out of the house so as not to run back and often I would put my boot at the door, that is until Dr. Dru Drury's wife would appear and say; "Git ye along to school will ya." To a youngster she was a woman not to be crossed! Gradually, I began to like school and did well. I showed a flair for sketching flowers and even now I remember with some pride when in Standard Five I was given 5s as a prize for my blue iris.

Before I left school, when my father was home from the war and after my grandfather had died, we moved further along West Street opposite Woadens shop sited on the corner of the approach road to the car park. This was mainly a sweet shop with some groceries. The man next door to us, Mr Langtree, owned some cows and each day before leaving for school my job was to take a gallon of his milk to the Bankes Arms. However, if the cows couldn't provide enough I would go to the Milk Factory instead. For this seven day a week job I'd be given one shilling. A few years later my father had the chance to buy this home but it wasn't to be, so we moved to 77 West Street.

My father, who was then working at the cordite factory at Holton Heath, had inherited from his father a grandfather clock, but in this thatched cottage the ceilings were so low that the clock would not fit. My father's solution was to dig a hole in the floor of the front room and lower the casement down. I could never understand why he bothered because it was so noisy. We only went in the front room on special occasions but from any room every hour and half hour the darn thing could be heard striking. As soon as it came into my possession I got rid of it.

At 14 years I joined Battricks Bakery at the Mill. My main job here was to care for the two horses. In summer I would collect them from the field, but in winter they would lie in so I had to clean them out which meant putting their bedding under the manger, brushing out, wheelbarrowing away the dirty bed and then at the end of the day bedding them down for the night. I can hear their wickering now as I would arrive to feed them at 7am. I gave them a mix of furze that had been through the chaff cutter, hay and oats that had been crushed at the mill. Once the horses were seen to I would help in the bakehouse. One of my jobs was to prepare the tins for the mixture to be dropped in. While the dough was proving I would put the rashers in the oven for breakfast. The old fashioned ovens were heated with a combination of furze cut from the Common and elsewhere and wood faggots. These were longer length sticks cut out of hedges. Rempstone Estate supplied 2,000 faggots each year for the bakery. Two men's winter job was to work from Challow over the hill cutting out these and leaving younger growth for the next year's supply of fuel.

Once the smell of the freshly baked bread wafted up from the bakehouse, nearby villagers would arrive – there was no shop so we delivered around Corfe six days a week. The loaves were mainly 1lb and 2lb with a few 4lb ones. Wholemeal and Hovis were also requested and we tried to oblige individual preferences. Some liked crusty, others browner on the bottom so these were left in the oven on the hot bricks a bit longer. Daily, the quantities were carefully prepared to supply our customers but also to avoid waste.

With the carts securely loaded and the horses harnessed, I would begin the rounds. However, that's enough recollections for now. More of my thoughts on November 20th.

FINE, BRIGHT AND DRY WITH AUTUMNAL CHILL

Name E. Mullett   Year of birth 1912

House 108   Street East

Today's weather:

Name

A Corfe Castle Resident

Year of birth

House

Street

Tuesday October 18th

9.10: Ooops! Bit late this morning. The 'phone's ringing and the workshop door has jammed - swollen by the damp as it always is at this time of the year. In spite of possessing nearly every woodworking tool invented, haven't used any of them on the door. Now the handle's come off. Answering machine cuts in - I can hear the message through the door. "We'll be in Poole all day Nick, can you come tomorrow?"
Customers I should have called at 8.30 have slipped the leash! Manage to prise door open and clutching redundant door handle, break in

9.15: Unexpected respite, what to do with the day now Make some driftwood furniture but first, coffee. Search for mug. Fall over careless tools on stairs. Find mug. Trip over tools, once again, on way downstairs. No coffee in works kitchen. Don high visibility vest in order to cross the railway line and avoid high visibility steam train Buy coffee from Clealls. Kettle's boiled and joy hot coffee. Workshop looks like aftermath of casual Corfe earth tremor.
Untidy workshop - busy untidy man. Tidy workshop - retired man.

9 30: Start new project. Down at Chapman's Pool yesterday to search for driftwood. The equinoctial gales have made up for the summer's dearth of flotsam and I've found some very interesting bits which will go into a 'flotsam Throne'. Here's a very peppered piece of gribbled teak for the front legs (teak is as rare as rocking—horse droppings, all used on Heals' coffee tables in the 1960's, I suspect). Dig out a big lump of 3 inch oak, ex. Swanage Pier, from my store, for the seat and some gnarled and curved bits of Holm oak for the back legs. The back is going to be a fantastical piece of oak found yesterday, I saw along its length and the edges, Joined together, make a 'V' shape.

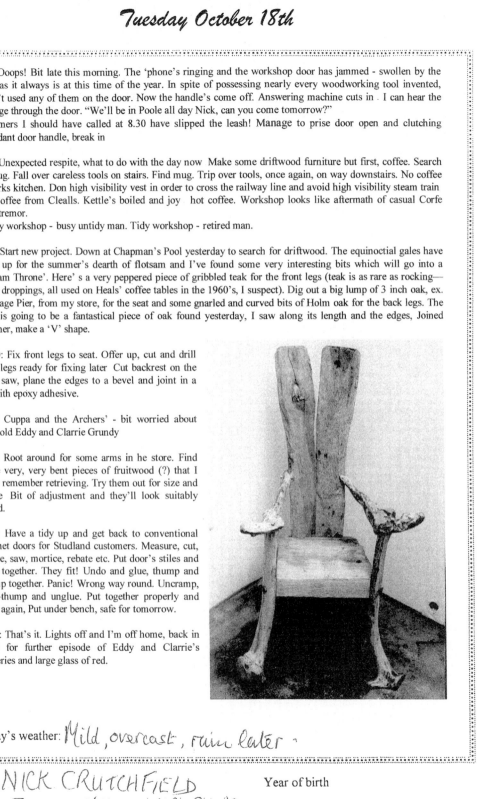

11.30: Fix front legs to seat. Offer up, cut and drill back legs ready for fixing later Cut backrest on the band saw, plane the edges to a bevel and joint in a Jig with epoxy adhesive.

2.00: Cuppa and the Archers' - bit worried about poor old Eddy and Clarrie Grundy

2.20: Root around for some arms in he store. Find some very, very bent pieces of fruitwood (?) that I can't remember retrieving. Try them out for size and shape Bit of adjustment and they'll look suitably weird.

3.30: Have a tidy up and get back to conventional cabinet doors for Studland customers. Measure, cut, scribe, saw, mortice, rebate etc. Put door's stiles and rails together. They fit! Undo and glue, thump and cramp together. Panic! Wrong way round. Uncramp, un—thump and unglue. Put together properly and glue again, Put under bench, safe for tomorrow.

6.50: That's it. Lights off and I'm off home, back in time for further episode of Eddy and Clarrie's miseries and large glass of red.

Today's weather: Mild, overcast, rain later -

Name NICK CRUTCHFIELD   Year of birth

House SANDY HILL WORKSHOPS   Street SANDY HILL
CORFE CASTLE

Thursday October 19th

The day started in bright sunshine and there was a green woodpecker on the lawn. There are a lot of trees at the bottom of the garden — thrushes and mistle thrushes nest there. I don't get so many birds for the last few years — I used to see blackcaps, goldfinches, a bullfinch, chaffinches and long tailed tits. I still have a wren near the house, tree sparrows, blue tits, blackbirds, starlings, very few swallows — but I have seen a rare tree-creeper , a very small pretty little bird, this year.

My kind neighbour, Bill Carter, brought in my paper which he has done for many years. We both live on our own so it 's a friendly face first thing in the morning. At about 8 a.m. I rang a Wimborne friend to ask her to add another name to the list of retired schoolmasters and wives who meet each year for a Christmas lunch in a country pub just north of Wimborne. We are all old friends who have worked together and known each other for many years. There will be about 25 of us I expect and some come 40 miles or more. I organise this with help from this friend.

After breakfast I took the box of vegetable peelings down to the compost at the bottom of the garden. It was very wet underfoot — we have had so much rain this year shrubs and trees have put on so much growth it will be hard work to tidy up this autumn. The apple trees have done well — I inspected the Bramleys but they still feel firm. I've already picked from two eating apple trees and from a cooking apple tree.

As it happened I was invited by friends to join them for lunch at the Priory Hotel in Wareham. It is a very beautiful house dating from the early 8th century. Later we walked round the extensive gardens which run alongside the river and include a good sized pool stocked with carp. We came back to my house for a cup of tea. After they left I walked across towards Blashenwell farmhouse — with all the rain we have had the duck pool was well filled.

When I got home I had a phone call from my sister in Poole saying he sciatica is very painful — will I take her some provisions for her tomorrow. After listening to the 10 o'clock news I went to bed.

Today's weather   Fine

Name   Betty Wigmore   Year of birth   1924

House   104   Street   West Street

Friday October 20th

My day started at 7.15am and having had breakfast, and opened some birthday cards and presents, received a phone call from my elder daughter with a rendition of HAPPY BIRTHDAY over the phone. I then walked our 4year old black Labrador called Flora, on brickyard common, where there are 10 bullocks and about 8 horses grazing.. My husband left for work in Bovington at 8am and I was out of the house by 8.25am. I drove down to the Village Hall carpark where the temporary doctor's surgery is situated in 3 portacabins.

Today I was working as relief dispenser, as the dispenser was on holiday. (I was the permanent dispenser for the village surgery for 3 years). My job is mornings only and I take orders on the telephone for repeat prescriptions, make them up to be collected by patients the following day, and order any necessary drugs, dressings etc. I was only there till 11am as I had another commitment later in the day and lots of preparation to be done. I was organising the food for a fund raising cheese, wine and pate supper party, for 150 people at Creech Grange, in aid of the local Conservative Party. On leaving work, I collected The Daily Telegraph as usual from the paper shop in the village, and bought myself a Danish pastry for elevenses at Dragons Bakery , as a birthday treat! I came home to do 2 flower arrangements and make some spinach pate. I then packed the car with the flowers and 2 other arrangements, and lots of bits needed for the party, (tablecloths, etc.) had a very quick sandwich for lunch and went to Creech to start setting up for the evening.

I was home by 4pm ready to welcome 3 B&B's who were arriving from London for the weekend. I repacked the car with pates, bread, and puddings that various people and I had made, ready to leave again by 6pm. Our daughter and her boy friend arrived at 5.45 from London with a birthday cake she had made for me, and a huge bunch of stargazer lilies she had bought at her local market stall at half the price of the same thing down here. My husband returned from work at the same moment, and we hardly had time to sit down, but managed a quick slice of delicious carrot cake, and cup of tea before a very speedy change of clothes.

Back to Creech where lots of willing helpers arrived to lay the table and prepare the salad, cut bread and cheese into portions and generally get ready for the arrival of the guests at 7.30. It was pouring with rain by now, but the party went very well and was enjoyed by all (I hope!) Creech Grange is a wonderful venue for a party. The owner generously lends the house to various organisations for fund raising events. It is a beautiful 17th century house, with period furniture and pictures. Some parts of the house have no electricity, so the candle lit hall added greatly to the atmosphere. The worst part was washing up 300 plates, 150 knives and spoons and 200 glasses in semi darkness! The scullery was very badly lit!

We eventually got home at 11.30pm and had to unload the car and put everything away. I then opened some more presents that my daughter had brought with her, from our other 3 grown up children and 3 grandchildren, who all live in London.

Sank in to bed at 12.45am, after an unusually busy day! Not a very relaxing birthday, but we will celebrate it tomorrow.

Today's weather: Dull and overcast – wet & windy evening

Name Anne Preston   Year of birth 1943

House Patchfield.   Street Valley Road

Saturday October 21st

As the wife of a retired Naval Officer, & totally proud of being British, today, however briefly, I remember, with my husband, this anniversary of the Battle of Trafalgar, 21-10-1805.

In our own Time, today has been tremendously busy in a very different way. After weeks & even months of persuasion, coercion, collection & wonderful support from so many people, we met together in Corfe Castle Village Hall where we held a Coffee Morning to raise funds for the Royal Society for the Prevention of Cruelty to Animals. The many stalls were manned (or womanned?!) by friends & neighbours, from Corfe & beyond, with the greatest energy & good humour, resulting in our being able to send a cheque for £619 to the Poole & East Dorset Branch of the Society.

By the afternoon the sun appeared briefly which encouraged us to do a little more work towards "putting the garden to bed" for the winter. A robin is most enthusiastic & pulls worms at great speed from the holes left by my husband's digging. There is still a surprising amount of colour — brilliant red Bishop of Llandaff dahlias, crimson fuschias, the lovely purple leaves of the Cotinus — even a last spray of the delicate pink flowers of the climbing rose Handel. Jack, my husband, is determinedly spiking & feeding our two tiny lawns — hard work that seems to go on & on, in spite of their being so small. The Everest crab-apple we planted in front of the house now has a good crop of scarlet little apples — with the various cotoneasters, — the birds are enjoying a real autumn feast.

Our much-loved elderly dog — a "rescued" Scottie called Sooty — had her daily walk, of course, albeit somewhat curtailed by the day's activities!

Now, this evening, after a little visit from dear friends & a nice restoring noggin, we relax over a picnic supper on our knees, watching the television news before bed — & STILL convinced that the year 2001 is the first of the New Millenium !!

Today's weather: Overcast with early drizzle, giving way to afternoon sunshine.

Name ELISABETH CARRINGTON-MAIL   Year of birth 1925

House No. 4   Street MEAD ROAD

Sunday October 22nd

I've had a terrible night! Hardly any sleep because my left knee has been painful, as Lisa the dog slammed into it last evening while we were walking on the Common! She was spayed on Monday and can't be allowed to run/jump off the lead. This is NOT a good day for me to be hobbling around with a stick!! My kind neighbour Gertie Welsh volunteered to walk Lisa this morning – a truly Christian Act!!!

My cousin Joy is coming today, so I tidied up my flat as best I can, then started to prepare for the afternoon. – whipped cream to put in the meringues I made yesterday, packed the meringues in boxes, also packed lemon cake, tea, coffee, sugar, big bag of crisps, paper napkins, 2 knives for cutting cakes, and a box of plastic bags. Also packed the large scrapbook of cuttings and other papers and photographs relating to the Corfe Castle Methodist Church, coloured photocopies of the Cradle Roll (for sale to interested families), and copies of a large picture of John Wesley (also for sale), two "single-use" cameras for general use. Must remember orange juice, apple juice and milk from the fridge, also my Bible for reading the lesson when we actually go to church this afternoon. Took bags in car up to church, as I don't want the car later – not enough parking space – and then back home to finish tidying.

11.10 am Joy arrived. She brought a large plant pot, with mystery plant already buried – had to cover with wire netting and a ½ brick to stop Lisa from digging out the contents! Joy said: "Wait & see what comes up". We talked for a bit, then walked down to the National Trust restaurant for lunch (table booked for 12 noon) - lovely meal (I had chicken, leek & mushroom pie, followed by apricot & ginger crumble with ice cream) All finished by 1 pm, back home to collect Lisa, then we both walked her on the footpaths round the bottom of the Castle (me still using stick). Returned dog home and walked up East Street to the church (complete with orange & apple juices, milk, Bible & stick) at 2.00 pm.

Left Joy to wander around with her own camera, while I joined the other ladies (Mary Wrixon from Church Knowle, Joan Hollister from Harman's Cross, and Barbara Smethurst from Swanage) to lay tables with cloths, paper napkins, plates, cups, saucers, teaspoons, sugar, and lots of plates of our home-made cakes ready cut into suitable sized pieces, plus scones, buttered and jammed. Just managed to get it all ready, and the Baby Burco boiler filled and heated, in time for the Service which started at 3 o'clock.

This was planned as a Special "Re-union" Service, before the closure, for people having family links with the Church - those who had been baptised or married, or attended Sunday School, or whose parents had been connected with it. Over 60 people came, some from as far afield as Derby, Birmingham and Malvern, including 8-10 children. The minister, the Rev. Sylvia Garrett based the service on the life of the church - baptisms, confirmations, marriages, funerals, fellowship - and the continuity of the Christian Church from 2000 years ago, in a succession of different buildings all round the world, passed on like a relay down the generations. The organ was played by Derek Brown Smith, from Wareham - he was our regular organist for a number of years in the 1970s and 1980s. The children spent some of the time colouring rainbows on special bookmarks for the rest of us to commemorate the occasion.

Afterwards the congregation regrouped in the hall to have tea (or juice) and cake, and a lot of conversation - catching up with friends and relations, some not seen for many years. Then we 4 (see above) had to clear up! Wash up, pack away the china, brush up the crumbs, stack the chairs, fold up the tables - we "borrowed" the 4 tables which belong to the Brownies who use the hall regularly- switch off heaters and lights and lock up. All finished by about 5.30 pm. What a great party! Pity the church only gets filled on such an occasion!

I'm afraid the rest of the day was a bit of an anti-climax - washed up cake boxes, watched TV, & went out for two more walks (plus walking stick) with Lisa.

Today's weather: MISTY START, BUT FINE AND SUNNY MOST OF THE DAY – HOORAY!

Name (HELEN) MARY WILLS   Year of birth 1938

House KESTREL COURT, No.56A   Street EAST STREET

A View from the Surgery

Another typical day if such a thing exists in Corfe Castle.

The Surgery has been situated in temporary accomodation in portacabins since I started eight months ago.

The practice has been through difficult times recently but is now enjoying something of a renaissance; it is only thanks to the supreme efforts and loyalty of the staff, combined with an amazing degree of support and tolerance from the patients, that the practice survived. Despite our leaking roof and lack of space the numbers attending the surgery have risen slowly but steadily. There are now 1260 patients registered, 30% of whom are over the age of 65 (well above the national average).

We employ five staff; a manager, two receptionists, a dispenser and a practice nurse. A physiotherapist, chiropodist and counsellor also attend on a regular basis.

Morale in the practice is high: we have applied for planning permission to develop a purpose built surgery on West Street and everybody is optimistic that we should be able to start building next year, planners permitting! Hopefully this will be the final time the surgery has to move.

There has never been a dull moment since I moved here. The variety of patients and their ailments never cease to amaze, as does the good humour and sense of community spirit trhat exists.

There are difficult times ahead for the medical profession, but I cannot think of a better place to practice than as a single handed GP in Corfe Castle.

Raining again. South easterly breeze.

Today's weather:

Name DR. STEVE HORSNELL

Year of birth

House TEMPORARY SURGERY VILLAGE HALL CAR PARK

Street EAST

The Youth shelter, being constructed by H.A. Stockley: Builders, in the Middle Halves playing field is now well on the way to completion thanks to the generosity of the donor, Corfe Castle resident, Joyce Armstrong, who also funded the sturdy metal football goalpost and basket ball facility in the same playing field.

It was the youths of Corfe Castle themselves who thought up the idea (see Diary March 19th) and subsequently helped to design the shelter which has been very youth orientated. The youngsters really feel it is theirs and have taken responsibility for looking after it. The brass plaque reads:

> PRESENTED BY
> MRS. JOYCE ARMSTRONG
> 2000

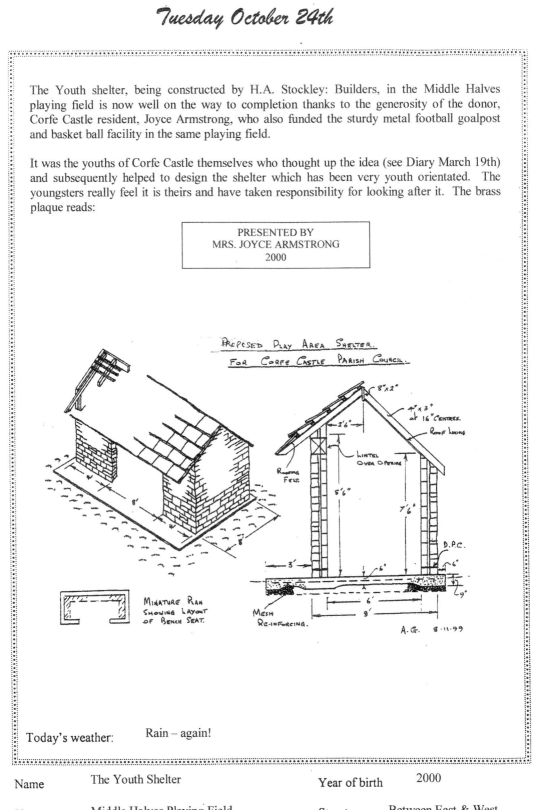

Today's weather: Rain – again!

Name	The Youth Shelter	Year of birth	2000
House	Middle Halves Playing Field	Street	Between East & West

Of course, Gill and I don't spend as much time in Corfe, since we emigrated to Canada in 1967. We now spend rather more time in Canmore, Alberta, (where we chose to retire, after years as non-academic staff at the University of Alberta, in Edmonton.) We do occasionally get tempted away from Canmore to various interesting places.

A fine sunrise to start my birthday; pink clouds, and red mountains: Grotto Mtn (E); Mt Lady McDonald (NE); the Rundle Range (W to NW); Ha Ling Peak (WSW) and the Three Sisters (S).

About mid-morning, we set-out on a walk up Stoneworks canyon; 75 min up the creek we reached the start of the canyon; the dark and cold of the bottom of the winding waterworn way contrasts with the parts that pop out into the sun; after 30 min, three narrows, a wall and a cliff (all with expansion bolts indicating where the sports climbs go) we sat in the sun for a break and a cuppa from the Thermos; and so back to Canmore!

Stoneworks Canyon

We had a late-lunch at the "Grizzly Paw" Brew-Pub: a jug of fall Boch; a Grizzly burger with back-bacon and 'cheddar' cheese; and chips.

The Three Sisters and Connor Church

The Ralph Connor Memorial Church, visible from (the non-smoking) bar upstairs, was built in 1891, by the Reverend Gordon, who wrote nearly 30 novels under the nom de plume Ralph Connor.

We took it easy and indulged ourselves for the rest of the day, with shrimps and avocado and fondue chinoise for dinner (we left the Black Forest birthday cake for later, because of lack of space).

Looking at the sky and stars from the hot-tub, was followed by cocoa, and so to bed.

Today's weather: Mixed sun and clouds.

Name FORD , PETER

House 8

Year of birth 1936

Street HALVES COTTAGES

This week is half term week for both our children William, age 7, and Toby, age 4. William attends Stoborough School and Toby goes to Fours' Nursery in Wareham. It's usually quite a relaxing week as it means no school runs and in and out of the car! Sometimes you feel like a taxi service!

We have my mother staying with us and today is her last day before she has to travel back to Lincolnshire some 250 miles away. It is quite a treat for the children as they don't get to see their "Nan Nan" very often. Also Jeremy is home for a couple of days from work. As he works in Henley-on-Thames it means he is away a lot so the children only really see their Daddy at weekends.

We decide to visit the cat sanctuary in Church Knowle as we are great cat lovers. William and Toby decide to go and look for a cat for their other grandmother who has just lost her cat. As well as having two cats, the children would love a dog so we spend time this morning explaining to them how much harder a dog is to look after than a cat! It's a mad rush when we get back, a quick lunch and then goodbye to my mother as she sets off on her long journey back to the north.

Next stage is to pack the children's bags as they are going away to their other grandmother's house. She lives in Devon. It's been a very busy week organising. Jeremy takes the children off to Torquay. "Grandma Bobs" is quite upset at having lost her old cat and as she lives on her own we thought seeing the grandchildren would cheer her up.

I have an evening to myself to relax, catch up on washing and prepare for work on Friday. I work in a busy hair salon on Fridays and Saturdays, which to me is like a day off!!

Today's weather:
Quite windy, chill in the air, occasional sunshine

Name	Year of birth
Sandra, Jeremy, William and Toby Wright	1964 1949

House	Street
Castle Keep Colletts Close	

The Storm Weekend at Sea

We had had a good season sailing from time to time in Brittany, and the boat, Shearwater had been left in Brest. The plan was to go over by ferry to arrive today to sail her back.

We had a good night crossing from Plymouth to Roscoff and took a taxi to Brest on arrival. The weather looked a bit iffy, but, strengthened by a local coffee, we thought we would be able to use the ridges of high pressure between the lows to make good progress at least as far as the Channel Isles.

However the weather forecast was just appalling. It started with strong winds and possibly gales. This quickly deteriorated as the day went on, until it was clear that there was no real possibility of sailing back to Poole.

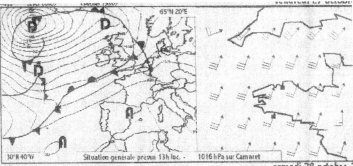

The situation when we arrived on Friday

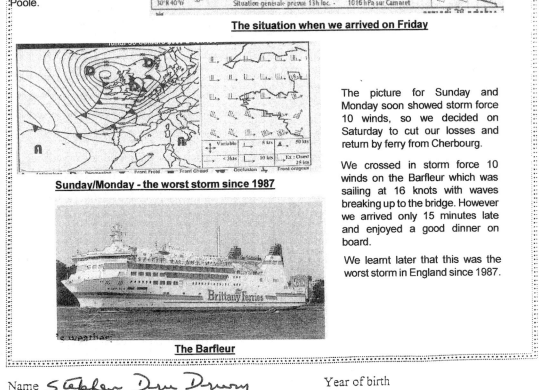

Sunday/Monday - the worst storm since 1987

The picture for Sunday and Monday soon showed storm force 10 winds, so we decided on Saturday to cut our losses and return by ferry from Cherbourg.

We crossed in storm force 10 winds on the Barfleur which was sailing at 16 knots with waves breaking up to the bridge. However we arrived only 15 minutes late and enjoyed a good dinner on board.

We learnt later that this was the worst storm in England since 1987.

The Barfleur

Name Stephen Don Drury and Richard Rierny

House Herons The Mount

Year of birth

Street East Street West Street

Saturday October 28th

We moved into our house in West St in very early Spring this year. Much work needs to be done, including the installation of a central heating system. We set off in the morning to a plumber's merchants in Poole to buy an immersion tank for the system. Around lunchtime, the weather began to deteriorate, so after buying Steve a new pair of wellies at Scats in Winterbourne Kingston, we took shelter in the pub for a couple of pints & some sandwiches.

Back at home, we spent most of the afternoon working on the house, in preparation for the imminent visit of the plumber to complete the pipe work & fit the boiler.

In Corfe, only a few hardened tourists could be seen milling about, & the National Trust shop looked quite crowded & steamed up at the windows.

Luckily in the late afternoon, the rain & howling wind took a break, & we got out for a walk with the dog, Barley, a young golden retriever. From Corfe Common, we headed across the fields towards Bucknowle, & then crossing the Church Knowle road, took the path up to Underhill. The young cows had really churned up the path, & we well & truly christened Steve's new wellies. Taking the Underhill path back to the Castle, we stopped off at the river to clean the mud off the dog, who was nearly swept away by the swollen & rushing waters.

At home, we decided that we deserved a 'hot toddy' of some kind to warm us up. Our neighbours Lorna & David appeared & together we huddled around the fire & enjoyed some mulled wine.

Later, after a surprise visit from Steve's son James, we sat down to tea. We had treated ourselves to a dressed crab, & then made a dish of tagliatelle with chilli tomato sauce.

Despite the awful weather, we had a very busy & enjoyable day.

Today's weather: Rain, sometimes torrential, with gale-force winds

Name Stephen M. Millar & Christie M. Perkins   Year of birth 1950 / 1960

House 53 West St, "Mead Cottage"   Street West St.

 THE NATIONAL TRUST

WINTER WORK ON CORFE COMMON

Is it really that time of year already? The summer seems to have sped by and thought has now to be given to the conservation work on the Common.

Much of this will involve scrub clearance to improve the flower-rich grasslands and small bogs used by a number of rare insects, such as the Southern Damselfly. Other projects include clearing debris from part of Byle Brook, clearing scrub from the Castle ditch and replacing various lengths of fencing.

To help achieve the programme of work I would be very grateful for any volunteer help. If you have any spare time during the middle of the week (Monday- Friday) and are keen to get involved in practical conservation, please contact me on 01929 481294.

Age is immaterial but a reasonable level of fitness will be needed. The National Trust pays travelling expenses and if you do a certain number of hours on a voluntary basis in a year, you become eligible for a Volunteers card which allows access to National Trust properties free of charge and shop discounts.

Phil Stuckey
National Trust Warden

Today's weather: A bright start then soon Gales, wet & Miserable

Name FROM the CORFE VALLEY NEWS   Year of birth

House   Street

Monday October 30th

I AWOKE ON MY DAY OFF FROM MY JOB AS STEWARD OF
THE CORFE CASTLE ROYAL BRITISH LEGION IT WAS A VERY
AUTUMNINAL MORNING, AFTER BREAKFAST AND HANGING
OUT MY WASHING AT AROUND 10AM I DROVE TO
BOURNEMOUTH TO VISIT FRIENDS, ON MY WAY THE
TRAFFIC WAS ATROCIOUS WITH SEVERAL ROADS
BLOCKED BECAUSE OF FALLEN TREES, DUE TO
THE WORST STORMS SINCE 1987 THE NIGHT
BEFORE.
I MET MY FRIENDS IN A BOURNEMOUTH PUB
AFTER SEVERAL GAMES OF POOL, WE MOVED ON
TO THE SECOND PUB IN BOURNEMOUTH SQUARE,
SPENDING AN HOUR OR SO SOCIALIZING, WE THEN
MOVED ON TO OUR THIRD AND FINAL PUB,
UNFORTUNATELY MISSING OUT ON MY FAVOURITE
ALE DUE TO ME HAVING TO DRIVE, LEAVING THE
FINAL PUB WE THEN WENT TO THE ORIENTAL CHINESE
TAKEAWAY, WITH MY APPETITE SATISFIED, I LEFT
MY FRIENDS AND HEADED FOR FLEETS BRIDGE
TESCOS FOR MY WEEKLY SHOP, FROM TESCO'S
ON TO MAKRO CASH AND CARRY TO PICK UP SUPPLIES
FOR THE LEGION, ON MY RETURN JOURNEY I POPPED
IN THE LEGION TO DROP OFF THE SUPPLIES AND
RETURNED HOME AT 8 O'CLOCK FOR MY VERY LATE TEA
SPENDING THE REST OF THE EVENING RELAXING ON THE
SOFA WATCHING THE TELEVISION AND CONSUMING SOME

Today's weather: STORMY CANS OF LAGER

Name BRIAN ANTONY VARNEY   Year of birth 1964

House 16   Street TOWNSEND ROAD

Tuesday October 31st

At last the ferocious winds have abated, it is not raining and the sun is shining so my first job today must be to tour the garden to see what damage has been done by the gales of the last two days.

Outside I find a fence down, the larger pots of hydrangeas and fuschias tipped over and some smashed. Ah well, I enjoy the air outside so the morning is spent in the garden, standing up the pots, collecting the broken spars of the fence and removing the begonias and summer bedding plants which are now finished. As the wind gets up again and lunchtime approaches I am glad to return to the warmth of my cottage. Whilst having soup and a sandwich I watch "Working Lunch" on BBC2. It is nice to sit down after my labours.

The time has come to start the bookbinding that I had promised myself for today. This is a very time-consuming activity. I started bookbindng when I retired and find it a fascinating and rewarding pastime, whether binding pages into a new book or restoring an old one. Many skills are involved and the concentration required is such that time flies and nothing else matters. There are mishaps and anxious moments but is immensely satisfying and brings pleasure too to the friends whose treasured books I am able to restore.

In hand I have a large Family Bible with its front and back boards and spine detached. I have already made new end papers for inside the boards, put in new cords to attach the boards to the text block, glued linen and a stout hollow on the spine. The latter is to facilitate the opening of the book. The piece of leather to cover the spine has to be inserted under the leather on the front and back boards without making an unsightly bump so it has to be carefully pared down to a sliver using a very sharp knife sharpened on an oil stone and honed on a leather strop. This sharpening has to be repeated many times during the paring process. Care must be taken to avoid making holes or weakening the leather but paring is so absorbing that I hardly notice the time. Already the light is fading. I stop for a quick cup of tea.

The next stage is to attach the leather to the spine. Firstly I paste the leather thoroughly, fold it up and leave it for thirty minutes so that the paste is absorbed. Then the damp, pasted leather is moulded to the spine and boards. Finally I tie up the book and leave it overnight to dry. The very enjoyable finishing stages remain but that is for another day.......

Time for supper - Chicken breast, mushroom sauce, carrots and calabrese followed by cheese, celery and fruit. After all my efforts today I think that a glass of Dubonnet is allowed. Tonight is Hallowe'en. I wonder whether the local children will be knocking at my door but in the event the stormy weather keeps them at home. I sit by my fire, 'phone a friend and watch TV.

Today's weather: Windy but fine until the evening when it rains again.

Name	Vi Howe	Year of birth	1928
House	"The Buron", Number 104	Street	East Street

Up at 7.15a.m. for early breakfast in the Hotel. I'm not too keen on these early starts until 1 pop across to the shop and get the paper. Walking across the square I always think how lucky we are to live in such a great place. I've been here ten years and the last two have been exiting due to my involvement with the Millennium Association. I have been on the Entertainment and Fund-Raising Committee and the whole year has been a fantastic success. Our last big event will be next Saturday when we are having a Grand Firework Display in the grounds of the Castle. We are expecting five to six hundred people and it should be fantastic. My main duties for the committee have been to organize two It's a Knockout competitions to raise some money, and organize the Celebration week-end at the end of June (look back to the diary dates for details). All were a great success which is very gratifying.

For a small village Corfe Castle does some incredible fund raising for a multitude of things: from the new Bells in the Church to parties for the children and Old Age Pensioners who live here. I am a great believer in the old saying Charity Begins at Home and I am sure the village does most things along these lines. The next big project is the building of a Sports Pavilion at the field in West Street. This will be a great asset for the children and adults alike. If you have bought a copy of this Diary then you have already put something towards the building because the Millennium Association monies raised are going to this very worthy cause.

Besides my involvement with the Millennium Association I have just got over organizing my eldest Son's wedding. He lives in the Lake District and met a lovely girl from County Durham and they decided to bring all the guests from all over the country to Corfe Castle to have the wedding here. I think it was a combination of, What a Great Place to get Hitched and Dad can do the Reception in the Hotel. That was ten days ago and we've just got over it. Everything went very smoothly and I'm looking forward to becoming a Grandfather in a couple of years, although I've told them not too soon.

Anyway, back to the Hotel. This summer has been very wet so Trade has not been fantastic but we are still here surviving. Alison and I are pretty fed up with the weather so I've just been on the Internet and found a holiday in Egypt for seven days in Luxor B/B at £199. I'm told that it only rains there once every three to five years and then only for twenty minutes so we are off in ten days time.

We don't have much to do today as during the winter we try to keep our full time employees on all year and during the week they can pretty much manage without us.
Golf is my hobby so if this rain stops I am going to pop up to the Isle of Purbeck Golf Club for 18 holes with a couple of friends. Jamie and Claire (my son and new daughter-in-law) have just rung from the Airport, they are on their way to Mombassa for a three-week honeymoon (lucky sods). Still, I can look forward to three weeks in Florida in February. Well we need some relief from our miserable winter weather.

Today's weather: *A Sunny, day but chilly day*

Name *Mike Perry*   Year of birth

House *Bankes Hotel*   Street *The Square*

Michael Barnes, farmer of 600 acres of land within Purbeck.

Main enterprise is dairy at Afflington Farm with 200 acres arable and 110 acres of floodplain grazing beside Poole Harbour.

Today I fed and checked all of my cattle as usual. I have around 350 cattle - 150 dairy cows, 100 beef animals and 100 calves and yearlings.

The dairy cows are already housed inside for the winter due to the very wet season and fed silage (preserved grass). All of the other younger cattle are outside in four groups and checked and fed daily from our quad bike or tractor.

Our Soil Association Organic Certificate arrived by post today. It is always nice to pass the inspection and receive the certificate. Afflington Farm is in Organic Conversion and will be fully organic on 1st April 2001.

Aerial Photograph of Farm 1974

Today's weather: _Dull with rain at intervals._

Name _Michael Barnes_   Year of birth _1956_

House _Afflington Farm_   Street _Valley Road_

"Minnie" has put in an appearance as a new Resident of Corfe Castle. She is a Convoy 17 seat Minibus warmly welcomed at a Special Tea at the Village Hall on Wednesday 11th at 5.00 pm. Corfe Castle Community was chosen by the Management of B.P to be the recipients of this Wonderful Gift - "a brand new Minibus". Mr Kevin Hostler, Business Unit Leader of

BP with his Wife and others from BP were with us for tea. Kevin Hostler introduced himself to the packed hall, and said this was the first Minibus they had given to a Community, and they were pleased it was Corfe Castle which was chosen, seeing we were so close to them, and they hoped it would bring a lot of pleasure to many people. Kevin then presented Mr Peter Apsey, Chairman of the Corfe Castle Charity with the keys. Peter, of course, accepted very graciously, and assured B.P. we were very thankful for such a generous gift, and commented that "B.P". could well mean "Best Present". Peter then handed the keys to Pastor David Foot, introducing him as the Chairman of the Committee responsible for "Minnie's" welfare, and I am writing this appreciation for "Minnie".

Also, as a Trustee of the Charity, may I on behalf of the Corfe Castle Charity, and the Community of this lovely village, say a very big "THANK YOU" to BP for this marvelous and wonderful gift, it really is superb, it has a dual tank, petrol and LPG (meaning "Liquid Petroleum Gas") which is a new cleaner and environmentally friendly fuel. So "THANK YOU" Kevin and BP. May I also say a big "THANK YOU" to Val Hodge, Public Relations lady for BP, she it was who made that first magic phone call - I remember it well "Would you like a new Minibus?". So thank you Val for all you have done in making this possible for us.

I also thank the Women's Institute for such a good spread of food. So "THANK YOU" WI. for arranging and preparing the tea, and BP who paid for it.

Our Village School was asked to propose a Name for the new minibus, so the children made a list - and what a list. Some funny, some strange and unpronounceable, but the best one was chosen as Minnie" the Bus, and was suggested by Canna Whyte, and she was given a £20 prize by BP. Canna was surprised, and very pleased with her prize, and again I would like to say "THANK YOU" to BP on Canna's behalf.

NOW ABOUT THE COMMITTEE There are 4 of us on the Committee - Beatrice Clarke (Secretary); Ann Hobson (Warden of Springwell); Roy Davies of The Halves, who will look after the maintenance, until an official servicing is necessary, and myself, having been asked to be the Chairman of the Committee.

MONEY - of course, this always comes into everything we do, doesn't it, nothing is free! May I at the very outset of this new experience for the village, set out a few points clearly:

Today's weather: DRY & A NICE BLUE SKY .

Name Minnie the Bus   Year of birth 2000

House Springwell Close   Street West

There are some people already who think that because "Minnie" is a gift to us, that every use is free, or very cheap. BUT as the Yorkshire men would say "there's nowt for nowt". Yes "Minnie" is a free gift and a very expensive present it is, she comes with a year's licence, full of petrol and L.P.G all paid for by BP. The first year's Insurance, Fully Comprehensive, for the use of all groups of people, and for any driver over 25 years of age costs over £1,200 (we will have a 30 per cent 'No Claims Bonus' after the first year if we look after it). The Charity has paid for one year's R.A.C. membership to safeguard our journeys, and for this I would like to say a "THANK YOU".

So as she stands on the car park, the weekly cost will be just on £30. Then we have to save up for servicing, and any unforeseen problems we may have, because we <u>Must Not</u> presume that someone is following on behind with an open cheque book. The scale of charges has been worked out by the Committee, to benefit first the School, which, because of new restrictions on parents carrying children other than their own to their special events in school hours, now needs to use a minibus. They will have a very nominal charge. Then the young people of the Youth Club, Cameo Club, and the other organizations will benefit. Then, of course, the Senior Citizens for their regular outings, then others from the Churches or Village. As a Community Bus, the use will be restricted to Corfe (including Kingston) and is for groups, not for family use. Just one thing to mention, in order that we do not take away trade from our own village shops, who I may add are very helpful in delivering goods to those who are unable to get to the shops, we have agreed that trips to the Supermarkets should not be made - our village shops need us to keep them going as well, and we must not abuse that benefit.

So I hope I have set out for you the fact that we have to be "Self Financing" from now on. The costs will be much lower than any other hirings, so let us all feel we are doing our bit in keeping "Minnie" going.

<u>AND FINALLY</u> "Minnie" has been given Council permission to stay in Springwell Car Park. I would ask you all, but especially the children and young people, to keep an eye on "Minnie", we don't want any rough characters frightening her and damaging her. Please report to me, or any of the Committee, if you need to.

Let us pray that "Minnie" will be not only be a benefit to the village, but also the source of enjoyment and fun for outings and holidays. "Minnie" will be seen by many thousands of people over many parts of our County in coming years, carrying the very attractive name of "Minnie", and of course, the name of the Corfe Castle Charity and the name of BP. May God keep us safe on the busy roads.

Today's weather:

Name   Year of birth

House   Street

Today we went shopping in Bournemouth, and it set me thinking that our whole region becomes totally transformed by the time the summer months arrive. It is something that has only struck me since we moved to Corfe in 1995. Having previously only visited in spring and summer, I had a perfect picture in my mind of bright sunny days, green fields and lambs, golden crops and inviting beaches, fresh air and exhilarating views. Of course there is also that other major addition -visitors -who add to the happy holiday atmosphere (as well as queues, traffic jams and nowhere to park!). As residents, we soon learned to pick our moments if we needed to pop to the shops or go to the beach. You can either beat the crush and grab your patch of sand early, but we prefer to go to Studland at around mid afternoon when the crowds start to thin, and yet it is still warm (hopefully!). Then when it starts to cool we have a barbecue on the giant stones, there for the purpose.

Another excellent way to end a busy day is to head for Swanage, pick up fish and chips at Herston and then picnic in Durlston Country Park. It is just so tranquil there, overlooking the lighthouse, watching the distant passing dinghies and diving boats at sea or observing the wildlife around us.

Sometimes we even feel a bit like moles popping up above ground, as we get to the end of our road and then decide to turn around and stay at home as it just looks too busy out there! Winter on the other hand is such a contrast -grey sky, grey stone, horizontal rain and fog! I still find it fascinating when our beautiful castle can totally disappear! Usually there is no more than a handful of people around most of the time, shops in Wareham and Swanage deciding to close half an hour or so earlier than their signs suggest (this can be so frustrating!). And some shops, especially in Swanage closing up completely for the winter. In fact, once, when visiting Swanage, it was so quiet you could almost see the tumbleweed blowing down the middle of the road!

But I must stop daydreaming! Having driven home from Bournemouth, we have just got time to put the kettle on before heading off across the Halves to the field by West Street car park, to watch the Millennium Association Fireworks Display!

It was a clear evening and the stars were out, and no wind -perfect! A large crowd had already gathered in anticipation, while music played and refreshments were bought and consumed. The bright floodlight half lit the milling figures, their opposite sides in blackness. We must have known many people there but the brilliant floodlights and darkness made it almost impossible to tell. And then the heavens opened -RAIN! The fire juggler did his best to entertain and the crowd watched and waited. After several announcements over the PA, there was a sudden explosion in the castle ruins and an orange glow radiated from the depths. Then silver fountains joined in as the display gathered pace. The flat silhouette of the castle suddenly, fleetingly had colour and texture. Shadows danced over the ruins as breathtaking sprays of colour flowered overhead and then were gone. Now this was a side of Corfe Castle that I hadn't seen before!

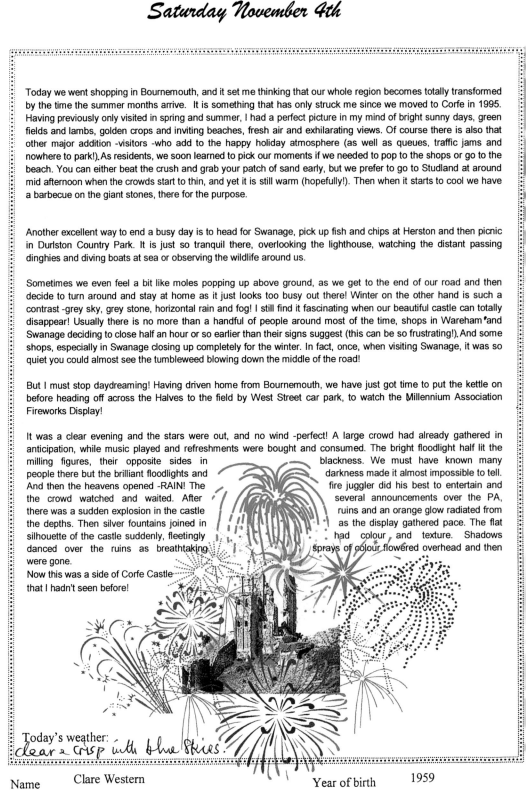

Today's weather: clear & crisp with blue skies.

Name	Clare Western	Year of birth	1959
House	Stonewood	Street	Calcraft Road

These pictures are by the young artists of the 1st Corfe Castle Rainbows. They are all our own work about the Millennium firework party held on Saturday 4th November and it was terrific and magic.

Lyndsey O'Brien (6)

Charlotte Anstey (6)

Lauren Davies (5)

Laurie Beardmore (6)

Emily Ward (6)

Lizzie Hole (5)

Chelsea Haskins (6)

Bethany Somers (6)

Today's weather:

Name *1st Corfe Castle Rainbows*   Year of birth *Founded 1996*

House *Methodist Church Hall*   Street *East Street*

Sunday November 5th

Early rise was made to undertake a convenient route to France for a holiday break. The car ferry from Poole to Cherbourg left at 08.35am and I knew that the weather would be a factor. At Poole Harbour the wind and rain started but it did not prevent me being on deck to see and admire the Purbecks even in a grey and windswept state.

By early afternoon I was in France having listened to increasing winds in the English Channel. The boat stabilizers meant that all passengers were very comfortable.

Cherbourg greeted me with very heavy rain which persisted for the rest of the day. In difficult driving conditions I was only able to reach Forgères before stopping to eat and rest. The weather depression was a large one covering Southern England, the Channel and Northern France.

Today's weather: WET, WINDY.

Name TREVOR G COLLINS Year of birth 1939

House VERGERS MEAD Street EAST STREET

Monday November 6th

Another Monday morning and what a morning! Rain, rain and more rain!

Our geese are having a wonderful time waddling around in the very large puddles but the chickens dislike having a swimming pool instead of grass to peck around in.

Another quiet, very autumnal day in the shop. Fortunately, despite the appalling weather a few customers came in to buy early Christmas presents. Very sensible of them.

Businesses here are very affected by the weather and the winter!

Arrive home to be greeted by the dog eagerly anticipating a long walk. She got a short one!

My son arrived home from rugby trials covered in mud. He had great fun.

Today's weather   Flooded

Name   Ann Cockerell   Year of birth   1955

House   Isle of Purbeck Gemcraft, The Old Reading room   Street   West Street

The War Memorial Arch – East Street Corfe Castle

The arch was designed by Francis G. Newberry, former Professor of Art at Glasgow University, some of its features being due to suggestions put forward by Dr. Godfrey Dru Drury. The cost was met by public subscription, and the work was entrusted to Thomas Luther, a well known local builder. The stonemason employed was William Arthur Day, who during the war had seen service with the Dorset Regiment in India and the Middle East and was one of the first to join the Corfe Castle Branch of the British Legion when it was formed in 1923..

'Do'set men don't sheâme their kind'

Stone for the walls of the arch was given by the Bankes Estate and came from the demolished West Mill cottages. The facing, lettering and carving work was done by a stonemason from Swanage.

The dedication took place on November 11th 1922, an occasion which is still remembered by some of the older people in the village who took part in it as children. The original wooden gates lasted until 1968 when they were replaced by the wrought iron gates in use today.

"IN SOME CORNER OF A FOREIGN FIELD ...."

There, in the corner, where the crab-apple
Leans lazily against the wall and watches
The honeysuckle and bramble
Scrambling over the rough stones,
There he lies, on his back,
With his face towards the
Everchanging sky from whence he came.

They shot him down.
He was threatening our harmless hills.
Him personally they bore no malice
But bore his body to the churchyard
And buried him in dignified austerity.

Not for him the nightmare pit
Of a sordid mass grave,
But an impassive, prosaic pardon
And an enviable resting place
IN a gentle landscape which
Trembles beneath nothing more
Terrifying than the plough,
Where the summer air throbs
With the drone and hum
Of the gnat and bumble bee.
                                        Mary Green
*Written in June 2000, sixty years after
The Battle of Britain*

Today's weather: Dry but dull

> AT THE GOING DOWN OF THE SUN
> AND IN THE MORNING
> WE WILL REMEMBER THEM

The picture above shows the former West Mill near the bridge on the Church Knowle road. The mill was demolished except for some remains of sluices and some of the stone was used in the war memorial arch.

Name	Compiled by Committee Members	Year of birth	Memorial Arch Dedicated 1922
House	Illustrations by Sheila Doyle-Stevens and Ken Williams	Street	East Street

Today the weather is fine, which makes a change , we have had nothing but torrential rain for weeks now. Mind you, we have been lucky here – there are parts of England that have had awful floods, people having to leave their homes or living on the upper floors.

I got up late today, I do like my bed, all snuggly and warm. I work part-time at the FOX INN in West Street, the oldest pub in Corfe Castle, dating back to 1568. I work in the kitchen and help with the waiting as well as behind the bar. I am a trained hairdresser but finding work around here is not easy without transport.

After I finished work at lunchtime I thought I would make the most of the good weather, so I went for a lovely long walk on the Common with my dog, Marney (an English Springer). She is meant to be black and white, but by the time we got back she was more the colour of mud, a little bit soggy on the Common.

Today's weather: Fine

Name   Fenella Louise Arnold   Year of birth   1960

House   94   Street   East Street

Thursday November 9th

I wish I could get up early in the morning, but I have always found it difficult to drag myself out of bed. Today is no exception and I reduce my feelings of angst at the lateness of the hour by having a second cup of coffee at breakfast, so it is past nine before I go into my small office room to make the usual phone calls and cope with the more urgent items of paper work. On my way from my house to my workshop I call in at the quarry for I need a piece of purbeck spangle to make a stone bowl It has to be three inches deep and although I keep finding pieces which look three inches they turn out to just a little less. In the end I see some quite different stone, which has a beautiful patterning of shells, so to justify my time I buy that instead. It will doubtless be added to the stack of similar impulse buys outside the workshop, which is opposite the railway station in Corfe. By now it is raining and although I will be spending the day being splattered by spray and chips from the stone saw, I nevertheless find this additional bit of damp depressing

I unlock the workshop and check the answer machine, but no messages. I am not sure which is worse, silence indicating that maybe all my customers have gone elsewhere or a stream of reminders about things I haven't done. I now begin dressing for work. They say Lawrence Olivier took two hours each evening making up for Othello, I have a fellow feeling as I laboriously put on overalls, waterproofs, rubber gloves, ear defenders and get the mask ready. Everything has to tuck into everything else in a special way, otherwise the water will get in and a horrid trickle make its way to my innermost and most private places. I check the equipment. Does the pump need priming? Is the saw table clear of chips etc.? At last I switch the saw on and the air is filled with a high pitched whistling scream as the motor gathers pace. I am making a polished stone lamp to be taken up to London next week to a shop in Pimlico, which has already sold it to a client in Germany for heaven knows what kind of additional mark up. I have made several such lamps and theoretically should be able to produce them with my eyes shut, but stone is a perverse and cussed material always waiting to catch out the unwary. If one is not careful the saw will pull it out of line or set up a vibration to cause a shell to hop out or start a crack making the whole thing unusable. After working for an hour or so everything seems to be going well. I look up out of the open door of the workshop — still raining, but this now seems quite encouraging. I am warm and relatively dry underneath all my clothes and those outside wearing the wrong clothes must be finding life grim. An outsider presents himself at the doorway. He is a salesman from a tool supplier. I try to limit my purchases, but I still can't resist buying some replacement grinding plates. This time he does not try to tell me one of those complicated jokes beloved of salesmen everywhere, which take so long in the telling that one's attention wanders just when the crucial punch line arrives, so that one laughs on cue without in the least knowing why. It is now lunchtime. I sit in my car and eat my sandwiches listening to the news on radio 4 Resisting the temptation to linger over a terrible comedy quiz programme I return to my lamp, which now has to be drilled for the electric wiring. The drill bit is shorter than the depth of stone so I turn it over and drill again from the other side, hoping that the two holes line up. Fortunately they do, so the Gods are smiling and I take advantage of their good humour by starting to polish the body of the lamp. This is a long and painstaking process. I use different polishing pads with a water cooled hand polisher. It is difficult to see the details of the stone through the stream of water, which tends to splash up round my face and cover my glasses. I will only be sure that the job has been successful once the last of the eight pads has been applied and the stone has dried off. I stop to have a drink of water and clean off my glasses and find that there are two faxes waiting printing on the machine. The first turns out to be an unsolicited advertisement for some kind of slimming regime, but the second is a request for a quotation. I pull off my rubber gloves and sit down with a pen and paper to work it out. It is soon clear that the stone they want is not available in the sizes. I ring round the quarries to find an acceptable alternative and then fax off a reply. In pre-fax days of course the sender would not expect any response for three days at least. Nowadays people want a nearly instantaneous reply. E mail and fax have a lot to answer for Back to the lamp, for the top has to be glued onto the middle and woe betide me if the holes don't line up. I now start to make the base. In no time atall I notice it is dark outside. Taking off my gloves again I see from my watch it is nearly 6 30 pm. I arrange things so that when I come back tomorrow it is obvious what needs doing next, otherwise I will waste half an hour muddling about before I finally get going It has stopped raining and most of the lamp is done On the whole not a bad day.

Today's weather. A lovely day.

Name Tony Viney   Year of birth

House Sandy Hill Workshops   Street Corfe Castle

corfe castle school

sophie

carys

meggie

Mrs gibson

r.

shuna

Today's weather: A BRIGHT COLD DAY.

Name shuna whyte

House 3 west street

Year of birth

Street   1995

Today is a very special day, when everything stops for a silence of 2 minutes in remembrance of those who lost their lives in both World Wars and many conflicts since, while serving their country. This is always at 11.00 am on November 11th, that being the time and date of the official end of World War I.

We have a ceremony in the Square with British Legion Standards and a gathering of ex-servicemen and women, and others who wish to pay their respects. The British Legion Chaplain, Herman Nuttall, and local vicar, the Rev. Maurice Strike attend, with Nigel Dragon who plays the "Last Post" before the 2 minutes silence and the "Reveille" after The Exhortation:

"They shall grow not old as we that are left grow old.

Age shall not weary them, nor the years condemn.

At the going down of the sun and in the morning

we will remember them"

is spoken by Col. V. Valle, president of our Royal British Legion, with all responding: "We will remember them".

Over the past week we have been Poppy collecting for the Royal British Legion whose aim is to give help to ex-service men & women whilst the Women's Section help their dependents.

Boxes are put out to all villages in shops and pubs, with volunteers calling house-tp-house with poppies. Joan Dunne and I go around the countryside calling at isolated farms and houses from 9.30 am to about 4.00 pm, stopping for a pub lunch at the New Inn, in Church Knowle.

Most people are pleased to see us and give generously. At the Blue Pool, Miss Barnard gives us a welcome cup of coffee, and at Doc Green's we get sweets from his pocket. One man, who was upstairs, was unable to come down, but threw money down to us from his window into the gravel below!

Today's weather: WET, WINDY ᴗ DARK

Name	Joan Marshallsay (Poppy Organiser)	Year of birth	1921
House	Corfe Castle Royal British Legion 76	Street	West

Today—Church Services will be held all over the Country to remember the people who died in both World Wars and various other conflicts since then, such as Ireland, The Falklands, peace-keeping in Bosnia and other places.

Our Service takes place in the Church of St. Edward at 10.45 am, the service being conducted by the Rev. Maurice Strike, with Pastor David Foot (Congregational), Rev. Sylvia Garrett (Methodist) and Rev. Herman Nuttall, British Legion Chaplain assisting him.

As Chairman of the Women's Section I will meet at the Royal British Legion Club with our Standard Bearer, Rosie Simmonds and Debbie Reynolds who carries our wreath of Poppies. We will walk down to the Church, where Rosie and Debbie wait in the porch with other Standard Bearers and wreath bearers, until time for them to come inside at the beginning of he Service.

The Standards and wreaths are presented at the altar for dedication. Part way through the Service a wreath will be laid under the Memorial Plaque, when the "Last Post", 2 minutes silence and the "Reveille" will take place. Towards the end of the Service the Standards and wreaths are handed back, the National Anthem sung, when the Standards are dipped, and on the closing hymn they parade to the Square followed by Legion men and women, Brownies and Foresters. We then parade to the War Memorial where a short service takes place to lay the wreaths.

After this all are invited to the Legion Club for refreshments - a gathering of friends old and new, some reminiscing, some just chatting.

Today's weather: Fine but cold

Name   Joan Marshallsay   Year of birth   1921
Corfe Castle Royal British Legion
House   76   Street   West

I'm on my way back to Nottingham today after spending a long weekend at home. I came back for my birthday on the 11th to celebrate with my mother and grandfather. We had a family lunch at Mortons House and in the evening I spent

my time with friends who I haven't seen since the summer break. We started at the Halfway pub and then came back to the Bankes Arms and the Greyhound. Nothing too hectic — just what I needed to keep my mind from the workload I have this year. I'm in my final year at Nottingham Trent University reading French and International relations.

Corfe was looking pretty as ever in the wintry sun. I love coming home, especially in winter when the tourists have gone. The village always seems so friendly and, mm - that lovely smell of wood fires from the chimneys as I walk up West Street towards home! I think how lucky I am to have the choice at the moment of living in a large city and the chance of coming back here as well.

There was the usual Remembrance Day church service and a special Millennium Tree was planted in the old Churchyard.

I'm having to travel back by coach from Poole which takes nine hours to cover 200 miles! Normally I would take the train, but after the Hatfield train disaster and with all the work now being done to repair the tracks there are virtually no trains running up north. Never mind, it was worth it just to get home to friends and family, not forgetting Tess, my little cavalier spaniel.

Today's weather.   Cold but fine

Name   Hannah Knijff   Year of birth   1978

House   Kerilee   West Street   Street

Tuesday November 14th

When the alarm sounded at 6.30 a.m., it was decision time. Is it fine or wet? Will I walk or swim? The recent spell of weather has been turbulent. So much of the country has been experiencing record breaking rainfall levels resulting in extreme floods. We are told it is due to global warming and there will be worse to come. Despite Corfe being fringed by a number of rivers and streams, only one or two households have been affected.

I had heard rain in the night and looking out of the window I could see rain drops or mist drops hanging from the trees. It was damp and misty but it meant I could walk. When we can, we like to take our exercise before breakfast. Jim, my husband, drives to Wareham to the public baths for the 'early bird' session where he swims his half mile. I sometimes accompany him but I love being outdoors, so, often opt for a walk/jog across Scotland Heath and Hartland Moor. It was peaceful and, as always, a joy to observe the wildlife.

We met up in Wareham and returned home for breakfast. The organic porridge oats had to go on hold though, as an SOS telephone call came from my mother to say her central heating was playing up and that her house was like a sauna. Indeed it was! Regulating the room thermostat made no difference, so it was time to shut the system off and reach for the British Gas helpline. My mother lives in a house built in about 1984. It is situated next door to Chapel Cottage in East Street which was her childhood home. When she moved into No. 50 in 1992, she decided to pay an annual fee of, at present, £127 to have a maintenance contract. A polite lady on the telephone assured us a man would come later today. Home then to a belated breakfast and some necessary domestic chores.

The sun was shining, so with overalls and wellington boots on, we took the opportunity to do some gardening jobs. Once, the small field that adjoins our cottage on the southern side had been a smallholding. Four years ago we were fortunate to purchase this, thus reuniting land and dwelling. It has been a satisfying conservation project. We have layed the roadside hedge which was badly overgrown and planted replacement hedging and trees. Within the field we plan to plant fruit trees and so reinstate it as a small orchard. The grass is lush but the weeds we inherited have been a constant problem. My brother, an agronomist, advised continual topping of the weeds as I did not want to use any chemical controls. We borrow a friend's sheep to graze the pasture. They are due back any day and they will eat the beheaded weed tops. We have a strimmer and the revolving strip of nylon rips the tops of the nettles, thistles and docks etc thus weakening them. It was Jim's turn today and it took him nearly two hours to strim the whole area. Meanwhile I dug out surplus perennials and gave them to a neighbour who is moving into a house with a large garden.

A light lunch of sandwiches and fruit sitting in our small garden room, watching the blue tits pecking at the nut feeder, was finished at 2.30pm. A phone call to my mother found the engineer was dealing with a faulty froststat. Tools put away, we set off to Swanage in our car. It was deadline time for paying for our holiday to the Canary Islands next year. Money drawn from the Building Society, we walked to Bath Travel, the local agent. A nice feeling to think about warmer, drier weather because by now it was again raining.

Time was rushing on so a change to the menu was necessary. A quick salad was assembled with pasta and cold chicken. This we enjoyed while watching the news – almost a week after voting and still it is not known who the new president of the U.S.A. will be, Gore or Bush.

The rain had ceased as I walked down the street to the sound of the treble and tenor bells being raised. It was practice night and the local ringers were gathering. Four of the men were in the belfry removing the muffles. It was Remembrance Sunday two days ago and as a sign of respect to those who died in the conflicts of the twentieth century, one side of each clapper had been covered with a leather pouch. This deadens the sound when the bell is struck on that side. The effect is solemn, yet beautiful. Although I am a relative novice, I am glad I am following in my grandfather's footsteps. He had been the Tower Captain for many years until the bells fell silent in 1957. He used to tread the stairs on winter nights to ring the curfew bell at 8pm. It was he who locked the door on the last occasion a rope was pulled. When I ring, I think of him calling the rounds and changes and my mother too, who listens from her bedroom window today as she used to when she was a child.

Today's weather: Damp start, fine and sunny with some showers later.

Name Mary Rosewarn   Year of birth 1949

House April Cottage 77   Street West

Like much of the autumn, today dawned grey and wet. Each day Gavin cycles the three miles to the Wytch Farm oilfield where he works. He spotted a couple of deer in one of the fields close to Old Thrasher's Lane but, although he thinks he is getting faster, as usual they managed to outrun him. He still finds it hard to believe that this is his commute to work, after having driven around the M25 for 6 years while he worked in London. Still, roll-on the summer.

At 8.43am Emily (6) sets off on her long journey to school. This involves opening the front door, saying hello to Jane the lollipop lady, crossing the road and going in the school gate – as you may have guessed we live opposite the school in the old tollhouse (see Gavin's drawing below). Preparations are beginning for Christmas but Emily won't yet tell us what her role is in the school play (The Very Hopeless Camel), not even a hint.

Amanda also started to think about Christmas, this morning nipping round to Poole to beat the rush – it seemed however that everyone else had had the same idea. She bought presents to send to the children of some good friends that we met while living in Australia, before we came to Corfe.

In the afternoon Gavin lead the 'upward feedback' for one of the senior managers on the oilfield. This means getting a group of staff to give what will hopefully be constructive feedback on their manager. Not a difficult task in this instance as the manager concerned is a very amicable fellow who seems to treat his staff well.

After school on Wednesdays Emily attends a swimming lesson at the Springfield Hotel. She started swimming lessons when she was three and now seems almost as confident under the water as on it. Amanda takes Charlotte (3) into the pool at the same time. She enjoys splashing (Charlotte that is) but we can't yet persuade her to take her own lesson.

Many an evening recently has been spent by Amanda in front of the computer finishing-off her doctorate in clinical psychology, and this evening was no exception. It has taken 4 years to accomplish and will be a great weight off her mind when it is finally done.

Gavin, Amanda, Emily & Charlotte Ward   1965, 1965, 1994 and 1997 respectively

St Edmunds House,   66, East Street

I woke up at 7.30 a.m. feeling refreshed after my beauty sleep, which needless to say I don't need much of!

I set about the day by attending to my horses, dressing accordingly as it's very muddy where they're kept due to all the rain we've been having.

Once the horses have been fed and watered, next is doing the rounds of checking my wild horses out of the Corfe Castle area and whether my Houdini sheep are still in their field. To my relief, yes, they are in their field and all on four legs, which make a welcome change. It's not so much me who minds herding, catching and treating the sheep, it's my helpers. They have the cheek to refer to them as "bloody poxing sheep". I tell you, they're sailing close to the wind, I won't stand for it much longer, calling my poor sheep that. I tell you, they're a pleasure to own. Mind you, even nicer on my plate – I suppose I agree with my helpers there!

Whilst checking my wild horses, I notice a couple of foals playing, which is reassuring in this hard weather. A helper spots a very well grown foal and comments on how pretty it is. I go on to tell them that I was pretty once and that back in my day...... but before I can continue they tell me to "shut up" – most charming!

Well mark my words, there are going to be some changes. I'll teach them the way to respect their elders! Again they tell me to "shut up" and call me a soft old fool!

Well the above took up most of my day, save a break for lunch (Mmm – had two Cornish Pasties).

Around 7 p.m. I settle down to see what's on the box. Of course that's a waste of time as I don't get a say: soaps it is and soaps it will always be! So at this time I decided to make a few phone calls to catch up on the gossip and do so as loudly as possible so they struggle to hear the TV!

Later on I have a topical discussion about my livestock management with my management team, planning for tomorrow after tea.

After watching my daily intake of the News, I tootle off home to tuck up in my bed and dream about my lovely sheep. Zzzzzzzzzzzzzzzzzzzzzzzzzzz

Today's weather:

| Name | L. C. Seager (Jumbo) | Year of birth | 1945 |
| House | Vineyard Farm Bungalow | Street | Church Knowle Rd |

Friday November 17th

This morning I travelled back from Swanage in my Vauxhall Nova. I stay with a friend on Thursday evenings so that we can go to a line dancing class. This type of dancing has become very popular over the last few years. I can see why, because it is relatively simple, appropriate for any age group and, most importantly, it is fun. I stopped off at Don's, the butcher, after picking up my Sun newspaper at the Paper Shop in the Square. I help Don with one or two chores most mornings for about half an hour or so. No delivering today, that was yesterday when I went to Herston and Swanage where I did two calls.

Having scanned the race meetings, I fancied a flutter on a couple of horses, so drove to Wareham to the bookmakers in North Street to place my bets. While there I picked up a few items of food from Somerfield, the supermarket, before heading homewards. I have lived here since 1952 and bought my house from the council in 1981 for £11,000. I like to keep the garden tidy, so this morning I spent a while raking up the last of the leaves. After a dinner of bacon and egg, I sat down to watch some TV. I enjoy following the 'soaps' and sport, especially football. Not always do I find there is much of interest in the daytime and invariably I close my eyes, sometimes dozing, sometimes just thinking.

I have appreciated my life as a resident of the village. I was nine years of age when I arrived here with my grandparents in 1929 and lived in Townsend Lane. My schooling was under Mr Mathews, the headmaster. Those days were so different from today, no television, no cars, so we had to make our own enjoyment which mostly was football and going to the pictures at Swanage. The village had many more shops then. We had four grocers, three butchers, sweet shops, a saddlery, Wegg and Tuck for women's clothing and Strouds for mens. Mr Day had an ironmongery and in all there were fifteen businesses. Many tales could be told of these and the two blacksmiths shops. Horses were the norm then. I was lucky enough to have a donkey and trap when I first came here.

My first job was as an apprentice painter to Mr George Day who then had a building business in West Street. He was also an undertaker which I had to assist with. I think I received one pound a week in wages, but we got by OK. The football club in the village had two teams, youth and minor. When we left school most of the boys played for these teams, they were happy days. Then came the war.

I was twenty, so I and one of my best friends, Wilfie Pope, volunteered for the RAF and it wasn't long before we were off. I was sent to Blackpool on the square training, then on to Boscombe Down near Salisbury. While there I was introduced to Peggy as a pen friend. She came from Birmingham and after regular correspondence, we got married in 1942. In November that year I went to North Africa and in time to Italy, Corsica and the Middle East. While in Italy I met Tony Groves, my old school mate. He was in the army at Taranto. There were some good times, but some were not, but that was life. These memories are fresh because on the eleventh it was Remembrance Day. I was attending a coffee morning at the Village Hall. Just before 11am, Lil Gibb, a member of the British Legion, halted the proceedings to ask for two minutes silence. She spoke the words: "They shall not grow old as we that are left grow old." My thoughts were of former comrades.

On returning to England after three years abroad, I was demobbed and returned home to Townsend. While there, my son, Tony, was born. He will be fifty-four tomorrow. I started working for J. Spiller as a painter in January 1947 until 1959 when I worked for George Brinton for a short spell. In 1963 I began working with Phil Chant until I retired in 1965. I still did some painting jobs because I found it so rewarding.

Sadly, my wife died in 1984 at Christmas. Since then by going to church either here at the Congregational Chapel or in Swanage at the United Reform Church, I have met some very nice people, and, of course, my job took me into a lot of people's homes. Many have since died but I shall always remember them and my dear wife, especially at Christmas time when this lovely village is all lit up with the decorations - there are some things you cannot change. I am proud to be a resident here, I hope I haven't written too much but there is no ending to a beautiful village, so much loved.

Today's weather:　　Chilly N.W. wind. Warm in sun. Fine all day.

Name _Charles John Butt_ 　Year of birth 7 - 7 - 20

House _10 WEBBERS CLOSE_ 　Street _WEST STREET_

Saturday 18th November

We are the Watson family and have resided in Wessex House since August 1993, having moved from Slough, Berkshire. Our eldest two daughters, Emma & Sarah (b. '76 & '79), have "moved on". Emma works in London (currently with CSFB bank) and Sarah is with her husband Rob, having been married at St Edwards CC 3rd June 2000. Both are employed at LloydsTSB bank in Wareham and reside in Poole. Our day started at 07:30hrs by taking Joanna to Wareham Sports Centre for swimming training with the Wareham "Water Rats" Club of which she is a member. Transport was "Dad's Taxi", a 1988 VW Polo.

It is the day of the Church Missionary Society Christmas Bazaar, which will be held in the Village Hall. Hilary is managing the cake stall, so starts the day icing her cake contribution that she cooked yesterday. By 10:00hrs she is in the Hall with Joanna (who has just been collected from her 1.5km swim – Dad's taxi!) setting up the table ready to display all the splendid offerings and price each accordingly! The sale went well. All the cakes were sold along with a few seasonal items. The event was well supported by local residents. A fine time was had by all.

Joanna left early to prepare for her afternoon of assisting at the Church Knowle animal sanctuary. Hilary remains at the hall to clear up. At home, David has been working on his latest update to the village amateur dramatic group web site, "Double-Act.org.uk". Matthew has by now "risen" and collected our Telegraph newspaper from the village newsagent. The avid Tottenham supporter next spends time working on his family football syndicate, which he has managed for a few years. Participants comprise a number of uncles, cousins and now, Rob (Manchester City). Members pass their predictions for the results of a sub-set of the weekend's games to Matt by phone, email and fax. All are collated, scores eagerly awaited and points awarded. The winner is the one with the highest score at the end of the season and receives the family trophy, kindly donated by Hilary's brother, Uncle Glyn. Matt won it last year!

Meantime, lunch is consumed – sandwiches constructed with the assistance of a granary loaf acquired from our local bakery, Dragons. After lunch David rehearses his lines for the forthcoming Double Act production "1066 And All That!" His principle characters are Julius Caesar and a scheming baron. All four of us have parts; Hilary, one of Henry 8th's wives and an air hostess; Matthew, Guy Fawkes (in trouble for failing to blow up the Houses of Parliament!) and Joanna as the Troubadour's wife – many lines to learn. David's difficulty is that he has two business trips away to Benbecula and Montreal (CAE) and will miss out on all the final dress rehearsals – arriving home jetlagged on the morning of the evening of the first performance! David Kemp, who has the lead role, assists by performing a read-through with David W that is recorded on a cassette tape. This will be replayed at 37,000ft on a personal Walkman – more than once!

It is Joanna's birthday on November 21st, she will be 15. It is customary at such events for us to have a family "party tea", nearly always principally consisting of egg sandwiches (though we don't remember why!) along with an array of sweet items including a cake made by Mum to the "celebratee's" specification.

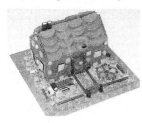

This year Jo has requested a "House cake" decorated with her favourite nibbles. The "party" will be tomorrow because Dad is departing on his travels Tuesday – her birthday. Whilst Hilary is constructing her latest masterpiece, David Kemp departs and Dad's taxi is re-launched to collect Joanna from the animal sanctuary; she having completed the housework for an assortment of rabbits, mice and rats! By relaxation we all half watch a film on Channel 4 – "Aces High" – judging it as average-to-good. Tonight is the Water Rat's club championships, member against member.

So, it's Dad's taxi back to Wareham! One of Hilary's pass-times is choral singing – currently with the May Day Singers based at Langton Matravers. Several Purbeck groups are preparing for a combined Christmas performance of Handel's "Messiah" at St Mary's, Swanage. Hilary rehearses for awhile in the afternoon. Dad starts to pack. Somewhere in the middle of that we prepared and enjoyed an evening dinner assisted by a glass each of our favourite Bordeaux. (Mum & Dad only!) The finishing touches were applied to the cake late on and we fell into bed at around 00:15 – and readied ourselves to do it all again!

......and yes, Joanna did come home proudly brandishing a medal (100m backstroke - Silver)....

......**via Dad's taxi.....**

(Today's weather: Damp & grey!)

Name: David, Hilary, Matthew & Joanna.   Years of birth: 19's 49, 50, 82 & 85.

House: Wessex House.   Street: Calcraft Road.

I was utterly electrified to see Corfe and Studland on Meridian T.V. at lunchtime today, and not least, to be given a superb view of "Penny Cottage"! They were featuring the present debate on second home charges.

As an octogenerian, fast becoming a 'nonogenarian', I can only translate myself back to 1925: It was in the summer of that year that my parents brought me on a charabang trip to Swanage for the day whilst on our Summer holiday at Boscombe. My vivid recollections of that trip were the old bridge over the Frome at Wareham, sadly demolished the following year, the Castle and the old Bankes Arms alongside the very poor road, and the pier at Swanage.

Exactly 22 years later I brought my wife, a Canadian whom I met in Manitoba, Canada where I was instructing on Tiger Moths, to Swanage for our Summer Holiday. We camped near the railway in a hike tent on Mr. Beavis's farm at Langton. Both he and his wife and niece, Nellie proved to be wonderful friends and we repeated our holiday every year until our 8 month-old second child came too and my wife flatly refused to camp anymore because Susan would insist upon exploring the cow-pats. By then, of course, Peter, now 3, had become a seasoned camper! After two days the Beavises insisted upon us staying in the farmhouse! In subsequent years it was our pleasure to stay at "Worcester Lodge" in Victoria Avenue with the Dunfords.

It was on a day's visit to see Corfe in 1964 that I took the two older children 'up the Castle' while my wife explored Corfe with the 'little one' (Matthew) in his push-chair. When we met up again Elisabeth told me how she had seen the most delightful cottage which was being refurbished in West Street. I thereupon asked her if she would like to be the owner of a second home. Her enthusiasm was obvious and we eventually became the owners of "Penny Cottage"! We then proceeded to make substantial use of the cottage and many friends and relatives came regularly. In fact, cousins from Canada thought it a wonderful place to have their honeymoon!

In 1995 Peter and Clare, daughter Melanie and big dog, Ben established themselves with Mother at the cottage and looked after her while establishing an electronics factory. Baby James was born after the move to their new home locally, relieving the pressures on Penny Cottage. Unhappily Elisabeth became too ill to look after herself while I was still trying to dispose of our home in Hertfordshire.

Time having taken its savage toll since then I have managed to live here on my own thanks to the unbounded kindness of many members of the community: I can honestly conclude that in spite of being 'foreigners' we were never made to feel outsiders!

Today's weather: Sunny and pleasant

Name Raymond Charles Western   Year of birth 1919

House Penny Cottage   Street East Street

Continuing memories of my time at the mill (see October 16th):

We had set routes on set days delivering every day except Sunday, sometimes two rounds a day. Our supplies were essential to the farmers and the villagers in the area. On Monday, Wednesday and Saturday my journey would be to Church Knowle, Puddlemill, Orchard Farm, Bradle, Cocknell and Barnston Manor. Tuesday and Friday, one cart went to Lower Bushey while the other went to Higher Bushey and Rempstone. On Thursday, Norden, New Line, Half-Way House and Scotland Heath were visited. We also went as far as Dunshaye Lane, Primrose Hill, Tabbits Hill, Woolgarston and Sandy Hills.

When delivering on Scotland Heath I would often leave six loaves for one family and ten for another in a shack from which the farmers would collect. Browner bottoms to loaves would supply an alternative if tea was short. The isolation of these farms meant wives would sometimes run low on certain items, so they would trim off the bottom of the loaf and put hot water with it so it looked like tea. Although I never tasted it, husbands would accept it and for the wives it meant further economy by not having to use so much milk.

It was on a Thursday, when heading along one of the many rough tracks on the heath, made partly from chalk cut out of the hills, that the cart wheel became wedged in a deep rut. The sudden lurch sent me flying through the air. The horse was struggling and in order to release him I had to cut the harness. Once Archie, he was a grey, was back on his feet, I had to tie up the harness with string to keep it together and then continue the round. We always did the deliveries despite even the harshest weather. Archie was particularly good on frosty ground when he had special nails put in his shoes. I remember the boss complaining about the cost of the repair of the harness which was done at the saddlery in East Street. Two men worked there and the moan from Mr Battrick was that the repairs cost as much as buying new harness. In those days for my week's work I was paid fifteen 'bob' (shillings).

At the age of 26 years, I had a complete change of scenery. My work in the war was at Eastleigh in the railway works helping to maintain rolling stock and rebuild coaches. Once the war was over, I worked for eight years at Wyatts of Upton which was a building firm. I had a small car by then, so this made the journey much easier.

When I was 27 years old I married my 23 year old bride, Maisie. She was one of thirteen children. We began our life together at 108 East Street paying seven shillings a week rent for our house. I am known as being thrifty and don't believe in overspending but to put a bit away for a rainy day – the sun won't always shine, I say. It was with a view to making a bit extra that I took up the idea of using my neighbour, Sid Paine's pig sties – he had two at the bottom of his garden. I started out with two piglets that I collected on my bike from Reg Curtis who was farming at Woolgarston. These were the first of many and the money I made I saved and this is how I was able to buy my house for a thousand pounds.

I have never had a holiday. I consider that life is one continuous holiday, even when working you get your fun out of it. I did go on a trip to London once to the Wembley Exhibition. It was a school outing. We went by steam train and it cost 7s.6d. I didn't go much on it, a waste of time for me because I didn't learn anything. I read enough about people and what goes on that I think I had just as well stop at home. I have two sons. David lives in Swanage and has three sons. Nicky lives at home and continues to grow vegetables in the back garden and allotment as I used to. I wander down to the Legion Club with Maisie about three times a week. Maisie has her whisky and I a beer or two. We meet up on different days with different people for a chat.

When asked what my secret is for a long life, Maisie jumps in with; "Being looked after and waited on." She is a good cook. Before the boys were born she made scones with her sister, Gladys, at Sheasby's Tea Shop in The Square. Between them they would make 300 to 400 per morning. We celebrated our Diamond Wedding Anniversary in March. We spent the day at home where we received lots of cards, several bouquets and people dropped in to see us. Our son and grandsons came and, together with Nicky, it made it a real family occasion. We drank sherry and even had champagne! It is one of many days that I shall remember for the rest of my life.

Today's weather: Dawned fine but damp, sunny with rain later.

Name E. Mullett   Year of birth 1912

House 108   Street East

Tuesday November 21st

This is the day that we moved to Corfe Castle in 1971. Having spent my previous 13 years in the Police Force either working on traffic duties or big towns I was about to embark on the rural way of life!

What an introduction! Having spent the day humping furniture about and hanging curtains I decided that it was time for a break. With family approval, we have three daughters, I set off to "The Castle Inn" with Sandy (the dog) in tow, for a pint.

It is a feeling that you get as your service increases but the minute I walked in the door everyone in the pub knew I was the new Bobby! Everyone that is except "Champ" who happened to be in the loo. When he returned, in the welcoming fashion that is typical of Corfe, he introduced himself and proceeded to tell me all about his poaching activities!

It was my turn to go to the loo and when I returned someone had put him wise! With a grin as wide as the fireplace in the bar he said, "Would you like a pint Sir?"

Today's weather: (In 1971) Cold. Still some snow on the ground

Name	Doug and Val Davies	Year of birth	1933
House	Formerly of The Police House (Now living at Sandford Woods)	Street	Townsend Mead

Wednesdays are busy for me in my retired life. I came back to live in Corfe having lived fifty years on the farm at Blashenwell one and a half miles outside the village.

I joined the Land Army in the war of 1939 to 1945. I was one of many young women throughout the country who replaced the men workers while they fought for their country. My job was to assist in the dairy. I had been trained to do this particular work which involved much of the cleaning and sterilising of the milking containers. Sometimes I had to chop the wood for the fire which heated the boiler. The milking units were placed in the steamy sterilising chest after I had thoroughly washed them. We had an old Fordson tractor but mainly the milk was taken in churns on a cart pulled by Bob, the horse, to the Milk Factory in Corfe.

I used to cycle to the farm to begin my twelve hour day at 5.30am. Sunday morning was my half day when I could have a sleep in and also sing in the choir at the Parish Church. This was the pattern of my life for five years. I still have a pay slip from January 1943. It reads: Pay £1.8s.6d. Tax and National Insurance Contributions – 7d and 8d. Net Pay £1.7s.3d.

It was after the war that I married the farmer, Tom, and continued to work long hours as well as becoming a mother of three children. It was as though I came home when I was widowed in 1991 and began life here.

Every Wednesday, and today is no exception, at 10.30am I go to the Communion Service at St Edward's Church, a place where I was christened and married. Afterwards I go to the Post Office to collect my pension and to the village shop to buy necessary goods for the store cupboard.

Twelve o'clock brought Mrs Nel, the chiropodist, to the front door. She spent ten minutes trimming my toe nails and massaging my feet. I have rheumatoid arthritis and this treatment makes me feel, for a while at least, like I am walking on air.

After dinner I go next door to the Congregational Chapel, to the Women's Bright Hour Meetings. Apart from it being a social get-together, we also sometimes participate in the presentations like reading poems, and using extra instruments such as tambourines to make music while we sing Songs of Praise. Today we listened to a speaker and, as always, finished with cups of tea and a chat. Actually the Chapel's south wall is the boundary of one side of my garden and the house where the Pastor of the Chapel lives, the other side of the building, is where I was born and lived for twenty-nine years until I married.

This evening I look forward to going to the Springwell Meeting Room to a whist drive. Our numbers vary, anything up to twelve. We are all oldies with infirmities of one sort or another, but we have fun as well as enjoying the games.

Before retiring I nibble a biscuit with my hot, chocolate drink and lie in bed listening to the relaxing music of Classic FM on the radio which often sends me to sleep.

Today's weather: Heavy showers until 11am, then dry all day.

Name _Joan H Palmer_   Year of birth _1918_

House _5b_   Street _East_

CORFE CASTLE MILLENNIUM ASSOCIATION
CAPITAL PROJECT – PAVILION & SPORTS FIELD IMPROVEMENTS

Below are the plans for the pavilion which will be erected on the West Street Sports Field. This, together with other enhancements to the field including a floodlit, all-weather multi-sport area, will serve as a lasting memorial to the Millennium whilst being a legacy of benefit to both present and future generations.

The plans, drawn by the architect Ken Morgan, have been approved by the Planning Committee of Purbeck District Council. On the dissolution of the Association, the project will be continued by the newly formed Corfe Castle Sports Trust. The Association wishes the Trust success in bringing the scheme to fruition.

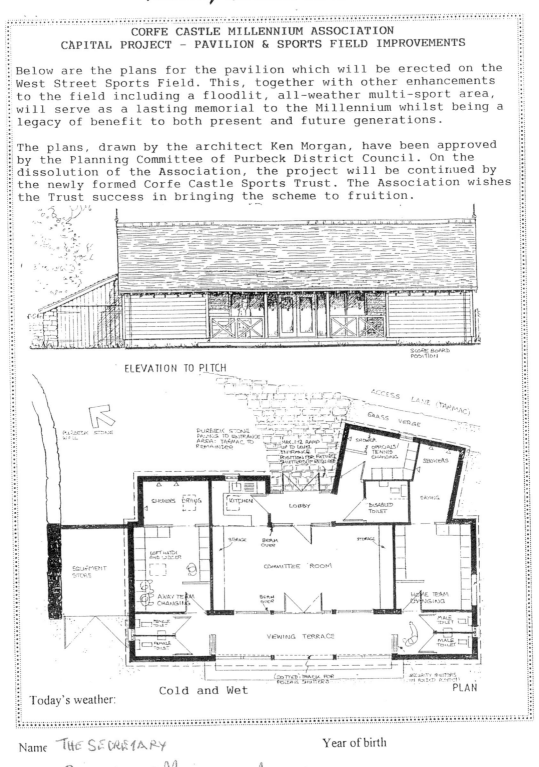

ELEVATION TO PITCH

PLAN

Today's weather: **Cold and Wet**

Name THE SECRETARY   Year of birth

House CORFE CASTLE MILLENNIUM ASSOCIATION Street

5.45am the day begins, the kettle goes on and whilst savouring our first cup of tea, we listen to the weather forecast and news on Radio 4. After showering, daily chores begin. The day is dawning, with just a hint of red in the sky, it looks as if it could be a nice day for a change or is it a warning of things to come.

7.00am the birds are waiting for their daily seed and Robin lands on the food box, that I'm holding, to snatch his first snack of the day.

7.20am We set off for Poole. Rubbish sacks are collected on Fridays, as we leave I take our's to the gate. There are black sacks lining both sides of East Street waiting for collection. Several people are walking towards the common taking their dogs for a walk. John at Cleall's Store is wheeling his barrow, full of plants and flowers, to the corner of the shop, we toot and wave as we go by.

There is very little traffic between Corfe Castle and Wareham but volume increases considerably at Sandford, never the less, we arrive by 7.50am at the Nuffield Industrial Estate, our place of work. My wife and I own a small label printing business and spend the day, as usual, printing and designing all types of labels mostly for industry.

By lunch time it's wet again - thought it was too good to be true.

On Fridays we try and close by 4pm. It's not always possible but today things have gone well and we leave on time.

4.15pm raining heavily and the traffic is creating a lot of surface spray - not an enjoyable journey home.

4.45pm stop off at Cleall's Store for milk and a few groceries and home for an early dinner as I have to be out again before 7.00pm for a 'N' Gauge Railway meeting at Pelham's Centre in Kinson. I hope to be home again by 11.30pm.

Another week over and looking forward to a weekend at home, enjoying the garden and Purbeck.

Roger Denning

Today's weather: A dark wet day.

Name ROGER DENNING   Year of birth

House A CORFE CASTLE RESIDENT   Street

As I sit here today on my sixty-ninth birthday and look out of my window, I feel very lucky to live in such a nice bungalow, which is owned by the Corfe Castle Charities. These were built in 1973 after the Charities had upgraded the original alms-houses to commemorate Queen Elizabeth's Jubilee. My bungalow is one of four lying at right angles to the main road and beside the First School. I get great pleasure from hearing and watching the children coming and going to school. The view from my window is great, with the railway, the fields beyond with cattle and horses grazing, reaching to the ridge of hills which run from our village to the outskirts of Swanage.

As I sit here I remember eleven months ago to the day when I had my accident, suffering a triple fracture of my right ankle and a chip to the main bone of the leg. This has made this last year very different. It has meant spending a lot of time backwards and forwards to the hospital at the beginning and then for the last six months having a nurse call quite often to change dressings. I think my leg will still be in bandages until 2001 but never mind the future is there to make what you will of it.

At last the postman has arrived with more cards and two parcels from family and friends. My family has arrived with more cards and presents from the grandchildren. I have been told to sit and see what my granddaughter, Polly, has chosen for me. The grown-ups have gone out of the room, something is happening but I have to undo Polly's gift. Oh! It's a stone badger for my front garden. Then my two daughters and son-in-law told me to choose a place in the garden for Boris, this is Polly's name for the badger. So, in the pouring rain I open the door and to my great delight the three grown-ups have bought me a lovely, stone bird bath. I shall have more to look at from my seat in the window. This has turned out to be a very happy day with more visits from friends and phone calls too.

Today's weather: Wet all day. Confirmed that this is the wettest autumn since records began in 1750.

Name Lilian M. Gibb. Year of birth 1931.

House 3 ST. EDWARDS CLOSE. Street EAST STREET.

Sunday November 26th

Our night's sleep was interrupted by the force of the severe gale and squalls flung at the house from the Tyneham valley and sea beyond - the price we pay for our stupendous views, including the Castle a mile below us to the west and Knigston Hill and Swyre Head to the south. The deer had as usual raided the garden in the night.

My husband set off in breezy sunshine to a working lunch near Chippenham (save your sympathy: lobster and organic lamb). This left me and our dog Daisy to spend a quiet Sunday together. Our first venture, a walk up Rollington Hill behind our house, lasted five minutes. Quiet was not the word. A stupendously loud 'crump' from the Army Ranges had the usual effect on the dog, she keeled over, apparently shot dead, and wouldn't move! I carried her home. Not much respite for her indoors either. The house shook with each thudding detonation.

The afternoon was more successful. I drove to Studland beach. The strong winds had attracted kite-flying enthusiasts (but no nudists!). A fine array of kites were tearing to and fro above the beach, threatening to dive-bomb and skewer casual walkers. Then there was a show-stopping sight. Caught between the Purbeck sunshine and a heavy shower over Bournemouth Bay we were treated to the brightest and most complete rainbow I have ever seen. What's more, thanks to its reflection in the wet sand, I may even have got the pot of gold!

Back home it was an ordinary dark November evening - husband safely home (not hungry); paperwork to deal with (my NHS work); long Sunday phone calls to our mobile from our son and daughter in London (our main telephone line has now been down since October 27th - a month, and the third time since we moved here permanently in July.); television news (the ongoing Bush/Gore U.S.A. Election Result Dispute and official confirmation that this has been the wettest autumn ever). Despite the rain - the foundations of our new sunroom look like a swimming pool) we love living here.

Today's weather: Very windy

Name Mary Sabben-Clare   Year of birth 1944
House Sandy Hill Barn   Street Sandy Hill Lane

Monday 27th November 2000 and the Davis family of 43 East Street begin another fun filled week.

The radio switches on at 6.45a.m and I nip into the shower first before waking everyone. Sam (14) and Josh (12) each have a shower followed by Rosie (10) and Poppy (8) then Dad –Paul (old as the hills). Spike (5) has to be woken as he is collected at 8 and he's not a mornings person! We go downstairs and let Woody our 8 month old Border Collie into the garden. I have to keep a close eye on him as he's developed great skills at escaping next door to play with Tristan, a mature collie and very reluctant playmate. Woody's also searching for Lady Bankes' treasure so I keep having to bang on the window to suggest other possible sites. I put the kettle on and help Spike to get into his school uniform. This can be a delicate operation as he can be a tricky customer. Spike has cerebral palsy and epilepsy and though he's fairly able physically– he can walk and dress himself- he does have a bit of an attitude problem and can be difficult and stubborn. On a good day he can be all sweetness and light but then…. He's finally dressed and has his breakfast of Weetabix. Rosie and Josh join him .Monday mornings can be awful, full of dreadful problems lost games kits, forgotten homework, no bread for toast, the shock discovery that a thief has stolen one school shoe and everyone in filthy temper. But today all's calm (well what passes for calm in our house). Maureen and Gerry arrive at 8 to take Spike to school in Dorchester. He goes to The Prince of Wales School which is a mainstream school with a unit for children with physical disabilities. It's a lovely school and his teacher Marian works really hard to keep us in touch through 'phone calls, home school link book and coffee mornings. Spike loves it there. I wave him "Good bye" then it's back indoors to get the others off on time. Josh and Rosie go to Wareham Middle and Sam to The Purbeck School . At 5 past 8 Davey arrives to call for Sam and Ben, Tim & Olly for Josh, so our front room is perfumed with umpteen different hair gels and deodourants, and full to the gills with boys and backpacks. Woody dashes in to join in the fun and I try to ensure that everyone (who lives in our house) has had their breakfast, brushed their teeth and collected their biscuit and drink for break. Sam, Josh, Rosie and Spike all have hot school lunches so I only have to do sandwiches for Paul & Pop thank-goodness. Rosie leaves to call for Lauren 3 doors down. Then

The 6 boys go leaving just Paul and Poppy , me and Woody. I make a flask of coffee for Paul and finish making his & Pop's sandwiches. Woody rushes round barking his request for a walk. Paul thunders downstairs looking for his glasses, camera, 'phone, keys and college work. He's in the second year of an H.N.D. course in Architectural Stone Masonry and Carving at Weymouth College which he's really enjoying. He used to be Corfe's electrician before he broke his back in1998 in a boating accident, but couldn't return to it as his back couldn't cope with bending and twisting. So now he's a mature student. This means there's yet another Davis clamouring for a turn on the computer and able to lose that vital page of homework. Poppy ambles down to have her breakfast then goes back upstairs to brush her teeth and find a band for her hair. Then back down for hair brushing, ponytail making, bag packing, coat on and off she skips up the road to Corfe Castle First School. I can see her all the way to the school gate. This is her last year there so after July I won't watch any more journeys up the road with warnings of "No running on the narrow bit"shouted to a departing child. Paul drops me and Woody at Cat's Eye Cottage Norden and we walk back through the soggy but still beautiful countryside while he heads off for Weymouth. Woody and I share an interest in birds, I like to watch them and he likes to chase them. To-day I see a buzzard and an egret . I'm glad I'm wearing my wellies as it's rained almost every day since the beginning of October. They are "Monsoon" wellies ,just as well, "Slight Drizzle" or "Bit of a shower" brand just wouldn't cut the mustard. I collect the paper and a loaf go home and it's so …….quiet. Lovely. I can listen to" Woman's Hour" whilst clearing away the breakfast things and sorting the washing. I put some on the line,ever the optimist, perhaps it'll dry before the next shower (Ha!) I have a go at clearing the chaos of a family week-end & hoovering & making the house a smidgen less messy. Where do all those "Ideal Home" type homes keep their clutter? Sometimes I feel like a hamster running round on one of those wheels. It's O.K. so long as you keep running but now and then something happens- someone's ill, you have to sort something out and it takes all day on the 'phone, and there you are bumping around in chaos- no-one's got any clean socks, you've forgotten to take the library books back and there's nothing for tea! Bedlam! Well today the wheel's running smoothly. I have a sandwich for lunch, listen to "The Archers", change the boys beds and take Woody for a walk along Sandy Hill Lane and across the fields behind Challow Farmhouse to meet Pop from school at 3. Josh & Rosie arrive back at 3.30. and Sam at 3.40. Everyone's starving so they have a biscuit or some fruit. Spike's taxi arrives back at 4.15,and Paul gets home an hour later. Everyone's got some news or gossip and they all tell it at the same time, so peace and quiet goes out of the window as youth comes in the door. We have our tea of pasta, peppers, mushrooms, onion, garlic, and leftover-from-Sunday cream & chicken followed by melon at 6. I then clear the debris and listen to various accounts of who did what to whom and why, and try to assist with bits of homework with facts poorly remembered from 30 years ago. Then I get into my aerobics gear. No I don't wear a leotard! Jogging bottoms and a baggy T-.Shirt as befits a young- at -heart but overweight lumpy. (Don't visualise Jane Fonda- more Teletubbies). I go with Joan from the bakery and Jennie from Church Knowle. After strutting our stuff we go to "The Halfway" and undo all that puff and sweat by knocking back a couple of drinks and eating cheese and onion Nutsters and we set the world to rights too of course. I'm home at 11.30 and everyone's asleep. Aaaaa Goodnight from Donna the dog-walking –aerobic-ing 44 year old mother of 5 from East. St.

Name **DONNA DAVIS +FAMILY**   Year of birth **14.9.56**

House **"THE OLD SADDLERY"**   Street **43 EAST STREET**
ALSO KNOWN AS "THE OLD HAIRDRESSERS"

Tuesday November 28th

Hi, it's my birthday today. My favourite present was probably a Sony walkman. Unfortunately, I still had to go to school ⸻ today! My lessons were: Lesson 1 art with Mr. Dixon (I had half the lesson off practising carols in the Hall with Miss Chaudhri for the carol service). After that it was break time and I got the birthday beats (it's where someone hits your arm as many times as you are years old and it hurts!) Lessn 2 was singing carols again and I was missing French with Miss Murfin. Lesson 3 – English – we were reading some of Charles Dickens' "A Christmas Carol".

Next it was lunch but I had to be picked up by Dad to go to the dentist to have TWO teeth out!! The appointment was for 12.50 and the lunch bell goes at 12.25 so I had to eat my lunch in the car.

Luckily the dentist is really nice, so she put some bubble gum flavoured numbing cream on my gum before she inserted the needle with the anaesthetic. It really helped because the needle only stung a little. It didn't hurt when the teeth were being taken out and the suction made a snapping noise.

I had the rest of the day at home and when I got there Mum said, "I heard some wild animal noises from your bedroom upstairs and I know you are brave!" I guessed she was joking so I went upstairs and on my bed was sitting a camel beanie baby called Niles.

When I had said thank you I worked out how to work my walkman and arranged some photos in my new album that I had as a present.

For tea we had mashed potato with a sausage casserole followed by butterscotch pudding. We had apple shloer to drink.

After tea I had a bath, watched "A Muppet's Christmas Carol" for a break and then I went to bed around 9 o'clock.

Today's weather: Cloudy and dull but it didn't rain!

Name   Holly Smith   Year of birth   1988

House   Larksgate   Street   Townsend Mead

Advent candles; hot chocolate in the Greyhound after Communion.

Yvonne and Roger take the guided tour of the castle.

Fresh baked bread from the famous Dragon Bakery.

A lovely beginning to my 75th birthday.

Today's weather: Fine and dry; new doors and windows are being fitted to our bungalows.

Name Sheila Doyle-Stevens

Year of birth 1925.

House No 8

Street Springwell Close.

30 November 2000.

This day I had intended to talk to people who knew the village and the estate well, but at the vital moment illness intervened and peoples' minds necessarily were in other directions.

It has been a sad year in Kingston. We have had a lot of illness. Three people have died. This may not seem very significant but in a community of 120 it takes its toll. Everyone knows everyone without knowing their business. We all care for each other and such losses hit hard.

The church was full for all the memorial services. There were village people, but many from Worth, Langton, Swanage and Corfe as well as relations. All three who passed away had taken part in numerous activities outside the village and were much loved and respected. They had also done much for the village.

Today's weather: Overcast - wet.

Name CHAPMAN   Year of birth 1935

House OLD POST OFFICE   Street 16, WEST ST KINGSTON.

What better a way for "Double Act" to celebrate the Millennium than with a production of "1066 and All That!". Friday night saw the dedicated cast into their second performance of the most memorable production with the most memorable date in the memorable history of our memorable country, produced by the memorable Christine Kemp .. ..

Following a few minor problems (i.e. the costume rail collapsing as a result of bearing too many exasperatingly heavy Tudor outfits) it was time for "curtain up". The first scene opened with the Hall of Fame, containing such noble beings from history as Nelson and Caesar. We hope that the audience also fully appreciated the suit of armour inhabited by Nicky Haswell as Hotspur. The other statues put a great deal of effort into developing an elite armour removal squad. By Friday we had got "removing" Nicky down to a fine art, to clear the stage in time for the Roman Road, and that memorable song, "We're Going Home".....

Several historic scenes later we somehow found ourselves at the interval. Anyone entering the changing room at that point might have been amused to see Oliver Cromwell and William the Conqueror (1066!) chatting over a cup of coffee, while Henry VIII chewed on a rice crispie cake. Soon the excited hush (hush being a rare occurrence here at Double Act) swept backstage as the curtain came up for Act II, beginning with Henry and his wives. Several more decisive battles were fought, Acts signed, wars won (or lost as the case may be) and fabulous dance routines executed. A definite highlight was the can-can fantastically choreographed, that brought huge cries of "encore!"

And we were at the finale: one more reprise of THAT song and then we were navigating our way out of those heavy costumes.

This has given just a small glimpse of Double Act. As well as an annual production, we participate in monthly workshops. Both are extremely rewarding and great fun too! We hope the curtain will be rising on Double Act productions for many years to come.

Today's weather· 'orrible! Surprisingly mild, but raining on and off all day. Soggy!

Name	Philly Byrde (age 14 from Kimmeridge)	Year of birth	Double Act Founded circa 1997
House	Rehearsals: Workshop Venue	Street	Corfe Castle Village Hall

Corfe Castle Christmas Festivities – Turning on of the Christmas Lights.

Well the lights look marvellous! What a spectacular sight! After several weeks of hard exhaustive work the Christmas Festivities Volunteer working party have succeeded. The village Christmas lights get better every year, and so says everybody that sees them. Little do they know or realise how much hard work and time goes into making the village look so good. It starts back in the summer when the volunteers meet in the Village Hall to check all the looms, wiring, bulbs, fittings and ornamental lighting, so that any replacements that are needed can be ordered and replaced in good time. When checking is completed the lights are all packed and safely stored ready for later in the year. The volunteers then regroup on the first Sunday in October at 8.30am to start the arduous task of erecting the street lighting, and this continues every Sunday until the beginning of December.

The work starts in East Street with volunteers climbing ladders, directing traffic, passing up looms and checking bulbs, and gradually continues to the Square and West Street during the following weeks. Whilst the work is going on some villagers and local tradesmen supply some much needed refreshments to the volunteers. With the majority of the work completed and the mainly intricate work left the deadline falls on the first Saturday in December when the lighting up ceremony takes place.

On the first Saturday in December the Volunteers gather at 8am in the Square to start what is a very long and busy day. An early start is essential, as there is a lot of work to be completed before the grand lighting up ceremony at 4.30pm. Thankfully the weather was kind being dry and bright, but there were a few showers later in the morning (the weather forecaster had promised dry with blustery showers and strong winds). The major worry is the large Christmas tree. This is always a cause for concern, and takes quite a lot of time but we are very lucky to be able to borrow a crane for the task of raising the tree into position behind the cross. Then to put up the small trees and ornamental lighting on the wall brackets, the crib is then assembled in front of the cross. At the same time the volunteers install the loud speaker system to ensure it will be audible for the New Year and Christmas celebrations. During the day local tradesmen ensure that the volunteers are well catered for by supplying morning refreshments and lunch whilst they carry on working. By late afternoon it is all in place (a race against time).

The High Sheriff of Dorset Mr Michael Bond (who lives in the village) had agreed to switch on the illuminations. He arrived by car, the Chairman of the Christmas Festivities greeted him. The High Sheriff made a short speech thanking the volunteers for all their hard work and switched on the illuminations. It looked magnificent! **Congratulations to you all!**

NB. Because the lights are in place and working it does not mean that the volunteers job has ended. A rota of names is drawn up to ensure that the lights are checked every night and any replacement bulbs or maintenance takes place quickly, so that the lights are at their best all over the Christmas period. Then in the spring the process starts all over again for the next year.

Today's weather: DRY, BRIGHT, FEW SHOWERS. (LUCKY, IN A YEAR OF RECORD RAINFALL)

Name MRS HELEN LAYTON   Year of birth 1951
Committee Member - Corfe Castle
Christmas Festivities
House MOONFLEET,   Committee.   Street HIGHER FILBANK

Sunday December 3rd

Advent Sunday

I suppose we all have our favourite days and seasons in the year. As Rector, I have always loved Advent Sunday which is the beginning of a new church year. There is a certain excitement and expectation in the air with everyone preparing for Christmas. In contrast to the hurly-burly outside, the church is subdued and remains undecorated until the last possible moment. Hymns sung in the Advent season are among the most beautiful, melodic and reflective.

Tonight the Service of Light takes place at St. Edward's, a candlelight service which attracts more people every year. It is so successful at Salisbury Cathedral, they have extended it over Saturday and Sunday.

The service begins in silence and in the dark with the exception of one candle representing the light of Christ to symbolise hope; in the Order of Service, I have written, "That light dispels the darkness but not without showing up the dark places of our world and lives". The silence gives way to holy scripture being read and an early anthem is sung from the baptistry. As the choir process east, candles in the nave and chancel are lit, in sight and sound it is an experience of great spirituality.

In our somewhat secular age, I think we underestimate the importance of the church year and its seasons, how the liturgy of music, poetry and prose reflects the natural year but above all the mood of our being and need.

Looking back it has been an exciting church year at St. Edwards. Last Christmas the bells rang for the first time since the mid fifties and we are overjoyed to have so many ringers too! With the new millennium it also seemed appropriate to put on a special presentation reflecting two thousand years of Christian witness. How can one celebrate without a thanksgiving to God ......for people like Wilberforce, Shaftesbury and Bonhoeffer and many who gave so much. With a cast of forty (adults and young people, ... The village school joining us) and one hundred projections it was a production to remember. A thanks to everyone for their expertise and patience with a demanding and highly strung director!

Looking forward, no doubt Christmas will be as joyous as ever. The Square, thanks to the Christmas Festivities Committee, is ablaze with fairy lights and I hear rumours of an award and a beacon on the hill for New Years Eve! An, yes, the bells will ring. I just hope the weather will be kind this year. Last Christmas we had no stop torrential rain on Christmas Eve. In Kimmeridge Church there was a stream running through the church and one had to navigate a waterfall to exit. On returning to Corfe in the mid evening the village was cut off by a rising river. With the midnight communion to take what is the Rector to do? Rolling up my trousers but keeping my shoes firmly on, I waded through a brown and swirling river to re-emerge in Corfe Square .....the church year must go on!

It is like a wheel that keeps turning. Advent, Christmas, Epiphany, Lent, Holy Week, Easter, Pentecost, Trinity ..... that's when I pause for a while, as if one has climbed a great mountain. It is the day on which I like to read that passage from the Book of Revelation, *"Now when the Lamb broke the seventh seal, there was a silence in heaven for half an hour"* .... If you like, a dramatic pause in mid summer before one prepares for Harvest, Remembrance and Advent again.

Without question, I would say the seasons of the church year are a real joy and should be rediscovered by society in the quest for greater understanding of our place and purpose in creation.

Today's weather:

Name	Maurice Strike	Year of birth	1944
House	The Rectory	Street	East Street

Today the Wytch Farm oilfield produced 60,258 barrels of oil. That equates to some 195 pints of oil per second for every second of the day. The oil is produced by nearly 100 wells from three different layers of rock which lie at depths of up to a mile beneath Poole harbour. Unfortunately, because the rocks are wet, we bring three barrels of water to the surface for every barrel of oil. All of this water, plus a volume of seawater equal to that of the oil, is pumped back down into the reservoirs to maintain their pressure The oil is taken by pipeline to a terminal at Hamble on the Solent. The nine million cubic feet of gas also produced was put mainly into the gas transmission system, some of which was no doubt used by residents of Corfe Castle today.

In order to lift oil to the surface we use electrical pumps at the bottom of most wells. All these pumps make Wytch Farm the biggest user of electricity in southern England after Heathrow airport. The pumps generally last for only a couple of years before they fail and need replacing. Today the main drilling rig, called the T65, was in the process of replacing the pump in well F21 – the 21st oil well drilled from F-site on the Goathorn Peninsula. Also on F-site, well F11 which has recently been re-drilled, has just started producing oil again at a rate of nearly 4000 barrels of oil per day.

On A-site (between Wytch and Shotover Moors) work was proceeding to prepare the way for the T65 to move there That may soon confuse unwary mariners who are used to navigating by the sight of the rig on Goathorn (the rig was added to admiralty charts in 1999 after having been on the same site for nearly 6 years).

Today most of the managers and supervisors from the plant attended a workshop at the Springfield Hotel on improving communication. The workshop continues tomorrow and then we'll see if they can put all those words into practice.

Finally one of the chaps, Phil Greenwood, was recently inspired to put pen to paper to help BP to raise money for Save the Children. This is one of the thirty or so limericks that he wrote about people on the site. (He has been given the task of installing a new gym on the site.)

> Some say that gentleman Phil,
> Is over the top of the hill,
> Perhaps the gym,
> Will reinvigorate him,
> I do hope that it will

Gavin Ward on behalf of the Wytch Farm oilfield   Discovered in 1974

Gathering Station, Thrasher's Lane

Instead of asking someone in the village to write about their day, it seemed it might be appropriate to describe Kingston in 2000.

Kingston started as an estate village. Everyone who lived here worked for the Encombe Estate and lived in an estate house as a tenant. However, things have changed. There are only about five people who work for the estate. There is no longer a village hall, school, football team or field, post office or shop. Two of our three churches are now private houses

The nucleus of the village at the top of the hill has 44 houses, roughly 55% belong to the estate and 44% are freehold. Of the latter, 57% are permanently occupied and 42% are holiday homes. In the main village there are only about 12 children who are of school age or below.

Kingston was previously closely tied to Corfe. Our Norman Chapel was looked after by the curate of Corfe. It was easier to go to Corfe than Swanage. When the railway came, Kingstonians went to Corfe to catch the train to Swanage. They went to Corfe to shop and to see the doctor. However, gradually Kingston moved away from Corfe. We are indeed in the civil Parish of Corfe and are grateful for what they and our councillor, Peter Bell, do for us – lighting and grass-cutting are the most recent problems they have solved and we benefit from the Corfe Castle Charities. But we are in the benefice of Kingston and Worth Matravers. Swanage has superseded Corfe for shopping and now we have cars, the top road is the quickest way there. We may seem not to be very involved with Corfe but spiritual and material matters pull us in different directions these days.

Today's weather: Overcast, wet and windy

Name	George Pitman	Year of birth	1935
House	The Old Post Office	Street	16 West Street, Kingston

THE NATIONAL TRUST

Today, despite being a grey, miserable day with steady heavy rain, several valiant visitors fought their way up to the top of Corfe Castle, no doubt determined, once here, to experience to the full the most important medieval monument in Dorset and one of the greatest Castles in England.

This much loved site was given into the care of the National Trust in 1981 on the death of Mr H J R Bankes, whose family had owned the Kingston Lacy and Corfe Castle Estates since the seventeenth century.

Although the ruinous state of Corfe Castle today is due to the Parliamentary engineers who were ordered to destroy it in 1646, erosion continues to attack the remaining blocks of stone, requiring constant monitoring and attention from specialist conservators.

The Castle is open to the public 363 days a year and receives around 170,000 visitors each year. A delicate balancing act has to be performed between the needs of visitors and their desire to understand the site, and the prevention of damage to the fabric of the property by wear and tear.

Led by Property Manager, Doug Whyte, the team of property staff today includes an Education Co-ordinator and Education Assistant who look after some 20,000 school visitors per year; the Retail Manager and staff who run the shop; Tearoom Manager and staff; Warden; and Visitor Services Co-ordinator responsible for visitor reception and recruitment. Seasonal posts include Membership recruiters and visitor reception staff.

This year, several exciting events have taken place in the Castle, including the Millennium Committee's glamorous Ball on 1st July, and the very livelyMillennium Disco on the previous evening.

The first open air theatre production in many years was performed on 6 August in the Castle grounds. Illyria's production of 'The Importance of Being Earnest' was a great success and they will be coming again next summer with two new productions.

The Castle grounds were a launch site and dramatic backdrop for the spectacular firework display in November, which was amazing, if perhaps, a little unsettling for some of the ghosts from the Castle's eventful past 1000 years.

Today's weather: *Wet and dull.*

Name *Rachel Rodman*   Year of birth

House *Secretary to the Property Manager* Street
Corfe Castle National Trust

Yet another wet Thursday which would mean yet another missed golfing morning! At 7.30am I begin tea consumption and deliver the first of the day to my wife, Amy, in her bed. It is pill time next, we both have medication to take. I have high blood pressure and angina both of which were discovered during an overhaul two months ago. Two years ago I had a tumour removed from my bowel but recently I received confirmation from the ultrasound scan that there is no recurrence, my next check will be 2003 - very good news.

This morning I had cereal for breakfast. On alternate days I have toast and marmalade, this is accompanied by more tea, up to four cups - which is enough to last the day, well almost! Phone calls to mates confirmed no golf today. Normally, we would tee - off at about 9ish or later, if convenient, and play in a four, tossing for partners. We are evenly matched and usually play eighteen holes round the Purbeck Golf Course. I have been a member for 50 years and play off a 20 handicap, my best being 14. After a brush up we have a coffee in the clubhouse, chat over the game and others often join us for a yarn.

No such luck today, instead I battled my way along the pavement in torrential rain to the doctor's surgery to have my regular check up. Amy is laid up at the moment with a swollen knee so I have a few extra chores to do. Wednesdays is our usual 'shop' day but we didn't go yesterday which meant with no golf, I was chief 'shopper' today. Amy talked lists of items, while we had a coffee then off to Sainsbury's at Wallisdown. I sped in my 'F' registered Ford Escort, which I bought ten years ago. She has 130,000 miles on the clock and goes like a bird. The reason we travel so far is because past colleagues from Merck Chemicals Ltd, of Poole, shop at the same time, around 12ish. This means we meet up and chat. I had been the assistant packaging manager and spent 40 years working for the company until 1990 when I retired. Previous jobs had been as a butcher with Ted Moss in West Street, a dispatch rider in the Fire Service and forestry work on Rempstone Estate. I look forward to seeing my pals to share old times and exchange news.

We generally spend up to £70 at the supermarket but still rely daily on the local shops for additional supplies. My timing was good at the petrol station, they had just decided to lower the price of unleaded from 81.9p to 79.9p per litre which slightly reduced my weekly fuel bill of £18. There would be no time to visit our daughter - in - law in Merley, as we usually do. I had to wait while they closed the pumps to alter the info on the computers which delayed my return and meant we had lunch around 3ish. Amy knows I will be late if I am out on my own but it was salad, so no harm done.

What was left of the afternoon was spent resting. Amy and I watch quiz shows on the TV together with the last cuppa of the day and a piece of cake. Amy is an avid crossword doer and spends many hours solving clues. She is a homemaker and looks after me well. I really knew she was the one for me when I met her at a sixpenny 'hop' in 1949 at Kingston where she lived. We married in the church there on February 3rd 1951 - I really must spoil her on our 50th anniversary next year. We spent our honeymoon in Bristol and have lived here at No 28 ever since. Apart from living in the cottage at the entrance to Webbers Close where I was born, I have only lived here, that is from the age of eleven. It was known as a Church Terrace then. Les Stockley the local coal merchant, used his lorry to move us. My father made wine and during the move I remember the men drank two barrels full. It is funny how when you are older you think back to the days when you were a boy and what clear memories they are too. I recall that at Corfe School I was caned more than once and how, in the holidays, I would join my father on the horse and cart to deliver bread to Bushey and Rempstone. My happiest recollection though was of making tents on the Common. I would smuggle out my father's saw to cut small river bank trees to use as poles. My mates and I would spend weekends and holidays camping out and imagine we were soldiers. This became a reality when in 1943 I was called - up. I was attached to the Fleet Air Arm in Northern Ireland based at the end of the runway of Eglinton Aerodrome. I saw many of the fighter planes come back damaged and some, of course, did not return.

Early this evening, relations visited and we found ourselves, as one often does, chatting about the past. Before we knew it the clock said 9.30pm and it was time to tread the stairs.

Today's weather: _Continuous rain_

Name _Ivan Orchard_   Year of birth _18 - 5 - 25_

House _28 East Street_   Street

Friday December 8th

I am sitting in my little cave like shop recalling my first Christmas preparation here eight years ago ..... it seems only a little while ago. So today I am going to change my window display and put I some of my seasonal items, such as my Steiff Winter Bear, which is on its own wooden sled, a Santa's elf bear, and of course the special Steiff reindeer-drawn Santa on a sleigh, not forgetting Muffy Vanderbear and her Family and Friends dressed in their finery for the Vanderbear Ball.

I want to make it as special as possible to link in with the village lights which are being put around the Square and along all the approach road.

Having caught up with some of my friends who have dropped in for a chat I went across to the Bankes Arms Hotel for lunch, as I always find putting in a new window display exhausting as it involves turning the shop totally around. It's very difficult to choose from so many, all of which demand my attention, but at this seasonal time I must give pride of place to my Steiff musical carousel, a beautiful piece.

This afternoon I must spend some time packing and posting Bears from the "Happy Cupboard" which have been laid away. The layaway service has been a great success this year, having to pay only a small deposit to secure the bear of your dreams has made special purchases possible for so many happy customers.

Just time now to sort out some enquiries regarding my web site and to prepare some material for an article on my shop in the February issue of the Dorset magazine. Then time to close the door and head for home after giving the Bears their bread and honey and tucking them up for the night!!! Sleep tight.

Today's weather: Heavy showers, some icy

Name   Heather Ghillyer   Year of birth   1944

House   Memory Lane   Street East. 18A .

Today I have been invited to go beating at Ashley Barnes Farm at Afflington Farm. I have never been before and was looking forward to it.

Mum dropped me off in the car and was met by Ashley's Mum.

We waited for the guns to get there. We drove to a field and beat the wood through all in a long line. Not many pheasants were shot on the first drive.

We had lunch in a barn with other beaters. I was starving!

After lunch we went to the big wood, followed by duck shooting on the duck pond.

In total we shot 70 ducks and pheasants, 4 pigeons and 2 partridge.

A cock pheasant

One of the guns dropped me home – I was filthy dirty and hungry.

After a bath and dinner I fell into my bed. Tired out.

Today's weather: Cloudy, bright, breezy

Name	Ben Jarvis	Year of birth	1989
House	37	Street	East Street

Sunday December 10th

What I thought was going to be another boring old Sunday, wasn't to bad. Usually I either work, in the fox inn just accross the road. Doing preperation work in the kitchen, its not to bad, I only do it for the money, £3.00 an hour, Spose its ok, I don't really espect much more at my age. Any way I didn't work that afternoon. Last night, which was the Saturday, 9th, I went to Swanage and slept round my freinds house Fiona. Paula my best freind was meant to come, but she couldn't come for some reason. Me and fi allready had tickets to watch this show in the mowlem, we were there to watch Tiffany, another mate, also there were other people I knew that were there.

It was really good actually, the ballet at the beggining was bit boring, but once we got past all that and got into the Jazz stuff, I really enjoyed it. There were a few freaks there, but that didn't put me off. Also I watched out for all those people that were out of time, and making fools of themselves. I had no idea Tiff was so good.

Well paula still hadn't showed up so me and fi went back to her house. There was nothing much on TV, apart from this documentry about Madona, that got boring after a while, we just went to bed and talked for hours, just about normal stuff. fi's dad took me home, I went to dads house, Me and olly went out on our bikes for abit, he showed me a few tricks, im not that good, but ill learn. Also Ben my brother was there. I hate him.

Today's weather: Wet start, followed by bright sunshine + strong winds.

Name Harriet Jarvis

Year of birth 9 2 86

House 37

Street East

This day dawned (for us) in Brittany, where we have a small cottage. We got out of bed very early this morning to catch the ferry from Roscoff to Plymouth, with the intention of being in Corfe in time to join in with the rest of the Festivities Committee for the 2nd Monday of our Annual carol singing around the village. As this was obviously our last visit to 'Ty-Kerneis' (our cottage in Finistere) until the Spring we had to make sure everything was locked up and the water & electricity turned off, also that the fire was not still burning. We drove to the ferry through torrential rain, but fortunately gave ourselves sufficient time. Although in Brittany the roads are very good, in that part (just South of Roscoff is a vegetable growing area) one can frequently encounter tractors. Our one task we always give ourselves before boarding the ferry, is to top the car up with diesel – it is much cheaper than in England (e.g. approx. 53p per litre in France, whereas here we are paying 85p).

The ferry journey was uneventful (6 hours), we had breakfast of croissant and coffee, couple of hours snooze and before we knew where we were it was nearly time to dock. As in Brittany, there was torrential rain for our drive back to Corfe. We arrived home at about 2pm all set to light the fire and switch on the Central heating and unpack the car. We opened the door and were greeted by a very nasty musty smell (a bit like overcooked cabbage!). On closer inspection we discovered that the whole of our living and dining room carpet was sodden. Having checked that this was not caused by burst pipe, overflowing cistern, faulty valve etc, there was only one thing to do – telephone the insurance company. We certainly had good service from them – an assessor arrived at 4.30pm, condemned the carpet and stayed to help us cut it up to make it easier to put in the garden. We have since discovered that, due to the extremely heavy rainfall which we experienced from October onwards, the water table (normally only 4/5 feet below the surface) was much higher: as our house is about 9 inches below the level of the pavement the water just crept up through the concrete floor. Needless to say, all thoughts of going out carol singing were gone! We spent the evening mopping up!

Note for later when it has all dried up: - in case we ever get this prolonged wet weather ever again, we think that it would be wise to have the level of the floor raised – don't want this to happen again!!

Moved here October 1994 from Burwash, East Sussex

Today's weather: WET & DARK.

Name   Chris & Lynn Evans   Year of birth   Born 1936 and 1939

House   114 East Street   Street

Tuesday December 12th

Today my long awaited aga is arriving; the space in the inglenook will be filled and our kitchen will be warm and cosy. A day for celebration. Little Woolgarston Cottage is our new home and this afternoon our daughters Bonnie and Kate are coming home for our first family Christmas here.

I am frantically busy unpacking boxes still piled high from our recent move, trying to find the girls' belongings so as to make their bedrooms familiar. Next is shopping and later, when the aga is lit, cooking. Ed, our youngest, and still living at home, is planting our Christmas trees in pots, one for the cottage and one for the barn. He is hoping to have the decorations up by tonight.

After supper we gather round our piano for a "singsong". My husband, Steve, and children are all musicians and we enjoy singing and playing together. We are so happy to learn that musicians Norman Knottley and David Brindley lived here, and built the barn as a music room in the 1930s. I wonder what they would think at the songs we are singing tonight from musicals such as Les Miserables, Cats, Miss Saigon?

Before bed we stand in the garden, admiring the amazingly clear sky, no light pollution here! Family home, aga burning, please God let us enjoy many happy years in lovely Little Woolgarston.

Today's weather: DARK ALL DAY!

Name   Caroline Royal   Year of birth

House   Little Woolgarston Cottage   Street

The Chamber of Trade and Commerce was founded in 1997 by a group of local business people, their aim to watch over and promote the interests and trade of the village of Corfe Castle and to maintain the integrity, ecology and reputation of the village.

This is one of those frantic days when the telephone never stops ringing and you realise that you have a deadline to meet – on this occasion an article on the village of Corfe Castle for the Dorset magazine February issue, and everything to be in by the 15th December and you need to get together with other members of the Executive Committee to finalise the details.

This article is to promote the village with input from over twenty businesses. This involves us in collecting material from our members and also ensuring that all historical data is accurate.

One of the events supported this year by us was "It's a Knockout", which was organised by the Millennium Committee, where we donated medals and trophies. This was a marvellous event and we were delighted to help support it.

Our web site is now completed and available for viewing and I have just received this mornign notification that our leaflets on the village will be available for distribution in the early part of next year.

A very busy but successful day culminating in a wonderful feature in the Dorset magazine with full representation from all.

Today's weather: Wet and dark

Name   Heather Ghillyer   Year of birth   1944

House   Chairman, Corfe Castle Chamber of Trade & Commerce   Street

Today saw the Annual General Meeting of the Millennium Association. It was a time to reflect on the year and consider whether good value had been provided. We believe the answer to that question is a resounding "Yes", and from the favourable comments received, this would seem to be a view shared by much of the community.

The following is a review of our activities over the past twelve months.

ARTS – In July, Angelika Seik organised a Stone Carving Symposium which was held in the church grounds and purposely timed to coincide with the annual Flower Festival. The two events complemented each other and were a great success. Local stone carvers displayed their skills and produced work of exceptional quality.

Double Act undertook their Medieval Midsummer Murder Mystery Walks in July and August. These were much enjoyed by those who attended. In November, the group staged '1066 And All That' in the Village Hall. An excellent, amusing reflection of our history. The group clearly goes from strength to strength and we wish them success for the future.

RELIGIOUS – The interdenominational services have, so far, been well supported and brought the various faiths together in common worship. The community play, 'Thy Kingdom Come', was held in April. The play, although hailed a theatrical and technical success, did not attract the audience numbers hoped for. Nonetheless, congratulations to Rev. Maurice Strike, the players and those who assisted back stage. All concerned worked so hard to produce the play which focused on two thousand years of Christianity.

ENTERTAINMENT – Despite threatening to do otherwise, the weather was kind to us for all our events. The Midsummer Weekend was a huge success with the Dance/Disco, Ball, Interdenominational Service and Children's Party well attended and thoroughly enjoyed. Everyone played their part and should be congratulated. The villagers should be recognised for coming together and generating the community spirit we so much hoped to achieve.

The Millennium 'It's a Knockout' in September was another event which saw the villagers combining to have fun together. The event raised in the region of £500.

November 4th saw the conclusion of the entertainment programme with a firework display with the castle ruins making a superb backdrop for some spectacular rockets and other pyrotechnic special effects. Some three hundred to four hundred people turned out to watch the show and the supporting act of Felix the Fire Juggler.

CAPITAL PROJECT – Having reached a satisfactory compromise with the Architectural Panel of the National Trust, the plan for the pavilion has been approved by the Planning Committee of Purbeck District Council. We are now in discussion with the Parish Council concerning the future development of the project, and the management of the Sports Field in general. The setting-up of a charitable trust is being explored.

TREE PLANTING – A yew tree was planted in the old cemetery on Remembrance Sunday by our Chairman assisted by 2nd Lieutenant Lisa Potts of the Royal Engineers. Some fifty or so people who had attended the laying of wreaths at the War Memorial, remained for the ceremony. The school planting was beset with difficulties. It was necessary to postpone the event twice due to bad weather. Rain came again on the third occasion, so members gathered in the School Hall to formally present the trees which will be planted later.

All 366 dates for the **MILLENNIUM DIARY** have been adopted. A truly monumental feat. Priority will now be given to publication. Roger White has offered to piece together the camera work of Jill Foley and produce our **VIDEO**, plans for which are well in hand.

We presented **COMMEMORATIVE MUGS** to all children up to the age of thirteen years living within the parish. Many were distributed by Michael Bond, this year's High Sheriff of Dorset, at the Midsummer Children's Party.

All the hard work of fund raising during the early years allowed us to sponsor much of the above activities from our own resources. However, our Treasurer was still able to report that £8,170 remained in our accounts, much of which will help towards financing the Sports Field Project, a lasting legacy for the future.

It was agreed that the success of the year was the result of excellent team work. An example of people working with and for each other for the benefit of all. Congratulations!

Today's weather: Lovely, sunny, dry day – at last!

Name Jim Rosewarn   Year of birth 1945

House April Cottage   Street West Street

My day started at 7.30 a.m. by preparing to drive to Swanage where South Dorset Coaches, owned by the Sheasby family is based and for whom I have worked for the past forty-five years. The business was started in Corfe Castle circa 1904 by the grandfather of the present owner who came to Dorset from Leicestershire. At that time horses and carts were used to transport corn, wheat and coal then cleaned out to carry passengers. Later, taxis, coaches and one lorry were available. During the war years troops were moved all over the country by coach. In time, foreign travel was also undertaken and places like France, Germany, Holland, Belgium and Austria for skiing were visited. In time there were as many as eight coaches and petrol pumps were installed on the premises to supply the coaches and private cars belonging to the general public.

The garage was opposite the old cemetery in East Street but has since been demolished. The new buildings, known as Uvedale, have been built by the Corfe Castle Charities to provide housing for older people of the village.

When I first began as a driver, one of my jobs meant an early start, 5.30 a.m. I had to collect sixty-nine milk churns from the Milk Factory near the railway station and deliver them to the United Dairies Depot in Bournemouth. Another regular run, which I did for many years, was transporting school children from Langton Matravers, Kingston and Worth Matravers to Wareham Upper and Middle Schools. During the afternoon, I made the return journey. Today, I also transported school children, this time to Dorchester and Maiden Castle to visit the museum and earthworks which were built to defend the people of the town many years ago.

The highlight of today has been to have our family, son Martin, grandson James, daughter Julie and son-in-law Aidan, join us at home for a meal. My wife, Pamela, has spent all her life in the village and since our marriage in the local church in 1956, I have been able to appreciate the village and be happy in Corfe Castle.

Today's weather: Some sun, cool and seasonable.

Name _Stan Smith_   Year of birth   1930

House _Pathways. 2. Tilbury Mead._ Street _East Street._

Saturday December 16th

Today is party day for Corfe Castle children aged 4 – 11 years. This annual event, organised and given by the Corfe Castle Christmas Festivities Committee (CCCF) is a village highlight. In the festooned Village Hall (annually decorated by the CCCF) the Christmas Tree lights glow on this dark afternoon. Bundles of balloons have been blown up and delicious party food laid out in the kitchen. It's a magic day but certainly all this does not happen by magic but by the dedicated hard work by the ladies of the Committee from earlier in the day and much pre-planning.

 And we're ready to open the doors ….

 The Village Hall is filled with the sound of music and about 58 excited children. Team games and musical activities are interrupted at ….

Tea time! The piles of pizza slices, crisps, sausages, hula-hoops, biscuits and fruit squash soon disappear. There was silence for a <u>short</u> time!!! The children then carried their chairs to form an audience to meet "Bobby The Clown" with his magic tricks and puppet pals. With much audience participation a great deal of laughter and serious shouting …..

and the party ended on a high note. Mums and Dads met their excited and tired little children each clutching a Christmas present from the Committee and a balloon on a string.

The lady helpers string along to tidy the Hall.

All agreed, a long but happy day. More fun next Saturday when Father Christmas arrives in Corfe Castle !

Today's weather: Dry and cold

Name   Compiled by Jane Windsor   Year of birth

House   Corfe Castle Christmas Festivities
                       Committee Member   Street

Saturday December 16th

Party dress for sisters Laura & Hayley Aylward

Crowning Glory for
Becky (Rebecca) Varney

Team games organised by Betty Carter &
Jane Windsor

Every picture tells a story!

Bobby the Clown and his young
assistants

One job that had to be done this morning was to remove the ashes from and lay up our coal fire which we have alight most nights during the winter months. The heat from this type of fire is so comforting on dark, dreary evenings - it gives a glow and such warmth that the central heating is not needed. Normally I would have done other jobs around the house but this morning I had to go shopping. Whereas this would usually be done on a weekday, for various reasons I was unable to make the journey to Tesco, a supermarket, near Poole. For convenience all our foodstuffs, baking, vegetables and fishmongery needs are obtainable from one premise, unlike in the past, when I would have had to buy these items from four separate shops.

Approximately one hundred years ago, my family, surname Woadden, started a grocery shop in a former bakery in West Street in the corner house of Cemetery Lane. My Great Grandfather, Great Grandmother and Great Aunt set up the business. In time they passed it on to my grandparents and finally my father and mother continued trading until 1956. Shopping at Woadden's was vastly different from the self service style of today. No helping yourself to cartons, tins, packets etc and placing them in your mobile trolley, customers would stand at the counter and ask for all their requirements. Village life meant everyone knew everyone and shopkeepers and customers would exchange news and local gossip.

At night the shop was restocked by filling shelves and weighing up various foods. Biscuits were weighed up from four pound tins and sultanas, currants and raisins were kept in large drawers under the counter. During the years of the Second World War there was rationing which meant each customer was allowed a two ounce portion of butter and sugar etc. Sides of bacon were boned and sliced by hand, these and other items were placed in a separate storeroom because there were no refrigerators or freezers. An example of the amount of money taken during one month from all the customers in 1932 was on average £62. Today we, as a couple, on average would probably spend at least £350 per month.

The highlight of my day was to entertain my family. I have one son, Martin, who is thirty-nine years old and is employed by Folgate Insurance in Poole as a computer programmer/analyst. He has one son, James, who is eight years old and attends Uplands School Parkstone. They live in Swanage. My daughter, Julie, is thirty-four years old and is the Chief Cardiac Technician in the Cardio Respiratory Department at Poole General Hospital. Her husband, Aidan, has a dental laboratory in Wareham and they live in Upton, near Poole.

For the last forty-five years that my husband, Stan, and I have been married, our lives have revolved around our family and it gives us great pleasure to spend time with them. We count ourselves very fortunate to be living here in Corfe Castle. There can be no better place!

Today's weather: Frosty start. Cloud with glimpses of sunshine.

Name   Pamela Smith   Year of birth 21-04-1932.

House 'Pathways' 2 Tilbury Mead   Street East Street.

Monday 18th December 2000

I awoke at 7 am and looked out of the window - oh dear - a grey day again - after such a lovely frosty one yesterday, it was so cheerful to see the sun. It's raining, I've never known an autumn so wet. I have lived in Corfe since just before I retired (I was a jeweller and antiques dealer for seventeen years, and before that a Yacht builder - I lived in Canford Cliffs and used to look over to Corfe Castle and tell my family ' that is where I was going to retire to' , I could look out of my window and across Poole Harbour and I could see Corfe Castle and the Purbeck Hills).I have three grown up children, Paul the oldest lives in Florida ,Jaqueline my daughter lives in Bournemouth - she has recently opened a shop in Westbourne & I get in most weeks to help, which is great fun. My youngest son Richard works in Kuwait, he has been out there for more than three years, but is home for Christmas as his wife Kate is expecting their second child on Christmas Day. She has been staying with me but they have just moved into their new home at Bankgate, Arne so they are very excited and this is where I shall spend Christmas Day - I LOVE LIVING HERE IN Corfe, I bought The Old Curatage in East Street (over three hundred years old) it was a marvellous house with a huge inglenook fireplace in the breakfast room, spacious panelled hall study and large sitting room and five bedrooms up a galleried staircase. I finally decided it was too large and reluctantly moved to a smaller house only built in 1931, but just off the main road (East Street) and which I find so very much quieter, especially in summer when there are so many visitors and cars about. The Chevin is a lovely little three bedroom cottagey type house with a small garden overlooking my neighbours much larger one. We seem to have about the only large trees in Corfe, and I can see three fine Horse Chestnuts, several Silver birch and six lovely Beech trees, one of which is a Copper beech. In the corner of my garden by the gate I have a huge old Oak tree. Needless to say there is a lively family of squirrels and lots of bird life around me, so I am constantly busy filling bird feeders and watching their fun. Until Friday when we had a hard frost I still had flowers blooming in the garden in fact they still look alright today Fuchsias some penstimmons and quite a few pink Kaffir lillies.

Now my fist job this morning after breakfast of cereals, coffee and toast is to go down and check out the horses. I share some fields and stables in West Street, where at present we have two mares Shadow and Charlie and two pony mares Rio and Sherry on loan from a trekking centre in Wales - they come down to me for a rest each winter. Also my grand-daughters fat little Shetland pony Flora. She is a cheeky little soul, very friendly and in winter loves to be out in the fields with the 'big' horses. Unfortunately in summer she has to be kept off most of the lush grass as she gets very fat and it is not good for her. She has a wonderfully warm coat and although she is a 'grey' she looks much more like a grubby, muddy fur ball this time of year. She hasn't been ridden for a few weeks, but now my grand-daughter Lottie, has broken up for the school holidays I am sure they will get some more outings together- they are a familiar sight walking round West Street and the Car Park (they enjoy jumping over the flat poles there (only about 6 inches high!)

Well it is lunch time and thank goodness the rain has stopped Lottie and I have . been up to Norden Farm to select a nice 4ft tree so we have come home excitedly with the Christmas TREE. Luckily it is quite dry and we are putting it in a large flower pot outside, before my son helps me to carry it into the place of honour in the sitting room.. We also bought a nice little holly wreath and after a snack lunch we will fix it to the front door.

Now we must get the large box out from under the stairs, where I have always kept all the Christmas decorations and lights . This always causes fun as some of the items have been saved since my children were very little and there will be lots of fun unpacking the box and deciding what we shall use now I have a much smaller tree than when I lived at the Curatage, we sorted the tinsels, beads and all the hanging silver and gold balls, and selected the best ones to put on the tree.(the old fairy doll goes on first) The lights went on, my son then threaded some outdoor lights round the bay window outside whilst we finished the tree. By the time this was all done it was time for a cup of tea, and we could turn the lights on and inspect our work. It all looked very pretty and festive. The room was also decorated with some fifty Christmas Cards I had received from old friends. We then decided to have a walk down to the Square and inspect the beautiful lights and decorations there. My little grandaughter had spent the previous Christmas's in a Moslem country, so she was thrilled and delighted to see all the little trees and lights and we had to go round and inspect all the beautiful decorations and the huge tree and the crib The church was also illuminated, Corfe Castle itself stood above us standing out against the sky. We walked back up to the house to enjoy the warmth inside the front door and sat down to a lovely warm supper. We felt we were all now ready to welcome Father Christmas here in Corfe Castle.

Today's weather:
Rain but clearing by mid-day - dull cloud

Name June Mary Anstey   Year of birth 1927

House THE CHEVIN   Street CALCRAFT ROAD,

An early start to the day as usual, about 8.30. Quite a miserable start to the day rather overcast and showery, but not too cold. After a cup of tea I take my chocolate labrador, Joe for a walk, not far these days, at nearly 14 he finds life rather a struggle so we don't over do things.

I wake my two children Harriet and Ben at about 7.15am to get prepared for school, they have a few more days left until they break for the christmas holidays so it's all rather an effort to enthusiastic about school with christmas just around the corner. After the children have left for school I decide what to do with my day off from work. I decide to go for one of my regular runs, but must first wait until the school bus is well on its way, apparently it is too embarrising to have a mum who runs in public. I start my run from East Street down to Castle View along the new path (which is now quite old) crossing the Church Knowle road and up Ollie Vyes Lane then along West Street to the common. Now the best bit through the common to Blashenwell, say hello to the ducks on the pond then head back but this time cutting across the top of the common to the Kingston Road, then along East Street and home. The rest of the day is spent catching up on housework and last minute christmas bits.

The children arrive home at about 3.30pm dumping school bags an annoueing that they are starving. The are both excited about christmas even Harriet who is nearly 15 is beginning to show signs. The christmas lights come on at about 4.00PM, they are better than ever this year, what a grand job our christmas festivities committee do.

After tea I make the effort to go to a Yoga class at the Springfield country Club rather an effort on a winters night, but worth it afterwards as I feel much better for a long stretch. Sleep comes easy after a long day.

Today's weather: Overcast with showers.

Name Sarah Jarvis

Year of birth 16.12.00

House 37

Street East Street

Wednesday 20th December,2000

Peter has an early meeting in Wareham, so I am allowed to get our animals up.
It is a DRY,mild,cloudy day, and the birds sound fresh and relieved the storms
are over   It is very wet underfoot, which is good for Poppy`s paw, the soft
ground is gentle on her injury.   The animals up, Peter returns with the great
news that Faith House,the new building has been passed by the Purbeck District
Planners.   This means that the next stage in the development of Holton Lee,
centre for people with disability to have wonderful holidays beside Poole
Harbour, can continue
Over coffee we open Christmas cards from friends, introduction to new members
of families, plans for the future ; my favourite cards are hand made
Plans for the day include making chocolate cakes and chocolate truffles as
Christmas presents   But we take a few moments off to walk the dogs from
Swyre Head Car Park up to Heaven`s Gate, looking at the Golden bowl, full of
sheep with new lambs
Home to a quick lunch, jacket potato, boursin cheese and salad, and then give
coffee to the builders who are converting an outhouse, to an annex.   Building
beautiful stonewalls, and taking such care to enhance the buildings.   Someone
knocks on the door.   The postman delivers the most exciting parcel from
Andrew`s friends, a huge Jasmine to go into the new conservatory.   Amazing
what can be delivered by post   Most of our Christmas shopping has been done
on the internet, through Amazon.
I have two lessons with children at the kitchen table.(I give individual help to
children, who are struggling with large classes of 35)   One goes very well and
progress is possible   One is tricky, as the child, finds it difficult to accept his
difficulties.
Quick change and off to a Christmas Party in Wareham   Met old friends and new
and have a class of wine and brilliant eats.   Wareham is looking very colourful
but Corfe Castle lights really are something else.   I am so looking forward to
celebrating New Year in the Square this year.
Home to supper of a Delia Smith special and to watch Jamie Oliver in Manhattan

Today's weather Dry, mild cloudy day.

Name BELINDA BELL   Year of birth 1945.

House Scoles Manor   Street Kingston.

Thursday December 21st

9.00 a.m. ..... the 'phone rings … Good morning, Corfe Castle (01929, 48038) Oh, Hello Sybil. I should say "Good Evening", it's 8 p.m. there in Melbourne isn't it? It's my eldest sister calling from Australia where she and her husband, Brian, both from Yorkshire, have lived since 1956. Sybil goes on to say ….

"… I was just thinking, it is 31 years ago today that we were in The Old Forge getting ready for Gary's 12th birthday the next day (22nd). That really was a great year, 1969/70, Brian's sabbatical year, when we all lived in Corfe Castle with you Eileen, and Mummy." (the late Elizabeth Crone). Having spent their Christmas' in Australia's hot summer with beach barbies for Christmas dinner, I remember how the children were all wishing for snow. *"You had the Christmas tree in "The Saddle.", the builders had almost completed the transformation of the stable in your garden into an attractive holiday house. The boys were all on school holiday, Gary from Swanage Grammar School and Tony and Mark from Corfe Castle School. Lisa was too young for school. They loved to go to the Corfe River by the Castle. Did you get my recent letter with the bit Brian wrote about that?"*

Extract from Brian's letter:
"I remember Corfe River as a stream that flowed and gurgled its way around the base of the Castle. Floating in the stream were twigs launched by our four children. For them, however, the "Stream" was the Amazon River in the depth of winter and the twigs were fearless boats racing with their precious cargoes to the finishing point about a mile down river. Hooting and shrieking instructions, the children encouraged their craft over blockages, down rapids and past lurking pirates. The winning skipper was rewarded with a treasure trove of lollipops from E. O. Holland's shop in the Square." (now the National Trust Shop)

"The cost of these calls is so reasonable nowadays! It's good to chat – can't beat it and neither of us has e-mail anyway. Please give my love to those who may remember us: Margaret Cooper, Mr & Mrs. Hopkins, the Percy family at the farm, Nigel was Mark's best friend. Thanks for your Christmas card with the picture of Corfe Castle Christmas lights, I'm going to frame it. Oh, and good luck with the Diary 2000 project.

Today's weather   In Melbourne very hot …. in Corfe Castle: dry, mild and dark

Name	Sybil and Brian Nettleton Gary, Tony, Mark, Lisa	Year of birth	1931 1929 1957 '61 '64 '67
House	Memories of: The Old Forge	Street	38 East Street

ORIGAMI

Origami is my hobby. Origami means paper folding, It is a traditional Japanese craft.

For origami you need thin paper or origami paper. I have many different sorts of origami paper in different sizes.

You can make all sorts of things with origami, from animals and birds to ornaments and models or you can make up your own design.

I once made an animal that looked like a cross between a dog and a rabbit!

This summer we went to Japan and mum bought me a new origami book with good pictures, (I can't read the writing because it's in Japanese)

I prefer Japanese origami books to English ones because the pictures and diagrams are easier to understand.

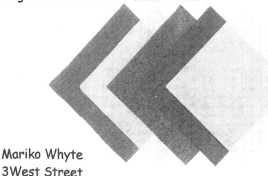

Mariko Whyte
3West Street

Year of birth 1990

Saturday December 23rd

Anne (Mum): It is a dry, clear night, the sky brightly starlit, a hint of woodsmoke in the air. The flag of St. George flutters gently from the church tower. The Square is filling with families awaiting the arrival of Father Christmas. Monica Williams and her two helpers do a roaring trade on their hot dog stall. Mr. White sets up his tripod; tonight is to be recorded on the Corfe Castle Millennium Year video - and it is also a chance to capture for posterity the Christmas lights erected by the Christmas Festivities Committee decorating the Square and much of East and West Streets. Rita Churchill has been heard on Radio Solent this morning, reacting to the news that Corfe Castle has won the national competition for the best Christmas lights of the year – Lyndhurst being second and Romsey third. They are indeed magnificent: miles of multi-coloured looms, Justin Cross's pictures-in-lights of candles, angels, sleighs, bells, and galloping reindeer, and about twenty small lit-up and decorated Christmas trees on the walls of buildings and the corners of streets. There is an enormous lit and decorated Norway Spruce towering above the War Memorial, with the Nativity at the its foot, reminding everyone what Christmas is really all about.

Chris Evans is visible in the Robing Room window dispensing Christmas music to the crowds below, and George Preston is weaving his way with a loud hailer between the traffic bollards holding back the crowd. Father Christmas has been sighted in Wareham. Ivan Orchard, one of the founder members of the Christmas Festivities Committee, the organisers of this event, is heard to say that this is the biggest crowd in 40 years, bigger even than Millennium New Year's Eve. Excited children warmly wrapped in bobble hats and bright jackets are restrained by parents, babies sleep in buggies and Jessica, aged 1, stares from her mother Emma's arms with enormous round, wondering eyes.

Alexander (aged 10): There's a rocket .... Whoo-oo-sh ... BANG! And another ... and three more. I can see golden stars and streamers and sparklers all over the sky.

That's the signal that Father Christmas is nearly here.

And here he comes now! Oh ... W – o – w ...!

'Course this is for the little children, I'm almost too old, this is my last year. Even so, it's brilliant. First it's the Fat Controller, then Thomas the Tank Engine, absolutely huge, it must be a tractor all dressed up or something, with Annie and Clarabel on behind. Father Christmas is sitting inside, I mean not the real one, everyone knows that's your parents, but ... well, anyway its not Ian at the Post Office 'cos this one's fatter ... anyway, there's Father Christmas with an absolutely giant sack, and a girl dressed up in a red mini-dress with fur on, and he gets out and everyone claps and cheers, and we all queue up, and some of the little children get squashed, and Alec and Joe and Michael and me get nearly to the front, and Father Christmas gives us our presents, and we go and sit by the church wall and open them – its sweets, and we all swap till we've got what we wanted – then we go and race around the war memorial shouting and bumping into people. Then we sit on the top step eating our sweets and watching. The castle is floodlit and looks like something out of Harry Potter – all ancient and misty and magic...and Jingle Bells is belting out from the back of Clarabel. "Jingle Bells, Batman smells ..." we sing but someone says shut up, and its such a lovely night that we do. ...

Anne (Mum): All too soon it is over. The hot-dog stall is being folded away. Father Christmas, his sack limp in his hand, climbs back into Annie and, escorted by Sir Topham Hat (alias Snitch Norman) marching in front with rolled umbrella firmly under his arm, Thomas the Tank Engine rolls away down West Street towards Blashenwell farm. As his lights fade into the distance, the strains of Jingle Bells hangs faintly on the cold night air.

Today's weather: Rather a dark day but dry.

Name Anne Bond
Alexander Bond

House Fizgeralds

Year of birth 1944
1990

Street West

Sunday December 24th

I awoke very early, 4.30 a.m., my birthday, Christmas Eve! Whatever age, always a feeling of special excitement and expectancy. I mused on the evening before – the arrival of Father Christmas in the Square, brilliant with our best Christmas lights ever (thanks to the Christmas Festivities Committee), carols, friends, celebration, standing nearby Ann Bond and one of her twin sons, Charlie – a birthday boy also – 21.

However early, I got up, lit the fire and positively enjoyed my small cottage bedecked in Christmas finery. Listening to BBC World Service, I knelt on the floor surrounded with paper and ribbon and wrapped up presents. A familiar voice, Nick Thorpe, BBC Eastern European Correspondent, son of a close friend, telling of the election defeat of ex-president Melosovitch in Serbia; the triumph of democracy over tyranny.

5.50 a.m. Radio 4 London awakened with the bells of St. Paul's. I opened a bottle of bubbly and had a Buck's Fizz with a mince pie and brandy butter. The telephone rang several times during the morning with birthday wishes and I busied myself preparing for a small gathering of friends at midday; William and Marion Ormorod, Chris and Lynn Evans, Eileen Van Lelyveld, Tess Robinson and Angela Reed came; a few could not. We happily imbibed bubbly and celebrated the joy of Christmas time. A slight sadness began to fill me as I was leaving my own nest, aglow with Christmas, to stay in Iwerne Courtney with my family for the next few days – but really I wouldn't have it otherwise and indeed was greeted by my two sons, Tim and Laurence and daughter-in-law, Lizzie, with much spoiling and celebration. Sadly my daughter, Melanie, was in Cumbria.

Delicious champagne, pheasant, excellent claret and a glorious pudding – what a birthday feast.

A chilly short walk to St. Mary's, a beautiful church and a wonderful, moving celebration of midnight service.

I remembered my dear ones and many friends in my prayers in particular Beth, wife of our organist, Ken Claxton at St. Edwards in Corfe Castle, assisting our Rector, Maurice Strike, at Communion. A very special occasion for her administering wine for the first time, and being Christmas, from our beautiful Elizabethan Chalice.

What a splendid day!   HAPPY CHRISTMAS

Today's weather   Overcast and chilly, Getting colder. Snow?

Name   Joy Kingsbury   Year of birth   1932

House   Wayfaring Cottage   Street   47 West Street

My First Ever Christmas   by Baby Luke

Hello my name is Luke and i am only ten weeks old.
Everything is new to me and i have just learnt to smile.
All i keep hearing about is a thing called Christmas and a week before a strange thing
happened.Mummy and Daddy started to hang up pretty bright things in our house
along with a big tree with colourful lights on it.
On the Saturday evening before Christmas Mummy dressed me up in my Teddy Bear
suit and took me to Corfe Square to see Father Christmas.Daddy was going to come as well
but had a nasty sickness bug which was going around the village.
Everyone down the Square was singing Carols and kept smiling at me and saying how sweet
i was.I was just busy listening to all the noises and stareing at the pretty lights.
I didnt get to see Father Christmas as just as he was coming i fell fast asleep in Mummies
arms.
Christmas Day i was woken up at six o'clock in the morning by Mummy and Daddy
opening presents.How strange i thought,isn't it supposed to be me wakeing them up on
Christmas Day.They told me Father Christmas had been and i had lots of presents.They
took it in turns unwrapping them and showing me what i had.How lucky i am i've now
got lots and lots of toys and rattles to play with when i'm a little bigger.
Later in the Morning we all went to Gran and Grampy Cowards House to have a big
Christmas Dinner, i had a nice big Christmas bottle of milk! but i wished i could have had
Turkey and Christmas Pudding like everyone else.After opening more presents and haveing a
big sleep i woke up to find myself back in Corfe Castle at my other Gran and Grandad
Lardners house.My Uncle Ben and my Great Granny Churchill was also there.Honey my
Grans dog was also there going mad ripping up all the Christmas paper which made me
smile.
In the evening i started to get very,very tired after my long but exciting first Christmas.
Mummy and Daddy looked absolutely shattered. I don't know why!.
As i fell asleep i smiled to myself and thought what a great first Corfe Castle Christmas
i'd had but next year will be even better.If Mummy and Daddy were exhausted this year
they'd better look out. Baby Luke will be a big boy then and i will be able to walk.
Wow just think ill be able to grab the pretty things on the tree and everything.I'll even
be able to have some mashed up Turkey and help put out some mince pies for Father
Christmas!. For now though i've got to concentrate on 2001 and a thing called Summer,
growing teeth?,crawling and giggling.I think i need a sleep.
Thankyou Father Christmas,i think i like Christmas in Corfe. night night.
                    lots of love Luke Coward.
        (son of Mandy and Martin Coward)

Today's weather: *Sunny Spells, very cold.*

Name *LUKE COWARD* (*PARENTS* *MANDY AND MARTIN COWARD*) Year of birth 24 - 10 - 2000

House   39   Street *EAST STREET*

Tuesday December 26th

Awoke as usual at 5.30 a.m. After many mugs of tea and a shower, took dogs for a walk on the Common – then home for breakfast.

Sought out boots for Boxing Day Tug of War in the Square. Our team is pulling for the Fox Inn. The team consists of Simon Robins, Tony Blackwell, Tom Harris, Trevor Hendes, Chris White, Dave and Richard Williams (my sons) and myself.

Arrived at the Square at 11 a.m. – only two other teams arrived, both from the Legion Club in East Street.

After winning first heats against Legion B we pulled against their A team and won by 2 – 0 after umpire wanted to change the rules half way through. He was told we would be back at 11 a.m. next Boxing Day if he still wanted to argue.

Next stop the Fox Inn for some light refreshment.

The landlady, Annette, had reserved the tables etc. for us. We were joined by the Legion teams and all made "jolly".

Left the Fox at approx 3.30 p.m.

Made way home with family for traditional bubble and squeak Boxing Day lunch.

The remainder of the day was spent in some peace.

Today's weather: Cloudy and dry

Name   Joe Williams   Year of birth   1944

House   94   Street   West Street

The sunlight broke through our deliciously small windowpanes this morning, beckoning in another day of possibilities for us. 96 East Street is our weekend and holiday retreat from our frenzied lives in Wimbledon. Whilst planning the day we, Paul and Sarah, together with the children, Antonia (10), Hugo (9), Madeleine (5) and Hedley (2) discussed the plans for the day, pinching ourselves to see if it really was all real.

The children then vacated our bedroom and went downstairs to join their Grandfather, Tony Cronk, long up and breakfasted. A quick chat with Antonia's pet rat, Bibi, and then the hubbub of breakfast.

No croissants from Dragon's this morning, as the village shops were rightfully closed for the Christmas break. This meant that Paul was not able to enjoy his morning walk across the Halves to purchase his newspaper and breakfast. Ah! The contrast to our morning rush to work, from our Wimbledon home. Granny Cronk, Audrey, joined us for the finalisation of plans for the morning but before we could proceed, there was the small matter of yet more Christmas presents beneath the tree! The tree really is the finest we have had yet. Each year we telephone to Norden Farm and confirm our order – one for the sitting room and one for the children's "den" upstairs. They keep the details of the dimensions and species in a little book and always put aside lovely trees for us. This year, however, they have surpassed themselves.

After the presents and with not a thought about our violin practices, homework and the like, we set off for a walk at Shell Bay – both the seaward side amongst the dunes and along the edge of Poole Harbour by the wonderful houseboats. It was cold and windy and by now, somewhat grey but, as ever, it was exhilarating to be by the sea at Christmas time. The ferry to Poole was running again, after its refit, and we decided to take a trip across to the Haven Hotel for lunch. The adults agreed the view was perfect, especially as the sun came out; but the meal was not one to be repeated. The children, however, loved it all, the best part being the hot chocolate in the lounge after lunch.

We returned to the cottage and later enjoyed tea, Christmas cake and mince pies in front of the fire. We talked of the village life we had known over the past five years, the local people we had met through Church, Sunday School, the weekenders we would be dining with later in the week (the Doolans, Roshiers, Saunders and others). Antonia proudly spoke of reading in Church on Christmas morning and Hugo showed Granny and Grandad the excellent school project he had done on the history of Corfe Castle.

Later we prepared for Dinner, a lovely Game Pie from Don Palfrey's, together with one of his delicious Dorset Apple Cakes. He too, takes our Christmas order each year, actually taking it home with him one year as we took five hours to travel to Corfe due to flooding in the area. Extraordinary that in this year of appalling weather, we managed to get straight through with no trouble.

Before Dinner, we all walked through the village to enjoy the Christmas lights, the floodlit Castle and the beautifully decorated windows along East Street. How magical it all looked – another "best yet" we all agreed. The children were late to bed, of course, savouring every moment in this most magical of places. We followed them to bed later, in a similar mood.

Today's weather: Cold with snow flurries!

Name	Paul and Sarah Docx Antonia, Hugo, Madeleine and Hedley	Year of birth	1990/91/95 & 98
House	Little Cottage (96)	Street	East Street

Today is our 5th day as "residents" of Corfe because we have rented a cottage in which to spend Christmas week in this village. Farriers Lodge, a 17th century listed building, renovated in 1998 is a superbly snug holiday home, wonderfully equipped – we love the "old" features so different from our 1955 bungalow in Eastwood, Nottinghamshire. We chose Corfe because on our previous visit to the area in "eclipse" week 1999, we had cycled from our campsite at Knitson Farm, Swanage, to the village, climbed up to the castle and watched the steam trains. It's an ideal centre for walking and enjoying the rare leisure time of a holiday.

The people too are most friendly. Emerging from the cottage, passers by greet us daily and the same openness was demonstrated on the evening of our arrival in two ways – at the carols in the village square preceding Santa's arrival and later by an invitation to a party next door. One morning walking to our car, a couple must have thought <u>we</u> were local as they asked us questions about Don Palfrey's butcher's shop.

Our day TODAY began late 9 a.m. (too tempting to lie in) and after discussion at breakfast, we had three journeys to make once we'd taken packed lunch, rucksack, jackets, coats, hats, gloves round to the car:-

1. To allow our son to photograph the 11.07 steam train, we parked by Afflington Farm beside the bridge, OS ref: 970806 for a perfect view of the steam train and embankment with Corfe Castle as the backdrop.
2. Weymouth, first ever visit, walk along lengthy esplanade and harbour front, crossing town bridge to west quayside (RNLI station). Picnic in gardens at Nothe Fort, Brewers Quay visit. Tim called it a "Wheelie" town as everyone's on wheels, scooters (the Xmas present of the years 2000), plus skateboards, rollerblades, wheelchairs and electric buggies.
3, Pre-sunset dash in car to Durdle Door; the steep down hill path much eroded by recent rain. Then back to Farriers Lodge for a relaxing evening.

As for Christmas Day, we attended mass at St. Edwards RC Church in Wareham at 10.30 then walked the town walls including a diversion into Lady St. Mary's C of E Church. The vicar and his wife awaiting any sign of life for their 12 o'clock service. One lady arrived. Other highlights in Wareham: (a) River Frome, high level at the Quay; (b) Photo of northern lights over Corfe in April 2000 in window of Celestial Skies shop;

Today's weather: Superb: clear sky, very cold - perfect "walking" weather.
Snow fell overnight throughout the country. Airports closed, road chaos

Name	Nora, David and Timothy Harper	Year of birth	1947, 1953, 1991
House	Farriers Lodge	Street	36 East Street

Hello diary my name is David and my father Roy Ford lives within the village, it gives me great pleasure to tell you all about our day today.

To begin with, I will just say a few words about my day-to-day life.

I am currently serving with the Royal Air Force at Lyneham Wiltshire repairing and maintaining the C130J Hercules aircraft; I live with my wife Natasha who works as an Admin assistant at the Honda plant in Swindon.

For Christmas this year we have gone back to Natasha's home to see family and friends in Metheringham Lincolnshire, this is where I met my lovely wife whilst based here with the air force.

Anyway on with the day in Metheringham…………………….

09.00 am

We both awoke this morning to a blanket of snow hoping for a trip to Grimsby to see some friends which we had not seen for at least 18 months, outside it was still cold, and reports on the the news were still saying that the roads were hazardous. The phone rang it was our friends from Grimsby to say that they had a lot more snow overnight and it was blizzards there at the moment. A decision was made, sadly we would not be venturing to see our friends, my wife and I were annoyed with the weather because the last time we saw them, their daughter was only a couple of months old. Molly is now 2 years old and is a real character so maybe sometime in the New Year we will see them.

12.00pm

Natasha and I had decided to go for lunch at the Red Lion in Dunston. It is a lovely village, which looked very picturesque in the snow. This pub brings back some good memories for us having visited it on a number of occasions with family and friends, but most importantly having held our reception meal here after our marriage nearly 2 years to the day on New Years Eve.

Our anniversary meal was superb we then headed home to relax.

Later that afternoon, we had a trip out to a furniture warehouse, within the village, to help decide on some bedroom furniture for my sister in law Phillipa, who is expecting her first child in February. The village looked pleasant it was still only just above freezing but the sun was shining and the snow had started to thaw, which made it, feel very Christmassy indeed.

8.00pm

We both went to see our friends, Benny and Vonnie, whom we have not seen since March. Benny was an old work colleague of mine who I worked with in the RAF whilst at Coningsby.

We had a really good evening talking about old times, what delights we got for Christmas also having the the odd drink or two, and topping up our food levels with all those Christmas snacky things!! Leaving at 11.30pm, we were ready for bed. If the weather holds, we are off home tomorrow, stopping off at Sleaford to see my wife's old school friend Anna for lunch.

Sadly, this is our Christmas holiday over, with the snow and the excitement of Christmas it has been wonderful. Hope you have enjoyed our day as much as we have. Roll on New Year and our anniversary.

Good night diary!!

Today's weather: Snow, Cold 1degree Celsius, sunny spells, -6 degrees tonight

Name David & Natasha Ford	Year of birth 1972 & 1973
House No: 8	Street Halves Cottages

Millennium Tree Planting

The Corfe Castle Millennium Association sponsored the planting of
6 trees around the village for a more lasting memorial:

    1 Golden Yew (Taxus baccata 'Standishii')
      at the Old Cemetry, East Street

    3 Birch Trees (Betula pendula)
      at the Playing Fields of Corfe Castle First School

    1 Hawthorn , pink
    1 Hawthorn , white (Crataegus monogyna)
      at the New Cemetry, West Street.

The exceptionally wet autumn and winter severely disrupted our
schedules of tree planting ceremonies. The First School tree
planting had to be put off 3 times and in the end the trees were
officially presented in the school hall on the 27th November 2000,
by Mr. Michael Bond, High Sheriff of Dorset.

On Remembrance Sunday, the Golden Yew was planted in the Old
Cemetry, East Street, by Lt. Lisa Potts, of the Royal Engineers,
who lives at Halves Cottages.

The Hawthorn Trees were officially presented to the Garden of
Remembrance on 14.1.2001 and will later be planted in the new
part, when it is ready to be opened.

Today's weather: cold, overcast

Name   David Roy Ford   Year of birth   1947

House   8   Street Halves Cottages

When I chose this date I expected to write in reflective mood, thinking back over the year, but now the day is over my thoughts are more of anticipation and looking forward.

A kiss from the grandson, Michael, who at eight remains an affectionate boy, was received while I was still abed. He knows the ritual well as he proclaimed it was time to make Grandad a cup of tea. This done I left the two 'men' in the bedroom with Michael reading a story to his Grandad who lay back on the pillow showing an early morning interest in Mr Pinkwhistle! I retreated to the bathroom, a room we constructed from the space on the landing. The cast iron bath now sits on reinforced joists, unlike its former precarious position which we discovered after we bought our cottage in 1986. The two layers of floorboards and the supporting half tree trunk joists were virtually powder in seventy percent of the structure, so, no doubt had we filled the bath it would have descended rapidly to the room below. We know our home was built before 1660 when it was two cottages, one room up and one down in each, but over the years many changes have occurred. We have made alterations and those that follow us will too, but, during the renovating, we have tried to conserve some of what we believe to be original features.

Breakfast eaten, Michael and I walked to the bakers for the next ritual - one farmhouse loaf 90p and a gingerbread man 40p. Up in the Ringing Room Michael settled himself in a corner ready to draw his chosen subject pulling a bell rope. Little did he, or I, know that later he too would be ringing a bell. He was invited to take the tail end which he did without hesitation. What a thrill for us and wouldn't he have something to tell his parents. He is waiting patiently for the brother or sister who was due on Christmas Day but who now looks destined to be a January baby. A joyous event to welcome the coming of 2001.

Before returning Michael home to Southbourne, Grandad suggested a walk along Studland Beach before taking the ferry from Shell Bay. We were nearly blown off our feet and had to struggle to walk on the sand against the force of the wind. It was cold too, so became one of the shortest walks on record. We paid our £2.20 for the one-way passage across to Sandbanks and found we were first on the slipway. Now, Grandma is no sailor, so having to wait and watch the stormy sea did not ease the quibbles. 'I-spy' was the antidote on the crossing! With Michael safely home we stopped en route at a local pub for lunch. Jim and I had intended to walk to Blashenwell Farm, my childhood home, where my father farmed for fifty years. I remember helping to deliver eggs to villagers including those who lived opposite our cottage, Mrs Riddle, Polly Andrews, Miss Matthews and Mrs Chaffey. Today only two of the terrace of five cottages have permanent residents, the other three dwellings are used for holiday accommodation. This is a growing trend which does affect the social balance. The weather turned very wet so we postponed our visit to the spot where we sprinkled my Dad's ashes and instead had a quiet afternoon indoors.

This evening we donned our wet weather gear and strolled to The Square. Just turned 11pm and all seemed quiet. We made our way to the tower impossible to believe it was twelve months ago the ringers gathered to ring in the year 2000. The tenor, half muffled, was to be tolled until 11.55pm. This would then give enough time to remove the muffle for the full ring to begin on the dot of midnight. So, Michael rang the treble for the first time, I had the experience of tolling the tenor, an achievement to take in to 2001. Ringers and friends partook of refreshments before wending their way down the stairway, some to continue their celebrations, others to head homeward for their sleep.

During the year, I have listened to some of the older locals' recollections of their younger days, as well as how they live now. It has made me realise the significance of social history and the importance of safeguarding such memories in this changing world in which the simple things of life can seem so trivial. What we take for granted now will be of interest to those who live after us. Being involved with the establishment of this diary has inspired me to scribe my personal, day-to-day thoughts and happenings. A radio programme, 'The Archers', an everyday story of country folk, has this year been broadcasting for fifty years, with interested listeners of all ages. Who knows our 'Corfe Castle 2000 - A Diary of the Village', may be a valued and fascinating read a half century from now.

Today's weather: Dry, cold and windy followed by rain.

Name   Mary Rosewarn   Year of birth   1949

House   April Cottage (77)   Street   West

INDEX

Corfe Valley News 27 Jan 17 Feb 26 Jul 15 Aug 29 Oct
Cotterell 13 Aug
Coward 19 Sep 25 Dec
Cowles 6 Mar
Cowley 12 Jan
Cox 3 Jan
Crabbe 12 Jan 6 Apr 3 Aug
Crackle 31 Dec ('99) 29 May
Creech Grange 20 Oct
Cricket Club 31 Aug
Crone 11 Aug 24 Sep
Cronk 27 Dec
Cross 8 Jan 30 Mar 18 Apr 1 May
Crutchfield 18 Oct
Cunningham 3 Jan
Curtis 20 Nov

Dallisson 5 Jan
Dames 1 Jan
Dando 6 Jun
Dankesreiter 15 Feb
Davies 3 Nov 4 Nov 21 Nov
Davis 5 Jan 15 Feb 27 Feb 6 Jun 2 Jul 24 Jul 27 Nov
Day 22 Jul 17 Nov
Dean 1 Jan 14 Jul
Denning 24 Nov
Diary 2000 Sub-Committee 1 Jan ('01)
Dixon 28 Jan 15 Feb 19 Feb 27 May 5 Aug
Docx 27 Dec
Double Act 12 Feb 6 Aug 1 Dec 14 Dec
Doyle-Stevens 15 Feb 16 Sep 7 Nov 29 Nov
Dragon 31 Dec ('99) 5 Jan 30 Jan 19 May 2 Jul
        29 Jul 12 Aug 11 Nov 29 Nov
Drane 2 Jul
Dru Drury 28 Jan 2 Feb 4 Feb 11 Feb 4 Mar 16 Apr
        29 Apr 11 Jun 27 Jun 13 Jul 20 Jul
        31 Aug 13 Sep 27 Oct
Druitt 19 Apr
Duffy 10 Jan
Dunne 12 Jan 11 Nov
Dupuy 13 Apr

Eady 26 Jun 4 Aug
Edwards 1 Apr 3 Jul 30 Aug
Egdon Heath 31 Dec
Ellison 2 Jul
Elmes 1 Jan 4 Jan
Elms 8 Oct
Encombe Fête 19 Aug
England 6 Aug
Esson 29 Mar
Evans 20 Jul 11 Dec 24 Dec

Fenney 30 Mar
Figgins 31 Dec ('99) 28 May
Fish Man 11 Apr

Flower Festival 20 Jul
Flower Show 18 Jul
Foley 1 Jan 25 Jan 19 May 23 Aug 14 Dec
Foley's Garage 25 May
Fooks 16 Feb 19 Sep
Foot 31 Mar 5 Jul 3 Nov 12 Nov
Ford 7 Feb 9 Feb 27 Feb 7 Mar 26 May 29 May 30 Jun
        2 Jul 18 Jun 29 Jul 8 Oct 25 Oct 29 Dec 30 Dec
Foresters 12 Nov
Fox Inn 31 Dec ('99) 11 May 8 Nov 26 Dec
Free 4 Feb 15 Feb 14 Apr 24 Apr 29 Jul 29 Nov
Freeman 2 Jul
Freer 17 Mar
French 2 Mar
Fretwell 2 Jul
Frost 14 Mar 26 Mar 5 Aug
Fry 6 Jun
Fuller 21 May
Furmage 10 Aug
Furzey Island 17 Jan 18 Feb

Gardening Club 21 Mar 29 May 18 Jul
Garrett 26 Apr 9 Apr 17 Jun 22 Oct 12 Nov
Garstang 2 May
Gaudin 14 Apr 29 Jul
Gemcraft 6 Nov
Ghillyer 8 Dec 13 Dec
Gibb 1 Apr 4 Mar 19 May 18 Jul 18 Nov 25 Nov
Gibson 12 Jan 10 Nov
Girkins 2 Jul
Glaister 11 Aug
Glassock 9 Apr
Glover 10 Sep
God's Acre 5 May 22 Jul
Golf Course 7 Dec
Goodall 5 Feb 6 Jun
Goodwin 7 Apr 9 Jun 28 Aug
Gopsill 20 Mar
Grace 31 Jan
Green 3 May 24 May 6 Jun
Gregory 8 May
Greyhound Inn 29 Nov
Groves 3 Feb 20 Feb 16 Apr 13 Jun 18 Nov
Gumbrell 27 Mar 30 Jul
Guy 8 Oct
Gynes 4 Jul

Haines 23 Aug
Hamilton-Fletcher 1 Oct
Hardy 14 Jun
Harley 1 Jun
Harper 28 Dec
Harriott 20 Jan 16 Apr 20 Jun 30 Jun 3 Sep 17 Sep 6 Oct
Harris 8 Jan 9 Jan 14 Feb 26 Dec 31 Dec
Harrison 6 Jun 2 Jul
Hartle 25 Jul

This Index has been prepared to help you explore the
Diary   We hope that you will enjoy amending and
extending it from your own research   RF

ACKNOWLEDGEMENTS

Michael J. Allen (Delpool Picture Library)
S.A.M. Chalmers (Sponsor)
Martin Smith
David C. Watson
Jenny Wilson

Corfe Castle Parish Council
Corfe Castle Post Office
Corfe Castle Society
Corfe Castle Town Trust
Corfe Valley News
National Trust
Telegraph Group Limited (Matt Cartoon 11.01.00)

All diarists 2000
The entire parish of Corfe Castle with Kingston
for your encouraging, patient, co-operation

Corfe Castle Millennium Association members:
Autumn 1996 – 2001
Linda Applin, Betty Carter, Rita Churchill, Stephen Dru Drury
Jill Foley, Angelika Ford, Roy Ford, Jan Harriott, Mike Harriott,
David Kemp, Joan Marshallsay, Mike Perry, Anne Preston, Kevin Reynolds,
Jim Rosewarn, Karen Spooner, Maurice Strike, Ian Tarbotton,
Doug Whyte, H. Mary Wills, Eileen van Lelyveld

And all others who have been involved over the last five years

Front Cover Artwork: Courtesy of:-
Paul Glaister: Graphic Designer
Ian Harris: Castle View Crafts (village sketches)

LIST OF SUBSCRIBERS

Linda APPLIN

Peter APSEY

Jill & Alan BEAVIS

Susie BOND

Joan BOWYER

Jane BURT

Betty & Bob CARTER

Jasmine CATTLE

Ruth & John CHAFFEY

Valerie & Sam CHALMERS

Anne-Marie COLLINS

Margaret COOPER

Mandy COWARD

June CROSS

Eileen CUNNINGHAM

Donna & Paul DAVIES

Sheila DOYLE-STEVENS

Diana & Stephen DRU DRURY

Angelika FORD

David Anthony FORD

David Roy FORD

Peter FORD

Yvonne & Roger FREE

Roger FROST

Heather GHILLYER

Lillian GIBB

Babs & Donald GLAISTER

Juliet & Michael GLOVER

Viv & Don GOODWIN

Tim HAMILTON-FLETCHER

Jan & Mike HARRIOTT

Dorothy & Ted HOPKINS

Vi HOWE

Queenie HURRELL

Tony IDE

Brian JOHNSON

David KEMP

Shirley LARDNER

Joyce LUMBUS

Derek H MATTHEWS

Connie & Danny McCRAE

Sybil & Brian NETTLETON

Ivan ORCHARD

Marion ORMEROD

William ORMEROD

Chris PERKINS

Anne & George PRESTON

Debbie & Kevin REYNOLDS

Marta & Rob REYNOLDS

Michael ROBBINS

Mary ROSEWARN

Douglas RYDER

Cynthia SANSOM

Eileen & Lucas van LELYVELD

Hilary WATSON

Clare WESTERN

Raymond WESTERN

Chris WHITE

Jenny WHITTLE

Misako & Douglas WHYTE

Betty WIGMORE

H Mary WILLS

Jenny & Barry WILSON

Personal Notes

Personal Notes